37.95

METHODOLOGY
for
land and housing
market analysis

METHODOLOGY
for
land and housing
market analysis

EDITED BY

Gareth Jones & Peter M. Ward

LINCOLN INSTITUTE OF LAND POLICY
Cambridge, Massachusetts, U.S.A.

First published in 1994 by UCL Press.

First published in the Americas in 1994 by the Lincoln Institute of Land Policy.

Library of Congress Catalog Card Number 94-075109
International Standard Book Number: 1-55844-123-9

Typeset in Palatino.
Printed and bound by Biddles Ltd, Guildford and King's Lynn, England.

Lincoln Institute of Land Policy
Cambridge, Massachusetts, U.S.A.

UCL Press Limited
University College London
Gower Street
London WC1E 6BT

The name of University College London (UCL) is a registered trade mark used by UCL Press with the consent of the owner.

In memory of
Matthew Edel

Everything is worthy of notice, for everything can be interpreted.
Hermann Hesse, *The glass bead game*, 1943

It may be that the whims of chance are really the importunities of design. But if there is a Design, it aims to look natural and fortuitous; that is how it gets us into its web.
Mary McCarthy, *On the contrary*, 1962

Contents

Micro-level methodologies: specific techniques in researching land markets and property prices

Assessing the impact of public policy upon land markets and property prices

Acknowledgements

We would like to acknowledge those who helped organize the Fitzwilliam Workshop held at the University of Cambridge, 14–19 July 1991. In particular, our thanks go to Edith Jiménez and Richard Trenchard. The Workshop was financed by The British Academy, The Economic and Social Research Council (ESRC), The Cultural Department of the French Embassy in London, The International Development Research Centre (Canada) and the Overseas Development Administration (UK). Support was also received from the Department of Geography and from Fitzwilliam College, University of Cambridge. We would like to thank Chris Pickvance for his assistance in producing the Workshop Memorandum so promptly.

The help of Guy Lewis in the Cartography Office at the Department of Geography, University College of Swansea, has been invaluable. The secretaries of the Geography department in Swansea and the LBJ School of Public Affairs at Austin, Texas, have been patient as our numerous and occasionally over-long faxes have kept up the line of communication between us. Finally, UCL Press was flexible with deadlines and sympathetic to the inefficiencies of academics producing hard copy.

Contributors

Dr Gareth Jones
Department of Geography
University College of Swansea
Singleton Park
Swansea, Wales

Professor Peter M. Ward
Department of Sociology & Lyndon B.
 Johnson School of Public Affairs
University of Texas at Austin
Austin, Texas, USA

Dr Willem Assies
CEDLA
Keizersgracht 395–7
Amsterdam, The Netherlands

Mtra Priscilla Connolly
CENVI
Violeta 27
Copilco El Bajo
México DF, México

Professor William A. Doebele
Graduate School of Design
Harvard University
18, Quincy Street
Cambridge, Massachusetts, USA

Professor David Dowall
Department of City and Regional Planning
University of California
Berkeley
California, USA

Dr Edith Jiménez
Instituto de Estudios Económicos y
 Regionales
Universidad de Guadalajara
Apartado Postal 2-738
Guadalajara, México

Dr Alain Durand-Lasserve,
Groupement de Recherche INTERURBA –
 CNRS
7, Rue Sante Garibaldi
Bordeaux, France

Mtra Beatriz García Peralta
Instituto de Investigaciones Sociales
Torre de Humanidades 2
Ciudad Universitaria
UNAM
México DF, México

Dr Manuel Perló
Instituto de Investigaciones Sociales
Torre de Humanidades 2
Ciudad Universitaria
UNAM
México DF, México

Dr Carole Rakodi
Department of City & Regional Planning
University of Wales College of Cardiff
PO Box 906
Cardiff, Wales

Professor Donald C. Shoup
Graduate School of Architecture and
Urban Planning
University of California
Los Angeles
California, USA

Dr William Siembieda
School of Architecture and Planning
University of New Mexico
Albuquerque
New Mexico, USA

Dr Martim Smolka
IPPUR-UFRJ
Prédio da Reitoria, Sala 543
Cidade Universitária – Ilha do Fundão
Rio de Janeiro, Brazil

Dr Ann Varley
Department of Geography
University College London
26 Bedford Way
London, England

CHAPTER ONE

Introduction

Gareth Jones & Peter M. Ward

From Fitzwilliam Workshop to work on methodology

Like many edited collections, this book arose from a conference, in this case held over a five-day period in July 1991 at Fitzwilliam College, Cambridge. Unlike most such books, however, this one was not a predetermined product anticipated by the organizers, nor was its central theme – methodology for land and housing markets – a priority item on the meeting's agenda when it began. Rather, the issue had been relegated to a half-day session as a prelude to the final plenary. The importance of methodology only emerged during the course of the substantive discussions, and came to the fore when we began to draw together our conclusions for the Fitzwilliam Memorandum (1991). Most of those who attended the meeting agreed that there was no real need nor justification for the publication of yet another collection on low-income housing in less-developed countries, not even one dealing specifically with many of the complex and fascinating issues related to land markets and land prices that we had debated at length. However, we were all excited about the need for a volume that got experienced researchers to think about the ways in which the methodology they adopted shaped their analysis of the land and housing market problem and how it drew them into a particular framework and orthodoxy of conclusions and policy prescriptions. A book that sought to totally recast our pre-prepared papers, pushing the substantive detail into the background while bringing to the fore an account of the methods and approaches used, would be worthwhile and new indeed. That is how this book was conceived.

The Fitzwilliam Workshop was organized by Ward towards the end of a major UK ESRC-financed research project directed by him to investigate land values and land valorization processes for cities in developing countries. With research associates Jiménez and Jones, that tranche of research had focused on three Mexican cities, but proposals were already under way to extend the study through independent research groups working in Kenya and in India. The "land values" project had four broad aims: first, to investigate residential land-price trends in Mexican cities. Secondly, to analyze the social composition and the rationale motivating the various different groups engaged in developing land for residential purposes, whether legally or illegally. Thirdly, we wanted to begin to gauge the effectiveness of state policy towards control and managing land. Specifically, too, we wanted to assess the impact of state intervention on land prices and, by extension, on the population living in different types of neighbourhoods. Finally, we recognized that answers to these questions would not be easily arrived at, and that we would have to develop strategies and methods of data collection, many of which would be innovative; and not all of which could be expected to work equally well. We hoped that, along the way, we would be able to offer some guidance about methodology and land-market analysis (Ward 1989b). The final product, however, was always targeted at a sharp synthesis of key conclusions and the identification of important issues for future resolution. These were drawn up on the last day, and were published in the *International Journal of Urban and Regional Research* some five months later (Fitzwilliam 1991).[1]

For many researchers methodology is, rather ironically, a "dirty word". Our point of departure was the realization of the need for a stronger research framework with which to transform rhetoric into data. Our own work and the discussions which emerged at the Fitzwilliam Workshop indicated that our understanding of the key research questions has often outpaced our ability to formulate appropriate strategies and methods to answer those questions. Moreover, in trying to assess land-market behaviour in cities, or in trying to produce nationally or globally relevant conclusions, we were all aware that a lot was being done within a single framework. As Ingram (1982: 109) notes, land-market analyses are characterized by the collection of data that are not equal to the tasks they have been asked to perform. Although many of us were unconvinced that a neoclassical approach could answer our questions satisfactorily, few of us were sufficiently convinced or confident of the alternatives to put in its place. Did Marxism offer a sufficient methodology to address service infrastructure? Were researchers trying too hard to fit findings into one model? Was the clumsy ideological and methodological baggage that all research takes on board seriously compromising the research we had set in motion?

These conundrums threatened to undermine the merits of much arduous empirical work that had already been conducted. Moreover, the competing methodologies and ideologies themselves do not facilitate an objective comparison of findings. Added to this there was often too much "noise" derived from the different methodological approaches. Little wonder, then, that the otherwise well documented field of housing research finds difficulty in providing comparative international statistics on market performance and land or housing prices (Gilbert 1991b). How could we talk to one another when often we were speaking different languages? Although it was tongue-in-cheek, there was also a note of desperation in Donald Shoup's plea for us to convert all "foreign" currencies into dollars, it being a medium and a comparator that he could understand!

This need for communication requires, we would argue, a greater awareness of the individually based "ideology" which each of us takes into the field. The morally comfortable position of the researcher in developing countries is increasingly the subject of ethical debate (Crocker 1991). It is critical, too, that in urban research an appraisal is made as to how the researcher intends to "see" the world which he or she sets out to study. This is never more important, of course, than when the results of the research feed directly into policy prescription. The question here is how the research is to be relevant and for whom (Gilbert 1987). As Sidaway (1992: 404) has noted, building a methodology requires a certain reconciliation with one's conscience and the appreciation that the questioning of "assumed knowledge" is not simply a problem for the researcher; it may also have a profound effect on the subject.

For these reasons, this book is not an attempt to convince readers and researchers of a particular methodological approach – our aim is not to convert doubters of the benefits of any one approach. All the contributors to this volume would support our contention that this would lead to sterility of findings and debate. Nor is it an attempt to standardize "mixed" research approaches or to suggest that for certain research questions only one line of enquiry is suitable. Nor is the book intended as a vehicle to suggest "single methodologies" as being more appropriate in certain societies or for certain types of study. Rather, the call is for greater awareness of methodology and how it affects research and research results. It responds to the need to advance scholarship with academic honesty.

The notion that methodology dictates results is not new. But it is surprising that so few of the many multi-authored books on housing have sought to address the issue head-on. An exception is the volume edited by Tipple & Willis (1991), but even this book focuses on specific methodological techniques used in housing analysis and social science research. It does not address the issue of methodology per se, nor the ways in which our paradigms and political persuasions may shape our research. Indeed, in commissioning revised papers, we, the editors, did not want a series of descriptions of methodologies employed in a disparate array of studies. Rather we have insisted that contributors present their research results in the context of an honest assessment of the advantages and disadvantages of competing methodologies and approaches. In order to achieve this our editing has sometimes been severe, but we have tried not to destroy nor to homogenize the individual styles of writing and presentation. Shoup's account, for example, captures the dry humour that he brought to the Workshop. We believe that methodology is, at least in part, about individuality, and should reflect the imagination that we, as researchers, apply to the intellectual problems that we set ourselves. We want the reader to receive the full flavour of that individuality as expressed in the contributors' writings. We also want the reader to enjoy, albeit vicariously, some of the pleasure we derived in working with other participants in the Workshop.

Collectively, we decided to dedicate this book to the memory of Matthew Edel, whom most of us had known, and whose work on land markets and house prices we all admired. His sudden death in 1990 deprived the Workshop of an invitee whose slightly quizzical seriousness and enormous experience were sadly missed. In retrospect it was doubly sad, since he would have greatly enjoyed the meeting that took place without him.

The structure of the book

The book is divided into three sections. The first outlines some of the debates from competing paradigms within land-market research. The structure of this first section pitches neoclassical against political economy approaches. In soliciting chapters for this book we have sought to include a broad selection from both camps. However, the balance is probably more heavily loaded towards the political economy paradigm for two reasons. First, most readers will be more familiar with the neo-classical framework since it has traditionally dominated land and housing market analyses, whereas examples of the political economy approach are less common and less well documented. Second, many of the insights drawn from the Workshop and reported in the Fitzwilliam Memorandum (Fitzwilliam 1991) were derived from those researchers who had eschewed more classical and traditional methodologies. Inevitably, therefore, the balance swung towards their studies when we came to put together the final volume. Broadly speaking, the work reported in the chapters by Dowall, Doebele, Amitabh, Siembieda, Perló and Shoup have their intellectual origins in the neo-classical urban economics school. The chapters by Durand-Lasserve, Rakodi, García & Jiménez and Connolly are firmly in the political economy camp. The remaining contributions (Assies, Varley, Smolka, Ward et al., Jones et al.) are rather more eclectic, but also lean towards the holistic, political economy methodology.

The chapters by Jones & Ward, and by Doebele, highlight the changing conventional wisdom and directions of land-market research over the past two decades. Both chapters indicate and question how this wisdom has become enshrined in global policy. The most recent policy relies in part on methodologies such as that presented by Dowall in Chapter 3, which adopts a neoclassical approach for land-market assessment. Durand-Lasserve takes an alternative line by highlighting, with reference to Conakry, the capital of Guinea, the insights a political economy approach can offer. An important element here is the uncovering of the effects of the transition from socialism to economic liberalism. Rakodi's chapter underlines for Zimbabwe the significance of a political transition from colonialism to independence, although in that case the socialist experiment reinforced rather than challenged the system of private property. Rakodi looks at trends in land and housing markets against a backdrop of post-independence socialist rhetoric and more tangible trends in falling real wages, housing shortages and structural changes in housing and land supply.

4

Nevertheless, Rakodi identifies a recent transition from post-independence socialism toward economic liberalism, albeit perhaps less orthodox than that witnessed in Guinea by Durand-Lasserve. How private sector developers respond to and shape market conditions is the subject of the chapter by García & Jiménez. This work, based on two independently run studies in Querétaro, Mexico, evaluates the degree of organization of land developers and the extent to which intervention in the land market can be considered to fit a theoretical logic. A very different approach is forwarded by Assies, who shows how land may possess different meanings constructed through the social and political conflicts that surround the mechanisms by which land is appropriated, acquired and responded to through positions adopted by various actors, including the public sector.

The second section takes up many of these points and shows how they may be applied at the micro-level. Varley questions the apparently neutral assumptions made on defining the household. She notes that the household is central to most social science methodologies, but that the definition is not without its problems. Her chapter challenges the concept by assessing the interconnectedness of the household and the house. Amitabh analyzes the usefulness of land-registration data which, at face value, offer many of the features commonly looked for in empirical investigation, but which many researchers have dismissed as weakened by severe shortcomings. Amitabh's analysis, however, argues that one must look beyond such all-too-easy-to-make pessimistic statements in order to uncover the usefulness of the data source. The chapter develops these points with reference to an Indian case study. Land-registration data are one of several sources surveyed by Siembieda for assembling land-price information. A further dimension is added by constructing estimates of land supply, thereby suggesting a mixed approach to combine temporal and spatial analysis. Ward, Jiménez and Jones review the efficacy of newspaper- and questionnaire-based data for measuring land-price trends. The authors point to an holistic methodology that includes insights from a top-down and bottom-up strategy, the inclusion of middle and elite settlements in addition to the more conventional focus on low-income settlements and the application of appropriate benchmark measures of land affordability. The chapter by Smolka introduces an under researched area of urban studies, the second-hand housing market. Looking at Rio de Janeiro, Smolka shows how fiscal and census records can be combined in order to uncover both temporal and spatial trends that include the effect of new housing supply on the market, the changing socio-economic composition of areas and the relationship to credit availability.

In the third section, four chapters set out to assess how research might address the impact of public policy on land and property markets. Perló develops an original methodological contribution from the experience of government attempts to rehouse the inhabitants of downtown Mexico City after the 1985 earthquake. Perló advocates a "before" and "after" approach within a model of transaction quantities and prices paid. The snapshot survey demonstrated by Jones, Jiménez and Ward also points to a synthetic methodology. Here, however, the aim is to provide insights into the apparent valorization of plots after public intervention and to stress the mechanism by which this is, or is not, achieved. The chapter argues the need to contextualize the explanations of public-policy impacts. Rather than identify misgivings in public policy, Shoup's aim is to use what is increasingly understood about the impact of public policy on land markets to adapt a tool known as the "deferred assessment" in order to attain the original set of policy targets. Paramount in Shoup's analysis, which is illustrated by experiences from the Venice Canals, California, is the ideal that payment for public services should be fair as well as replicable. Lastly, Connolly takes the example of a planned city, Cancún, Mexico, to illustrate how public intervention produces the structure of segmented markets which earlier chapters had identified. Connolly argues that in order to understand the nature of the land market one must appreciate the political forces that created and administer each land-market segment, the interrelationship between the respective segments and the accuracy of economic theory in informing understanding of the market when economic forces are so clearly mediated by politics.

This book is not presented as the culmination of academic research which offers either new theoretical insight and/or empirical findings, although sections of each chapter do both. Rather, the book attempts to provoke such academic research by laying out some of the methodological concerns that have shaped recent investigations and by suggesting some tentative ways forward. In so doing, it is hoped that readers will be increasingly aware of the narrow line between objective and subjective research, with the implications this has for socially, politically and ideologically neutral research. Such awareness for conducting research into urban problems in the developing world is perhaps timely, given the statement of the World Bank that "urban poverty will become the most significant and politically explosive problem in the next century" (World Bank 1991: 4). If true, such an outlook suggests that for social scientists and policy-makers alike, the stakes for adequately appreciating the methodological constraints on land and housing market analysis will be higher in the future than they have been in the recent past.

Notes

1. Others present at the Workshop, but not involved in the final making of this book were Antonio Azuela, Michael Ball, Paul Baross, Alan Gilbert, Emilio Haddad, Daniel Hiernaux, Chris Macoloo, Michael Mattingly, Modupe Omrin, Johan Silas, Allyson Thirkell and Richard Trenchard. The chapters by Assies, Siembieda and Varley were solicited afterwards, since none was able to attend the Fitzwilliam meeting.

Macro methodological approaches
Neoclassical economic theory versus political economy perspectives

CHAPTER TWO

Tilting at windmills
Paradigm shifts in World Bank orthodoxy[1]

Gareth Jones & Peter M. Ward

Introduction: tilting at windmills?

Since the middle of the 1980s there has been a growing awareness of the desirability of better management of urban development in less-developed and relatively poor societies. At all levels – local municipal administration, state and federal government – the message is one of how to achieve better value for capital expenditures in providing urban services, utilities, land and housing; how to cut wastage through removing inefficiencies and "leakages"; how to improve cost recovery; and how to ensure a greater level of financial replicability for such programmes, so that these are ongoing, rather than one-offs that end when the money runs out. As we shall demonstrate, this changing awareness reflects a broader paradigm shift away from large-scale urban projects, in which government expects to be the principal provider, towards a position in which the rôle of public administration is to facilitate equitable and replicable urban-development processes, in part by offering conditions conducive to the involvement of privately raised capital. Increasingly, a major concern is to ensure self-sustaining environmental management. Often, too, it involves a complete revision of taxation and consumption charges in order to remove subsidies. In principle, we applaud this broad shift in approach, and we note that most working-class householders whom we have interviewed over the years in the course of several research projects are usually willing to take these costs on board. They do not expect something for nothing; their major concern, however, is that such charges be realistic and affordable given local wage levels, and that any measure should be applied equitably across all socio-economic groups.

This chapter has three principal aims. First, to document the paradigm shift and describe the antecedents to the conventional wisdom embodied in the New Urban Management Programme (NUMP) now being actively promoted by the World Bank. Secondly, we want to demonstrate how the underlying premise of the NUMP is drawn almost exclusively from the neoclassical economics para-

8

digm. The programme flows directly from the neoliberal economic orthodoxy, which emphasizes the withdrawal of the state, operation of a relatively free and unconstrained market and notions of efficiency, productivity and growth. Finally, in anticipation of the methodological discussions and debates contained in the following chapters, we propose to raise questions about whether the NUMP can be made *to work* without a more nuanced understanding of the way in which local land and housing markets are produced and commercialized, and without some considerable degree of direct authority being exercised by state and municipal government in order to ensure that urban development is achieved equitably. Our view is that even under the neoliberal economic orthodoxy and the so-called "rolling back of the state", governments cannot divest themselves of responsibility for protecting lower-income groups and exercising effective planning controls for the wider good. Just as "trickle-down" economics did not achieve greater equity for wage labour during the period of rapid industrialization in contexts such as Mexico and Brazil, so handing over responsibility to the private sector and to the marketplace is unlikely to make substantial improvements to their housing and land-acquisition position. Improved public administration, progressive systems of taxation and consumption charges may help considerably, but the local state must also hold the ring between the many competing interests and actors identified by different authors in this volume if the urban development process is to proceed equitably and smoothly, and if people's basic needs are to be satisfied. The challenge, in our view, is to reconcile what is technically desirable with what is politically feasible (Ward & Macoloo 1992).

As we shall describe in a moment, the World Bank has provided an important leadership rôle in setting the agenda for land and housing market analyses, and for identifying policy approaches. Rather like windmills, these policy positions stand out as important markers within a broader landscape of urban-development programmes. But more than signals, they have also done a great deal to prime the pump for the implementation of new urban-policy approaches. In developing this introductory critique, our aim is not to blindly tilt at and knock down these policy positions, but rather to encourage a more cautious and locally sensitive consideration of what elements among them may be expected to work. There are no easy answers, nor is the information readily come by – as contributors to this volume will attest. To assume that a new strategy is the answer to our current needs would be reckless indeed. Moreover, it would ignore historical precedent, which suggests that the World Bank has offered a sequence of strategies underpinned by conventional wisdom throughout the past two decades. The latest paradigm is not necessarily the best, nor is it likely to be the last.

But in order to achieve a better understanding of land and housing market dynamics we believe that new methodological frameworks and approaches are required. This is not solely our view – as we mention in the introduction to this volume, it emerged as the most important conclusion of a major international

9

meeting of experts (Fitzwilliam 1991). Certainly, neoclassical economic models and philosophy no longer appear to be sufficiently sensitive to economic and political reality in most contexts, and certainly not in Mexico where we conducted our research. Although such models have a theoretical elegance that is attractive and capable of multivariate modelling, they do little to uncover or explain the processes we have described, which are largely formulated according to social and political criteria and considerations, not purely economic ones. We prefer a more actor-centred approach that starts by looking at the political economy in which land production takes place. We also believe that while standardized land-market assessment data for neoclassical modelling are useful (see Dowall 1991a, and this volume), they are only the first step to be complemented by more in-depth actor-oriented and local household survey type information, and they are not sufficient for any meaningful analysis that will promote sensitive policy formulation. The attraction of neoclassical models, of course, is their replicability in different economic contexts. But that seems of little utility if they don't work, or if they lead one to narrow and misleading conclusions.

Although the methodology that we adopted is less easy to replicate and adapt than neoclassical models, it has allowed us both to identify key areas where action and public intervention might be appropriate, and to provide some indication of the direction that policies might take. In short, we argue that our work will lead to outcomes that are workable and sensitive to the needs of different groups. However, ours is not the dominant paradigm, and much of what follows comprises an analysis of the changing nature of World Bank thinking in recent years, together with an evaluation of why we consider it to be fundamentally flawed.

The shifting paradigm: from "urban projects" to the New Urban Management Program

There is already an extensive literature on the organization and structural weaknesses of the World Bank itself (Ayres 1983, Toye 1989), its limitations with regard to housing policy (Burgess 1992, Campbell 1990, Payer 1982) and the inadequacies in its methods of forecasting (Cole 1989). A recent survey of overall World Bank and IMF policies since Bretton Woods in 1944 by the *Economist* (1991) listed 10 criticisms. In short, the *Economist* argued that the Bank and IMF have tended to apply identical remedies, as doctrine, irrespective of a country's circumstances, with the result that programmes continue to be supported and promoted even after it is clear that they do not work. Contrary to the broad aims of both institutions to foster development and to improve the conditions in which the poor live, the result is often the application of austerity measures that are anti-growth and harm the poor.

Nevertheless, since the early 1970s the World Bank has been very influential: initially in effectively recasting housing policies in developing countries (Ward 1982, Payne 1984), later during the 1980s at developing lines of urban development strategy (Linn 1983), and most recently it has begun to promote the NUMP (World Bank 1990). These policy shifts have been achieved through the dissemination of its publications and technical expertise, through demonstration projects, through lines of credit and through structural adjustment policies. Very briefly, we propose to review the two phases prior to the NUMP.

The structure of World Bank urban policy was initially laid out in the 1972 *Urbanization Sector Working Paper* (World Bank 1972). The document was one of the most lucid evocations of the urban crisis in developing countries and the potential of self-help policies. Moreover, it outlined the Bank's philosophy of the *urban problem*, and although in other areas of activity the philosophy may have changed radically, we believe that so far as urban policy is concerned it remained largely unchanged over the following two decades. An analysis of that original *Urbanization Sector Working Paper* reveals an early incorporation of phrases with which observers today would be familiar: "urban efficiency", a "harnessing of market forces" (1972: 6), the "improvement of urban management" (1972: 7), and so on. Today's urban policies are more of the same rather than a radically new departure. In some respects it appears to be different because the Bank is caught in a round of "faddism" – doing the same thing differently. As Ayres (1983: 75) puts it, the greater emphasis on poverty alleviation was "pasted onto the prevalent ideology without, however, altering its fundamental slant". Thus, while the Bank appears to have become more sceptical during the 1970s of the ability of market forces alone to provide urban solutions without guided state intervention, cost recovery was still the driving force behind all its projects. On the specific issue of land, the Bank argued in 1972 that in view of "the inherent divergencies between private decisions and social benefits in urban land use, the very limited public financial resources and the importance of land costs in public projects, it is abundantly clear that market values are usually not an efficient allocator of urban land" (1972: 39). Yet it failed to formulate or adopt a land policy at this time, and preferred instead to define the urban problem in terms of housing. What emerged, therefore, was a vision of World Bank policy as a curious hybrid of neoliberal thinking and practical welfare economics from which two consequences sprang. The first, identified by van der Linden (1992: 341), is that Bank policy has done precisely the opposite of "learning by doing", and instead has acted to reinforce previous weaknesses instead of overcoming them. The second, admitted by the Bank itself in relation to its "new" programme, is that the direct link to poverty groups has tended to become steadily "fuzzier" (*Urban Edge* 1985: 2).

The 1972 *Urbanization Sector Working Paper* identified four key areas where Bank policies could improve the urban environment. First, it advocated low-cost solutions so as to make shelter affordable to more households. In essence, this meant moving away from completed housing "packages", towards actions and "elements" that would support self-help and so-called sweat equity approaches (Turner 1976). As a result there was an upsurge in programmes such as sites and services, core units, upgrading and so on (Ward 1982, Payne 1984). Institutionalization of these programmes was often accompanied by the development of major new housing finance institutions, some of which later developed into second-line financing for worker housing of different forms.[2] Secondly, services were to be extended without – so the Bank hoped – a need for subsidy. Rather, financial aid from the Bank was to act as pump-priming for provision and greater capture of the installation costs and consumption charges by local authorities. In fact, service installation often remained heavily subsidized, whether out of political expediency, or because local authorities lacked the wherewithal to recover local contributions that would ensure replicability. Thirdly, it promoted the growing desirability of urban planning and investment procedures in order to improve the technocratic nature of policy formulation and application in developing countries. Technical assistance and orientation provided by the Bank was designed to be a catalyst for changes in consciousness in urban planning. Increasingly, too, it was hoped that "technical" criteria would shape urban decision making over political expediency. Where the World Bank was a major provider of funding, then it sought to use its influence on the board of management in order to press the paramountcy of "technical" over "political" criteria (Gilbert & Ward 1985). Fourthly, as mentioned above, programmes were required to be self-financing and therefore, to be replicable.

The rôle that the World Bank played in reforming urban policy in the less-developed countries is well known, and it produced a sea change in attitude among governments and other agencies, inducing a shift toward self-help as more than a "politically rhetorical pledge" (Pugh 1989: 251). This turnaround, however, did not lead to the Bank adopting the policy recommendations made by Turner and his followers (Nientied & van der Linden 1983). Although Turner's ideas were seen as compatible with the Bank's own perception of the problem, the specific arguments and policy recommendations won less attention (Burgess 1992). Ironically, this time it was the Bank's turn to adopt policy in rhetoric and jargon only. While accepting that the poor are constrained from providing their own solutions, the Bank viewed this as more the result of unsound pricing policies and the lack of an adequate understanding of markets by agencies and the state (Nientied & van der Linden 1983). In order to exemplify this throughout this chapter we propose to concentrate on World Bank policy with reference to land.

As Pugh (1989) notes, the early Bank literature was cautious on land policy. The *Urbanization Sector Working Paper* placed its discussion of urban land policy into an annexe (World Bank 1972). Yet this section was perhaps the most detailed in the document and was the only one to mention *specific* policy alternatives, especially some confidence in "land banking" as a possible policy solution. Nevertheless, overt land policy was quickly dropped from the Bank's agenda and only re-emerged as a key policy area a decade later with the publication in 1983 of Bank economist Johannes Linn's *Cities in the developing world: policies for their equitable and efficient growth*. Although privately authored, it closely reflects World Bank thinking during the 1980s. While the land problem was now identified as a major impediment requiring government intervention, Linn maintains an approach consistent with standard Bank ideology – as revealed by the subtitle. The land market presents an impediment because it is inefficient, defined in terms of supply and demand. Thus, while there is a concern with equity throughout the book, there also remains the emphasis on efficiency. But as our recent analysis of land prices and trends has stressed, a neoclassical approach centred around principles of supply and demand is too simple (Ward et al. 1993, 1994). Rather, as various authors argue in this volume (see especially Chs 5, 6 and 7), one must take account of the complex relations and processes engaged in residential land production and distribution.

For Linn, the problem is largely one of inefficiency and bottlenecks in the supply of land, particularly fully serviced land. The policy prescriptions that arise, therefore, are those that will facilitate the smoother operation of the (largely) privately produced land market. It is the market-supply mechanisms that have become "blocked", and the rôle of public-sector intervention is to clear those blockages. Specifically, Linn (1983: 182) proposes a range of actions which include:

(a) the "regularization" of illegal ("clouded") land titles, ostensibly to provide tenure security to de facto owners;
(b) limitations to be imposed on the monopoly control of land by a single group or land-owner, and which may result in artificially created scarcity and high land prices; and
(c) the development of effective land registration and cadastre, from which clear property ownership and taxation responsibilities may be identified.

The Bank no longer considers the public supply of land through low-cost residential subdivisions to be an appropriate response, except where these are used to enable the relocation of residents from downtown areas which have a high redevelopment value, i.e. to facilitate greater land-use efficiency, and to free up land sites for commercial or other uses.

This policy approach was very influential, especially proposals (a) and (c) above. In Mexico, for example, "regularization" has been vigorously promoted and implemented since the late 1970s, but instead of being viewed by local authorities *as an end* (i.e. the provision of clear-cut property title), it is now seen as a *means to an end* – namely incorporation into the property register and the subsequent application of property taxes, valorization charges, consumption costs and the many other levies that the local state is empowered to adopt (Ward 1986). These two policy development areas are tied to the notion of cost recovery, but in Mexico since the 1983–4 Municipal Reform they have begun to offer an important mechanism for generating resources necessary for city development programmes and for reducing dependence on state and federal lines of credit (Rodríguez & Ward 1992). But we acknowledge that, in Mexico at least, there has been a marked improvement in the capacity and efficiency of city administrations during the past 10 years and levels of servicing nationally and locally have improved, notwithstanding continuing rapid urban growth, recession and the exercise of austerity in public expenditure (Ward 1993). Mexico, at least, has successfully managed to do more with less, but increasingly these funds are expected to be generated locally.

The New Urban Management Programme

This brings us to the latest promotional "orthodoxy": the New Urban Management Programme. This began in 1986 as a 10-year project to raise levels of professionalism and the image of land management in the developing world. It was designed in two phases. During the first phase (1986–90), the aim was to develop the thinking and techniques of land management, infrastructure management and municipal finance. The second phase, from 1990 onwards, was promotional: to develop and promote awareness levels and to develop the quality of urban research and guides to more practicable policy alternatives. This is where we are today. Thus, NUMP signals the end of "urban" projects as we have come to know and understand them (i.e. direct hands-on intervention). Now the primary concerns are overall public administration. In the Bank's own words it focuses "urban operations on citywide policy reform, institutional development and high priority investments and . . . [puts] *the development assistance in the urban sector in the context of broader objectives of economic development and macroeconomic performance*" (World Bank 1991: 4, our emphasis). The new focus accelerates an already existing trend within the Bank for policy emphasis to concentrate on support for national housing finance systems, urban management and local government revenue generation and move away from urban "projects" and the "urban product" (*Urban Edge* 1985: 1).

Some researchers have suggested that this is a much more limited and less ambitious approach than either of the two earlier phases (Toye 1989). We believe that it is quite the reverse. The NUMP seeks to address total management and government practices, not just individual projects or lines of funding, and does so against the backdrop of more neoliberal macroeconomic management. It is actually very radical. Moreover, although to our knowledge this has not yet been made explicit, it is likely to lead to the application of total quality management principles (already widely used in business and industry) to urban administration, in a similar vein as is already occurring in many US cities (Austin, Texas, being a prime example).[3] Today, the question about the NUMP hinges on whether it is what cities in developing countries want, and whether it will work.

Table 2.1 Priority issues in land management under the New Urban Management Programme.

NUMP subject area	Emerging "priority" issues
1. Municipal finance	Central–local relationships (allocation and functions, financial flows, access to credit)
	Assignment and administration of revenue sources (including user charges)
	Municipal organization and administration
	Community participation, the informal sector and responsive urban management
2. Infrastructure	The linkages between urban infrastructure and service performance and macroeconomy
	Administrative, financial and technical means to improve infrastructure maintenance
3. Urban land management	Urban land and related markets: identifying and rectifying constraints
	Institutions and instruments to support land markets: the rôle of land registration, information management, urban planning and informal land management and administrative practices
	Urban land tenure and property rights
4. The urban environment	Improving urban waste management capacity and operational efficiency
	The legal and regulatory framework for environmental protection: assignment of jurisdiction for legislation, monitoring and enforcement. Use of economic instruments as alternatives to command and control
	Environmental implications of land-use control and property rights

Source: World Bank 1990.

In Table 2.1 we have reproduced the emerging "priority" issues related to different areas of the NUMP. These are relatively straightforward and embrace a wide gamut of activities that were often incipient during the "urban projects" phase, and became more visible during the 1980s emphasis on "market efficiency". Interestingly, municipal finance is at the top of the agenda. Under this heading three categories deal directly with finance and institution-building, while a fourth category identifies community participation and the need for urban managers to respond to public needs. The second subject area sets out the broad categories of Bank thinking on infrastructure improvement, and again presents these in terms of financial management. The third subject area advocates the removal of "constraints" from the land market. Thus, while the NUMP confirms the importance that the World Bank attaches to land markets, the policy outlines developed under this heading are essentially those mentioned by the Bank in the early 1970s. It is only the emphasis on land management, most obvious at the level of the three subcategories, that appears to have changed. Here, the Bank argues for "management" over "administration". Land markets are to be freed from constraints, supported and formalized. Although the Bank places land tenure and property rights in a separate category, we would argue that these issues are more closely linked to land registration mentioned in the category above. Effective land management also requires institution building (planning offices, land registries, etc.) as well as the development of administrative capacities and regulatory measures that will allow the effective implementation of those institutions' programmes. In the arena of urban environmental issues the Bank sees the need for *more* regulation for environmental control. Although the Bank seems willing to assert the need to improve and increase the amount of legal controls, there is a consistent emphasis on management, operational efficiency and property rights.

Urban productivity as a way forward?

The underlying motive for World Bank concern to adopt the NUMP is not entirely evident. Certainly, the concern appears to go much further than that of an urban programme per se. One suspects that the Bank is concerned by data leading up the 1990 World Development Report which indicated that the poor in some socialist countries fared better during the economic crisis of the 1980s than those in capitalist ones (Corbridge 1991). One also suspects that an underlying area of concern is that urban poverty "will become the most significant and *politically explosive* problem in the next century" (World Bank 1991: 4). The policies invoked to deal with the structural problems of many less developed economies, however, and which were supported by the Bank and the IMF in the early 1980s, required the adjustment of national economies toward more sensible pricing mechanisms, less welfare expenditure (especially if this required deficit spending) and real interest rates, and the whole package became known as structural adjustment loans (SALs). While these policies have had some impact in controlling the structural problems they set out to address – inflation, negative balance of payments and public sector revenue-debt ratios – they have inevitably hit the poor hard (Cornia et al. 1988). By the mid-1980s it was clear that SALs were not sufficient to provide economic growth, and the so-called "lost decade" of the 1980s was in danger of being repeated in the 1990s. One way around this has been for the Bank to promote the idea of "urban productivity". In market economies the Bank sees the need to raise productivity as a key mechanism to bring about growth. Although urban productivity has emerged as a rather nebulous term, it is the nub of the NUMP and thus the policy agenda for the 1990s.

The Bank's emphasis on the economic dimension of the city, its contribution to the wider economy, has been an element of policy since at least 1985. Before that the Bank tended to see the city as a net drain on resources; as a consumer of investment and subsidy rather than as a producer (Cohen 1990). Having in 1991 appointed a banker as president (Lewis Preston) it is hardly surprising that the Bank sees the raising of urban productivity as the greatest hope for improving living conditions and management of cities. To do so, it has adopted much of the thinking behind de Soto's (1989) work on informal urban, labour and transport markets in Peru. This argues that the poor, and more specifically the informal sector, have enormous economic potential and are contributing ever larger sums to the national economy. Moreover, it is the urban poor that have done most to keep developing economies afloat during the 1980s. The rise of the informal sector has taken place, however, in the context of institutional and political constraints: bribery, corruption, legal restrictions and the arbitrary use of power. Optimism about the ability of the poor to lead economic development rests on the fact that the poor have survived somewhat better than might have been expected given the severe economic crises of the past decade. Thus, the Bank places "paramount importance" on reducing the constraints to urban productivity (see Doebele, this volume). It advocates that governments should strengthen the management of urban infrastructure and reinforce the institutional capacity for the state to operate and maintain this system; improvements to the urban regulatory framework in order to increase market efficiency and to enhance the rôle of the private sector in shelter and infrastructure provision; improvements to the financial capacity of municipal institutions through the more effective division of resources and responsibility between central and local government; and a strengthening of financial services for urban development (World Bank 1991: 54).

In our view there is a major contradiction here. We acknowledge that the informal sector (or the "unregulated" sector) may be highly productive and sensitive to low-income needs. But the danger in developing a regulatory framework (even in ways that are more appropriate and conducive to unregulated activities) is that it ignores the fact that the benefits and productivity of the unregulated sector derive precisely *from their lack of regulation*. Attempts at regulation may expose the poor to costs that they did not have to face before – at least as soon as they get a job or a house plot (Ward & Macoloo 1992). Looking at de Soto in detail, Lehmann (1990) also argues that confidence in the ability of the poor to improve conditions for all is based on a false perception of the informal economy. First, Lehmann notes that the neoliberal analysis leads to the inevitable conclusion that a greater freeing of the poor from the constraints imposed by the state would raise productivity and, with it, economic growth. Yet the informal sector relies on the protection that the state itself imposes on the economy: the informal sector is created by regulation. Secondly, he notes that the neoliberal and de Soto's perception of the state as the only source of market imperfection is absurd – the state does not have a monopoly on bad decision-making, arbitrary or outdated systems of control, divisive policies, or regulations that lead to negative or illegal outcomes. Moreover, the preference for placing urban policy in terms of productivity and regulating arrangements for the market has meant that fundamental questions about welfare and equity are unmentioned in the NUMP. The resemblance to modernization theory thinking is quite clear: what is good for urban productivity is deemed unquestionably good for the poor as well. Urban productivity is linked to macroeconomic growth to raise the rate of the latter and not, in the short term, the welfare of those who will have contributed to the former. Thus, urban productivity is part of a trend that ignores issues of welfare and equity in favour of growth.

Let us continue with the land theme, and examine how the World Bank might raise productivity through the land market. The aim would be to formulate a regulatory framework that was appropriate to each city or administrative unit, and which would develop:

(a) fiscal incentives derived from land sales (e.g. capital gains and land transfer taxes) as well as from taxes and regulations – property taxes, valorization (betterment) taxes and many other possible levies, fees and charges;

(b) legal institutions to exercise land-use controls, land tenure, land registration, land allocation instruments and so on; and

(c) institutional arrangements to provide better information in order to assist in the smooth flow of market transactions: e.g. valuations and assessment systems; monitoring land ownership, land-price trends and plot turnover etc.

In short, instruments that will inform us about the nature and operation of segmented land markets. Dowall's (1991a) manual *The land market assessment: a new tool for research and policy analysis*, was explicitly for this purpose, and he discusses it in further detail in Chapter 3 of this volume. Excellent though it is in technical terms, it is firmly cast within the neoclassical economics paradigm of supply and demand, and as the various contributions to this volume demonstrate, it is by no means certain whether this approach and methodology are appropriate to the analysis of land and housing markets.

As we argued previously, there is nothing especially "new" about many individual elements embodied in the NUMP, but when taken overall as an integrated package it represents a quite radical departure from the urban projects and from the efficiency and equity approaches of former decades. In addition to the fundamental contradiction outlined above, it is possible to identify four other principal areas in which we believe the NUMP to be flawed.

The NUMP: a technical instrument for political problems?
Many of the researchers who attended the Fitzwilliam Workshop and whose work figures in this book understand the desirability of focusing not on supply and demand but on the *production of land*. Specifically, this means a focus on

land developers of rich and middle-income subdivisions – their patterns of ownership, practices of dividing up and promoting residential land, their discretionary practices, the relative profitability of land versus other investments, the opportunities to disestablish "community" land, and so on. For low-income groups the focus has been on the production of land by illegal practices of company-led or private landlord subdivisions, squatter invasions, and on the myriad ways in which community land is introduced to the market. In short, these are considered to be segmented land markets in which there is a wide range of actors, agents and social relations; degrees of formality and legality; variation in the size of holdings and practices of subdivision; different methods of financing land acquisition; and complex patterns of negotiation and regulation with local institutions. Thus, it is unhelpful to seek to diagnose the land problem in the rather simplistic terms of supply and demand, or to formulate policy interventions that do not begin to address the underlying causes, but which, at best, touch only on the effects.

Therefore, our argument is that methodologies must be designed so that the analysis focuses on the production of land, and seeks to identify the processes mentioned above, as a first step to any public-sector intervention. Land production is also an arena familiar to many politicians, and it embraces many of the considerations often made paramount when they formulate their decisions. Supply and demand accounting is not likely to impress politicians except at a general level. By way of a brief example, let us take the recent changes in Article 27 of the Mexican Constitution which deals with the Agrarian Code. Under the new provisions of the law, formerly inalienable (social property) land held by the *ejidal* community may now be sold by the users, provided that the maximum authority (the designated users in the community) vote to support the sale. In an urban context a "land market assessment" approach would be helpful only in so far as it identified the location of land considered ripe for transfer, the levels of local demand, and the forms of possible supply. It would not offer insight into the processes likely to occur in reality (and which are probably already under way beneath the surface). Here, the key considerations will be the extent of interest of private developers and the specific spatial location in which each has an active interest. The ability of those developers to work in concert is also likely to be crucial, and this would require sensitive and painstaking investigation into their social and business relations. Another crucial factor is likely to be the relative level of organization of the *ejidatarios* themselves, and whether they are likely to act in concert or individually; the support that they may receive from corporatist bodies such as the CCI, CNC, or from the agriculture and agrarian reform departments, etc. In Chapter 12 we provide evidence of how this local level of organization can be a crucial determinant of land-price fixing, and if the local state or dominant political party holds sway over these local *ejidal* interest groups, then the price of land supply may be much cheaper. The point is that although there has been an important rise in recent years in the technical capacity of Mexican government institutions to respond to residential land demands, implementation remains firmly in the hands of politicians, and is often highly politicized.

The "efficiency" of existing informal land markets

A second major problem with the NUMP and with approaches extolling urban productivity is the fact that in many countries land markets are actually working rather well (Angel et al. 1983). We disagree with Dowall's premise in his "Land Assessment" document that "in many countries policy-makers are concerned that urban land markets are not operating efficiently and that land is in short supply, land prices are high or combinations of the two". Although there are important exceptions where the absolute availability of land is short supply, or monopoly controls over the production of land induce scarcity, our experience is that often land is quite freely available, albeit through illegal modes of acquisition. Moreover, it often remains affordable (see Ch. 12), although it may also be relatively expensive since it is often produced illegally and without service provision. In these circumstances, insensitive regulatory controls that impede the supply of land, or demand compliance with servicing norms from the outset, may actively undermine many of the benefits and "efficiencies" of the informal/illegal system (Baross 1991, Ward & Macoloo 1992).

The need for market control, not market management

The third difficulty we have with the NUMP derives from our belief that the issue of equity needs to be addressed directly, rather than being left to the marketplace. In some respects we are seeing a return to the modernization theory of yesteryear in which it was believed that the benefits of growth would gradually "trickle down" to workers and to less-advantaged groups. There is abundant evidence worldwide that this did not happen, and that an important rôle of the state is to ensure some level of redistribution of the fruits of development – through protective policies, positive discrimination, progressive taxation and consumption charges, etc. The idea of subsidy has, however, become anathema to most governments and we agree that in the past many forms of subsidy and protectionist policy did encourage inefficiency. But there is also a rôle for sensitive subsidization where it indirectly facilitates productivity. For example, subsidized infrastructure will encourage self-help housing investment on plots even where the land is held without title, and this stimulates fixed investment in the urban landscape. (In keeping the costs of housing down, and the health of the worker population up, it also cheapens the reproduction costs of labour power – of direct benefit to productive investment.) This goes much further than what the World Bank has considered to be legitimate "lifeline" subsidies (i.e. those that led to direct reductions in public expenditure elsewhere, e.g. subsidized vaccination programmes to reduce down-line expenditures on expensive treatment for preventable diseases). Therefore, we need more explicit consideration of equity in urban development based on principles of progressive redistributive functions, rather than regressive ones. In our view, this requires greater state intervention, not less, and our belief is that markets must be controlled much more than they should be managed.

Our knowledge and level of expertise to manage urban development remains uncertain

Finally, notwithstanding the marked improvement in our knowledge of the urban development process, and the heightened sensitivity shown in the formulation of public policy interventions, we remain remarkably ill informed and uncertain of our ability to manage urban development effectively. A simple methodology gives a false sense of confidence in dealing with urban problems, hence our argument throughout this chapter that we must adopt more analytically aggressive approaches that will go to the heart of complex problems, even if that makes policy formulation more difficult and more time-consuming. Let us take the example of "betterment" taxation on the privately appropriated benefits of land valorization brought about by public intervention – to improve or to develop infrastructure, etc. The application of valorization and betterment taxation has become a key feature of the conditionality clauses attached to new lending as part of the practical measures designed to achieve adequate cost recovery (Pineda n.d., *Urban Edge* 1986: 10). Thus, this particular policy has attracted considerable attention and has much to commend it. Shoup's contribution to this volume (Ch. 16) offers an interesting and reflective account of how this may be made to work in less-developed contexts (by deferring the application of the tax/charge until the capital gain is mobilized on sale or transfer). But a problem arises since the amount of valorization is very difficult to ascertain and is often quite unpredictable. Our work in Puebla, Mexico, suggests that the determinants of valorization are complex and often obscure; that it is often non-existent or marginal; that the benefits may be considered dubious (i.e. a highway may be good for some, bad for others); and there is often a considerable and unpredictable time lag between implementation of a project and any discernible impact on land values (see Jones et al. this volume, and Jones & Ward 1994). In short, we don't know what the valorization impact may be, nor have we developed adequate tools to disaggregate and measure so-called windfall benefits brought about by betterment programmes. (In this respect we applaud Shoup's proposal, since this at least imposes a time delay, which may be considerable, and allows some effort to be made to assess the actual valorization impact, rather than guessing what that might be in advance.)

Our argument, drawn from this one example, applies equally well to several of the "priority issues" of the NUMP identified in Table 2.1. However, we are not saying that these are not legitimate lines of policy consideration, rather we want to urge caution about being overly confident, and not to overstate what can and cannot be achieved in the arena of urban management. The conclusion we derive from the example of betterment taxation is that it is probably safer (at this stage at least), to charge *users* of a public good or benefit, rather than purported "beneficiaries" in the land and housing markets. This echoes our earlier point about equity and the state's rôle in ensuring that fair play is achieved on a more or less level playing field.

Conclusion: learning by tilting

In medieval times the tilt was the divided track or field along which knights practised and refined their skills in attacking their enemies on horseback at full charge with lance in hand. We hope that this chapter will be perceived as an attempt to refine the current World Bank paradigm embodied in the NUMP. We have demonstrated that the Bank's philosophy stands out rather like windmills on the horizon, and that the conventional wisdom has shifted significantly over the years. Given historical precedent and the important proven rôle that the World Bank exercises in setting the overall lines of urban policy, it would be absurd (and unhelpful) were we to seek to "trash" this latest line of thinking. Rather, our comments are designed to stimulate debate and discussion and to urge, perhaps, some restraint about being overly ambitious about what may be achieved by the NUMP. Specifically, we should be wary about "wholesale" acceptance of the principles it contains, and of the idea of management rather than control. In matters of urban development the state should not unthinkingly abrogate its rôle as market controller, in a rush to conform with neoliberal orthodoxy.

We need also to develop our understanding of segmented land and housing markets and their behaviour in cities, and systematically to gather information that is both analytically strong and offers some degree of comparability between areas. In our opinion, this requires that we go beyond methodologies based on neoclassical principles of supply and demand, and develop approaches that focus on the production of land. Finally, we should consider very carefully possible regressive outcomes that regulation and "efficient" management of informal systems of land supply might have for the poorer economic groups. Although heavy subsidization is no longer an option (nor a demand of the poor), city administrations should seek to develop regulatory controls that unequivocally operate in a progressive distributional direction.

We recognize that in this chapter we are probably swimming against the tide of conventional wisdom. In bringing several partial examples of Mexico's land-market behaviour and urban politics to the fore, against the backdrop of our perceptions about current and past World Bank thinking, we hope that we may have provided an appropriate context for several of the more detailed discussions that follow. We hope, too, that the reader might have been persuaded to put the politics back into any assessment of land and housing market behaviour, as well as into the formulation of public policy. Surely, if these were primarily technical problems, then our past track record would have been very much better?

Notes

1. An earlier version of this paper was presented by Ward at the "Strategic Urban Management" conference organized by the Lincoln Institute of Land Policy and the Universidad Autónoma de Nuevo León, held in Monterrey, Mexico, 16–17 June 1992. We have borrowed the title, "Tilting at windmills" from an unpublished position paper written by Bill Bell as part of a major research project co-directed by one of us (Gilbert & Ward 1985). In that paper, Bell reviewed the various theories of the state and their principal academic protagonists.
2. In Mexico, the creation of INFONAVIT in 1972 led to a dramatic rise in formal housing production for blue-collar workers, financed as it was by tripartite contributions on the wage bill from state, employer and employee (Garza & Schteingart 1978, Ward 1991).
3. Total quality management is based upon the principles devised by Demming in the 1940s, embraced so successfully by Japan and only latterly, in light of its success, adopted in the US. In essence, the aim is to develop a client-oriented approach, to involve the whole of an organization's workforce in the decision-making process, and also to instil a greater sense of responsibility and identification with whatever products or services a particular enterprise produces. These principles are now actively being adopted by city management because they have been so successful in the private sector – Xerox, Motorola and the Cadillac branch of General Motors. Although there are inherent difficulties in implementing TQM in the public sector, there have been some notable advances towards successful adoption – for example, Austin, Texas. We anticipate that these principles will soon be tied into the NUMP and will become the leading "fix" for city administrations during the latter half of the 1990s.

CHAPTER THREE

An overview of the
land-market assessment technique

David E. Dowall

Introduction

Population and economic growth do not take place in thin air; they require land, and lots of it. Taking Asian cities alone, the rate of land conversion to urban use is enormous. In Bangkok, for example, between 1974 and 1984, urban growth requirements in the metropolitan area needed 32 km^2 of agricultural land per year (Dowall 1989a). In Karachi, over a similar period, 24 km^2 of land were needed per year for urban use (Dowall 1989b). Even in small and medium-sized Asian cities such as Bangalore, a rapidly growing city, land-conversion pressures are tremendous – about 13 km^2 of land per year (Srinivas 1989). In Kathmandu, the pace of land conversion to urban use meant a doubling in city size between 1971 and 1981 (Doebele 1987a).

Cities in developing countries are facing serious challenges as they attempt to cope with population growth. In most cases, public policies have been launched to relieve the symptoms of poor urban land and housing market performance. Public housing authorities have been set up and multilateral agencies have invested heavily in new programmes as part of national economic development planning (Menezes 1988). Nevertheless, urban development is overwhelming the capacity of local institutions, both public and private, to respond adequately to development pressures. As a result, policy-makers throughout the world are asking such questions as: Will there be enough land to support urban development? If not, how can the government mobilize resources to finance the construction of infrastructure? Is the land market operating efficiently? Will the prevailing patterns of population and housing density continue into the future or are there alternatives to urban development that require less land? How can agricultural land surrounding cities be preserved without driving the price of land beyond the reach of low- and middle-income households? Should the government attempt to aggressively control land development?

Against the backdrop of rapid growth and the questions posed above, policy-makers are beginning to recognize that efficient land-market operation is essential to maximize the potential delivery of affordable housing (Malpezzi et al. 1985). There are two fundamental impediments to this. The first is the absence of a workable model with which to understand the land market. The second is the lack of accurate and up-to-date information about urban growth. No-one knows the shape of land prices across the city, how far infrastructure or regularization of tenure change land prices, or how much government revenue could be raised from more efficient land taxation. In the absence of such knowledge the assumed existence of a land-price spiral in many developing-country cities is based on perceived price changes often informed by reports in transactions at the urban periphery or in the city centre (Dowall & Leaf 1991).

This chapter aims to contribute a methodology for collecting land-market information which can be used to improve the efficiency and effectiveness of urban land markets – The Land Market Assessment (LMA). This technique is a structured survey and analytical protocol that collects, organizes and analyzes information about local land-market operations. The LMA incorporates surveys over time of land-use and urban-development patterns, land prices and housing developments (Dowall 1991a). It is also grounded in the principles of the neo-classical tradition. It assumes that the land market is fundamentally a competitive mechanism for distributing land. Competition among users sets prices and determines the pattern of land use (Walters 1983). The market operates to allocate land on the basis of price: the potential user capable of paying the highest price will occupy it. Collecting and disseminating information about the land market will make the market more efficient, bringing faster market corrections, reducing risk to developers and balancing profits.

The LMA is also of use to the public sector. It is based on the assumption, however, that public policy that interferes with the dynamic process of the land market, while it may offer amenities, can create adverse conditions for urban land supply and prices (Dowall 1991a). The LMA has illustrated this last point by comparing Karachi and Bangkok. In Karachi, the Karachi Development Authority (KDA) underprices residential plots and thus limits its financial capacity to fund infrastructure, thwarting access by low-income families in the long run. In Bangkok, the absence of strict planning and development controls has been an incentive to an aggressive private sector and lower overall land prices (Dowall 1991a, Dowall & Leaf 1991).

The following sections outline some of the key issue areas where LMAs are especially useful in helping to clarify problems and identify initiatives for increasing land-market efficiency, and provide a description of the tool. A complete description of the LMA can be found in *The land market assessment: a new tool for urban management* (Dowall 1991a).

The benefits of LMA

The purpose of the LMA is to provide an accurate and up-to-date database on the operation of the urban land market in terms of prices, supply of serviced land and present and projected projects. LMAs can be used to support a variety of broad activities: providing information for governmental planning and decision-making; serving as a foundation for evaluating the economic and fiscal impacts of government policies and actions; and providing information for private-sector investment and development decisions.

The most significant benefit of the LMA is that it can vastly improve the quality of land development planning and policy-making by providing public officials with basic assessments of the state of the land market. In planning, as in medicine, diagnosis is the first step in problem-solving. The LMA is a method for assessing the *current* condition of the land market and can therefore indicate whether the supply of urban serviced land is capable of meeting growing population needs. As the so-called land problem is not solely an issue of residential land, the LMA can gauge whether other, competing, land uses are growing the faster. As the LMA can be adapted to include a spatial assessment, it can answer questions concerning where urban land conversion is taking place or where land prices are highest or increasing the fastest. The LMA also offers a straightforward method of analyzing whether land prices are increasing faster than the overall rate of inflation. From here, the LMA can afford insights into questions of welfare and access: how much land is being provided with minimum services for future urban development; is land and housing affordable; and which segments of the population do not have access to housing from the formal private sector?

LMAs can also be used to provide baseline estimates of future urban land requirements. They can be used to guide infrastructure programming and investment decisions and the development of land use planning policies. For example, LMAs can be used to estimate the demand for residential plots and commercial and industrial space requirements associated with projections of population and employment. Armed with these estimates, the adequacy of the current supply of land for urban expansion can be gauged and plans for expanding the supply of serviced land developed.

Many governments, when they create plans to guide future development, do not base them on a firm understanding of how their cities are growing. As a starting point, it is useful to assess the current performance of the local land market using a technique such as the LMA. This will begin to help set an agenda for government action to make the metropolitan area's land and housing markets more efficient. In San Pedro Sula, Honduras, an LMA was carried out to help the city prepare a new development plan (PADCO 1989).

The San Pedro Sula LMA identified the critical issues affecting the performance of the city's land market. It revealed that it was becoming overheated and that substantial increases in real land prices were occurring. Projections of land

26

demands for residential, commercial and industrial uses clearly suggested that considerable land will be needed for urban development over the next decade. The situation called for a fresh approach to land-development planning, including a more aggressive posture by the public sector to stimulate land development and infrastructure financing for urban growth. As a result, the establishment of a powerful land-development agency was proposed for San Pedro Sula and is now under consideration (PADCO 1989).

In Bangkok an LMA suggested that the National Housing Authority's (NHA) current policy of building large housing projects on the fringes of Bangkok was inappropriate for current market conditions. Based on the LMA, it was suggested that the NHA shift its housing development efforts to smaller-scale projects located closer to the central city. Also, since the private sector was moving into the lower price range, it was suggested that the NHA concentrate on increasing the supply of low-cost land for private housing development and not attempt to compete directly with private developers as long as they are moving "down market". LMAs can be used to evaluate the competitive position of government housing programmes vis-à-vis private-sector projects. The LMA played a critical rôle in illustrating the need to alter government housing and land-development programmes (Dowall 1989a, 1992).

Using LMAs to evaluate the economic and fiscal impacts of government policies and actions

Governments exert great influence, both positive and negative, over land-market outcomes. Through investments in infrastructure and regulations over land development, governments powerfully shape the operations of land markets, potentially creating substantial increases in land values. In other cases, government actions are less beneficial, with plans and regulations unintentionally causing serious negative side-effects on land-market operations. Given the important rôle that governments play in shaping land-market outcomes, it is extremely important for the implications of their investment and regulatory decisions to be understood.

Unfortunately, this is usually not the case. The way planning regulations adversely affect land-market outcomes is complicated and frequently difficult to estimate. The biggest impediment to gauging the effects of government regulations on land markets is the lack of information about land prices, and demand and supply conditions. With the LMA, an information base can be established to monitor land markets so that the potential effects of new government policies and programmes can be evaluated. The LMA can be used to answer questions such as: Are there specific public policies or actions that are constraining the land market? Is infrastructure placement limiting residential development? Are greenbelts or agricultural land preservation policies limiting development? Are planning standards and building codes pushing up housing prices?

As local governments begin to seek out new approaches for financing urban development, techniques such as special assessment districts and beneficiary charges will come into currency. In order to develop these fiscal tools, accurate information about land values and the impacts of infrastructure developments on land values will be needed. The LMA, by systematically cataloguing land-value information, can play a critical rôle in supporting the application of these new financial tools. As a first step, the LMA can serve as a foundation for gauging land-price trends. Over time, as data on land prices are tabulated, the government can gauge the impact of public investments and use the information to set taxes, fees or user charges.

In Karachi, an LMA was conducted to assist the Karachi Development Authority (KDA) in assessing urban land and housing market conditions in the metropolitan area. The KDA is Karachi's major land developer, charged with the responsibility of developing and distributing residential plots to residents. Over the past 10 years, the agency has had a difficult time financing the construction of serviced plots, claiming that it lacked sufficient resources to provide necessary infrastructure. Based on the information gathered by the Karachi LMA, the market value of fully serviced plots was estimated for 1980 and 1985, and used to project potential revenues that could have been created by the KDA had it priced and sold plots at their full development value (Dowall 1991b).

Table 3.1 compares the actual allotment revenues with estimated developed market values of plots allotted in 1980 and 1985. In 1980, the KDA allotted 2,477 plots by computer ballot. Based on the 1980 allotment-price schedules for the schemes in which these 2,477 plots were located, the KDA received a total of Rs81.3 million. Of this amount, Rs12.3 million was from the allotment of "small plots" below 120 sq. yd; the remainder was from larger plots. Based on regression model estimates, the total value of these plots, if fully developed would be Rs339.7 million. This is the total market value of the plots with infrastructure, taking into consideration their location and size. Thus, the difference between the Rs81.3 million and Rs339.7 million represents the development gain created by the KDA.

By setting its allotment prices at cost recovery, the KDA is transferring a development gain of Rs258.4 million to the allottees. Since there is no guarantee that the allottees are of low or moderate income, the transfer of this gain serves little social purpose. The KDA would have been better off to charge full development value prices for the allotments and use the additional revenues to build low-cost housing or cross-subsidize the purchase of plots by accurately targeted low-income households.

The situation for 1985 is much the same, in terms of the relationship between allotment revenues and actual developed market value. A total of 10,210 plots were allotted in 1985. They generated total revenues of Rs362.7 million, an average of Rs35,500 per plot. The projected total development value of these plots based on their size and location is Rs552.3 million, or Rs54,000 per plot. The difference between development gain and allotment price is Rs189.6 million, or Rs19,000 per plot. In this case, plots are being sold at a 34 per cent discount to their market value.

Table 3.1 Comparison of KDA allotment revenues and developed value of plots allotted by KDA in 1980 and 1985 in 1988 Rs, Karachi.

	1980	1985
1. KDA plot allotment Revenue:		
Small plots	12,300,000	142,700,000
Large plots	69,000,000	220,000,000
Total KDA allotment Revenue	81,300,000	362,700,000
2. Developed market value of plots:		
Small plots	58,400,000	171,300,000
Large plots	281,300,000	381,000,000
Total developed plot value	339,700,000	552,300,000
3. Potential additional revenues $(2-1)$		
Small plots	46,100,000	28,600,000
Large plots	212,300,000	161,000,000
Total potential revenue	258,400,000	189,600,000

Source: Dowall (1991b).

The results of the Karachi LMA reveal the enormous impact of the public sector's production and allocation of land to citizens at prices below market values. The difference in values creates an enormous incentive for speculation, and merely transfers the benefits of development gain from the public sector to private individuals. As a matter of public policy, the KDA should consider shifting the disposal of plots from allotment by balloting to auction for all but the smallest plots, which should be carefully targeted for delivery to low-income households.

By using auctions to dispose of most of its plots, the financial condition of the KDA would be vastly improved; production of schemes and serviced plots would accelerate. At the same time, a portion of the additional resources could be used to subsidize the production of low-income housing. In addition, the administrative burden would be reduced, allowing the KDA to concentrate on conveying plots to low- and moderate-income groups.

This example illustrates how the outputs of the LMA can be used for setting the prices of publicly provided plots. The same method can be used to determine the total land value increase created in an assessment district by the development of public infrastructure. Such estimates provide the critical foundation for setting taxes and beneficiary charges.

Providing information for private-sector investment and development decisions

Unlike stock, bond and commodity markets around the world, land markets are disorganized. There is no central clearing house for information about land prices, land conversion and demand for land. Most private-sector land developers must take substantial economic risk when launching projects. Unfortunately, the lack of information about land and property markets in most cities in developing countries has thwarted attempts by private-sector developers, bankers and consultants to prepare feasibility studies of potential projects.

The level of housing or property demanded in the market can be determined by the rate of sales of housing units or commercial units over the past year. This level of "absorption" will suggest that so many housing units or square metres of office or commercial space can be sold in the marketplace over the next year. If the current level of units available for sale in the market exceeds a full year's amount of absorption, then the market may be oversupplied. In Bangkok, the results of a project survey indicated a strong and demonstrated demand for housing units priced below US$10,000 in the northern corridor of Bangkok (Dowall 1989a). Units produced in this price range sold well, at about twice the rate of the overall housing market. The survey helped the development community recognize the potential profitability of building houses in this price range in the northern corridor.

LMAs can play a critical rôle in helping to inform private investment decision-making. For example, by illustrating the effective demand for low- and moderate-cost housing, LMAs can help stimulate the production of such units by the private sector. On the other hand, LMAs can identify when the production of certain urban uses far exceeds effective demand, thus helping to bring about faster land-market corrections. In the long run, with improved information about the market, the risk associated with development is reduced and developers may be able to operate with lower rates of profit (Walters 1983).

Surveys of housing and commercial property development projects can be used by developers to gauge the current level of supply by geographic area. If detailed project-level information is gathered on the types of housing or product types currently for sale, and tabulated by price and location, private as well as public developers can compare the current level of supply with demand to determine whether an additional project is feasible.

The LMA as a tool for institution-building and public–private sector partnership

As should be clear by now, the benefits of LMAs are significant and are likely to generate widespread support among public- and private-sector planners and decision-makers. A key implication of these broad-ranging benefits is that support for LMAs can be generated from many quarters of the public and private sector. Even so, when organizing for the LMA, care should be taken to involve the full participation of benefiting agencies. Before the LMA process is even begun it is important to develop broad support for it. The best way to do this is to establish both public- and private-sector participation in the planning and execution of the LMA. To avoid conflicts between competing line agencies in government, the responsibility for execution of the LMA should be lodged with the executive office of the local government and include the full participation of the private sector.

Obtaining full co-operation from the private sector is critical. To obtain support, a LMA steering committee should be established, containing prominent professionals from the private-sector development community. The group should be established at the start of the LMA process to discuss how the LMA can be used to increase the performance and efficiency of both the private and public sectors. There must be agreement about which types of data to collect and the frequency of collection. Firm protocols should also be set for preserving the confidentiality of sensitive market information. Obviously, it is absolutely essential to address the concerns of citizens that the government is snooping. Here, the most effective method is to take the time to explain the purposes for which the surveys will and will not be used (for example, for land-use planning purposes, but not for tax-collection audits). Special attention is needed to explain how the anonymity of those interviewed will be protected (for example, the survey teams are not to submit the names of those interviewed to the government agency managing the LMA).

Another organizational issue is to ensure that the surveys are conducted in both formal and informal areas of the city or town. The process in both areas is essentially the same. But it may require the slight modification of surveys or the types of information collected in informal areas. Experience in Karachi, Jakarta and Bangkok indicates that informal land brokers can be identified quite easily and that they have little difficulty responding to questions about land prices. The housing-project survey discussed below may also need to be modified to capture accurately relevant information about informal land and housing developments.

As the LMA offers a vehicle to bring the private and public sectors together to co-ordinate land-use policy, procedures for periodically disseminating LMA reports also should be drafted. This can be accomplished by way of seminars, reports and briefings to public- and private-sector professionals. In the long run, it is desirable to issue an annual report on the state of the land market. This report should pinpoint key constraints in the land market and identify actions for removing land-supply bottlenecks. The report should be widely distributed to both public and private decision-makers. Increased information and knowledge on all sides should ensure a more efficiently run land market.

Timetable for conducting assessments

The time required to prepare an LMA will depend on the size of the city, the level of detail of analysis and the number of professional staff assigned to the project. If the city is starting from scratch, it will take approximately one to two years to complete fully an LMA. However, usually much of the information needed has already been collected, shortening the time required for completion. The LMA should be updated every three to five years depending on the rate of urban growth and available resources.

The first step in launching a land and housing market assessment is to review available reports and data sources compiled by public and private agencies on

31

the land and housing conditions in the metropolitan area. Based on these preliminary efforts, the study team can proceed to define the precise scope of the land and housing market assessment, including the size and shape of the study area, the types of data to be collected and analyzed, and the specific policy questions to be addressed (Dowall 1980).

One of the most important early questions is defining the area of study. This will often require a political decision to be made, as the area may depend on the political boundaries of the local government, the spatial organization of tabulated data (such as population, infrastructure, cadastral and building activity), and on the location of employment centres and commuting patterns in the metropolis. The size of the land and housing market assessment area should depend on how far into the periphery households will search for housing to purchase or rent over the next 10 years. In most cases, information is tabulated at a district or subdistrict level and these units form the basis for defining the study area from a data collection and availability standpoint.

Establishment of geographic zones for data organization
For the LMA database to be useful in assessing precise land-market conditions and to gauge the impact of government policies and investment decisions effectively, data must be collected on a spatially disaggregated basis and the study area must be divided into zones for tabulation of these data.

On a conceptual level, these zones should be defined so that each provides a homogeneous pattern of land and housing market characteristics. For example, the boundaries of the zones should be set so that the land-use patterns within zones are roughly similar, not a mixture of commercial, industrial or residential areas. In outlying areas, the zones should be similar in terms of the pattern and density of urban development. The zones should also be similar in terms of social and economic conditions such as household income. The finer the grain and the more homogeneous the zones, the more accurate the database and the assessment of the effects of government policies and investments. On the other hand, the greater the number of zones, the more difficult and expensive it will be to collect and update data.

Another consideration in defining zones is that their size and total number should be based on the underlying base of existing data. While it is impossible to delineate different zones from those in the database, it is possible to combine zones into larger groupings. In large metropolitan areas (over 1,000,000 in population), where the potential number of zones is large and is likely to be difficult to manage, it is appropriate to combine zones. The zones should be small enough, however, to illustrate the activities of fundamentally different land and housing markets but not too large to mask important differences in market activity. (On the problems of large-scale urban models, see Lee 1974.) In Bangkok, a metropolitan region with a population of over 6 million, a land and housing market information base of 344 zones was developed. Figure 3.1 illustrates the zone system used for the Bangkok LMA. In Karachi, 271 were tabulated. In other cities, the number of zones for urban modelling has ranged from 100 to over 1,000. For purposes of analysis, given computer and software capabilities, the total number of zones should be limited to less than 500. The limitation of a maximum of 500 cases should not present any significant problems for developing a clear assessment of a metropolitan area's land and housing market.

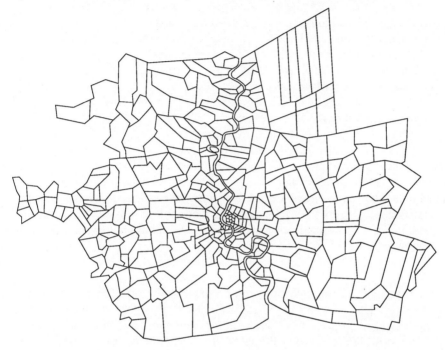

Figure 3.1 Division of land market zones for Metropolitan Bangkok.

Basic land-use and population data for tabulation

For each geographic zone, data on land use and population should be collected for at least two points in time: a "base year" and "current year". The base year is normally the last year in which either aerial photographs or satellite images are available for analysis. Ideally, the two years should span a period of 5–10 years. The following data should be collected:

(a) zone identification number
(b) size of zone in hectares
(c) "x" and "y" co-ordinate of the centroid of the zone
(d) total urbanized land in base and current year in hectares
(e) total residential land area in base and current year (gross area)
(f) total housing units in base and current year
(g) commercial land area in base and current year (gross area)

(h) industrial land area in base and current year (gross area)
(i) institutional land area in base and current year (gross area)
(j) vacant land area in base and current year
(k) vacant land with infrastructure in base and current year
(l) change in urbanized land area, base–current year in hectares
(m) change in residential land area, base–current year
(n) change in total housing units, base–current year
(o) change in commercial land area, base–current year
(p) change in industrial land area, base–current year
(q) change in institutional land area, base–current year
(r) change in vacant land area, base–current year
(s) change in vacant land with infrastructure, base–current year
(t) population in base and current year
(u) change in population, base–current year
(v) population density in base and current year
(w) change in population density, base–current year

By providing baseline data on land-use changes, infrastructure availability, and population by geographic zone over time, a very detailed assessment of the spatial patterns of urban development in a metropolitan area can be determined. The data can be tabulated from land-use surveys, aerial photographs or satellite images.

Land-value information

The next step in data collection is to assemble land-price information by zone and year. This information is available from a variety of sources. Many countries levy property taxes and therefore compile information on land-value assessments. While in many instances these assessments lag or understate the market, they may provide a usable measure of land-price inflation (although see Amitabh, Smolka, this volume). In cases where private land-value information is also available, it can be used to verify the public land-value assessments. Land-value information can also be directly collected from interviews with real-estate brokers. Only a few agents in the land market can be relied on to provide accurate information and then only for specific areas of the city about which, ideally, they have an intimate working knowledge. A variety of methods can be used to identify brokers. For formal-sector brokers, membership lists of professional organizations can be used. Since the objective of the land-price database is a comprehensive coverage of the metropolitan area's active land markets, interviews should target most (over 50 per cent) of the neighbourhoods in the study area. This requires informal-sector brokers to be interviewed as well. They can be identified by seeking advice from village headmen and residents. In all cases only experienced brokers are surveyed. In both Jakarta and Karachi, for example, approximately 100 real-estate brokers working in either the formal or informal sectors were interviewed to obtain land-value information on plot prices.

The first step is to design a suitable questionnaire which contains a series of questions aimed at getting brokers to appraise the current probable selling price of several specific types of residential plots. The basic plot is a typical hypothetical plot, $120\,m^2$ say, located on a collector street. Other conditions control for the influence of other variables. The hypothetical plot is assumed to be located mid-block to avoid assessment of corner positions. It is assumed that there are no existing buildings on the plot in order to eliminate confusion over building and pure land value. It is also assumed that the hypothetical purchase price for the plot is made in a single payment, thus eliminating implicit interest conditions in the final price.

The appraisal process is repeated for plots with different types of land tenure and levels of infrastructure. Once the appraisals are complete, the brokers are asked to estimate the probable selling prices of plots for the base year. All prices should be tabulated in terms of price per square metre and adjusted to constant price levels.[1] In order for a representative price to be arrived at, three brokers are asked to assess each area, and the middle value (median) in each case is taken. Including appraisals for standard plots, plots with infrastructure and plots with and without tenure security, within each neighbourhood median values of between three and nine types of parcels should be acquired for each year.

It is a straightforward exercise to organize the land-price data according to zone. This can then be combined with additional information on land use and population. In most cases, data on land values (based on appraisals) by type of land can be tabulated. For example, an ambitious collection of land values for serviced and unserviced land for residential, commercial and industrial use might include, for each zone, the median land value (constant prices per square metre) for serviced residential plots, the change in median land value (constant prices per square metre) for serviced residential plots, median land value (constant prices per square metre) for unserviced parcels, change in median land value for unserviced parcels, median land value for serviced commercial and industrial plots located on main streets, and change in median land value for serviced commercial and industrial plots.

Once the land-value information has been coded into the spreadsheet (see the appendix to this chapter), patterns and trends of land values over time and space can be calculated. This information can be used to determine where land values are increasing fastest and also where land is priced low enough to make the construction of low- and moderate-cost housing feasible. Basic land-use, population and demographic information can be added to compare land-value changes with the spatial distribution of zones experiencing the greatest population increase between the current and base years. Such calculations generate useful information for identifying growth areas in the metropolitan region.

Tabulating housing, commercial and industrial uses

Since governments in most metropolitan areas do not compile detailed information on changes in housing stock or land use by small area, it is necessary to interpret and tabulate aerial photographic surveys. If aerial photographs are not available, then the acquisition of satellite images should be pursued. As outlined in a technical paper by Marie-Agnes Bertaud, satellite (SPOT) images can be acquired for less than US$2,000. SPOT images have been available since 1986 and offer good resolution of 10m in panchromatic mode. Combined with a thorough ground survey, SPOT images can be used to develop land-use typologies for assessing land-use and urban-development patterns (Bertaud 1989). Ideally, two aerial or satellite surveys that closely correspond with the time interval of the assembled demographic data listed above can be utilized for the housing and land-use analysis. Based on field surveys of the metropolitan area and preliminary assessments of the aerial surveys, a typology of housing types, including both informal and formal housing development, can be defined for detailed tabulation, differentiating slums and squatter settlements, land subdivisions, formal private housing developments, and public housing projects. Non-residential uses, including industrial areas, commercial districts and institutional uses, can also be tabulated.

Once the typology has been established, tabulations of housing by type of unit should be made for each zone.[2] A suitable breakdown of typologies would be:

(a) informal housing settlements
(b) public-sector housing projects
(c) formal private-sector, low-density housing estates
(d) formal private-sector, medium-density housing estates
(e) formal private-sector, high-density housing estates

For each category of housing, an estimate of the number of habitable units should be made for the base and current year aerial photographs or satellite images. Comparison of the tabulations provides a clear picture of changes in the housing stock over the period. Calculations of absolute changes in the type of housing and change in housing by zone and by type will identify the specific patterns of housing supply dynamics.[3]

Using the same photographic survey or satellite-image information, the rate of land conversion within each zone over time can easily be established. By calculating the area converted from agricultural to residential and other urban uses, and correlating it with housing-unit changes or changes in commercial and industrial employment, an estimate of the land required to support urban growth can be made. With this type of information, estimates of annual requirements for land can be developed. Figure 3.2 illustrates land-conversion patterns for Metropolitan Bangkok between 1974 and 1984.

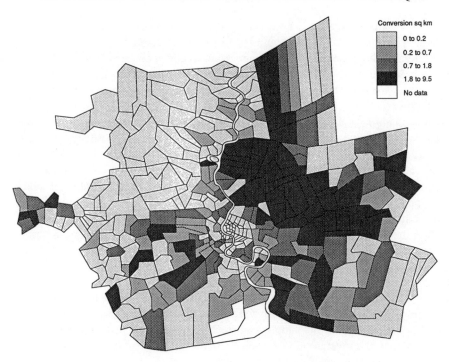

Figure 3.2 Land conversion in Metropolitan Bangkok 1974–84 (km²).

Estimating current and future developable land supply

The most critical element of the assessment is an estimate of the current and future supply of developable land. This is defined as land having reasonable access to roads and other critical infrastructure such as water and electricity, and not constrained by physical impediments such as steep slopes, or by governmental limitations on development. To determine which lands are potentially developable, assessments of parcels must be made according to physical constraints, governmental policies and the location of current infrastructure. Additional assessments should be made of the potential for the redevelopment of urban areas. While difficult to gauge precisely, redevelopment potential can be measured by determining past redevelopment activity and extrapolating into the near future. Depending on the type of infrastructure and the cost required to extend services, land located within one-half to one kilometre of existing infrastructure should be classified as developable, assuming there are no physical and governmental constraints. By combining this information with land-use data on vacant parcels, the potential supply of serviced land can be estimated (Dowall 1980, 1981, 1989a).

To estimate future supply conditions, proposed infrastructure programming by local government must be assessed and mapped. If a parcel is to receive road and water systems access within five years, and has no other constraints, it should be classed as developable in the future estimates.

In determining land supply, it is important to consider vacant and under utilized parcels in built-up areas. Although many vacant parcels do not have road access, or are not well suited for development, their location and potential for infill construction make them important sites to consider when estimating land supply. Gauging the potential of under utilized parcels is more difficult. Here areas with low-rise older buildings should be evaluated and estimates made of the net urban development potential.

By comparing land-supply estimates with future demand, assessments of future land-market conditions can be made. For example, the number of years of supply of serviced land should be estimated by dividing the annual urban land requirements by the current supply of serviced land. A table showing the annual increase in the stock of serviced land and the annual urban land requirements should be prepared to illustrate whether the current and future supply of serviced land is sufficient to meet urban growth requirements over the next five to ten years.

The estimates of land-supply inventory should be tabulated for each zone. This information can then be analyzed to determine the spatial patterns of land supply. Levels of current supply can be compared with past and anticipated patterns of land conversion to determine whether there is sufficient land in high-demand areas of the metropolitan region.

Adding housing project information to the land-market database
Detailed information about the price of housing units offered in the market as well as detailed information about their characteristics can be obtained from a survey of projects currently on the market. This section describes the basic strategy for carrying out a survey of housing projects, but the same technique can be applied to commercial and industrial projects.

To gauge current market activity, a compilation of housing projects, both formal and informal, currently offering units should be made. The universe of projects should be assembled from newspaper advertisements and interviews with bankers, community organizers, government officials, real-estate brokers and other key informants. All of the identified projects should be grouped into the same housing typologies used for the aerial photographic or satellite-image interpretation. Based on the relative share that each type of housing represents of the total number of housing units selling at present, a stratified random sample of housing projects can be drawn for further research (Malpezzi et al. 1982).

Detailed interviews with the sales personnel at each of the sampled project sites should be conducted by field interviewers. The interviews should concentrate on quantifying the land area of the project; the number of housing units or plots by model type or size; the selling price of units or plots by model type or size; the sales rate of units or plots per month by model type and size; the terms of financing available for the project; and profiles of buyers of units or plots including income, occupation, prior residence, and whether they were first-time buyers (see Dowall 1991a for a complete description of the survey including a questionnaire).

The project surveys provide detailed information on the current supply of housing on the market that can be used to assess the affordability of the current supply of housing relative to current household incomes in the metropolitan area. It also provides a clear picture of the types and locations of units selling most quickly. The housing-price information and land-value information can be used to gauge overall housing affordability in the metropolitan area. Based on current financing practices and lending terms, estimation of the monthly payment necessary to finance the purchase of a house is straightforward. By comparing monthly housing costs with monthly current household income, housing affordability can be determined (Malpezzi et al. 1985).

LMAs in practice

Allowing for modifications to local conditions, the LMA has been applied to three Asian cities, Bangkok, Jakarta and Karachi, as well as to San Pedro Sula in Honduras. The results for the first three cities have been most widely disseminated and will only be briefly summarized below (Dowall & Leaf 1991, PADCO 1989). Price changes conform to the expected pattern. In all three Asian cities prices were lower at the periphery than in the centre. The land-price gradient appeared to be flattening. Prices were lowest in Bangkok and highest in Karachi. This conforms broadly to the city with the most open and the most restricted land supply system. Comparing prices with GNP per capita indicates that land in Karachi requires a far greater proportion of income than the difference in land price would imply.

Land-price rises were calculated for each city. In Karachi real prices rose by an average 11 per cent between 1985 and 1987. The prices of large residential plots rose less rapidly (Dowall 1989b). In Jakarta real prices rose 20 per cent between 1987 and 1989 but were considerably higher (37 per cent) on plots without clear land title or infrastructure, and in informal settlements (Dowall & Leaf 1991). It has been calculated that improving plots in Karachi by providing infrastructure raises plot prices by about 100 per cent, while in Jakarta the increase is between 80 and 110 per cent, and improving security of tenure raises prices by 40–50 per cent (Dowall 1989b, Dowall & Leaf 1991). In Bangkok prices appear to have risen from 1977 to 1986, with price rises slowing from 1980 onwards. Affordability, however, has improved for both middle- and low-income households (Dowall 1991a). In San Pedro Sula, price rises were 15 per cent despite an enormous increase in land supply, particularly through invasion and illegal subdivision (Dowall 1991a).

As indicated in the sections above, the LMA takes a broad view of the land market and makes assessments of housing as well as land supply. In San Pedro Sula, for example, the LMA predicted that a total of 2,650–3,555 ha of land would be required for future growth between 1989 and 2001. This means that the city is expected to grow by one-half to two-thirds in 13 years, a rate 3.5 times faster than its historical average growth rate. From such predictions the LMA is well placed to make policy prescriptions. In San Pedro Sula, it was decided that the government should adopt a more aggressive posture to stimulate land development and infrastructure financing. In Karachi, the LMA identified a serious barrier to efficient market operations in the form of the government agency entrusted with land-development control. The LMA found that the Karachi Development Authority (KDA) underpriced the land it sold on the market, creating an incentive for speculation. The LMA concluded that the government should privatize the KDA's land holdings (Dowall 1991b). In Bangkok, the situation is different. The land market is substantially private-sector led and developers appear to have been adept at reducing costs and moving down-market when conditions have required it. It was appropriate, therefore, for the LMA to recommend that the government curtail its current policy of building large housing projects at the periphery and concentrate on smaller projects nearer to the city centre.

Conclusions

The land and housing market assessment is an essential first step towards making local land and housing markets more efficient. The information base generated by the assessment can be used to gauge market performance, identify future needs for infrastructure, assess housing affordability, and assess the impact of public policies and actions. By providing accurate land-market information the LMA should remove one of the major obstacles to the operation of rational economic behaviour in the land market. It should also pose questions about appropriate government policies: what level of urban land-use regulation is needed for effective management of urban development in fast-growing cities in developing countries? To what extent should policy-makers rely on economic market mechanisms or use government policies and programmes to determine or control how land is allocated and used? What is the optimal division of labour between the public and private sectors regarding the provision of urban services and low-cost housing?

Governments around the world pursue urban land-policy objectives that rely on a vast range of policy tools and institutions to achieve them. Many cities use master plans, zoning, subdivision regulations, building codes and other public policies to shape development. These regulations are normally adopted to help protect the urban and natural environment, gear infrastructure investments with development, and maintain and enhance property values. Other objectives are more difficult to achieve: providing the poor with access to land, and controlling land speculation and land inflation. In the minds of many policy-makers achieving these goals requires stronger medicine: nationalization of land, public-land development, and highly centralized property registration systems to control and monitor land-ownership.

A global assessment of these urban policies reveals troubling evidence that many government urban land policies are ineffective and, perhaps more alarmingly, frequently result in significant adverse impacts on social welfare and economic productivity.[4] In the course of adopting these and other well intentioned regulations, little consideration is given to their potential cost-effects. For example, few attempts are made to answer such questions as: how will master plan and zoning designations, if enforced, affect the supply of land for residential development? Similarly, how will minimum lot-size standards affect lot costs? How do cumbersome and redundant formal and customary land-registration systems distort land-market operations and encourage informal and unregulated development? Failure to address these questions is unfortunate, since there is ample evidence that overly stringent land-use and development controls and poor titling and registration systems reduce land-market efficiency and push land prices above what would prevail under competitive conditions.

Because many government interventions are inefficient and lead to suboptimal distributions of land resources, some policy experts argue that the best way to "manage" land-use and development patterns is to rely on market forces. On the other hand, without planning and regulations, land markets are likely to generate enormous external costs and fail to produce public facilities such as parks, open spaces, major infrastructure and urban services that the private sector cannot profitably produce and sell. Thus, the solution to ineffective and counterproductive urban land policies is not to do away with government interventions and policy initiatives, but to find the proper balance, or division of labour, between the public and private sectors regarding urban land development and management. This chapter has argued that striking this balance will not be easy. But, if we are to get close to answering such important questions, having an appropriate methodology and knowing how that methodology might "colour" our interpretations become central to our understanding.

Appendix
Resources necessary for setting up an LMA process

To carry out the LMA several types of professionals are needed, including a land economist with market survey research experience; a land planner with aerial photographic and satellite-image interpretation experience; a statistician with computing and database management experience; two data analysts for coding, data entry and fieldwork; a draftsperson; and a team of research assistants for conducting field surveys. In smaller towns such a team will not be necessary. The minimum level of staffing is probably one urban planner who has been trained in applying the LMA and one to two survey assistants.

In large cities and metropolitan areas, developing the database and conducting statistical analyses will require a computer system. The minimal system is an IBM AT compatible system with 640K of RAM, two disk drives and a 20 Mb hard disk. The system should have VGA graphic capabilities and have either a colour or mono monitor. A high-speed, dot-matrix printer is necessary and it should be able to handle continuous-feed paper up to 14 inches (35.5cm) wide.

For large metropolitan areas, the best method of presenting land and housing market information is by using a computer mapping system. Such a system can be run on the IBM compatible system with a type "A" multi-colour pen plotter and a 12×12 inch (30×30 cm) digitizing pad. The total cost for the computer equipment is between US$6,000 and US$7,000, or between US$4,000 and US$5,000 without the computer mapping capability.

The software required to run the computers and develop the database and map files will be: Lotus 1-2-3 or a comparable spreadsheet system, an advanced statistical package such as SPSS- PC+ or STATGRAPHICS, and ATLAS GRAPHICS, a computer mapping system. A word-processing system such as WordPerfect or WordStar and a graphics programme such as Harvard Presentation Graphics will be needed for preparing reports. The prices of these software packages vary considerably, but should cost less than US$2,000. Thus, for under US$10,000 a complete computer installation can be created for conducting the land and housing market assessment. This system can also be used for other management and research functions such as financial modelling, demographic projections, database management and report production. In smaller cities and towns, the data can be analyzed manually using a pocket calculator and/or adding machine.

With the delineation of land and housing market study zones, a database system should be established for coding data. The database should be developed on a microcomputer, using a spreadsheet system such as Lotus 1-2-3 (Landis 1986). Basic information for each zone should include: (a) zone identification number; (b) size of zone in hectares or square kilometres; and (c) an "x" and "y" coordinate for locating each zone.

Notes

1. The results of each interview should be tabulated on a questionnaire form. Information recorded on each form is then computer-coded using a spreadsheet such as Lotus 1-2-3, and verified for accuracy.
2. Satellite imagery offers a level of differentiation that is much more coarse than aerial photographic interpretation.
3. While trends of past housing construction provide a partial assessment of future housing activity, a separate projection of housing demand is a more accurate method of gauging the

future. Projection models of regional housing demand, such as the USAID system (Struyk 1987), should be considered more fully to incorporate demographic factors that shape housing demand. With consistent projections of future housing need, land requirements for residential development can be determined.

4. The range of policies is staggering: land nationalization in Tanzania; massive slum eradication in Kenya; slum regularizations in Pakistan and the Philippines; breaking up large landholdings in India; speculation taxes in Taiwan; preservation of agricultural areas in the USA; and green-belt designations in Seoul.

CHAPTER FOUR

Urban land and macroeconomic development

Moving from "access for the poor" to urban productivity

William A. Doebele

This chapter attempts to evaluate aspects of the current level of understanding of urban land and property markets. It begins with a brief comment on the prerequisites for an effective literature and a critical examination of three intellectual premises that have shaped current research. It then proposes three new research priorities and discusses the problem of relating land markets to urban production and macroeconomic development. I outline these as the broad methodological goals for the future.

Introduction: the prerequisites of an effective literature

The body of literature on any subject may be roughly divided into two types: that which advances knowledge for its own sake, and that which attempts to advance knowledge in a way that will have an impact on policy and actions in the real world. Research and writing about urban land markets in developing countries serves both ends, of course, but by and large its exponents hope to fall into the second category. However, if this is the case, one must ask if the work in the field has in fact been well designed for this purpose.

There are four prerequisites if research is to have an impact in the consciousness of policy-makers. First, it must resonate with issues that have priority on the mental agenda of the policy-maker concerned. Secondly, the work must be done within an established and reasonably rigorous intellectual framework that makes it comparable with work by others on the same subject. Thirdly, it must have the ability to be predictive. And fourth, it should be in a form that suggests prescriptions for policy.[1]

Considering the first requirement, it is important to understand that the world urban policy-makers confront in 1993 is a quite different place from that of 20 years ago. The 1970s were times of considerable optimism about economic development, and equity issues were assigned a specific priority, even by the World Bank. However, the disappointing progress of most developing countries in the 1980s and the current worldwide recession have tended to give contemporary policy-makers a darker outlook. Specifically, the failure of urban economies to generate employment at rates comparable with the increase in employable populations has been a particularly intractable problem. Urban unemployment rates are ominously high and growing in almost every developing-country city. With such a shift in the external environment, it is not unexpected that priorities are now more heavily focused on macroeconomic development and job creation than on equity. Prolonged and massive unemployment has a social and political urgency that cannot be denied.

Much of the research being done on urban land markets and land policy in developing countries has not yet specifically responded to the need to incorporate macroeconomic analysis. Researchers who have devoted much of their effort to the issue of "access to land for the poor" naturally insist that equity concerns must not be overlooked. Obviously, a middle ground must be sought. If it is true that urban policy-makers are concerned with job creation and productivity as the *sine qua non* for political stability, the research agenda must be expanded to include the question of what types of land policies and land markets would lead to these results. By the same token, if, as Jones & Ward suggest in Chapter 2, there is evidence that an obsessive concern with the deregulation of markets may be counterproductive, equity issues must not be swept aside in the new enthusiasm for efficiency.

This is not the place to elaborate on the intricate and perhaps reciprocating relationships that exist between equity and macroeconomic development. The point is that new policies of nations and international agencies are being driven by quite unpleasant realities to develop new approaches. They do not spring solely from an abstract ideological commitment to "privatization" or "neoclassical" economics.

Three intellectual premises in current research due for re-examination

Emphasis on the rôle of a unitary state

Whether the approach is "structuralist" or "instrumentalist", writing in this field often assumes a "state" that is an extension of the interests of a ruling (capitalist) elite, with policies towards land driven primarily by the goal of the accumulation of excess capital, and maintaining the class structure as defined by Marxist theory. Although this approach has led to much useful analysis, it tends to become misleading to the extent that it assumes a unitary state, when it is clear that in reality such an entity does not exist. The governmental agencies of all countries, however hierarchical they may appear on organization charts, in fact often promote policies that are far from consistent either with each other or in effectively advancing the interests of any single dominant class, as Peattie (1979) noted in her classic article, "Housing policy in developing countries: two puzzles". Only in highly totalitarian regimes, happily, decreasing in number, is this likely to be even plausibly true. Gilbert & Healy's (1985) careful study of the political economy of the land market in Valencia, Venezuela, provides an interesting example of how much the paradigm of "the state" must be modified to cover the realities in the field. Venezuela is a nation with a well established elite, which has had the additional advantage of nationalized petroleum as a source of wealth and power. Nevertheless, the general picture that emerges is far from a simple dichotomy. As Gilbert & Healy (1985: 146–7) point out:

> Although the powerful in Venezuela use the state to develop and protect their interests, our analysis shows how the state, caught as it is within the tensions of Venezuelan society, maintains a considerable degree of autonomy from any one group or class faction . . . [I]t is in no sense a state for itself . . . There are . . . the pressures that come from Venezuela's unequal society, the demands for better living conditions from the poor and for continued largesse from elite interest groups. The social and economic networks of the elite may allow members privileged access to the state machine and they certainly strongly influence state policy, but in no sense do they determine it.

This is, of course, not to argue that the relations between the governmental apparatus and the socio-economic elites who control so much of the political power in many developing countries is not important. However, what may be more important is that the modern "state" is an extremely complex set of institutions and agencies, with overlapping, contradictory and not always enforceable powers, increasingly decentralized and geographically distributed. Whether its leaders like it or not, the modern state is subject to the need to at least appear responsive to community demands, while at the same time it is frequently unable, given the current technology of communications, to hide its weaknesses and errors.

There are obviously immense disparities of power, which lead directly to the gross social injustices so readily observed in developing countries. However, this is somewhat different from the notion that any contemporary "state" can speak with a single voice with respect to policies concerning such complex issues as the markets for land and housing. Gilbert & Healy's summary, quoted above, would apply to most countries.

Emphasis on a two-party paradigm and underestimation of the complexity of the actors involved in urban land markets

As long as land is viewed as the object of a struggle between the poor and the state, sometimes with various non-governmental organizations (NGOs) appearing as third-party intermediaries, policy recommendations have tended to concentrate on the reform of the state, either through positive interventions (such as aggressive infrastructure policies, land-banking, etc.) or "negative" interventions (such as lower building standards, expedited procedures for "regularizing" subdivisions, etc.) There has frequently been a failure to adopt these recommendations. The reason generally given is that "the government lacks the will" to reform. The flaw of the "two-party paradigm", which recent research is beginning to make clear is, first, that there are numerous and complex systems of private intermediaries between the poor who aspire to land acquisition and the state, and second, that the bureaucrats of the state itself have strong personal interests (as opposed to protecting the power of the ruling elite) in maintaining the status quo.

The statement that "the government [the state] lacks the will to reform" is, of course, no real explanation at all. Its use obscures the fact that reforms may be failing because the problem is more complex than our present paradigms. It now appears that there are layers of vested interests, both inside and outside "the state", that have the potential to undermine and defeat any attempt at change. For example, the Khuda-ki-basti project near Hyderabad, Pakistan, attempted to deliver low-cost plots to the poor by imitating the process followed by private (illegal) subdividers, but without the bribery and excessive profits of the private system. However, the public agency was unable to recruit the type of applicants it desired and enlisted the help of private land brokers (the *dallals*). These brokers seized the opportunity to undermine a programme that threatened their interests and were apparently able substantially to limit its success (Badshah 1992: 232–43).

Other work summarized, for example, by Payne (1989), Serageldin (1990), and Baross and van de Linden (1990) has shown that the informal delivery system for land and housing in many cities in developing countries is a major business. It delivers, in one form or another, hundreds of new dwelling units or plots of land every week in almost every major city. It is complex, with many layers of actors, interacting with each other in highly structured ways. It has usually penetrated into, and is interlaced with, municipal, provincial and national bureaucracies. It normally operates with the passive or active support of individual public officials, local politicians, and national political parties. It represents flows of money and power that are intricate and often very large. Overall, it exploits the poor, often exorbitantly, but it also delivers an almost infinite variety of "products" at a range of prices to fit almost every pocketbook. It provides some sort of place to live for more than half of many urban populations. It is in itself a significant source of employment for large numbers of people and is an important part of the informal employment sector, which is one of the main means of livelihood for the poor. It is also sometimes an avenue by which the entrepreneurial poor can escape poverty. Above all, it is a massive web of vested economic and political interests that have a major stake in the status quo.

In other words, to the extent that the two-party paradigm leads us to see the world as "the government" (or "the state") versus "the poor", we will be unable to understand the complexity of the reality with which proposed reforms must deal. Instead, most reforms fail, not because "the government lacks the will", but because the proposed reform is itself based on a highly oversimplified perception of the situation and the many vested interests that must be satisfied before change will be accepted.

An emphasis on the importance of security of legal tenure,
as opposed to the security of "a claim on the system"

A seminal article by Baross (1990) entitled "Sequencing land development: the price implications of legal and illegal settlement growth", is built around this theme. Other recent research is showing a growing number of examples where legal tenure is not highly valued by the poor or is even rejected by them. In Peru, 100,000 titles were offered for issue, but they were not valued by the recipients (Serageldin 1990: 28). In the Cairo governate, title was offered, under certain conditions, to some 600,000 squatters and only about 5 per cent of the requests were filed. In Lusaka, illegal occupants of land have had little interest in titles once services had been installed (Serageldin 1990: 54, 70). In Sant Nagar, Delhi, illegal settlers are far more concerned with protection of their rights from "land grabbers" (other claimants) than with having formal title from the government (Joshi 1991). In illegal subdivisions outside Amman, Jordan, plots with full legal title have less value than those with no title but better location with respect to services (Razzaz 1991). Conversely, Hoffman's (1990) work in Jakarta shows that only 55 per cent of persons with full registered title feel "very certain" about their security of tenure should the government wish to displace them.

Current research, rather than depicting a duality of "legal" and "not legal", delineates a real world that contains very complex mixtures of formal and informal systems with infinite variations in between. The interlacing and interdependence of the formal and informal, with special local variations depending on customary law, appear to be the norm rather than the exception. This should not be surprising. The general literature on the nature of "formal" and "informal" economic sectors in cities has long painted a similar picture.

Re-ordering research priorities

Giving more attention to understanding the rôle of
"the entrepreneurs of the urban land boom"

As implied in the preceding discussion, one of the most interesting aspects of recent case studies of urban land markets has been the documentation of what might best be called "the entrepreneurs of the urban land boom". These are the too-often forgotten figures in the literature of urban land markets in developing countries, who do not even receive much attention in the extensive literature on the so-called informal employment sector. Yet, as Serageldin (1990: 2) notes in referring to Egypt: "The evolution of the informal land development process into a planned and highly lucrative business operated by specialized agents and bringing together lawyers, brokers, land officials, court clerks, kin groups, and local civic and political leaders should not be overlooked".

Entrepreneurs in this context may be defined not only as businessmen, but also as all those who take advantage of a unique historical situation to make their fortunes (large and small). As noted by Payne (1989), more and more single-city case studies are beginning to identify the importance of these intermediaries in urban land markets, and the richness of the variety of their operations in different locales. (See also Baken & van der Linden 1992: 21-39).

Four studies are particularly interesting: Hansan (1987, 1990), van der Linden (1989), Joshi (1991) and Benjamin (1991). A short and incomplete list of the entrepreneurs in this literature would include land-owners, colonizers (subdividers), brokers, residents turned developers (Joshi 1991), industrialists who must create "vote banks" to get the infrastructure services they need for production (Benjamin 1991), bureaucrats involved in illegal subdivision, organizers of "chit" funds, leaders of community organizations and pressure groups (van der Linden 1989), and local politicians (Gilbert & Ward 1982). We are now beginning to understand the operations of these elaborate systems, which expedite, often in byzantine ways, the delivery systems that furnish most new land supply in the large cities of developing countries. So far our understanding of these operations is limited; we are even more in the dark about how they contribute to total urban economic productivity and national macroeconomic performance.

Urbanization is a wealth-producing process. An era of rapid urbanization (like the one we are now living through) represents an historic upsurge in the production of wealth through land valorization, as it has been in every period of rapid urbanization in human history. But, by and large, scholarship has failed to trace and quantify this process, even though it has obvious and major macroeconomic effects. It is not uncommon for property values to increase, in real terms, at rates of 10 per cent or more per year. At the scale of a large city, this can easily represent transfers of wealth amounting to many millions of dollars. One calculation, made by a parliamentary investigation committee in Korea, estimated that the total capital gain from land-price appreciation in 1989 was as much as 35 per cent more than the aggregate income earned by all urban workers in the same year (Korea Research Institute for Human Settlements 1989). While this is, of course, an extreme case, there is no doubt that increases in property values are major economic factors in every developing-country city that have seldom been systematically analyzed. Such transfers may or may not have beneficial macroeconomic effects. The point is that they simply have not received the attention that their magnitude deserves (see also Choi 1993, Dowall 1991a, Ward 1990, Ward et al. this volume).

Fortunately, recent field experience seems to indicate that gathering basic data may not be prohibitively difficult or expensive. If a reasonably confidence-building approach is taken by the researcher, many entrepreneurs appear willing to talk about the details of their operations. A suggestive piece of fieldwork on this subject is that of Benjamin (1991). His monograph is a first step towards documenting the connections between the land conversion (and valorization) process and the creation of a major industrial subcentre on the periphery of Delhi. While he was fortunate in having chosen a study area that had much more potential for industrial development than most peripheral settlements, his work could become a seminal example of how land-market studies (at least one class of them) should proceed. He provides a methodology for linking land valorization to productivity and the alleviation of urban poverty through land policy. While his study has many flaws, it is a significant prototype (see also PADCO & the Land Institute Foundation 1990, Dowall 1991b).

Alternatively, there is the method of the Instituto Libertad y Democracia in Lima, Peru (de Soto 1989) of simply having the researcher go through the process of purchasing a plot. Aside from the work of the Instituto, there appear to be no large-scale studies of land markets in developing countries that have adopted this technique.

Achieving a greater understanding of the
"second-hand" housing markets of developing country cities
A related issue, discussed at the Fitzwilliam Workshop, is the rôle of successive ownerships, or what may be crudely called the second-hand market for plots, dwellings, and small enterprises in informal settlements. A great many cities in developing countries now have large areas of long-established and well consolidated settlements, in which there is considerable de facto security of tenure and a reasonable level of basic services. Under such circumstances one might expect a fairly active real estate market to be developing. Anecdotal evidence, however, suggests that this market is not well developed, or, if it is, is not very much studied (see Smolka, this volume).

There are a number of important questions for research. Why do so few resales appear to be taking place in informal settlements (if indeed such is the case)? When do they occur, to whom are the plots or properties sold and how is the price fixed? How do sellers use the proceeds of their capital accumulation, and what economic consequences result? For example, are the proceeds from such sales generally used to purchase better housing, to capitalize micro-enterprises, or to fulfil one-time social obligations such as weddings or funerals? Does the exclusion of land and housing from formal markets actually cause them to appreciate in value more rapidly than they would were they formally marketed (Ward 1990: 155)? Is the absence of a second-hand market constraining an efficient urban property market in general? How does sluggishness in such a market affect the famous "succession" (or filtering) phenomenon, in which marginal housing stocks receive and pass up successive categories of urban migrants? The Lower East Side of New York is a classic case.

It is often noted that in all but the very youngest cities the existing housing stock outnumbers, by many multiples, the new stock being created each year.

By contrast, the literature of field studies has had a converse focus: on the process of conversion of agricultural to urban land, and new housing generally, not on how to improve the efficiency of the market in the enormous stock (much of it informal) that is already there. It is arguable that achievement of greater liquidity in this enormous stock of assets might be more important than many of the measures now being suggested to improve the production of new stock or land. If, in fact, the illegality of informal settlements (whether squatter or illegal subdivision) makes people afraid to transfer them, an additional powerful argument for the formalization of tenure (even in new complex ways) can be made. Perló's study, reported in Chapter 14, suggests one methodology by which this question may be investigated.

Understanding inheritance and the settlement of land disputes
Another area of sparse information, also discussed at the Fitzwilliam Workshop, is the issue of inheritance. In the absence of formal titles and registration systems, how are property rights passed to others when the original possessors die? Little research appears to have been done on this issue, or on how intergenerational claims generally affect security of occupancy and tenure. On the surface, it appears curious that this problem seldom comes up in interviews when fieldwork is done on questions of tenure in informal settlements.

Similarly, we know surprisingly little about the resolution of conflicts about land rights, either of the conventional sort (for example two claimants to one parcel), or of the sort that must almost surely arise among "presumptive heirs": for example, did the possessor of the rights really leave them to the eldest son, or did she or he write a letter two months before dying stating that the youngest was more deserving? One of the very first studies of land rights in squatter settlements (Karst et al. 1973) gave considerable attention to how conflicting claims were settled, but these questions have received considerably less attention since.

The question is not trivial. Obviously, as pressure increases for more formalization of rights, these conflicts will be pushed to the fore, since the act of formalization constitutes a declaration of who has true and definitive rights. At a more fundamental level, Razzaz's studies in Jordan (1991) constitute an interesting demonstration that one of the best ways of understanding the reality of a nation's institutions is to focus on the way they resolve conflicts, because it is in conflicts that the parties refer to basic principles to justify their causes. Operationally, these issues are critical in the debate on what forms of tenure should be available, and on who is to bear the burden of the taxation that is likely to follow.

Urban productivity and macroeconomic development

The current perception among policy-makers and a growing number of researchers is that cities are no longer negative – the consumers of scarce resources better deployed in other economic sectors. Rather, cities are perceived to have been highly successful in creating employment and economic development – the most urbanized societies have the highest national income (World Bank 1991: 18, Peterson et al. 1991). However, as Jones & Ward argue in Chapter 2, acceptance of this premise still leaves open the question of exactly which specific urban land policies will lead to improved macroeconomic performance.

The assumption that markets that are "formal" or "regularized" are more efficient and productive is not yet proven. On the one hand, some of the literature argues that "informality" and illegality reduce the costs of land and housing for the urban poor. Others argue that as long as the poor are insecure as to the legal status of their homes, their major assets in life, they will never enjoy full access to the economic and political system. One of the most interesting reviews of this issue, by Gilbert (1991a), concludes that the current state of research does not permit prediction of whether a more formalized land market is likely to benefit or harm the poor.

There is possibly an important difference between short-term and long-term effects. The regularization of a plot will obviously create a superior commodity that will demand a higher price and may cause displacement of existing occupants, at least in the short run, as, for example, has occurred in Klong Tuey in Bangkok. On the other hand, if regularization can be both rapid and massive, supply may be sufficiently plentiful to drive prices down. Certainly, evidence would seem to suggest that more efficient land markets result in lower land prices. A selective survey by the World Bank points to a lower ratio of price to income where markets are less restricted (World Bank 1991: 40). But we do not know enough about how this works and how much is attributable to market mechanisms.

Can regularization ever be rapid and massive? The answer may lie in the responsiveness of the actors in the complex processes that now operate the land markets in most developing-country cities – precisely those persons about whom we currently know relatively little. As implied in earlier discussion in this chapter, several issues are involved. At the most fundamental level, we are largely unaware of the numerical size of this sector – all those who operate or lubricate extra-legal land-acquisition systems, and who lend the money that is essential to their functioning. Secondly, we are poorly informed on the sums of money that change hands in this sector. Exactly how profitable is land development? What makes it so? Thirdly, as a consequence, we do not understand what opportunities may exist for enhancing the operation of urban land markets as a means for generating employment, nor how land markets relate to the so-called informal sector in general. Perhaps most importantly, we are unable to judge the political power of such vested interests to delay and distort proposed reforms.

Reforms work best when they appeal to the self-interest of those most affected. However, tempting carrots cannot be created unless we know more about the mechanisms that we desire to change. Unfortunately, the record to date has not been encouraging. Forty case studies commissioned by the World Bank and UNDP/UNCHS by eight research teams in nine major cities in Asia and Latin America described, with some notable exceptions, projects that affected only a few thousand, a few hundred, or a few dozen families, took a great deal of time, and involved organizational/professional inputs at an intensity that would be difficult to replicate at a large scale (Durand-Lasserve & Pajoni 1992). These studies constitute real-world vignettes of the layers of vested interests that exist in low-income land and housing markets and their resistance to change.

Conclusions

Two trends of thought are converging and require reconciliation. One is the recognition that macroeconomic performance is an indispensable consideration in making all types of urban policy. The current economic crisis and priorities of policy-makers require the establishment of a new normative criterion: that the success of a project or land policy for the poor be measured by the amount of increased income it produces as well as by the total number of persons housed. The second trend consists of an increased documentation and understanding of the complexity of the informal systems that deliver land and services to the majority of the inhabitants of major cities. These trends intersect in several ways:

(a) If, as appears to be the case, informal systems dominate the creation, improvement, and transfer of a substantial portion of the property market in cities, these systems are in themselves a major employer and an economic phenomenon whose current macroeconomic consequences should be better understood.

(b) If, as also appears to be the case, many entrepreneurial individuals, commercial firms, bureaucrats, and local and national politicians have substantial vested interests in the existing systems, attempts at reform in the name of improved macroeconomic performance are unlikely to succeed (at any appreciable scale) unless such interests are accounted for in the implementation of reform.

(c) In general, there is very little understanding of who gains and who loses by the process for land and property valorization that is a prominent economic phenomenon in almost all cities. The valorization of property is not, of course, equivalent to the production of immediate income, but understanding its nature would at least provide suggestive data relating to the maximization of both macroeconomic and microeconomic productivity. Paradoxically, two of the most economically successful countries, Japan and Korea, have had land policies that have created astounding social and economic inequities between urban land-owners and non-owners.

(d) The literature of international agencies and a worldwide movement to more participatory democracy have created pressures for the "regularization" of existing settlements and of the processes creating new ones. It is by no means obvious from the current body of knowledge that forcing existing informal systems out of business will either increase supply or contribute to macroeconomic growth, at least in the short term.

At the beginning of this chapter four prerequisites for effective research were listed. Much of the chapter has dealt with the first of these, designing research that resonates with the priorities of policy-makers. It should be clear, however, that the other three should not be forgotten. For example, research on the operation of land and housing markets has been notably idiosyncratic. Future Fitzwilliam-type conferences might profitably concentrate on developing a common methodology and agreed-upon set of research priorities. Certainly the funders of research will be more comfortable when these are established.

In addition, stronger discipline should be imposed on the growing number of case studies to prevent them from being particularistic descriptions, which resist generalization and thus reduce their potential for predictivity. Involving the participants themselves in the preparation of such studies has obvious advantages but sometimes makes it difficult to keep the details in perspective.

The ultimate objective is to achieve a new level of predictive and prescriptive reliability in urban land-market research. Specifically, research results should be able to prevent the unpleasant surprises that have characterized past international urban programmes, which have generally failed to obtain real national support even when pilot projects appeared to be successful. Truly useful studies must not only be better informed in their economic premises, but must also understand that the reform of land and housing markets is, in the last analysis, a political process.

Notes

1.   The author's thinking on the issue of relevant research was stimulated by discussion with Dr Ismail Serageldin, vice-president, environmentally sustainable development, World Bank, 17 March 1993.

CHAPTER FIVE

Researching the relationship between economic liberalization and changes to land markets and land prices
The case of Conakry, Guinea, 1985–91

Alain Durand-Lasserve

Introduction

This analysis of the land market of Conakry, the capital of Guinea, is based on a political-economy approach. The land market is not seen to result directly from demand and supply, in the abstract, but rather as being deeply tied up with the process of distribution and politics. Thus it is argued that the land price may depend as much on with whom one is dealing as on "pure" supply and demand. In this way it is possible to appreciate that land prices are as much a social construction as they are the technical interaction of demand and supply factors. Land price may not, therefore, be necessarily constructed in the same way for each type of land or land market. Moreover, the same land price may reflect wholly different procedures whereby those prices are fixed.

Along with Congo and Zaire, Guinea must be one of the countries of francophone sub-Saharan Africa where the state monopoly of land is most strongly affirmed. Those who support the state monopoly draw their arguments from postcolonial socialist principles: independence, equality, social justice, solidarity. Until the first half of the 1980s, state-controlled land subdivision was the only legal, formal means of developing urban land for housing. Since the end of the Sékou Touré regime in 1984, however, there has been only a limited transition to a liberal economic system. One area where this is most apparent is land management. Even though the state-controlled land-delivery system has been in disuse since 1985, the procedures and practices for land allocation remain intact. The legal situation was still, in 1991, based on texts that declare that the land is the exclusive property of the state. Yet today, informal land production and allocation agents are responsible for virtually all land development in the city. Conakry thus provides an ideal setting in which to observe interactions between land markets and the mechanisms by which land prices are fixed in a situation where different land-delivery systems are operating simultaneously with different logics.

Transition from socialism to liberalism in Guinea

In 1958, Guinea was the only colony in French sub-Saharan Africa to reject the transition formula towards independence proposed by the French government. Full independence and sovereignty were the logical conclusion of the nation-building exercise embarked upon by the Parti Démocratique de Guinée led by Sékou Touré between 1958 and his death in 1984. Such a move, however, brought retaliation from France and isolation in the international community. The result was that Sékou Touré increasingly aligned Guinea towards Eastern Europe, implementing a series of socialist economic policy measures. Despite only moderate annual economic growth of 1–2 per cent during the 1960s and 1970s the regime continued steadfastly with the socialist programme.

It is in this context that, one week after Sékou Touré's death in March 1984, a military committee (Comité Militaire de Redressement National) took power in Conakry. The new regime immediately began to install economic and political liberalization through a structural adjustment programme. State monopolies were dismantled and political opponents offered amnesty. With guidance from the World Bank and IMF, the new government attempted to attract foreign investment and reduce the budget deficit (République de Guinée 1986). A drastic monetary reform devalued the sylli to one-fifteenth of its former value and then, in a move designed to undermine the illegal currency markets, it was replaced with the Guinean Franc (FG) (Cheneau-Loquay 1988, Sodetegi 1987).

The administrative system was less easy to reform. For a mixture of political and technical reasons, among them the absence of a trained managerial group, the previous administrative model largely survived. The services provided by the state, however, were cut back. The heavily subsidized food and basic-services allocation system, which operated until 1984, was dismantled. The impact on the poor of this and other economic reforms was dramatic. Thus, while economic growth increased to 4 per cent, two household expenditure surveys reveal that between 1984 and 1987 the combined income of two wage earners, where one is assumed to be in salaried employment, fell from 40 per cent to 20 per cent of budget requirements for a nine-person household (Koivigui 1986, République de Guinée 1987, Cheneau-Loquay 1992). The practical impact of the liberalization programme, therefore, appears to be to accentuate existing hardships and to perpetuate public-sector mismanagement practices.

The institutional and legal framework of land management in Conakry

In Guinea, legal land tenure and planning legislation are governed by the Civil Code and a body of long-established statutory texts, some dating back to independence (République de Guinée 1980). As far as land is concerned, these texts recognize overall ownership by the state. Article 543 of the Civil Code states that all land in Guinea belongs to the state. Decree 237 of 1983 restates the following legal principle: "the land is the exclusive property of the State of Guinea and can never be definitively given up to anyone". This principle dictates that all land allocation or transfer of occupancy rights has to be authorized beforehand by the government.

Accordingly, private land rights are limited to the value of improvements (construction or plantation) carried out by the legally authorized occupant. In strictly formal terms, housing, construction or any other form of physical and permanent development is the only way for an occupant to obtain occupancy rights on a plot of land which is officially authorized by only three types of legal document: the "land title" registered in the Land Book; a leasehold – called the emphyteutic lease (*bail emphyteotique*); and the occupancy permit.[1] The occupancy permit is the key document, giving the right to occupy an unbuilt piece of land in order to live there. It can only normally be granted in respect of urban plots with areas of less than $1,000\,m^2$.

Land law is thus fairly straightforward from the lawyers' point of view (Tribillion 1985). However, it must be said that no provision has been made for the technical or economic requirements of urban development; social constraints have been underestimated or even ignored. Thus the overall supply of land has proven to be inadequate. This has not been because of speculation, but mainly because of the gap between technical and human resources on the one hand, and the need for serviced land for housing on the other. As a large majority of those requiring shelter do not have access to housing through a state-controlled allocation system, they have turned to "illegal" land-delivery systems.

The land for housing-delivery systems: archaism and effectiveness
A very active land market has now developed throughout the urban fringe of Conakry. This market has two basic features. First, land transfer is not legal. Secondly, the market nature of the transaction is denied by all parties concerned, and especially by the state, which does not formally recognize the existence of any market outside the sphere over which it has control or would like to have control. In Conakry, the public sector has an important rôle in the direct supply of land. Between 1963 and 1985, plots developed under large-scale public land subdivision schemes accounted for one-third of the extension to the city's residential area and covered 28 per cent of the whole urban area. A total of 1,837 ha in 20 subdivision schemes were developed up to 1985, when public-sector land development was temporarily suspended (République de Guinée 1989). In 1989–90, the state resumed its land development activities by creating the Société de Logement à Prix Modéré (SOLOPRIMO), a special unit within the Ministère de l'Urbanisme et L'Habitat (Ministry of Urban Planning and Housing) for a pilot site and services project implemented under UNDP funding (ACT-Consultant 1988, World Bank 1990).

One factor influencing the survival of the public system is that land serves to reinforce and justify any resistance put up by certain sectors of the administration to reforms limiting the state monopoly. By their support of the status quo, or their declared hostility, some key sectors of the state administration have managed to delay any plans by the state to reform the law relating to land-ownership, and this against the advice of the Ministère du Finance (Ministry of Finance), the Ministère du Justice (Ministry of Justice), the city of Conakry, private investors and international finance institutions. Clearly, the state monopoly has led to an impasse. The state is unable to provide the population with the land it requires for housing, nor can it allocate the few plots it has been able to produce or recover, nor even maintain a minimum level of land management and registration. In 1989, the Direction de l'Aménagement Foncière (Directorate for Land Management – DAFO), part of the Ministère de l'Urbanisme et l'Habitat, was able to cope with only 9 per cent of the 15,000 demands for regularization of irregular settlements, allocation of new plots, and registration of transfers.

It is in the interests of a certain category of state officials to support the monopoly in land matters for other reasons. These officials hold a key rôle in that they are the main producers and, at the same time, the main users of land information. This facilitates bribery by agents in the different administrations involved in land management. Close clients of the state or party apparatus were allocated plots against payment of a nominal lump-sum tax. Members of the Commission Nationale Dominale (National Land Commission) and officials who issued occupancy permits took bribes for their services and thus contributed to the establishment and consolidation of a land market. However, as illustrated below, this results to some extent in a balance being achieved between prices in the reference market (the resale of registered plots) and those found in the state-controlled land for housing delivery systems and, more commonly today, in the customary plots market. However, the 1960–85 public land development and allocation system progressively led to the emergence of a submarket, as allocated plots were resold.

The second process of land acquisition is via the allocation of customary land (Durand-Lasserve & Tribillion 1986). Although private land-ownership is illegal and transfers of property rights are formally subject to state control and approval, the quarter of a century of the state apparatus run on socialist lines has, to a large extent, contributed to the survival of customary arrangements in land development and allocation. Thus, while customary practices are seen as relics of the past in most francophone West African countries, this is not the case in Guinea. Indeed, customary practices are so pervasive that the very first team to go to Conakry in 1985 to prepare the Guinea First Urban Project concluded that the transfer and allocation of urban land was not governed in any way by market forces, but was implemented by the exchange of symbolic gifts, marking the formal submission of the receiving party to the customary occupant. It was not until a year later that a survey of land management practices revealed the existence of a true market structure.

In fact, the customary system of land allocation has tended to function more and more along the lines of a market system, especially since the beginning of the 1980s. This has meant that the relationship established between a newcomer and the customary occupant is increasingly one in which the land has a "price". This price is now negotiated in much the same way as land in a private and formal setting would be: according to location, access and so on. However, when the price is agreed, the customary occupant sells the land, but the actual transaction is obscured by a facade of customary procedure. The "sale agreement" is signed before the village council or its representative, who will attest if necessary, in the case of litigation, to the reality of the transfer. In this way housing plots have been developed and allocated in sufficient numbers, within acceptable time limits and at prices that matched the revenue and savings capacity of the majority of the urban population. In fact, customary practices and principles have adapted quickly and effectively to market mechanisms and constraints.

Price-adjustment mechanisms between the state-controlled land-allocation system and the customary land market

There are two possible interpretations regarding state land-management practices and administrative agents. The first view, held by most government officials in DAFO and by clients of the state apparatus, is that there is a need to maintain strict control procedures in order, officially, to reduce the risks of embezzlement or misappropriation during the land-allocation process. Those who hold this view tend to be in favour of modernizing (but not necessarily simplifying) procedures and rationalizing the state's actions in land matters. The aim, however, is not to lessen the state monopoly.

The second view is held by the private sector and some sectors of the administration. It recognizes the existence of several land markets with different price levels. Those who hold it stress that price-adjustment mechanisms usually work to the advantage of state agents and their clients during the various stages of the land allocation process. It is thus in the interest of these agents to complicate and draw out these procedures and reinforce the state monopoly. Those who hold this second view tend to favour the setting up of a liberal land policy and the free development of a land market.[2] For methodological purposes it is possible to reduce these contradictory views on the rôle of the state in land management to a single question: how and to whose advantage do the present price adjustment mechanisms currently operate?

The administration as a predator: does it negate or regulate the market?

As the production and allocation of plots by the state has virtually ceased since 1985–86, let us consider the two most common transactions in land development. The first is where land previously granted to its holder by the state, for example, in a public land subdivision scheme, is transferred to someone else. Officially, it is not the land that is sold, as private ownership of land is not authorized, but the improvements made on the land by the original recipient of the plot and the right to settle on the plot. In principle, the recipient of a plot cannot resell the land that has been allocated to him. However, since only one-third of demand was satisfied in the period when the state was most active in land development between 1978 and 1985, a very active submarket emerged.

With the end of the Sékou Touré regime and new conditions under the Second Republic, the predatory nature of many sectors of land-development administration has become even more pronounced. The new regime has not greatly modified the existing set-up: the only aspects to have been reviewed are the composition and functioning of the Commission Nationale Dominale, which is responsible for land allocation and for issuing occupancy, regularization and transfer permits, and for collecting the single lump-sum tax payment. Between 1974 and the first half of the 1980s, when the state was still actively allocating land, those people receiving a plot had to pay a single lump-sum tax, which was fixed by a ministerial decree in 1974 at 7,500 sylis.[3] This was only a modest sum at the time, and, following the period of hyperinflation experienced between 1983 and 1986, became a token amount. This has been replaced by a land tax (*redevance domaniale*) which increases in proportion to the area of land being allocated. Since 1987, in Conakry, it has been fixed at 50,000 FG (US$141) for a plot of less than 500 m² and 75,000 FG (US$211) for a plot of between 501 and 1000 m² – this is the most common plot size in the Conakry suburban area.[4]

The second most common transaction is the right to settle on a plot of land, and the right to build a house on it is granted by a customary occupant. As we have observed, under customary law such a practice is tolerated. In fact, this customary allocation is a sale: in other words, a plot of land is sold by a customary occupant who sees himself as the customary owner of the land. The purchaser then makes a request to the relevant section of DAFO to regularize his occupancy; after an investigation and lengthy procedures, the administration will issue a transfer permit or a provisional occupancy permit that will later be changed to a permanent occupancy permit after improvements (i.e. a construction) are carried out on the land and testified. In principle, for the purchaser, the cost of the plot will be the amount paid to the customary owner, plus the cost of taxes and levies paid to the administration to obtain the occupancy permit. In addition, agents of the administration require bribes, which become greater as demand for urban land increases. Only when this is understood can one begin to disentangle what price implies in this context: namely a complex mixture of varying social prices not solely associated with demand and supply.

Although a very active market has developed, its existence is not openly acknowledged. Nor is the notion of a land price. However, the plots do have a price, or more precisely several prices, according to the land-delivery system being considered and the guarantees offered for security of tenure. Moreover, it is possible to identify and even quantify with some precision the various components of urban land prices in Conakry in 1989–90, as I shall demonstrate below (Author survey 1989, BCEOM 1990).

Components of the "price of land":
the reference price and mechanisms for adjustment

Whatever the type of land-delivery system, the price of urban land is always established in relation to a so-called reference price. This is the ceiling to which all urban agents refer, and it represents the price used in the very narrow market for the resale of registered and legally occupied plots. Occupancy may be authorized when the plot has been transferred or allocated (this is the case in state-owned developments) or when rehabilitation-upgrading programmes have been carried out.

In these cases, security of tenure is guaranteed even though, supposedly, "the land is the exclusive property of the State of Guinea, and can never definitively be given up to anyone". Intervention by DAFO is limited to issuing a permit to sell or to transfer with a stamp duty of 1,000 FG. This authorization can usually be obtained quite easily if the two co-contractors put enough pressure on the administration and agree to press (usually with bribes) the officials dealing with their case. If their application is not contested by a third party, this payment is usually a fairly modest sum, compared with the value of the property that is being transferred. When the sale has been approved, the purchaser must pay the land tax which, at the time of fieldwork (1990), was 75,000 FG (US$127) for a plot of between 500 and 1,000 m².

In fact this land market is fairly limited. Less than 20 per cent of the 56,000 plots in Conakry are registered either in the Land Book, which includes only land for which land titles have been issued, or in the land roster, which records permits granted by DAFO and are mainly situated in and around the city centre. Moreover, these transfers affect only 2 per cent of stock annually. It is thus with reference to this very limited market of plots that have been allocated, registered and occupied in the regular way that the reference price for urban land in Conakry is determined.

Since 1986, state production of developed plots has virtually ceased. The right to use a plot is granted by the state under certain conditions. In the case of state-run allocation procedures, the "price" (remembering that the term is in fact inappropriate) represents the sum of the legal taxes and fees and the illegal charges (bribes imposed by administration officials). The first component of the land price is the reference price at resale. All the agents in the urban sector know the base price for an allocated plot of, say, 600 m². They also know that such a plot could be resold in 1989–90, depending on its location, for between 800,000 FG (US$1,215) in the eastern part of Conakry, 15 km from the city centre, and 2,500,000 FG (US$3,796) on the northern coast road or on the southern road and with a sea view. In other words, the resale price may be 11 to 33 times what the applicant had to pay the state.

This reference point is important. Administration officials are obviously going to try and keep for themselves some of the expected profit from resale. There are two possible courses of action open to them. First, they may allocate plots to themselves under various borrowed names. An analysis of occupancy permits for plots in public land subdivision schemes shows that they are distributed in a very subjective way, with the main landholders occupying the highest positions in the administration (BCEOM 1990). Secondly, they may take a certain amount at each stage of the allocation process from the applicant. This amount is described as the payment (called a gift) that has to be given to officials to encourage them to deal favourably with requests.

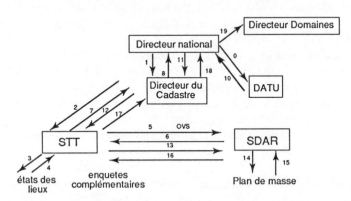

Figure 5.1 Procedure for approval of a layout plan.

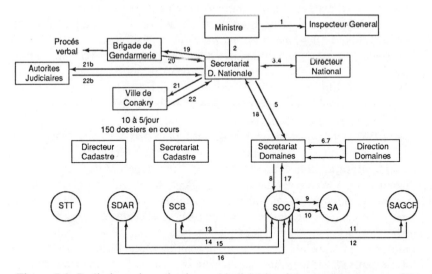

Figure 5.2 Preliminary investigation and judicial inquiry procedure in case of litigation.

The extent of this system of extra payments can be illustrated by looking at the required procedure to make a request for either an occupancy permit (Fig.

5.1), or the even more circuitous route to obtain a layout plan (Fig. 5.2). The shuttling back-and-forth within the offices of the Ministère de l'Urbanisme et l'Habitat, encourages the client to make some kind of payment in order to expedite the issue of a permit. The allocation of plots procedure also require a financial input from the purchaser. Legal texts are often contradictory, and the administration can thus justify any decision made. The final allocation is done by a committee, which arbitrates in the name of the minister as to the applicant's creditworthiness, considering the request according to its "priority rating".

The regularization procedure, too, is especially complex – deliberately so – in order to provide officials of DAPO with many opportunities to profit from applicants. Custom has codified such practices and has often even fixed the going price or rate for the gifts and other bribes that applicants must provide if their case is to be processed. Illegal levies, bribes and the level of corruption have a significant impact on the final price of a plot. Although these exactions can vary and are thus difficult to quantify, several factors influence the administrative decision-making process: the personality of the applicant, his relationship with members of the state apparatus, the degree of seriousness of the irregularity in which he is involved, and the length of time he is prepared to wait.

The system for the delivery of customary land fixes prices in a different way, although it is qualitatively similar. The state has no effective control over delivery, but legalization of transfer and the formal occupancy permit do ultimately depend on it. In this case, the price represents the sum of the price paid to the customary occupant, plus illegal charges imposed by administration officials, plus legal taxes and fees if the occupancy permit is issued or the transfer approved. This type of arrangement merits particular attention for two main reasons. First, it caters today for virtually all the demand for housing plots. Secondly, from several recent studies (ACT-Consultant 1989, BCEOM 1990) it is possible to evaluate relatively accurately what proportions of the final price of the plot are represented by the different levies (legal and illegal). The final price that the purchaser must pay for his plot can be broken down into the following components: (a) the amount paid to the customary owner; (b) taxes, levies and administrative costs; (c) illicit payments and bribes demanded by government officials to regularize transfer and/or occupancy.

Studies of prices in 1989 indicate that this final price is 20 per cent to 30 per cent less than the so-called reference price. To some extent, this price difference represents the cost of the additional risk involved when the purchaser deals with a customary occupant. The customary land market is rife with irregularities and misappropriations such that the amount to be paid by a purchaser to officials in the appropriate departments to obtain a favourable decision and to legitimize the situation may be high (Fig. 5.3). Table 5.1 shows how the final price is arrived at. We have taken the example of a plot of between $501\,m^2$ and $1,000\,m^2$. Its reference price can be estimated, in 1989–90, at 1,000,000 FG (US$1,689), depending on its location.[5]

Several observations can be made. The most important is that illicit payments

Table 5.1 Components of plot prices in Conakry in 1990.

Stages of the allocation process	Amount to be paid (in FG) to:		
	Administration (taxes, fees, etc.)	Officials in administration (illicit levies, bribes)	Customary occupants (sale is illegal but tolerated)
Payment for purchasing (rights on) the land			P
Topographic works	30,000	30,000 (land surveyor DAFO)	
Plotting, production and submission of a layout plan	9,000 (one engineer) 6,000 + 6,000 (two assistants)	42,000 (DAFO)	
Investigation and control by DAFO		7,000 to 25,000 (DAFO)	
Investigation by DAFO		15,000 to 30,000 (DAFO)	
Transcription of transfer on land register		50,000 to 200,000 depending on the estimated value of property	
Payment of land tax	75,000		
Settling of disputes or litigation	Court fees	Depending on the case and requested support	
Total (if no litigation)	126,000	144,000 to 327,000	P

are higher than taxes legally levied by the state. This is significant because, according to different ground hypotheses, the total of taxes, costs, dues, levies and illicit payments can represent about a quarter (23 per cent to 27 per cent) of the reference price of a plot. This is only a rough estimate. If we do not count the legal state levy (land tax of 75,000 FG), which must be paid in all transactions to be regularized, then this represents about 20 per cent.

Considering the reference price, it is suggested that the price of plots in the customary market can be broken down as follows: where R is the state levy plus dues, taxes and costs (in theory the same in both cases); Pr is the reference price through the formal and legal markets and Pc the price in customary land markets (Fig. 5.4). The difference between the reference price and the price in the customary market is represented by I, the illicit payments (15 per cent to 16 per cent of the reference price in this example) and R, a risk factor in case of litigation. This difference is estimated at about 20 per cent to 30 per cent, but it may vary considerably. The purchaser of a plot can keep most of this for himself if he is lucky or if he has the right contacts. He may, on the other hand, have to pay more than the reference price for his plot, especially if there is any dispute in law over the ownership of the plot.

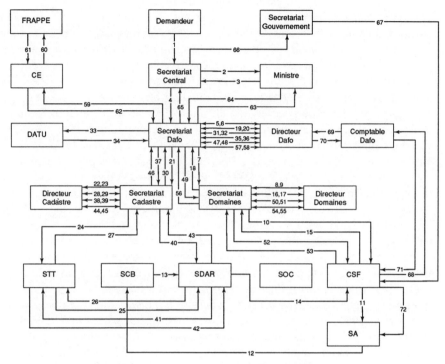

Figure 5.3 Procedure for obtaining a Regularization Permit.

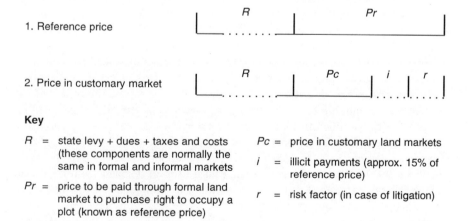

Key

R = state levy + dues + taxes and costs (these components are normally the same in formal and informal markets)

Pr = price to be paid through formal land market to purchase right to occupy a plot (known as reference price)

Pc = price in customary land markets

i = illicit payments (approx. 15% of reference price)

r = risk factor (in case of litigation)

Figure 5.4 Components of plot prices on the formal legal market and the informal customary market.

Changes in the price of land

The only data that can be used for an analysis of land prices was gathered during field studies between 1986 and 1990. Most prices refer to prices in the suburban areas of Conakry, in the urban "commune" of RATOMA, and around the village areas of Yimbaya, Simbaya, Nongo and Kaporo, 15-20 km from the centre of old Conakry (Kaloum peninsula). These villages are accessible by motor vehicle and since 1988 have had a regular bus service.[6]

Land prices started to rise very rapidly from 1985–86 throughout the suburbs of Conakry. In 1986, an 800 m² plot in an ideal location in one of four villages was sold for between 700,000 and 800,000 FG (approximately US$2,113). A plot in a less than ideal location, far from the road, with poor topographic conditions fetched 250,000-300,000 FG (US$775). By comparison, in 1989, the price of a 600 m² plot, depending on its location, was between 800,000 FG and 2,500,000 FG (US$1,351-4,223). Overall, therefore, between 1986 and 1989 the prices of plots like these increased between threefold and fivefold in nominal terms (during which time inflation rose by approximately 370 per cent). Because of these price increases, demand turned to smaller and smaller plots: from 800 m² in 1986 to 600 m², 400 m² and even 300 m² in 1990. Several observations, however, confirm that mid-1989 marked a turning point. The rate of increase in the price of land began to fall. This trend was still continuing in the first part of 1991, as is the other trend, towards smaller plot size. The first six months of 1991 saw a stagnation in current prices. During 1990 the prices rose in line with inflation (about 30 per cent for the year). As no systematic monitoring of prices has ever been carried out, it is difficult to assess all the contributory factors. The most critical problem is that there are no rational criteria for defining social actors in the market nor determining their influence. It is not known, for example, whether the systems of alliances or of clienteles can be quantified or otherwise taken into account when land prices are fixed. Nonetheless, it is possible to make three principal observations about the functioning and pricing of the land market in Conakry since 1986.

First, the best-situated and most expensive plots have increased in value most significantly and continue to rise at a rate that is somewhat higher than inflation. This points to a relationship between the increase in the price of land between 1986 and 1989 and the emergence of an urban middle class – itself a by-product of the liberalization of the economy. It also reflects the arrival of foreign capital (specifically development aid and Guinean exiles returning home from abroad) and a favourable political and economic situation. In the same way, the lull in 1990–91 is symptomatic of a drop in demand from the urban middle classes, a gradual deterioration in the economic situation due mainly to an increase in inflation and a reduction in purchasing power, and a fairly unstable political situation since the beginning of 1991. Secondly, there has been an almost total paralysis of the administration in charge of land management, which is quite incapable of carrying out the most basic and simple functions. Thirdly, there has been a crisis of confidence in the customary land-allocation system after many instances of embezzlement were uncovered during the period of high speculation by customary occupants. Especially rife were multiple allocations or customary sales of plots belonging to state-owned companies, as was the case with land earmarked for the construction of a refinery at Nongo.

Conclusion

This chapter has suggested a framework with which we can look closely at the land market. This framework stresses the interaction of an economic model and an understanding of the structure of power in society. Through the concept of a reference price I have argued that one can observe how social and political, as well as economic, factors inform land prices. There is a close relationship between what are, apparently, separate land markets. Although quantifying this approach has its difficulties, and I have not attempted to identify them all here, it can be readily appreciated that there is a need to embrace these considerations: (a) who supplies the land; (b) using which logic; (c) under which conditions; and (d) the relative interaction of middlemen.[7]

Many of the observations made in Conakry confirm others already noted in other francophone countries in sub-Saharan Africa. One is the co-existence of structures for the production and allocation of urban land that function according to different systems. A failure to appreciate fully the mechanism of land delivery means that the range of prices for land on the market becomes taken as a matter of fact when, in reality, the price of transferring the right to occupy a plot in a public land-development scheme and the price of that plot on the market, and the difference between the fees that the new holder must pay for a plot and the price of this same plot on the market, can be in the ratio of 1:10 or even as much as 1:40.

This is, again, broadly similar to the situation elsewhere in sub-Saharan Africa. In Ouagadougou, Burkina Faso, for example, a 1986 enquiry showed that the negotiated price of plots allocated by the state at the beginning of the 1980s was 24 times the amount of fees demanded for allocation (Boly & Zougrana 1988a, 1988b). In Bamako, Mali, in 1987, a "letter of allocation" giving the right to occupy an urban plot and considered by the population as an authentic title deed could be negotiated for a sum amounting to 10 to 20 times the fees the recipient had to pay the state (Touré 1988). In 1984, the going rate was 5 to 11 times the state fees (Cremont 1984). In Brazzaville, Congo, plots allocated by the state are resold for 20 to 40 times what was paid in fees and taxes by the recipients, (even though the sale was not legal). In Nouakchott, Mauritania, a highly active market has developed around the state land allocation system: in 1987, the final purchaser paid 10 to 20 times the price that was originally paid to the state for registration and land conservation fees (Bakani &

Theunynck 1988). In Tilabery, Niger, plots allocated by the municipality were "resold" in 1990 for 30 to 40 times their transfer "price" (Issa 1991, verbal communication). Many more examples could be given.

In these countries the reference price of a plot, registered plots and/or plots for which an allocation or occupancy permit has been regularly issued compared with the prices charged in the customary, informal or irregular markets differs by about 20–30 per cent when facilities and location are held equal. This rate varies, it would seem, according to the degree of risk attached to the irregularity and the amount of trust placed in the customary owners. The price difference between the two markets would widen if, for instance, the authorities had a repressive land-development policy.

The case of Guinea is of particular interest as it illustrates the consequences of a transition towards a liberal system of urban land management. Although a very active land market exists, the administration in Guinea insists on maintaining the fiction that "the land belongs exclusively to the state and can never be definitively given up to anyone". However, the state no longer has the means, even the repressive means, of ensuring its monopoly in land matters. Despite resistance from certain sectors of the administration, the transition towards a liberal land-management system is well under way in Guinea, particularly a price system integrating different components (prices in the customary land market, plus the various levies). This emerging land market paves the way for the transition to develop more fully.

The adjustment and balancing of prices between the state-controlled land delivery system and the private market system is currently operating to the advantage of, first, the officials in administration (through corruption) and state clienteles (through preferential allocations); secondly, the customary owners; and, thirdly, and more recently, a new property owner stratum of society (officials with some influence, and especially tradesmen, professional people, lawyers and surveyors) who operate at the limits of both state legality and customary legitimacy in the hope that there will be a liberal reform in land management legislation inherited from socialist Guinea. The influence of this third group seems to be spreading at the expense of the other two.

Several conditions are combining today to enable a legal land market to develop. In the last two years, the debate on the implementation of a liberal land policy has focused on reform of the Land Code (Code Domanial et Foncier). This matter so far remains unresolved, while the debate has moved forwards. At the end of 1989 the state approved the adoption, in principle, of an amenities fee to be paid by the occupier of a plot in public site and services development schemes. This fee should, in theory, cover the cost of servicing the plots developed by SOLOPRIMO. This idea of recovering land development costs is a new one. But it is by no means certain that the strong opposition to change comes only from officials, who derive so much direct benefit from the state monopoly, mainly through corruption. Indeed, if the system were to become more liberal, there would be other opportunities for this group to benefit. Thus, while this chapter has mentioned corruption a great deal, and it is a subject that merits closer scrutiny, it is worth considering what changes will be induced by the move to more formal land markets and a changing economic model. Hitherto, one might argue, corruption has served to redistribute land income, and although morally questionable and not very productive, it has proven nevertheless fairly effective (see also Ward 1989a). However, some high-ranking political officials fear that this transition will lead to a situation of total chaos, specifically in the formation of land oligarchies, soaring land prices and many more land disputes. This risk is perceived to be all the greater since the authorities do not have the human, material or financial resources to control the situation, the judicial system is inadequate and there is no land information system. From their perspective the future looks bleak.

Notes

1. The titling procedure is no longer enforced and no title has been issued since independence. An emphyteutic lease is a 20- to 99-year lease given by the state or public body. In most cases, the lessee gains a right to occupancy, and to develop, mortgage or transfer the land.
2. The new Land Code in 1992 is a compromise arrangement reached after extensive external pressure. The code recognizes the primacy of the private land market over the public allocation of land, but does not deprive the state of its prerogative regarding land management. It is not yet clear whether the new code will put to an end the conflict between advocates of public monopoly versus private free market, but information gathered by the author in 1992 indicates that the code is raising serious technical and political problems.
3. There are problems converting the syllis into either US dollars or Guinean francs. Before monetary reform in 1986 one dollar was equivalent to 25 syllis at the official rate but 400 in the parallel market. The syllis has been replaced by the Guinean franc.
4. The rate of exchange for conversion of Guinean francs to US dollars is as of January of each year. In cases of incomplete data the nearest or mid-point is used.
5. This example was provided by an official at the Ministère de l'Urbanisme in 1990.
6. One point of reference is essential. The average income and expenditure of a household according to a 1987 survey, which was updated in 1988, estimated that in Conakry an average household of nine people would need a minimum monthly income of 106,000 FG (US$298) in 1987 and 120,000 FG (US$338) in 1988 (Ministère du Plan 1988). In fact an unskilled salaried worker in Conakry earned 30,000 FG (US$85) per month in 1988, and a qualified government employee with a higher education diploma had a starting salary of 50,000 FG (US$141) net per month.
7. Illegal land plots are cheaper than legal ones, but not by much.

CHAPTER SIX

Applying a political-economy approach to land and housing markets in Zimbabwe

Carole Rakodi

Background and aims of the research[1]

Land availability for new development and trends in the property market are influenced by a combination of physical factors (topographical and geological suitability of land for development), economic factors (demand and supply), administrative factors (the legal, institutional and procedural framework for land administration, and land policy formulation and implementation) and political factors (both the underlying structure of a country's political economy and everyday political imperatives). In this chapter the aim is to illustrate the usefulness of a political economy approach developed at the micro-scale that is able to disentangle the variety of influences mentioned above and assess their relative importance as explanatory factors.

Urban land and housing markets based on private property ownership and subject to a greater or lesser degree of government regulation are generally held to be capable of both meeting the demand for land to accommodate a full set of urban land uses and satisfying the needs of each income group for adequate housing. Policy intervention that adversely affects supply and gives rise to large-scale evasion of land regulation is variously attributed to the inherent inefficiency of administrative systems compared with market forces, to incoherent policy formulation and unco-ordinated implementation, and to the vested interests of powerful property owners (World Bank 1983). Increasingly, the relative failure of government attempts to control the supply of subdivided and serviced land, and to provide low-income housing in sufficient volumes to meet demand, as well as the resource inefficiencies that accompany such policies have been unfavourably compared with the adaptability of the private market (both large- and small-scale). These comparisons have been used as a basis for advocating greater reliance on private resources, in addition to ways of making existing supply mechanisms more efficient. Although the concentration of land-ownership, development capital and housing finance in the hands of large-scale enterprise is recognized as a constraint on the ability of the small-scale sector to continue to provide adequate access to land and housing through informal processes, the ability in principle of the property-ownership system to reconcile efficiency and equity criteria is rarely questioned by policy-makers (see UNCHS 1986, Doebele 1987b).

There have been isolated studies of aspects of land markets in sub-Saharan African cities. However, there have been few systematic studies of land-market processes in particular cities. Yet the operation of the land market is crucial to the supply of housing. With respect to housing, as to land, basic questions are the extent to which the private market produces housing in sufficient quantities to meet effective demand, the need for government intervention, and the effectiveness of particular policies and projects in relieving constraints on supply and demand. Most research on housing in African cities has studied particular segments of the housing market, especially unauthorized areas, and the outcome of policies to improve conditions for the poor, some of which have, in practice, benefited middle-income groups (Sanyal 1987). Not least of the reasons for this outcome is the neglect of constraints on supply for middle- and upper-income households, which has resulted in them outbidding low-income residents for land and housing that was originally targeted at the latter. The shortage of accommodation for "middle-income" households had been recognized as a problem by the second half of the 1980s. Rent control introduced soon after independence had inhibited new construction for rent and led to the sale of middle- to high-rent flats and apartment blocks. At the same time, most former municipal rented housing has been sold to sitting tenants since the early 1980s, while serviced plot schemes were designed for owner-occupation. The unsatisfied demand for housing from middle-income households made small apartments, new serviced-plot schemes and existing high-density housing areas attractive to middle-income buyers. The Zimbabwe research project, therefore, accepted the need to take into account the housing situation of middle-income households, their socio-economic characteristics, housing needs and aspirations having direct bearing on the explanations of conditions and policy recommendations for the low-income segment of the market. To understand how policies that attempt to improve the land and housing situation of the poor are hijacked by higher-income residents, more systematic studies that concentrate on the city scale and the nexus between land and housing markets are necessary (Rakodi 1992a).

An earlier review of gaps in the housing literature identified a number of important points of departure for the current research (Rakodi & Mutizwa-Mangiza 1989, Rakodi 1990a). Since independence, formal racial barriers to residence in low-density areas have disappeared, giving rise to considerable in-movement by black Zimbabweans, especially in the early 1980s, when excess supply depressed house prices. Even so, the falls in real wages since then, together with a tightening of the market leading to rapidly increasing house prices and a limited supply of new dwellings, have probably led to increased difficulty for even relatively high-income households in obtaining access to housing.[2] The project aimed to collect information on the processes of change in typical low-density areas and to explore the social feasibility of densification which, it has been suggested, would improve the efficiency of urban land and service provision and use and decrease inequities between existing low- and high-density areas.

The aim of the study on which this chapter is based was to assess the extent to which market mechanisms, together with government intervention, have succeeded in supplying adequate land for housing in Zimbabwe. Zimbabwe provides an interesting if in some ways untypical setting for a study of land and housing markets in urban development. The colonial legacy has afforded Zimbabwe an urban-development process that is relatively orderly, largely because public authorities have considerable capacity for planning and implementing urban- development projects and the strains on the system imposed by rapid urban growth have so far been contained. Zimbabwe, therefore, provides a relatively favourable environment for policy implementation and urban management. Nevertheless, problems do exist. For example, it has been assumed by the state that demand for housing for high- and middle-income groups can largely be satisfied by the market, despite clear evidence of market failure in recent years. Further understanding of private-sector house production, constraints on supply, alternative strategies for obtaining access to housing and the housing demand and aspirations of these groups is necessary in order to explain why supply is not meeting demand.

Specifying and implementing the research project

In this section, the process of designing and implementing the research project will be outlined in greater detail. The operation of land and housing markets is most developed, and the severity of problems with which urban management systems need to deal greatest, in larger cities. In Zimbabwe's urban system, the two largest cities, Harare and Bulawayo, face problems of similar dimensions, although the pressures for development have been far greater in Harare, leading to its choice as the primary focus of the study. There has been relatively little research on the operation of land and housing markets in second-order settlements in Africa and so the extent to which these operate in a similar way to those in large cities is largely unknown. At the same time, most countries, including Zimbabwe, have adopted policies to encourage the growth of secondary cities, as a tool of regional development and in order to provide intervening opportunities for migrants (Hardoy & Satterthwaite 1986). For these aims to be achieved, such settlements must provide an adequate level of infrastructure, services, and access to land and housing. Appropriate policies must be devised for these settlements, which may differ from those needed in the largest cities. A second settlement was, therefore, selected for study which is, as far as any town is, typical of second-order settlements in Zimbabwe: the provincial centre of Gweru.

In the Zimbabwe context, research on land has focused almost entirely on rural areas, with the exception of historical accounts of the development of Harare (then Salisbury) (Christopher 1970, 1972, 1973) and a geographical survey of the city (Kay & Cole 1977). The land-use and development control system is slightly better documented (Whittle 1979, de Valk 1986, Underwood 1986, Wekwete 1989a), the local government system is described in Jordan (1984) and Mutizwa-Mangiza (1991) and local government finance in Harare is covered by Wekwete (1989b). In the absence of published material, the project's first aim was to document the land allocation and development processes, the ways in which urban residents obtain access to land, the property tax systems and the system of land use guidance and control. This was done by collecting and reviewing secondary material, including relevant legislation, published materials and central and local government reports, in addition to interviewing key officials in relevant central and local government agencies.

In the first instance, a series of questions was posed with the aim of building up a *description* of the land-development process and the land-administration system. These related to tenure and ownership, land-use planning and regulation of development, property taxation, public participation in the land market, the changing administrative structure at the central and local level for dealing with land and its relationship to political decision-making, private-sector actors in the property sector and paths of land development. The questions relating to each of these aspects were subdivided into those likely to be answerable on the basis of existing knowledge and documentation and those likely to require additional information. At the same time, the basis on which the outcomes of these administrative systems, legislative provisions and policy interventions were to be *assessed* was specified by means of a series of research questions, posed in terms of efficiency and equity (Table 6.1). Out of a variety of possible frames of reference, the question of whether land and housing markets are capable of efficiently meeting demand and equitably satisfying the needs of each income group was chosen because it is a significant concern in the literature and in wider debates about the relative rôles of the state and markets in achieving economic growth and distributing its benefits equitably (Cornia et al. 1988, Killick 1989).

Secondly, *explanations* were sought both of why Zimbabwe has adopted particular land policies and devised specific administrative systems through which these are executed, and of the outcomes of this implementation. Explanations, it was anticipated, would be derived from the characteristics of markets in privately owned land and property; the ideological, political and economic characteristics of Rhodesia/Zimbabwe; the policy-making process at central and local levels; and the degree of administrative efficiency. As the land policies and administrative measures adopted by the state in Zimbabwe are understood as having an impact on market processes, a greater knowledge of the land and housing market was required before policy outcomes could be assessed or understood. The second main aim of the research project, therefore, was to study land-market mechanisms and processes, in particular, trends in develop

Table 6.1 Criteria for assessing land policy.

	Efficiency	Equity
Tenure	Does the system encourage a smoothly functioning and responsive land market in which adequate land is available to accommodate urban growth?	Does the system provide access to land for all income groups and is it able to recapture increments in value when desirable?
Land-use planning and regulation	Does the system ensure a supply of land for all urban uses, in appropriate locations at reasonable cost and with necessary services?	Does the regulatory system impose standards or other requirements that inhibit the access of low-income groups to land?
	Is it adaptable and able to cope with urban growth and change?	Does it provide a non-discriminatory means of resolving conflicts between uses and users of land?
Taxation	Does the system generate local revenue for general purposes and/or finance expenditure on particular services?	Does the system reduce inequities in the distribution of benefits from public investment and actions, and increases in land values?
	Is this revenue buoyant in relation to growth of population and average income?	
	Does the tax structure provide disincentives to speculation and keeping land vacant and incentives for the efficient use of land?	
Public participation in the land market	Does public participation in the land market result in an improved supply of land for new urban development, generation of revenue to finance infrastructure provision and improved land-use planning of newly urbanized land?	Is land subdivided and serviced by public authorities or public/private-sector partnerships equitably distributed to all income groups?

ment and construction activity and prices, and the actions, motivations and opinions of private-sector actors in the land-development process.

In all cities the residential property market is dominated by exchanges of the existing housing stock; purchases of new dwellings form a relatively small proportion of total transactions. This is true of most Third World cities, although their rapid population growth makes the supply of new housing much more important than in the cities of industrialized countries, where demand for new housing often arises out of changes in income levels, household structure and preferences, rather than from population growth. Land is thus both essential for new building to cope with urban growth and an element in the value of residential (and other) property. The urbanization of undeveloped land and associated valorization, therefore, cannot be understood without analyzing trends in the property market as a whole.

This is particularly true in Zimbabwe, where changes in historic circumstances that have greatly influenced the demand for housing and an administrative and urban planning system based on the particular requirements of a settler society have been reflected in the land-development process. A review of trends between 1890 and 1979, relying on easily available historical analyses and planning documents, concluded that in examining recent trends in land development in Harare, the legacy of the pre-independence political economy as it was reflected in urban development is still of overriding importance. Thus the cross-cutting divisions by race and class were embodied in legislation related to tenure, planning and infrastructure standards, housing policy and administrative systems. In particular, inherited land-development processes and their expression in enduring physical development forms the context within which post-independence trends must be analyzed.

Parallel to documentation of the land-administration system, sources of information that could be used to provide indicators of demand and supply were identified, leading to the design of possible data collection procedures and survey instruments. Indicators of demand, it was considered, might include numbers on local authority waiting lists, development pressure as indicated by rates of application for development permission by area and type of development, rapidly increasing land and property prices, and speculation. Supply indicators could include new house construction and subdivision. In addition, it was considered necessary to analyze factors affecting demand, especially housing finance, and factors affecting supply, especially the motives and behaviour of land-owners, developers and intermediaries in the property sector.

Understanding the political economy of land and housing in Zimbabwe
The aspects of the political economy briefly referred to above are reflected in attitudes to and policies in the urban areas. During the 1980s, the country's government aimed to achieve an important transition, from an inegalitarian society based on race, in which government intervention ensured that urban processes served the needs of the settler economy and society, to an avowedly socialist society, in which prosperity was to be more equitably distributed, in particular, by measures to increase the access of the black Zimbabwean population to land and services. In reality, the socialist rhetoric outlasted practice, as the constraints imposed by capitalist economic organization, the Lancaster House Agreement, the desperate need for foreign exchange to replace outdated industrial and transport equipment, and drought narrowed the economic options open to the government. Increasing economic difficulties and inability to sustain

75

high levels of investment in social and redistributive measures led to attempts to implement structural adjustment policies similar to those imposed on many other African countries by the IMF and the World Bank, albeit in a context of greater economic prosperity, self-reliance and administrative capacity than elsewhere. Dependence on the international agencies, accompanied by their greater influence on policy, has increased in the 1990s.

The management of transition in the years immediately following independence is crucial in establishing the political and economic basis for post-independence society. Moreover, the ideology and goals of the new government have had direct relevance for managing urban development in Zimbabwe as attempts have been made to reconcile socialist aims with an inherited economic and social structure and an enduring built environment. Before independence, African urban dwellers were permitted to dwell in towns only on a temporary basis, as and when their labour was needed. Rental accommodation was therefore provided for them by local authorities or employers. Attempts to curb rural–urban migration included policies to prohibit squatting (almost entirely successfully) and limit (much less successfully) multi-occupation of authorized dwellings. Given the tensions that these constraints imposed, as well as the forcible confinement of most rural people to the Tribal Trust Lands, access to land was a critical issue in the independence struggle and afterwards. The response to this in urban areas took the form of converting existing rental dwellings to owner-occupation and selling a continued supply of serviced plots. No contradiction appears to have been recognized, however, between socialist ideology and private property ownership, or, in terms of efficiency and equity, between reliance on the market to match the supply of high-cost housing to demand and reliance on administrative controls to prevent the market (albeit small-scale and unauthorized) filling the gap between public-sector supply and growing demand from low-income groups.

As far as the low-income population is concerned, land supply has historically been and still is a purely administrative process. Land in municipal ownership from the outset or purchased from farmers who are willing to sell has been used for public-housing schemes. Compulsory purchase powers have not been used, partly because there has been little need to do so, partly because lengthy legal procedures are involved, and partly because, since independence, a proportion of the purchase price has had to be paid, where desired by the seller, in foreign exchange (Butcher 1989). The proceeds of land sales in serviced-plot areas are thus insufficient to finance new land acquisition, partly because prices are set at less than the market price for new land being acquired and partly because the number of plots being serviced and sold is far below the incremental need for new development. Most land purchases which, therefore, cannot be undertaken using the local authority's own reserve funds are financed by borrowing from central government.[3] The reluctance of central government to approve loan funds for advance purchase of land prevents local authorities from developing medium-term land-purchase programmes (Butcher 1989).

Although land made available for purchase by low-income households is, therefore, relatively cheap, land prices in Harare in recent years have typically been set at less than 12 per cent of serviced-plot costs (HCMPTT 1988), the associated costs of servicing and house construction are very considerable, while supply has been limited primarily because of financial constraints. As might be expected in this situation, squatting has occurred. The first government of independent Zimbabwe inherited a number of squatter areas in Harare and continued with the earlier policy of eradication and control. Small settlements continue to form today, but they are only tolerated briefly, do not generate widespread working-class support and are subject to frequent demolition, at the cost of considerable hardship to their residents. One result has been an increase in the number of homeless people sleeping rough in both Harare and Gweru. Only in one area just outside Harare's boundary, a long-standing settlement at Epworth, which originally belonged to a mission, has the notion of regularization and improvement been grudgingly accepted (Patel 1984, Butcher 1986). Here, a programme of infrastructure upgrading is gradually being implemented, although standards and procedures are in many respects inappropriate. Another form of illegal construction that is proving harder to eradicate is the construction of wooden sheds in the back yards of existing high-density houses. The HCMPTT found that in 1987 15 per cent of the population in Harare's high-density areas, mainly those nearest the city centre, and 18 per cent in Chitungwiza, were tenants in outbuildings (HCMPTT 1988). Unless the supply of affordable plots is increased, it may be only a matter of time before residents take the matter of access to land into their own hands on a much larger scale than hitherto.

The aims of the research were to increase understanding of the extent to which land and housing market mechanisms, together with government intervention, have ensured the availability of land for urban uses and enabled Zimbabwe's towns and cities to cope efficiently with urban growth at the same time increasing access to land and housing by the disadvantaged, notably low-income black Zimbabweans. Concern over the costs of low-density urbanization, the need to provide serviced land for low- and middle-income housing, the inherited segregated urban structure and the financial basis for local government and urban development had, by the later 1980s, led to a recognition of emerging problems with respect to the supply of land and housing.

Sources of data

The potential sources of data available in Zimbabwe include published sources, the city councils' valuation rolls, the deeds registry, information from the development-control system, advertised prices and information from individual and corporate actors in the land- and property-development process. Below I discuss the strengths and weaknesses of these sources and the quality of information available from each.

Published statistics

Regular digests of statistics published by the Central Statistical Office (CSO) contain some figures relevant to the analysis of land and housing markets. Figures are given for the total value of building plans approved, including additions and alterations, for each of Zimbabwe's main towns, other areas grouped and the country as a whole. National figures are also given by type of building (industrial, commercial, residential and other). The number of high- and low-cost houses and apartments represented by these building-plan approvals is given for Harare, Bulawayo, and other municipalities grouped.[4] Low-cost units are defined in the Local Government Laws Amendment Act (1979) as being flats in blocks of flats costing not more than Z$5,000 (US$7,000), and semi-detached houses or separate houses costing not more than Z$8,000 (US$11,000). These figures, now very outdated, with new four-room, low-cost houses costing over Z$20,000 (US$6,800) to build, have not been revised, reducing the value of the statistics.[5] Likewise, the figures for low-cost houses do not reflect all building, as building control is not exercised at the core house-construction stage, but only when approval is sought for extensions. The CSO property sales figures at date of registration are given by value for Harare, Bulawayo, Gweru, Mutare and other urban areas, with totals for urban and rural areas, while the number of sales is given for urban and rural areas. As with most other published data in the Third World, all the values are reported in current prices and no indices are constructed. Values can sometimes be deflated by use of other statistics published in the same source, for example, low- and high-income urban household consumer price indices and a building materials price index.

Valuation roll and census data

The city council valuation roll, which covers only middle- and high-income areas, was last reviewed for Harare in 1975. New properties have been added based on 1975 valuations. The roll specifies whether land is in public, private or municipal ownership, land-use, area of the plot, rateable value and development (market) value, and is used as a basis for the collection of the property tax, which contributed 18.6 per cent of the council's revenue in 1984–85 (Wekwete 1989b). Although the roll is computerized it is not used for generating data for planning purposes. A summary database was produced in about 1989 by the Department of Rural and Urban Planning and can be used at district and sub-district level to produce information on land-use, land in public and private ownership, average residential plot size, rateable value per square metre for developed and undeveloped land, and average market value per developed stand (plot). In some cases, it might be possible to add census figures to the database if a suitable method is found to reconcile boundaries and adjust the figures appropriately. Again, the values obtained from this source do not include low-income areas and the analysis will be of historical interest only.

Revaluation has by law to be carried out within 15 years and currently this exercise is taking place. In line with the policy of unifying the formerly separate administration of African housing areas with the rest of the city, these areas are being included in the valuation roll for the first time, although whether valuation is being based on replacement costs of houses and services or market values (the latter being difficult to estimate where few if any open-market transactions have occurred) is unclear. Previously, allottees in these areas paid supplementary charges or combined charges for services and a flat property rate. It was expected that the new roll would come into effect in January 1992, the same year as the census. Potentially, therefore, the database could be updated and could then form a valuable tool for studying changes in land use, values and population density.

The valuation roll in Gweru has been recently updated (1986). As part of the exercise, all transfers that occurred between 1981 and 1986 were recorded and used to construct a table of average annual prices per basic unit for each of the 13 areas within the municipal boundary. In addition, indices of residential values in each area were obtained, using 1974 as the base year, for each area and for the town as a whole. Revaluation of industrial and commercial areas was carried out using the investment method, mainly based on market rentals, but taking zoning into account. In residential areas, land and improvements were revalued separately: for the former the first $600\,m^2$ of a stand were valued at z$1.692 (US$1.02) per square metre and the additional area at z$0.84 (US$0.50) per square metre, while for improvements either the market value or the cost of construction was used. Unrateable property includes that owned by the government, schools, crèches, and property owned by the city council and eligible parastatal organizations. The valuation roll is generally similar to the Harare roll, but uses a different set of land-use categories linked closely to the Gweru town-planning scheme. Although it is not computerized and contains errors, mostly typographical, it has been possible to summarize it by hand and to create a database to study ownership and use of land in the city.

Title deeds

Deeds to all freehold or leasehold land have to be registered and can be transferred only by means of a registered deed of transfer. The register is open to public inspection and is a stand-by-stand (plot-by-plot) record of transfers, giving stand number, size, ownership and amount paid at the time of each transaction. Zimbabwe is legitimately proud of this accurate and reliable, if rather cumbersome, system. However, the register does not specify whether the plot has been developed and what it is used for, nor does it subdivide the trans-action price into land and improvements, and, once again, it is not computer-ized. Using it to provide information on land-ownership city-wide would therefore have been a tedious and costly exercise.

The possibility of attempting to combine data not recorded in the title deeds with available data from the valuation roll was rejected. Nevertheless, it is possible to identify *undeveloped* stands from the valuation roll or by inspection on site and then to ascertain ownership from the deeds registry. In addition, prices at the time of exchange could be obtained from this source. Such an exercise has been carried out for undeveloped stands in three study areas in Harare with the aim of identifying trends in the land market, the extent of post-independence speculative activity and trends in prices since initial subdivision in the 1920s. Also open to public inspection is a personal index file on every individual who enters into a registrable transaction, in which all such transactions are recorded.

Development-control records

The development-control system is a potential source of information on land-use change and emerging pressures for development. The register of development-control activity for Harare includes the register of subdivision applications. This gives the name of the owner and his/her agent, title deed description (including location), town-planning scheme zoning, date received, date and nature of decision, conditions attached to the permission and stand numbers allocated. In 1989 there were about 100 applications in Harare, mostly for two or three plots. Unfortunately, obtaining permission to subdivide is no indication that subdivision has actually occurred, although it would be possible to check whether subdivided stands have been sold by cross-referencing to the deeds registry.

A second development control is the development-control/building-control schedule which contains the stand number, zoning under the relevant town-planning scheme, nature of buildings proposed (and whether new, addition or alteration), the area and estimated cost of the main building and outbuildings, owner or agent, dates of submission and approval and conditions of development and building permission. Because the development- and building-control systems are very detailed and strictly enforced, relatively little illegal development occurs. The register would, therefore, be a potential source of information on new residential development, but extracting that information city-wide would have been a very time-consuming process, especially as development-control registers are kept in the relevant district offices. Instead, a study of special consent development applications (those requiring a change in zoning) and approval/refusal rates is being undertaken in an area to the east of the city centre, where pressures for change of use are considerable, to give an indication of development pressure and the way in which the planning system copes with this.

Advertised prices

Using information given in advertisements, property can be differentiated: houses for rent and sale in low- and middle-density areas, residential land for sale in low- and middle-density areas, apartments for rent or sale, and houses for sale in high-density areas. The price analysis of developed property, however, is difficult for a number of reasons: the price of land itself is affected by location, aspect, topography, plot size, etc.; these locational and physical factors also affect the value of the dwelling. The quality, age and size of the house clearly affect the price realized, and so does the presence of other buildings (servants' quarters, workshop, garage) and amenities (swimming pool, tennis court, wall or fence, etc.). Thus the prices of houses advertised for sale vary enormously, while insufficient information is given in the advertisements to control for the determinants. Prices for middle- and high-cost houses can, therefore, only be used in an indicative way. However, the range of prices within which dwellings (265 in June/July 1990) are offered for rent or sale enables both comparisons of successive years and urban areas and detection of broad relationships between typical private- and public-sector salaries and house prices. The much greater uniformity of dwelling units in areas of apartments and high-density housing makes these prices more comparable than prices in low-density areas, although prices for similar high-density units do vary widely so averages were mostly used.[6]

Data were collected on a daily basis during the two main fieldwork periods (June–August 1990 and January–August 1991) and used to analyze plot prices and sizes on offer in terms of monthly averages. In a city of Harare's size, and with an average of just over 60 pieces of land being advertised for sale each month, this exercise was easily manageable and yet yielded sufficient data to detect short-term trends and broad geographical variations. To study longer-term trends, advertised prices of land and high-density houses for sale were obtained from archive copies of the main newspaper for the June–August period for 1985–99. Time constraints prohibited working back further than 1985.

Actors in the land-development process

Actors in the land-development process are a potential source of information, including price information. In some circumstances, a postal survey and/or interviews with owners of undeveloped land may help to ascertain their attitudes and motives and the constraints on bringing land forward for development. Similarly, interviews with developers and contractors involved in the development of new residential property may reveal the nature of their financial calculations, factors taken into account in decision-making, motives and experience with the land-development process and its regulation. Plans are being formulated to extend the research in this way. The estate agency sector in Zimbabwe is well developed and respondents in selected larger agencies in both Harare and Gweru proved to be useful commentators on general trends in the land and housing markets, as well as on administrative procedures governing transactions.

Estate agents are also a source of information on trends in the emerging market in houses in ex-municipal rented and aided self-help housing areas. The price paid by allottees is a submarket price, regardless of whether land has historically been in council ownership or specially acquired, and can be added to the cost of constructing a core house. Present-day sale prices are inflated by the shortfall of supply and bear little relationship to initial costs. In high-density areas for which title is not issued at the outset, transactions in undeveloped plots do not occur as such stands are reallocated by the council. The selling price and purchaser of partly or fully developed stands transferred before title deeds are issued (cessions) are subject to council approval, but in practice the council acknowledges that if it interferes with prices set by the market, under-the-counter payments are likely to occur, and many such transactions may proceed without approval.

Direct collection methods

Ideally, perhaps, city-wide statistics on the socio-economic and housing conditions of the population together with more detailed household sample surveys, and interviews with relevant actors in the process of house development and exchange would be used to build up a picture of city-wide housing markets. Census information is of value in this respect, but long intercensal periods render it outdated at least half the time, while the absence of income and expenditure data is a clear disadvantage for the purpose of studying housing. In Harare, limited information had been tabulated from a city-wide household sample survey carried out in 1987 as part of the Combination Master Plan preparation process, but much of the information collected appears never to have been analyzed. City councils also regularly collect figures on the municipal housing stock, albeit with fairly large number of inconsistencies.

In the absence of resources for city-wide samples of households sufficiently large for areas to be analyzed separately, the decision was taken to carry out household sample surveys in a wide range of selected areas. Four criteria were used for selection. The first was typicality and the desire to obtain a picture of city-wide trends. Areas representing the main income groups and types of housing were selected. With respect to high-income housing in Harare, for example, a typical low-density housing area in the northern suburbs and a typical low-density housing area in the southern suburbs, the latter subject to considerable black in-movement, were chosen. The second criterion was a prior knowledge of important market processes thought to be occurring in an area. For Harare, an area of upper-middle-income housing that had experienced black in-movement was chosen in addition to an area of apartments near the city centre where a process of transfer from rental tenure to owner occupation was under way. The third criterion was to identify areas subject to policy interventions, including areas of former municipal rental housing now subject to private purchase, recent employer-assisted sites and services and contractor-built, "low-cost" housing for sale. Examples of the first were located in both Harare and Gweru, of the second in Harare and of the third in Gweru. Control areas of existing municipal rented housing and a well established area where extensive private renting has been in existence for a considerable time were also chosen.

Fourthly, areas that had not experienced recent surveys were selected in order to maximize response rates.

A total of 15 sample surveys were carried out in 13 suburbs, nine in Harare and four in Gweru. Surveys could not be carried out in Chitungwiza or a low-density area in Gweru because of time and resource constraints, while expected resident resistance prohibited surveys in Mbare, the area in Harare with the most extensive subletting and in which the council had recently carried out a survey. In most cases, however, the target sample of approximately 50 plots was completed. This number was considered to be adequate for general conclusions to be drawn. Importance was also attached to interviewing every household on the plot, as the characteristics and housing aspirations of tenants were a major focus of study. The relatively lengthy questionnaire had a number of purposes other than illustrating trends in the land and housing markets, including collection of information on household socio-economic circumstances, past housing history, the current housing situation, housing aspirations and, in the low-density areas selected, attitudes towards densification. It was hoped also to identify a limited number of typical households willing to be interviewed in greater depth, to supplement information obtained in the structured question-naire and to assist in its interpretation, although once again, time was not available to follow up this intention.

Trends in the property market in Harare and Gweru

Space restrictions preclude a detailed description and analysis of property market behaviour and price trends derived from the aforementioned sources. Rather, I am able to provide only a brief summary of the trends detected across several dimensions of land- and property-market operations. First, through analyzing the prices at which exchanges of houses in high-density areas are occurring, we were able to gauge the state of the housing market, and the implications for access to housing by low-income households. Average prices of houses advertised for sale in high-density areas in Harare increased gradually between 1986 and 1988, then more rapidly, with the nominal price in 1989 being 17 per cent above the average for 1988 and the average price in 1990 more than double (103 per cent) that in 1989. The same pattern is evident in the price per room. Estate agents in Gweru reported that demand from potential purchasers far exceeds supply, although prices are lower than in Harare.

Secondly, building-plan approvals give some indication of public- and private-sector residential construction activity and thus the demand for housing – even though approvals are, of course, not necessarily followed by construc-tion. Looking in detail at Harare, while on average 2,289 high-cost dwellings were approved each year between 1970 and 1973, this then fell off dramatical-ly, declining to only 149 in 1979. Private-sector, high-cost dwellings fell from

26 per cent of the total in 1970 to 3 per cent in 1979. This represented a decline in the rate of building in the early 1970s from approximately 22 per 1,000 to 1 per 1,000 in 1982, calculated from the census data.[7] From an average of 231 high-cost dwellings per annum between 1980 and 1985, a faster but still relatively insignificant rate of new construction commenced: 824 in 1986, increasing to 1,057 in 1989 (average 878 per annum between 1986 and 1990). From 1980, in Harare, a marked increase in the value of building plans approved occurred, but very few of these were for high-cost dwellings (defined as detached or semi-detached houses with a value of z$8,000-plus in 1979 or apartments valued z$5,000-plus). Instead, construction was of industrial and commercial as well as government buildings. Nationally, only 28 per cent of the value of this construction was residential, compared with 53 per cent in the previous year. By the mid-1980s, the downward trend in the real value of building plans approved was reversed and in the second half of the 1980s both the real value of all building plans and the proportion attributable to residential development increased. However, although the value of building plans approved increased markedly in Harare during the later 1980s, this did not represent an increase in real terms, if compared with 1980 rather than 1983, as the cost of construction escalated. The pattern in Gweru was less clear, as the value of approvals swung between very low in 1984–85, to higher in real terms in 1987–88, and to decline dramatically again while the overall upward trend in Harare continued.

A third area of findings upon which I wish to report briefly relates to property sales and house prices. During both the 1970s and 1980s, prices and values were generally stable or declining slightly in real terms – at least until around 1985, when the National Property Association estimated that house prices in low-density areas began to rise dramatically. This dramatic increase in house prices resulted partly from a decline in emigration and thus the supply of second-hand housing, and partly from increased demand. Towards the end of 1986 prices briefly stabilized, in a climate of general economic uncertainty, uncertainty over the capital-gains tax (from which sellers of first residences were given exemption in 1988), a shortage of building society mortgage funds, and greater caution on the part of buyers as the cost of building materials for improvements and repairs began to increase more rapidly and availability declined.[8] The slowing-down of emigration and lack of availability of small houses and apartments for smaller, elderly households reduced the supply of family houses on larger stands, while demand for these remained strong, including demand from embassies, foreign investors and companies at the luxury end of the market. Advertised prices in Harare from 1987 to 1991 show that these rapid price increases continued for the whole range of high-quality housing.

A fourth area of market activity for which we have data relates to rental housing and the sale of apartments. However, the market here has been severely distorted by an anti-inflationary measure of rent regulation from 1982, which has reduced investment returns upon the production of rental accommodations. Despite recent increases, the impact of rent control, especially in the 1980s, restricted rent increases to less than inflation and led to changes in the supply of rental housing. One indication of this is the fall in new construction for rent. From 3,236 high-cost apartments (a unit in a block of apartments or terrace of relatively modest houses costing more than z$5,000 in 1979) built in Harare from 1970 to 1981, accounting for 28 per cent of all approved building plans, between 1980 and 1988 only one major development had commenced. Disinvestment by financial investors, which accounted for 85 per cent of dwellings in 1980, also took place, with the share falling to only 40 per cent by 1988 (Pritchard 1989). The lack of opportunity in rental housing has also encouraged landlords to sell blocks of apartments to employers or for other uses, or to dispose of individual apartments under share transfer or sectional title. By 1985, therefore, an acute shortage of rental accommodation was reported.[9]

Finally, we collected data about transaction land-price trends in three privately developed subdivisions: Mount Pleasant, one of the oldest private residential areas in northern Harare; Borrowdale, a newer and higher income suburb; and Hatfield, an older residential area to the south of the city. Overall average prices for all three indicate rising prices in the late 1940s and the second half of the 1950s, a fall in the mid-1960s, and a recovery and gentler increase throughout the 1970s. Falling prices in the first half of the 1980s are succeeded by increases in the second half of the decade, but to little more than the 1980 level, even in cash terms. Because of the absence of consumer price indices before 1970, these figures have not been corrected for inflation. However, they do bear out the general analysis of trends in the property market discussed earlier. In order to ascertain geographical patterns in the price of undeveloped land and recent trends, data on the asking price of land offered for sale was collected for June–August 1990 and January–August 1991. The size of plots advertised for sale and the price per square metre were analyzed for Harare as a whole and separately for five segments of the city. Price data relative to the Consumer Price Index between June 1990 and August 1991 show that the increase in land prices for much of that time was markedly higher than the rate of inflation.

Conclusions

This chapter has dealt with trends in private-property markets. However, it was also intended to assess the outcome of government intervention in land markets with respect to the criteria of efficiency and equity. Operationalizing these concepts for this purpose presents certain difficulties, which have not yet been overcome. Neoclassical economic approaches to the study of land markets have given some attention to definitions of efficiency, but these are rarely of immediate use in policy evaluation, especially for a commodity as atypical as land;

while equity is conceptually problematic, particularly in the context of a capitalist economy and system of property ownership. Common-sense definitions have had to be adopted, and the policy evaluation to be carried out in general, rather than precise, quantified terms (Rakodi 1992b).

The analysis has revealed many of the problems that commonly occur in the use of information sources on land and property but has also given some idea of the scope for making the best of what publicly available information sources there are. It has enabled us to build up a picture of trends in the land and property markets, some of which can be explained by the use of typical concepts of neoclassical economic land rent theory, particularly demand and supply. However, it is clear that other levels of explanation are also needed. These relate to the policy-making process and Zimbabwe's political economy and ideological views of property. To some extent the former can be analyzed using policy statements and records of implementation, as well as interviews with informants in the public bureaucracies and private-property sector. However, the politics of central and local government, a sensitive area at the best of times, proved difficult for outsiders to penetrate. While accounts of national politics and the country's political economy by other analysts made up for this to some extent, the dearth of studies of the local state has resulted in neglect of this source of potential explanations, except as hypothesis. In addition, just as with analysis of other aspects of society and government, structural explanations cannot be found in easily observable phenomena and involve interpretation that inevitably depends on a degree of subjectivity. Finally, the meaning attached to property affects the attitudes, motives and actions of actors in land and housing markets. Again, an element of subjective interpretation is involved in suggesting values and ideologies that may be relevant to understanding, but which are implicit rather than explicit.

Notes

1. The research described in this chapter was funded by the Economic and Social Research Committee of the UK's Overseas Development Administration and carried out in conjunction with the Department of Rural and Urban Planning, University of Zimbabwe. The assistance of Penny Withers, Vincent Hungwe and students in the department with data collection, and Joel Lloren with analysis of the Harare valuation roll database is acknowledged. Useful comments were received from Dr Chris Mafico on an earlier paper.
2. One response, both to increased costs of living and to excess demand for middle-income housing, it was claimed, was that high-income families were resorting to the subletting of rooms and servants quarters.
3. In theory, the city and municipal councils can borrow from building societies, and Harare and Bulawayo are permitted to borrow on the open market.
4. In the late 1970s, a new town called Chitungwiza was developed several kilometres to the south of Harare. Although lip service was paid to developing economic opportunities there, the great majority of its workforce travel to work in Harare. Chitungwiza's 1987 population was estimated to be 263,000, compared with Harare's 994,000 (HCMPTT 1988). Shortage of time and resources prevented its inclusion in the detailed studies.
5. Effective and actual devaluations have made the US dollar equivalents misleading representa-

tions of the real price changes of housing units.
6. The profile of data collection for Harare was 40–50 apartments per month advertised to rent, 40 apartments advertised for sale, rising to 110 per month, and approximately 30 low-cost houses offered for sale per month.
7. Assuming the non-African population of 106,000 in 1969 (Kay & Cole 1977: 42) stayed fairly steady.
8. One estimate for 1980 was that only 20 per cent of properties offered for sale changed hands, mostly in Harare, and at the upper end of the market, supplying accommodation for embassy staff (RAL September 1980). The lifting of the prohibition of African freehold ownership in urban areas and the depressed property prices made it possible for black Zimbabweans to buy into the low- and medium-density areas, although constrained by the shortage of mortgage finance. Not until 1987 had savings increased sufficiently for most prospective purchasers to be granted mortgages.
9. To meet demand there was increasing evidence of lower-rent accommodation coming onto the market, notably houses near the town centre converted to lodging houses (at rents of Z$65–95 (US$26–38 per month in 1990), and the rental of servants' quarters and guest cottages.

CHAPTER SEVEN

Social agents in
land and property development
Relating approaches to findings in Mexico

Beatriz García & Edith Jiménez

Introduction

The main aim of this chapter is to describe the methodology used in two independently run studies of the social agents involved in land and property development in Mexico.[1] Unlike those who pursue neoclassical studies, we are interested in historical processes and trends (see Fitzwilliam 1991 for a discussion of the relative merits of neoclassical and Marxist approaches). The proposal here is that the study of land and property markets is too broad a topic to consider in isolation from other factors and without proper account being taken of the urban process as a whole. Furthermore, the contention developed in this chapter is that the form this process takes is determined by many political, economic and ideological factors that change in the course of time. In our approach, an important rôle has been given to the social relations (such as negotiations and struggles) between different groups (Ball et al. 1985) and to the search for profit in different "circuits of capital accumulation" (Harvey 1985, Ward 1989b). It needs to be stressed, however, that the findings presented are insights rather than incontrovertible conclusions. Only those findings necessary to illustrate the methodology are presented here, along with a self-assessment of the strengths and weaknesses of our work directed specifically at the methodology used.

The focus and the choice of research agenda
The point of departure for the studies in Mexico was an attempt to understand real estate development and the acquisition and commercialization of land through the study of the central agents involved in the land market. Both studies were particularly concerned with looking at changes over time from the earliest land-development projects in the 1920s, through a phase of more sophisticated real estate production in the 1960s, and to the economic crisis during the 1980s,

which had important repercussions on activities in this sector. It is proposed here that the most appropriate way to "map" these changes is through a focus on the structure and rationale of land-market agents – particularly those who promote land development.

Several authors have identified the promoter as the central agent of their analysis. Topalov was the first to consider promoters as a separate category and as the hub around which key explanations of real estate development in France were to be made (Topalov 1975, 1979). For Topalov (1975: 15) the promoter is a social agent distinct from, and independent of, other agents participating at the circulation stage of capital. The promoter's main rôle is to speed up the rate of circulation of capital and, in order to achieve this, the promoter invests in land to liberate it for building (by making it available on the market) and then finance construction either directly or through the banks. At each stage the promoter appropriates some of the profit of both the land-owner and the constructor. The promoter is thus the classic middleman.

Topalov's work has had a great influence on studies by Mexican scholars (Schteingart 1989, García Peralta 1988, Hiernaux & Lindon 1991). However, there appear to be three central problems in a direct application of Topalov's work to the Mexican case. The first concerns the application of the category of promoter without taking into account its specific meaning in Mexico. Schteingart (1989) appears to do this in her work on Mexico City, capturing within the category of promoter many large enterprises that include, among a variety of activities, the subdivision and development of land, and the construction of houses. The result of this indiscriminate application is that a great variety of agents have been forced into this category even when they do not belong to it. Furthermore, by bringing these agents together it is frequently implied that a broadly similar rationale applies to each. From our analysis of the city of Querétaro we conclude that it would be wrong to consider as promoters all large-scale enterprises. Similarly, it is equally confusing to give the term an all embracing connotation to include other social agents such as illegal land developers, as Legorreta (1983) has done.

The second problem in the application of Topalov's work is the ability to generalize from findings based on studies carried out in one city, especially the Metropolitan Area of Mexico City, to other rather different cities. It is by no means certain that the land and property development experience of Mexico City is common to all Mexican cities. Concentration of analyses on a "similar" set of agents makes this appear to be so. Indeed, the greater experience of land development in Mexico City and the more sophisticated agents involved in the process would suggest that this generalization cannot be maintained. It remains to be investigated whether there are more differences than similarities in this process. Our references to and analyses of other cities aim to diversify the academic research on the development of land and real estate in Mexico so as to make it less centred on the capital and help to avoid making unrealistic generalizations.

For this reason, the Cambridge group (Ward, Jones and Jiménez) employed a comparative framework. While here the city of Querétaro is used as the central case study, reference is made to other case studies in Guadalajara, Puebla and Toluca. From the outset it is acknowledged that comparative studies can cause methodological problems. Above all is the subjective decision of which features are compared from one example to those from others. This approach was adopted, however, in order to highlight what the authors consider to be the crucial methodological importance attached to the cross-reference of approaches and results, analysis of the similarities and the differences of specific cases. This allows a wider applicability to be given to the findings than would otherwise be possible (see Gilbert & Ward 1985, Gilbert & Varley 1991 for an elaboration of this approach).

The comparative studies attempted to uncover the principal land agents and, wherever possible, to conduct semi-structured interviews with them. Such a methodology would be severely constrained were it to be applied to a study of Mexico City on any scale where the size of the city and the lack of intimacy would militate against such an approach. The very local and sensitive nature of the land-development process lent itself to the analysis in a smaller city. The close association of Querétaro, Puebla and Toluca with Mexico City, however, is important. There have been consistent attempts to decentralize industry and administrative functions away from the capital. Moreover, it was believed that the processes occurring in the smaller cities might be representative of changes in Mexico City. One reason for this, which the studies hoped to expose, was whether real estate developers from Mexico City had been active in investing capital in the smaller study cities.

A third problem found in research in Mexico is a bias towards the so-called formal or legal market in the search for rationality and an understanding of sophistication. This relegates the informal or illegal segment of the land market to be regarded as irrational, or of some undefined rationality. In fact it is through illegal sales, particularly of the *ejido*, that land has become available in Mexico. *Ejido* land represents 69.3 per cent of the total land area in the municipality of Querétaro and dominates the north, south and west of the city (Fig. 7.1, and García Peralta 1988). However, only a fraction of this land was developed at the time of our research: 6.5 million m^2, equivalent to 30 per cent of the area said to have been developed by private subdividers in the municipality (García Peralta 1988: 32).

The principal methodological aim, therefore, was to bring together a less rigid definition of the term "promoter", and to include within the land-development analysis a broader scope incorporating the illegal and informal sector. The methodological starting point was that the land market did not consist of a single market, but was segmented. Each segment has its own characteristics – particularly since we agree with Azuela (1987a) and Ward (1989c) that legality and illegality are socially constructed terms.[2] It is this segmentation of land markets that, we argue, gives rise to distinct agents of land and real estate

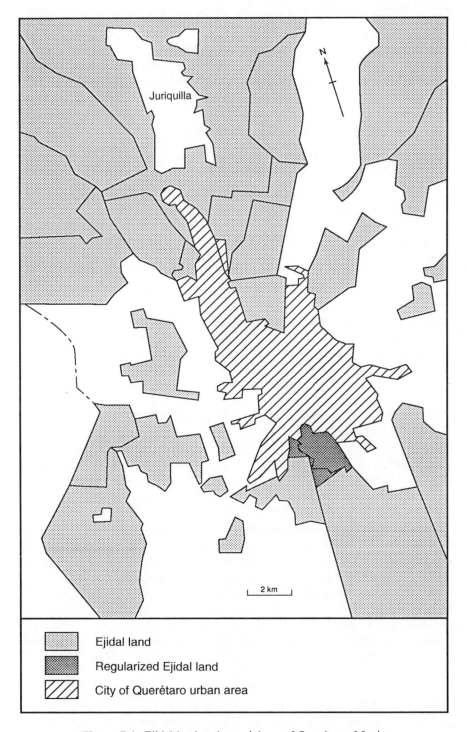

Figure 7.1 Ejidal land at the periphery of Querétaro, Mexico.

development; for example *ejidatarios*; smallholding owners; small-scale in-fill developers; and large-scale developers. The methods that each agent employs to commercialize land clearly vary in degree of sophistication and in the articulation each has with other land-development agents, the state and financial institutions. To refer to an earlier point, one can see that this commercialization is likely to vary from city to city according to the political situation, the level of organization of the different groups and the patterns of land tenure and land subdivision.

Summary of the methodological and technical steps taken

An analysis of land markets based on social agents needs to specify those agents whose actions influence city growth. Identification can be related to the amount of land developed and whether this had a specific impact upon the direction of urban expansion. Through semi-structured interviews with key agents such as property appraisers, real estate dealers, land-owners, high-ranking public officials in planning and urban works departments and politicians, including governors, municipal presidents and party leaders, one can begin to identify the links between land-market agents and other areas of investment (circuits of capital), such as the financial sector, industry and agriculture, and ties to groups in the public sector. With these interviews the aim is to get a *consistent picture* of the relevance of those considered to be central agents, and the factors that contribute to facilitate or hinder their actions in land and real estate development. To assess their relevance, the Mexico studies looked at a number of factors: the origins and changes in the tenure of the plots developed by the key agents; the size of territorial reserves; and links with the public sector and with social groups with whom conflict was common (neighbouring settlements, political parties, public officials). Also, a systematic review of the most important daily local newspaper from 1975 to 1989 was a useful way to place the principal land and real estate developers studied into a social, political and historical context, showing links with local and national elite groups.

Finally, in order to know the study city in some detail, a list of all the subdivisions was made, noting the name of the subdivision, the date when the developer submitted his application for the development, the date when permission was granted, the extension and number of plots and the name of the developer. This information was collected from the Department of Land Development of the state government and complemented with information collected on personal "tours" around the city. It should be mentioned that some invaluable "windfall" contacts and information were acquired through the city tours. These contributed to better-quality interviews later on.

The city of Querétaro

Querétaro is the capital city of a state that bears the same name. The city experienced a moderate process of industrialization during the 18th century, particularly in the textile and food-processing industries (Ward et al. 1994).

Large-scale industrialization, however, began only during the 1950s, with the rate of expansion increasing during the 1960s with the establishment of leading multinationals (Chant 1991, García Peralta 1988). The attraction of the city motivated immigration which, until 1970, was in excess of emigration, and concentrated an increasing proportion of the state's population in the capital (Table 7.1).

Table 7.1 Population growth in Querétaro.

Year	State population	City population	Percentage
1950	286,238	49,440	4.7
1960	355,045	69,058	19.45
1970	485,523	112,993	23.27
1980	738,605	215,976	29.24
1990	1,051,235	385,503	36.67

Source: VIII, IX, X and XI. INEGI, population census.

Much of the physical growth of the city during the period of study (1960 to 1989) was determined by two factors. The first of these was the control exercised over a large amount of private land by three land and real estate developments catering to the upper- and middle-class market. The total area acquired by developers here was 22 million m^2, the equivalent of 45 per cent of the total area of the city at the time of purchase (García Peralta 1988: 55; Fig. 7.2). Up to the 1950s, however, the land and housing market in Querétaro was characterized by the absence of any specific agents appropriating the profits derived from transactions on urban land development. It was only between 1950 and 1960 that the first private subdivisions by local owners of agricultural land began, mostly by conversion of hacienda cores (*cascos de hacienda*) or ranches. By 1982 Querétaro had 149 private subdivisions (García Peralta 1988), with an additional 18 developments to 1989 (Ward et al. 1994). The second determining factor was the availability of a large amount of cheap land in the surrounding *ejidos* and *pueblo* cores which was on offer to a low-income market and which represents more than 60 per cent of the municipal area. A more detailed examination of the strategies, rationale and market intervention in these two market segments is developed below.

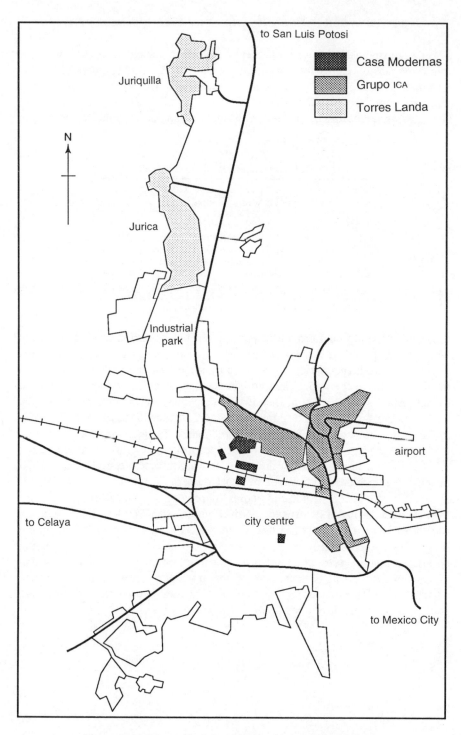

Figure 7.2 Private land development in the city of Querétaro.

94

Detailed case studies:
strategies, rationale, and market intervention

Developers of private land

In order to illustrate the diversity of land-market interventions by the private sector, this chapter focuses upon three detailed case studies. Each, we believe, is in some way characteristic of a general, but local, process of land development. The case studies do not, therefore, represent typical patterns of development for the city in general. The three examples are chosen according to the agent structure of each. The first is the most important land and real estate developer in Querétaro, known as Parques Industriales de Querétaro. The second is a family-run development which has responsible for Querétaro's two largest sites, Jurica and Juriquilla. The third is a privately run company known as Casas Modernas, SA, which has concentrated on smaller "in-fill" sites and has identified a niche by specializing in owner-occupied housing for lower-middle-income families.

Parques Industriales de Querétaro is a subsidiary of Mexico's largest construction firm, Ingenieros Civiles y Asociados (ICA). ICA is known to have close links with the government, which is the group's single biggest client for the construction of large-scale infrastructure, such as hydroelectric dams, thermo-electric plants, motorways, ports, airports, housing, and the Mexico City underground. In this sense, Querétaro is no exception to this large spread of activities and Bernardo Quintana, ICA's president for more than 40 years, had close personal associations with Querétaro's governors. Use of these contacts allowed the company to set up industrial estates in the city and win prestigious contracts, such as the construction of the Mexico City–San Luis Potosí highway (*libramiento*).

In terms of land development, ICA initially operated in Querétaro through a company called Parques Residenciales de Querétaro. Unlike the majority of real estate operations in the city, Parques Residenciales set out to create a planned and long-term project (Ward et al. 1994). Again, the company had the support of the state government. In a complicated deal struck between the state, ICA and a group of the city's leading landowning families, over 500 ha were acquired for real estate development.[3] The motive for the families appears to have been a lack of liquidity and an insufficient knowledge of land-development procedures (Ward et al. 1994). In return for the land, ICA allowed the families to become shareholders in smaller companies specifically set up to develop each individual estate. Thus ICA's activities have determined the urban growth of the city in terms of both the land use and the direction of growth.

The second case study is the development of Querétaro's largest private subdivision by the Torres Landa family.[4] Jurica was first conceived by the patriarch Juan José Torres Landa as an agricultural enterprise because of the good quality of the soil and the possibilities for irrigation. Torres Landa developed the land through a firm of developers known as Inmobiliaria y Constructora

Bustamante (INCOBUSA), with whom he had a formal interest. INCOBUSA planned to develop the site as a *fraccionamiento campestre* (country park-style subdivision) aimed at high-income families. The installation of some of the infrastructure over the site appears to have been conducted by the Public Works Department of the government of Guanajuato where Juan José Torres Landa was a former governor (Ward et al. 1994).

A number of other shady deals appear to have occurred. In 1974 Torres Landa sold Jurica to Ignacio Bustamante, the son of the most important shareholder of INCOBUSA. Nominally, at least, the reason appears to have been to avoid the risk of losing the land to the neighbouring *ejido*, which had made frequent applications to the Department of Agrarian Reform asserting rights over the lands. It also appears from interviews with the Torres Landa family that the site development to this point had not made any money.[5] In 1978 the holding company for Jurica created by Bustamante filed for bankruptcy and was passed to a liquidator of the Secretary of the Exchequer (Secretaria de Hacienda y Crédito Público). To manage the site Jurica was transferred to the Somex bank, which was then unable to sell the development for two years. In 1980 a buyer was found in Mexico's second largest bank, Banamex, which was planning the decentralization of its central offices from Mexico City to Querétaro. However, this plan was abandoned when the banks were nationalized in 1982 (García Peralta 1988). Finally, the Torres Landa brothers bought the development back.

In comparison to the national development projects contemplated by ICA and the fraught projects surrounding the Jurica subdivision, the third example reflects a local land developer with an unambitious development strategy. Casas Modernas was formed in the 1960s and began its real estate operations in 1967. In contrast to the other two agents, Casas Modernas is a local company that has not acquired large extensions of land; in fact it holds a land reserve of no more than three years. Rather, it has preferred to specialize in in-fill: buying already urbanized vacant plots within the city area.

Semi-structured interviews with the director of Casas Modernas conducted as a part of the Cambridge project revealed something of the rationality behind the company's operations. While a typology of Casas Modernas suggested that the company had been exceptionally successful in identifying and exploiting a market niche, the interview did not produce such a clear-cut perspective. Indeed, the main reason for acquisition of in-fill sites appeared to be one of conservatism on the part of the company's directors. While Casas Modernas is a local company, the company's capital formation is from a nationally based business family and the owners of one of Mexico's leading chains of food supermarkets. Acquisition of small areas of land, therefore, appeared to be related to the minimization of risk rather than the maximization of profit. If there were a rationale, it was the correct identification of social-interest housing as supplying the company with subsidized credit and quick sales. Location and strategy, nevertheless, were once more based on a notion of "personal choice".[6]

These findings suggest a need to reappraise the conventional wisdom of a straightforward linkage between macroeconomic changes, land prices, and real estate markets. The repercussions of the devaluation of the currency, the nationalization of the banks and the economic crisis, with inflation of more than 150 per cent in 1987, high interest rates, and restricted credit for middle- and high-income housing, were the most important reasons why the development of large-scale subdivisions came to a virtual halt in the 1980s. At the same time, however, supply was also affected by tougher regulations on land subdivisions, such as legal sanctions against illegal subdividers, guidelines for a higher proportion of donated areas to the municipal authorities and, increasingly in the case of Puebla and Querétaro, social pressure on the government not to authorize the building of more condominiums due to a scarcity of water. Thus, private developers moved from large-scale subdivisions to smaller-scale operations for which there was credit and where the risks were less pronounced. The combination of macroeconomic factors, changes in government practice and "personal choice" by the promoters draws together the tighter link of land development to financial cycles and institutions (Jones et al. 1993).

A further dimension is the changing territoriality of land development. In order to minimize losses during the crisis there has been a move out of the larger urban centres such as Querétaro, Guadalajara, Toluca and Puebla, to other municipalities, surrounding *pueblo cores,* and other cities in the state. Here, the demand for housing is more easily identified, laws are less strict and less strictly enforced, and land acquisition is cheaper – a spatial reorganization that the study cities share with the Metropolitan Area of Mexico City (Schteingart 1989).

The analysis of promoters, land-owners and developers in Mexican cities reveals a more diversified structure than has hitherto been suggested in the literature. Attempting to apply Topalov's typology of promoter would be accurate only in the case of INCOBUSA and, to a lesser extent, in the Parques Residenciales de Querétaro (ICA) case. In the latter, however, one must note that the decision to develop land in Querétaro was partly the result of a windfall political deal with the state government. INCOBUSA derived a significant amount of its business operations from defrauding purchasers and financial institutions alike. The point to be made is that a typology based upon the structure of operations may obscure a more complex rationality behind those operations.

The picture that emerges of an absence of promoters (in the strict sense of the term) in Querétaro is also evident in the other cities studied, Toluca and Puebla, even though these included a number of large subdivisions of over 100 ha. Most of the developers in these cities were not, to begin with, owners of the whole extension of land developed. A great many were owners of a core piece of land who then acquired surrounding plots to make the large subdivisions possible. In all three cities, the origins of the capital for land development included industry, agro-industry and commerce – but very few concentrated on land development as a principal business activity. Most could be categorized as businessmen in the wider sense rather than as promoters in the sense used by

Topalov. Diversity is also evident insomuch as most of the larger developments include golf course, tennis and clubhouse facilities. In such cases the development is often formed by a "civil association", where the initial land-owner or developer is quickly superseded by the residents themselves, who complete the final stages of the complex (Ward et al. 1994).

The case-study example of the Torres Landa family points to the overlap of local political influence and the real estate business. Despite political "clout" and some evidence of "creative" business practices for the installation of services and the receipt of hot money, it is by no means clear that the family has made much from real estate development. The opposite might be said of Casas Modernas. Here a small company has identified a niche in the land and property market and exploited the opportunity in a highly rational manner. As with the Torres Landa and ICA experience, the original capital was acquired from outside the real estate business; the land developed by Casas Modernas was not part of a family estate. Despite access to sufficient capital for land development, public and bank finance has been used to assist operations.

Ejidatarios

While the typology of promoters supplied by Topalov and others can be seen to be only partly useful in the case of the formal sector, land-market analyses that have investigated private land development have tended to ignore other methods of land delivery. This has contributed to a methodology split between the private sector, which is regarded as conforming to some formal and rational structure, elements of which the previous section brought into doubt, and the informal or irregular sector, which tends to be regarded as lacking an economic rationality. Here, we concentrate on the form of land development by a specific group of social agents, *ejidatarios*.

It was found that *ejidatarios* sold land for urban uses because it was more profitable to do so than to continue to use it for agricultural purposes. The main reason given by the *ejidatarios* for having to sell their land cheaply was a feeling of vulnerability. In Querétaro, particularly, a factor was the lack of a strong political organization among the various *ejidos*, which contributed to the absence of strong contacts with politicians in the local government or the Department of Agrarian Reform. The *ejidatarios* were threatened by a number of factors. Paramount was the action of government itself on the *ejido* community. Expropriations of land for public projects in the 1960s had yet to fulfil obligations of paying compensation in 1989. In Puebla, some *ejidatarios* were selling fast in order to dispose of land before rumoured expropriations took place (Jones 1991b). The sale of land cheaply assures the *ejidatarios* of some income from land, which, although low, is nevertheless more than would be paid by the government in the event of expropriation. Thus, while the *ejido* has a near monopoly of the land at the periphery of the study cities (Toluca is the exception), the pressure to sell, the illegality that this accentuates and the client group to which *ejidos* must sell, all contributed to the cheap sale prices.

The development of settlements on *ejido* land has clearly been motivated by factors very different from the apparently more rational, but often by no means more successful, development of private land.[7] The process, however, is not without its economic logic, but the relationship is a qualitatively different one. This angle is suggested by comparing the experience of *ejidatarios* and private developers in accessing financial assistance. As noted by Topalov (1979), private developers rely on capital at two key stages: for the initial outlay to develop a site and, later, to offer mortgage or credit for plot purchases to occur. No such opportunity is available to the *ejido,* which has to rely on cash flow to cover any minimal expenditure. Our approach has been to regard this difference in the context of the economic crisis of the 1980s. Based on a preliminary analysis of the data, it appears that the *ejido* sector has been subject to tougher negotiations over price, has been obliged to offer smaller plot sizes and has increasingly been required to offer buyers more *facilidades* (informal credit arrangements, usually in the form of staggered payments). The economic crisis has appeared to make the land market more commercialized, although the recorded land sales of the *ejido* seem to include a significant number of offers of down payment in the form of cars or other goods (Ward et al. 1994).

By comparing the price at which *ejidatarios* sold land in the three cities, one could come to some tentative conclusions about the degree of advancement of a commercialized land market in each city as well as discover the political relations between *ejido* and state. *Ejido* land sales in Toluca and Puebla, for example, were susceptible to rises and falls of up to 100 per cent, far larger changes than those in the sale price of private land.[8] While the overall trend is clearly the consequence of wider economic processes (Jones et al. 1993), the difference in proportion may reflect local dynamics that are distinct between private and *ejido* land tenures. We would argue the point that *ejido* land is more susceptible to changes at a local level than private land, which is much more tightly linked to national and international economic changes.

Conclusions: assessment of methodology

The strength of our work comes from the use of a temporal (longitudinal) and comparative perspective. Nevertheless, we are aware of shortcomings in our own methodology. One of the main problems faced is the great difficulty of enquiring into and demonstrating facts about such a sensitive topic as land development. Our study has identified the source of capital as a critical variable in determining market intervention, yet it is difficult to get access to reliable information on the source of capital invested in land and real estate development other than when it is linked to bank finance. This further weakens the ability to evaluate to what extent macroeconomic or more idiosyncratic agent-led decisions dictate the performance of urban markets. The data that have so far been collected permit only tentative insights into the relationship between land

and real estate investment and the wider cycles of the economy. While the economy may dictate overall performance, the studies have not been able to prove conclusively that the motive for investment decisions is wholly, or even largely, economic, for example, that land and real estate has been used by large-scale companies as a way to claim losses on the balance sheet. In the absence of reliable data on the prices of purchase, value or taxation, even a crude calculation of the rate of profit is beyond our means.

A second problem is related to the sources of the qualitative information gained through the semi-structured interviews. An obstacle to overcome here was obtaining interviews with high-ranking politicians, such as present and past state governors. The purpose was to identify the decision-makers behind the unfolding of events, rather than the agents or individuals who could do no more than inform us of the events themselves. Where top-ranking decision-makers could not be traced, alternative interviews were set up with those who appeared to be best informed and close to specific events as they occurred. These interviews were especially successful because most of the interviewees, although generally careful with the information they gave us, were more open and direct in answering our questions.

The further obstacle relating to the qualitative information in semi-structured interviews was to obtain good information during the interview. This was aided considerably by recommendations from influential politicians, close family relations, business partners or associates. So that interviews could be directed towards specific events rather than general discussion, for all semi-structured interviews, as much background information on the individual or company as possible was compiled. This allowed information offered by the interviewee to be compared, counterfactually, with what was already known or believed to be known about an event. On occasion, this led to interviewees reinterpreting what "really" went on rather than our relying on secondary sources. As this often involved dealing with sensitive information, it was necessary to put the message across very clearly that the work was of an academic nature and that the results were not to be used in making declarations to the newspapers or in setting up real estate businesses!

Finally, our attempt to concentrate on the whole land market – formal and informal segments – can be seen as a weakness. While this balanced approach was advocated by the Fitzwilliam Workshop, and in Mexico proved successful in understanding each segment of the market more fully, a comprehensive approach is clearly not the same as analyzing the interaction between the many segments (see Connolly, this volume). The need to illustrate the dynamic of interaction rather than to provide balance is what is most urgently required. In Mexico this has taken on a particular significance with the recent decision to liberalize the structure of the *ejido*. New questions are emerging on how the *ejidatarios* are going to respond. Will the *ejidatarios* sell cheaply to the land and real estate developers? Will the more organized *ejidatarios* become land and real estate agents? Is it then true that small-scale methods of land development will now be overtaken by large-scale ones with formal capital – a vision of the future long foreseen (Ward 1989b: 51, Baross 1983, Durand-Lasserve 1983, 1990, Angel et al. 1983) and hitherto postponed?

The idea in Topalov's work that we took up in this chapter is to analyze the land and real estate market through a study of the social agents involved. We found that an explanation based on the concept of the promoter was not, for the period 1962 to 1991, applicable to the city of Querétaro. The study failed to identify a true "middle man" between land-owners and constructors and found that, in the case of private land, its acquisition and commercialization are carried out usually by the same person or agent. This is not to propose the bankruptcy of Topalov's approach, but to call for a more sensitive and place-specific reworking of it.

Notes

1. This chapter is the result of work by two independent researchers on land markets in Mexico. García's fieldwork covers the years 1960–82 and was carried out during 1983–84. Jiménez's fieldwork covers the period 1974–91 and forms a part of a major research project based at the Department of Geography, University of Cambridge, between 1988 and 1991.
2. By "socially constructed" we mean that there is no absolutely clear-cut application of illegality or legality; rather an action considered illegal at a particular historical and political moment is considered legal at others. Equally, an action carried out by a particular social group can be considered illegal, while the same action is considered to be legal if carried out by another social group. For example, the transformation of *ejido* land to urban uses carried out by *ejidatarios* is considered illegal by government officials. However, the transformation of *ejido* land through government officials and influential groups in favour of high-income residential areas is considered legal.
3. Included in the deal was 196 ha of state land expropriated from the *ejido* that was ceded to the company (*Sombra de Arteaga*, 13 February 1964).
4. Jurica and adjacent Juriquilla total 1,300 ha. The two sites have in excess of 1,487 plots based around golf, social and hotel facilities.
5. This is despite the provision of major credits to the development through Financiera Intercontinental. The consolidation of the site, however, appears to have been very slow (García Peralta 1988). Bustamante became renowned for making money out of land development through purchase of sites with credit, selling the plots on mortgage facilities and transferring the mortgage to the banks. Having received commissions and profits to this point the development would then be declared bankrupt. (Interview, Juan Jose Torres Landa, 25 September 1989.)
6. While clearly profitable over a number of years, the company recently had difficulties with the development of a large *campestre* subdivision, Amazcala, located between Querétaro and the state's second city of San Juan del Rio. During the 1970s *campestre* developments were very common in Querétaro and were regarded as a logical strategy. The experience, however, appears to have confirmed the feeling of the directors that they should avoid large-scale developments that imply the conversion of rural land to urban land.
7. This point is based on a number of observations made by the team including one of the authors is a member that, notably in Querétaro, many private developers believed that the development of *ejido* land was more profitable than private land for an equivalent capital outlay (Ward et al. 1994).
8. As was the case with private land, *ejido* land was cheaper in Querétaro than in the other two cities. It is believed that one of the main reasons for this was the lack of organization of the *ejidatarios*. *Ejidatarios* in Querétaro were less able to negotiate with the different groups acquiring, or making possible the acquisition of, land relative to their counterparts in Toluca and Puebla (Ward et al. 1994).

CHAPTER EIGHT

Reconstructing the meaning of urban land in Brazil
The case of Recife (Pernambuco)

Willem Assies

Understanding the meaning of land

This chapter seeks to open discussion of an area of land and housing research that has all too often received little attention in the literature. As demonstrated elsewhere in this book, there have been major advances in land research in recent years, resulting in a refinement of techniques for the analysis of land markets and land-price developments. Assessment of such advances may be framed in terms of neoclassical theorizing or a political-economy perspective, which, in turn, may yield different views on the rôle of public policies. However, such approaches, which take as their starting point cither utility-maximizing individuals or interests attributed to structural positions in the accumulation process, run the risk of neglecting the way in which meanings of urban land are socially constructed and reconstructed.

With regard to low-income settlements, Ward & Macoloo (1992) have noted that we actually know very little about what houses and plots mean to their users or how people perceive land rights. Usually the issue is approached from a rather top-down perspective of mechanisms of co-optation and integration employed by the state. Concerning land rights, for example, it has been argued that their presence is functional to politico-ideological control, but their absence has been attributed with the same virtue. Some contend that the state will seek to increase the number of property owners as an ideological buttress for continuation of the capitalist system, which promotes a petty bourgeois mentality and pre-empts collective action (Burgess 1985b, Harms 1982). Others, however, have argued that the absence of legal rights provides the political system with an ultimate weapon for controlling the urban poor and enforcing political allegiance. Here, it is argued that vulnerability and dependence on political patronage explain the high levels of docility and conformism (Perlman 1976: 261). The dependent city, as Castells (1983: 212) concluded, is a city without citizens.

Such views seemed to have been challenged by the new generation of urban movements that emerged in Brazil in the course of the 1970s. These movements explicitly refused to submit themselves to the position of subordinated participation that was characteristic of the populist period. Rather, they sought to challenge the very social organization inherent in capitalism (Nunes & Jacobi 1982: 195, Singer 1980: 91). The new urban social movements, so called in order to distinguish them from the earlier generation of neighbourhood associations, contributed to a reshaping of the political culture (Mainwaring & Viola 1984, Mainwaring 1987).[1] The movements, through the transformation of needs and unacceptable privation into rights to be vindicated, were expected to construct new forms of citizenship (Durham 1984).[2] More specifically, authors have discussed the rôle these grassroots movements played in affirming the sociopolitical right to decent housing and the challenge this may constitute to the established property rights in which the commodification of urban land is rooted (Falcão Neto 1985, Panizzi 1989, Santos 1992).

These assessments draw attention to an important feature of the debate on social movements: the development of a powerful critique of the reductionist views of poor people's needs as if they are exclusively or even predominantly material and predetermined, and the consequent call for a retheorization of the "politics of needs" that includes non-economic dimensions (Alvarez & Escobar 1992). Social movements, as Escobar (1992: 69) has put it, "must be seen equally and inseparably as struggles over meanings as well as material conditions, that is, as cultural struggles". In short, social movements can be viewed as "spaces for the production of meaning". These meanings cannot be assumed as "given", as simple reflections of structural positions, but should be viewed as emerging from a complex field of competing and overlapping discourses and practices.

An interesting contribution to the development of analytical tools for examining such discursive practice has been made by Laclau & Mouffe (1985) in their discussion of the articulatory or hegemonic form of politics. This, in their view, emerges "in societies in which the democratic revolution has crossed a certain threshold" (Laclau & Mouffe 1985: 166). They differentiate between relations of subordination and relations of oppression.[3] Relations of subordination, considered in themselves, cannot be antagonistic relations. Subordination merely establishes a differential position between social agents, but it can be subverted and reconstructed as oppression through discursive intervention. They illustrate the process by referring to the displacement, through a logic of equivalence or "demonstration effect", of democratic discourse from the field of political equality between citizens to the field of equality between the sexes. The availability of a democratic discourse made it possible to reconstruct women's subordination as a relation of oppression, i.e. a site of antagonism. While this is one way in which antagonism may arise, a second possibility is that acquired rights are called into question as a result of certain social transformations that destabilize the established system of differential positions.

103

However, the logic of democracy, as Laclau & Mouffe assert, is one of the elimination of relations of subordination and inequalities. The antagonisms it produces are polysemic and can be articulated to very different discourses. Anti-bureaucratic struggles, for instance, may be articulated by the "New Right" to its programme of dismantling the welfare state, but they may equally be articulated to a socialist project. The dispersed democratic struggles provide the raw material for popular struggles where certain discourses tendentially construct the division of a single political space into two opposed fields. It is through this political practice of hegemonic articulation, the integration into a chain of equivalences, that democratic antagonisms acquire their meaning. To put it differently, one might say that the process of hegemonic articulation is one of boundary construction along symbolic lines (Cohen 1985).

One problem with Laclau & Mouffe's contribution is that, in the effort to overcome the simplistic or reductionist nature of the Marxist account of the origins of political issues, they seem to be victims of the law of the pendulum (Salman 1990: 129), at least where advanced industrial countries are concerned. The theoretical stress on contingency reduces the rôle of conditioning factors and the systemic or structured character of subordination in this part of the world.[4] On the other hand, Laclau & Mouffe's (1985: 131) view that in developing countries imperialist exploitation and the predominance of brutal and centralized forms of domination tend from the beginning to endow the popular struggle with a centre, with a single and clearly defined enemy, and that therefore the division of the political space into two fields is present from the outset, is questionable. It cannot be assumed that the meaning and the unity of struggles in developing countries is self evident, and, in contrast to Western societies, determined by conditions. It is a Eurocentric view that represents developing countries as having a different type of historical agency, somewhat reduced in relation to that of European society (Escobar 1992: 79). Here, too, articulatory practices must play a rôle.

A related problem is that Laclau & Mouffe take the conversion of liberal-democratic ideology into the "common sense" of Western societies as a point of departure. By doing so it makes somewhat circular the search for the "discursive conditions for the emergence of collective action, directed towards struggling against inequalities and relations of subordination" (Laclau & Mouffe 1985: 153). Moreover, though democratic imagery derived from the 1889 Revolution certainly plays a rôle in Brazil, this seems to be too restricted a perspective and one that fails to take into account that the Democratic Revolution itself was articulated from disparate elements. It is, therefore, necessary to broaden the perspective on "common sense", the way it informs collective action, may contribute to democratization and is itself transformed in the process. The rather opaque terminology Laclau & Mouffe often employ conceals the affinity with the notions of proactive and reactive forms of collective action (Tilly et al. 1975: 50–51). Whereas the former may be related to an extension of rights or the construction of new rights, the latter refer to the defence of acquired positions. This brings into focus the experienced collection of popular assumptions and expectations that inform reactive collective action and sensitizes us to the interplay between the old and the new, constituting discursive conditions for collective action.

In this chapter I shall focus on the articulation between the discourse on land proffered by the urban poor and other social agents involved in land conflicts, and debates on the issue of land rights. Analysis of the interaction between various enunciations is a key to understanding the social construction of meaning: the process whereby relatively structured discursive totalities are modified in such a way that the elements of which they consist are re-articulated to produce new meanings and significations (Laclau & Mouffe 1985: 105–14). This entails a close examination of conflicts and debates and the course which they have taken. Such an analysis of the production and negotiation of meaning involves a rather eclectic use of techniques, including archive research, (more or less participant) observation, eavesdropping, informal chats and more formal interviewing, and oral history (Silva 1990). The discourses or "texts" gathered through these techniques have to be contextualized – assessed against the background of historical macro-structures and conjunctures, as well as at the micro-level of institutional contexts and who speaks to whom. Thus it becomes possible to interpret the way discursive resources are appropriated, reproduced and transformed by people tailoring them to their needs in specific circumstances and engendering new meanings in the process.

To illustrate the social reconstruction of the meaning of urban land I briefly discuss some cases drawn from my research on the rôle of urban movements in Recife in the context of the democratic transition (Assies 1992a, 1992b). In Recife, as elsewhere in Brazil, this process coincided with a crisis of urban management, a crisis that can be viewed as a dialectically related aspect of the crisis of the political regime and the economic model (Vainer & Smolka 1991). While the breakdown of urban policies became particularly manifest in a proliferation of neighbourhood associations as well as a rapid spread of collective land invasions from the late 1970s, the urban question once again became a matter of public debate that forced the various social actors to a discursive articulation of the project each pursued. This provided a privileged opportunity to examine the conflicts, practices and discourses involving the definition of rights to the city and influence in local decision-making, including the issue of urban land use.

The profound roots of the illegal city

An insight into the "profound roots of the illegal city" (Bitoun 1991: 10) is indispensable for deciphering urban conflicts and the change of meanings. One has to take into account the long-term demographic and spatial development of a city and the ways by which they are shaped by economic and sociopolitical factors. Recife initially was a relatively compact city where social distinctions were expressed in the vertical segregation of mansions towering over the shanties, located in nearby but less desirable areas liable to flooding. This vertical pattern, which reflected the patriarchal relations of a slave society, was altered in the course of the 20th century. While rural–urban migration started to increase, Haussmann-style urban engineering and a policy aimed at the expulsion of the shanties from the central city areas, particularly in the early 1940s under the *Estado Novo*, generated a new pattern of horizontal segregation and peripheral growth.

Expulsion policies abated under the left-wing administrations of the 1955–64 period, but were resumed after 1964 with the technocratic-developmentalist urban project of the authoritarian regime. The road system and the city centre were main concerns of the municipal administrations, which thought of urban space in terms of shopping malls, leisure areas, huge traffic terminals and private transportation facilitated by large avenues and monumental viaducts. In this project there was no place for the urban poor and the pattern of extensive peripheral growth cum segregation continued, spilling over to the surrounding municipalities. The late 1970s, however, saw a counter-tendency with the spread of collective invasions. The pattern of extensive peripheral growth, which had left substantial tracts unused because of speculation and deprived the urban poor of access to employment opportunities and urban services, was to a certain extent being subverted. The legitimacy crisis of the regime, compounded by an economic crisis, provided the context for this new tendency and for the more general proliferation of conflicts over urban land.

These developments were accompanied by changing forms of access to urban land. The process of extensive peripheral growth had been characterized by piecemeal occupation of land by the urban poor. One possibility was "natural" occupation, often involving the production of land itself by gradual landfill in the peripheral swamp areas of the city. Another relied on informal transactions with private actors, the large leaseholders of the *terras da marinha* (marine lands), and people who claimed to have inherited the lands of colonial sugar plantations on the hill areas to the west of the city.[5] Often, "naturally" occupied land would subsequently be claimed by some large landholder, resulting either in expulsion of the settler or an informal arrangement sanctioned by the payment of an occupation fee (*foro*).

These forms of access to land came increasingly under pressure with the gradual reduction of opportunities for natural occupation and the increasing formalization and monetarization of the land market, often involving the very construction of "illegality". The tensions engendered by these developments were exacerbated by the urban policies of the authoritarian municipal administrations that, as a poet expressed it, "nailed the city to the cross of the new avenues". As noted, these policies were accompanied by the active eviction of *mocambeiros*, while private owners, or people who claimed to be owners, also started to recover terrains now being valorized. In 1977 the Archdiocese of

Olinda and Recife estimated that 58,000 families, totalling some 300,000 people, lived under threat of eviction. While these developments provided the fuel, it was no coincidence that conflicts erupted at a determined moment, the late 1970s, just as the power of the authoritarian regime was being eroded.

The "Nobody's Land" Movement

One of the most significant movements was the Movimento Terras de Ninguém (the "Nobody"s Land" Movement) directed against one of the "major urban *latifundios* in the country". An occupied area covering 350ha to the north-west of Recife was claimed by the inheritors of a sugar plantation. The legitimacy of the claim had been contested by the inhabitants, who said it belonged to a Catholic lay brotherhood. The conflict had been triggered by the establishment of a real estate enterprise by the presumed inheritors of the land and the subsequent reorganization of the payment of occupation fees in the 1950s. This implied a formalization and tightening of procedures and an increasingly exploitative relationship that was strongly resented by the settlers. While the first protests had been quelled with the military takeover in 1964, people started to discuss their problems again in the 1970s at meetings of the local variety of Ecclesial Base Communities (CEBs). Although the Communist Party was traditionally influential in the area, the moral indignation over the exploitation by the real estate enterprise was expressed in strongly biblical discourse that stressed God's creation of the Earth for all people without distributing deeds to the land. In a speech delivered in 1977, when the second anniversary of the movement was celebrated at the church on the Morro da Conceição, a centre of popular religion, it was said that: "This hill is to us what Mount Sinai was to Moses. Here we plant and here we will harvest liberation. That this land, which belongs to nobody, may really be ours, because God created it for us."

In the speeches, as well as in a letter to the President of the Republic, frequent reference was made to the "poor and humble" and their expectations about "Justice". The central demand of the movement was that the area be expropriated and then sold to the inhabitants at prices compatible with their means. In 1979, with the democratic transition under way, the government claimed to be willing to attend to the needs of the people. Negotiations began and, after the movement had rejected the government's offer to mediate a sale-purchase arrangement, the area was expropriated to facilitate transfer to the settlers.[6] In the wake of the Movimento Terras de Ninguém victory, payment of occupation fees sanctioning informal arrangements based on, at best, dubious ownership claims ceased in many areas throughout the city.

Invasions

While the occupation of land by the urban poor had traditionally been a piece-meal process, a change took place in the late 1970s with the spread of collective invasions. Between 1978 and 1981, about 80 "new" invasions were recorded, involving between 150,000 and 250,000 people (Barros e Silva 1985, Falcão Neto 1985). A number of conditions contributed to this new dynamic. Whereas earlier land occupation had mostly been related to rural–urban migration, intra-urban factors had become increasingly important. The population density in older settlements increased, meaning that the sociability that had developed over the years provided some of the conditions for collective action. At the same moment, the transition to civilian government got under way, electoral politics gained significance and press censorship relaxed, and the earlier repressive attitude of the state became a less practical option. For the squatters, there was also effective outside support. Church organizations constituted an important framework for mobilization and a particularly important rôle was played by the local Justice and Peace Commission which made the legal defence of *favelados* one of its priorities from 1979 onward. The Commission argued that the right to a dwelling should be accorded priority over property rights. By promoting squatter organization and mobilizing public opinion, the Commission sought to politicize the legal proceedings (court suits) involving land conflicts, aiming to move beyond the confines of the juridical arena (Santos 1992). This increasing-ly resulted in complicated negotiations involving squatters, state agencies, possible private parties claiming ownership of the land, and lawyers of the Justice and Peace Commission.

The "new" invasions have been interpreted as an instance of juridical plural-ism, whereby the property rights consecrated in the Brazilian Civil Code are challenged by the normative system of the squatters insisting on the right of dwelling (Falcão Neto 1985). Such an interpretation seems merited to the extent that squatters will justify their actions by pointing to their needs and the fact that the invaded area is unused. The opposition in terms of rights, however, conflates the discourse of the squatters with that of their lawyers (Carvalho 1991). In the juridical arena, lawyers and judges argued over the property rights and the right of dwelling, resulting in a postponement of the verdict or of its execution – effectively a non-decision. Meanwhile, in parallel negotiations involving the squatters, lawyers, private owners and state agencies, discourse tended to be framed in terms of the needs of the squatters and the responsibil-ities and obligations of the authorities and the rich. Different discourses were therefore developed in different institutional contexts, sometimes revolving around rights and at other times around needs and obligations. The discursive framework of needs and obligations provided a common ground for a practical solution to the conflicts.[7] Though this discourse of needs rather than of rights is the most common among the squatters in the Ecclesial Base Communities or other organizational contexts, they may switch to a discourse of rights. The conflicts triggered by invasions and the eventual resolution involved a complex dialectic of politicization, and the strategies of trivialization and integration adopted not only by state agencies in the context of the democratic transition (Moura 1990: 29), but also by the squatters.

Stubborn Brasília

Among the many disputes of the late 1970s, the mobilization of the Brasília Teimosa (Stubborn Brasília) settlement stands out for its mode of operation and its articulation of an alternative to the urban policies of the authoritarian regime. The settlement derives its name from the inhabitants' resistance to attempts at eviction ever since the settlement's formation by invasion in the late 1950s: at the same time as the new Brazilian capital, another "new settlement", was being constructed. Brasília Teimosa is located on the coast near the Recife city centre and bordering the neighbourhood of Boa Viagem which has been subject to rapid valorization since the 1960s. Brasília Teimosa consistently figured as a target area in the Integral Development Plans drawn up by the authoritarian city administrations of the 1970s. By the mid-1970s its inhabitants learnt from newspaper reports that, except for some "picturesque fishermen", they were to be relocated to make way for hotels, a "sea aquarium like the one in Miami", a shopping mall, bars, restaurants, boutiques and 1,800 housing units for people who would contribute to the *nobreza* (literally, nobility) of the area.

These plans triggered one of the most significant social movements of the period. Sponsored by the local *padre* (priest) and with the help of a private consultancy firm whose members dedicated part of their time to "support popular projects", the Residents' Council elaborated its own project for urbanization and regularization with extensive discussion by the residents (Moura 1987). In its manifesto, launched in 1979 on the occasion of a visit by President Figueiredo to Recife on one of the goodwill tours that accompanied the democratic transition, the Council stressed that most of the residents were poor people and that "therefore our urbanization must be for poor people. Without luxuries, without motorways. But with the comfort we were denied during the long hard years". Besides running water in the houses, hygienic sanitation, a school, a health post and a maternity ward, this included "the comfort of God's blessing, having the legal guarantee that we cannot be sent away due to egoistic and paltry interests".

As the area belonged to the *terras da marinha*, which cannot be sold or donated, regularization through a leasehold arrangement (*aforamento*) was proposed. The leases were to be free of charge since "God gave the land without asking a penny from anybody". The option for leasehold rather than private ownership was significant, since it was not only related to the fact that these were *terras da marinha*, but also represented the operationalizing of a priority of the right of a dwelling over property ownership rights. The idea was that the residents would receive individual leases to plots not exceeding 150 m². Tenants would be enabled to buy the dwelling they lived in and also receive a lease to the plot. The leases were to be transferable, but only to persons of the same economic conditions as the average resident. *Benfeitorias* (constructions, improvements or investments) on the plot could be sold, but the land itself would have no price. The leasehold arrangement would provide the Residents' Council

109

with leverage to monitor, approve or disapprove transfers and thus impede the buying-out of residents by real estate interests. As a result of local mobiliz-ations, favourable public opinion and the municipality's need to show its new concern with the poor at a time when electoral politics was becoming more important, the municipality endorsed the urbanization and regularization project in 1980.

Although the implementation of the regularization proposal proved to be a particularly convoluted process and is still not concluded (Moura 1990: 38–49), the form of the communitarian land management experiment in Brasília Teimosa was to be a main source of inspiration for the Regularization Plan for the Special Zones of Social Interest (PREZEIS), which was adopted by the Recife City Council in 1987.

The Regularization Plan for the Special Zones of Social Interest

The PREZEIS was elaborated by the Justice and Peace Commission in collabora-tion with the popular movement and, as such, was regarded as the outcome of a popular initiative in the field of legislation that, significantly, occurred before the 1988 Constitution legalized this form of democratic intervention. The initiative constituted an attempt to carry into the political arena the land disputes that had proliferated since the late 1970s.

The PREZEIS was grafted onto the policy of urban zoning that had been intro-duced in Recife in 1983 to provide a legal framework for a World Bank spon-sored project for improvement of the city. One type of zone distinguished in the new legislation was the Special Zones of Social Interest (ZEIS), characterized as "consolidated areas of spontaneous settlement where special urban norms are to be applied in view of the social interest of promoting their legal regulation and integration into the urban structure". Though the municipality acknowledged the existence of 72 "subnormal settlements" from the more realistic unofficial fig-ure of about 100, only 27 settlements, located in areas that were rapidly increasing in value, were designated as ZEIS. This choice, and the fact that the municipality failed to define the special norms to be applied to the ZEIS, aroused the suspicion of the Justice and Peace Commission, which asserted that the intention was to clear these areas by the combined impact of upgrading and market mechanisms. Toward the end of 1984, the Justice and Peace Commis-sion called a meeting with the popular movement to discuss the issue and find ways to remedy the situation.

In the course of 1985 and 1986, a series of meetings took place to discuss with representatives of the neighbourhood movement and local non-govern-mental organizations (NGOs) a draft version of the PREZEIS drawn up by the Justice and Peace Commission. The Recife branch of the Movement for the Defence of Favelados (MDF) was an ardent participant in the discussions. The MDF originated in São Paulo in the late 1970s and had started to act nationwide during the early 1980s. It was strongly related to the progressive Catholic current. At its 1982 Congress in Campinas, which coincided with the Brazilian

Council of Bishops' (CNBB) Conference at nearby Itaici where the issue of urban land was being discussed (CNBB 1982), the MDF adopted the *Concessão do Direito Real de Uso* (Concession of the Right to Real Use – CDRU) as the preferred form of legalizing landholding in *favelas* (Boran 1989).

The PREZEIS was based on the doctrine of the social function of property in the light of Liberation Theology. It stated that the right to a dwelling should be given priority over property rights and included the *Concessão do Direito Real de Uso* as an important feature of the new law (CEAS 1990). The legal mechanism of CDRU was created in 1967 by federal legislation, without any intention of its being used in the regularization of *favelas*. It was a form of leasehold used to cede public land to civilian organizations or enterprises for purposes determined by contract. Progressive sectors of the Church and left-wing groups reinterpreted the CDRU as a means of regularizing land in *favelas*, as a mechanism through which "the most advanced sectors of the popular movement could avoid the system of private property" (Gohn 1988: 328). In her analysis of the MDF in São Paulo, Boran (1989: 91) described the CDRU as "a socialist, collective type of land ownership which did not allow for the sale of land per se, but did permit the sale of any structure built upon it. Land-ownership based on land purchase was rejected".[8]

For similar reasons the Justice and Peace Commission and the MDF in Recife viewed the CDRU as a highly significant feature of the PREZEIS law. In a comment on the PREZEIS, the *Jornal de Casa Amarela* (Ano II, no. 14), edited by a federation of residents' organizations in the Casa Amarela neighbourhood, presented its implications for "the ideas on property" in the full translation that I reproduce below as follows:

. . . **4. The advantages of the right to real use of urban land** –
The capitalist system of private property creates better opportunities for the people who possess the most. The people who struggle for an egalitarian and fraternal society want equal opportunities for all. Whosoever struggles to create a fraternal society should know about the advantages of the DRU [*Direito Real de Uso* – Right to Real Use], which are: (1) whoever receives the land can negotiate the *benfeitorias* he constructs; (2) the Public Power and the Residents' Council control who can and who cannot live in the area; (3) the Public Power and the Residents' Council will have to approve the sale of any *benfeitorias*. This is a guarantee to keep real estate agents or bourgeois persons from entering land improved by the people. There may be sales, but not just any sale. This may seem like an oppressive prohibition, but in reality it is a correct way to guarantee that the community be defended. Not allowing just selling in any way is a means of assuring that the interests of the community prevail over individual interests. It is in this way that an egalitarian community distinguishes itself: the wellbeing of the community prevails over the advantage of individuals.

5. The ideas of capitalism inside ourselves –

The world we live in is dominated by capitalism, which penetrates everything, even our own minds. Capitalism invented private property with deeds registered at real estate registry offices. Private property is one of the values of capitalism. The powerful have succeeded in planting the idea of private property within us, to the point of making us forget that God is the owner of the earth and that we are only strangers and pilgrims (Leviticus). To combat the capitalist idea we should deepen our understanding of the advantages of the DRU. . . .

An earlier issue of the *Jornal de Casa Amarela* (Ano II, no. 12) had already heralded the adoption of the PREZEIS – the "law of the *favelas*" – by the City Council as proof that the people "have ceased to be a mass which can be taken one way or another, a mass which allows itself to be governed as if it has no opinion or a project of itself".

The PREZEIS was adopted under a progressive Popular Front municipal administration that had been elected in 1985. The law stipulated that areas not yet considered as ZEIS could request designation through the residents' organizations. This procedure was to ensure an active community initiative. In addition to the 27 existing ZEIS, seven more ZEIS were created during the Popular Front administration (1986–88) and an existing ZEIS was extended. Negotiations slowed down under the subsequent neo-liberal administration (1989–92). By December 1990 there were 36 ZEIS covering a total of 1,819ha or 8.3 per cent of the municipality. Fifteen ZEIS had formal Urbanization and Legalization Commissions (COMUL), consisting of representatives of the local residents' organization, the municipality and civil organizations such as the Justice and Peace Commission, the Brazilian Bar Association or local NGOs. These commissions, whose model was the Legalization Commission that had been created in Brasília Teimosa as a result of the struggle of that settlement, were instructed to define the urbanization and regularization projects for the areas and to monitor their execution (Lostao 1992a, 1992b, CEAS 1992).[9]

To assess the support for, or involvement with, the PREZEIS among the local population, three groups of ZEIS may be distinguished among the areas effectively integrated into the PREZEIS: namely, those with a functioning COMUL (Lostao 1991: 77). The first group consists of the areas where a legalization and urbanization project already existed before the promulgation of the law, for example, Brasília Teimosa. In these cases the local residents' associations were aware of the political dimensions of the PREZEIS, which was set up after the outcomes of their "historical" struggles. This also reflects a certain commitment to the CDRU as a form of land regularization. A second group consists of ZEIS that had existed since 1983, but where a COMUL was only created after the promulgation of the PREZEIS. In these cases the incorporation into the PREZEIS scheme mostly resulted from the initiative of technicians of the municipal urbanization company or of the NGOs. Residents' associations, in this case, are usually less aware of the functioning or the broader aims of the PREZEIS and

112

commitment to the CDRU is less significant. Organizations in these areas seek support among the population for what they generically refer to as "legalization of the land", without much explanation as to the nature of this legalization. The third group consists of the ZEIS created after the PREZEIS was made known. Here the involvement was often the outcome of a recent conflict over the permanence of a *favela*, and the organization involved had actively applied for the designation of the area as a ZEIS. The primary objective of guaranteeing permanence in the area resulted in some familiarity with the functioning of the PREZEIS, but the mode of land regularization is secondary to the guarantee of permanence of the settlement.

The commitment of local leaders to the CDRU also reflects the attitudes of the local population. For many local leaders the difference between property and the "Right to Real Use" is a complicated matter and explaining it to the local population more complicated. It often gives rise to controversy where the intervention of the residents' association in the transfer of plots and *benfeitorias* is concerned. This is regarded as a nuisance by *favela* dwellers, who are wary of control placed on the wheeling and dealing which is part of their household strategies (Lostao 1991: 111). In one of the ZEIS, for example, 60 per cent of the 8,000 housing units were owner-occupied. While only a small minority of the house-owners had a document sanctioned at a registry office to establish ownership, the majority were in possession of municipal tax receipts, a sale and purchase contract, or water and electricity bills to prove the claim to the house and occupancy rights (UMP 1986). Such documents, which may be transferred to third parties can serve as evidence for indemnification in case a legal owner reclaims the land. These are sufficient to turn the *benfeitorias* into a legally sanctioned "substitute commodity" while, juridically speaking, the value of the plot is not taken into consideration because no legal property rights are involved (Banck 1986). Rather than through a type of parallel legal system created within the community in the absence of official legalization, as Moura (1990: 148) has argued, transfer of plots occurs through transactions on the fringe of the established legal system. The fact that in the case of the above-mentioned ZEIS 25 per cent of the house owners could show a sale and purchase document is an indication of the vivid trade in "substitute commodities" among low-income groups. In such a context the individual CDRU and the supervision by the public powers and the residents' organization it entails, may not be attractive to the individual residents. The residents aspire to full property rights (GAJOP 1987: 8, 14). At the same time, however, this does not mean that the designation of their settlement as a ZEIS is irrelevant to them. The residents welcome the security of permanence it provides for the settlement as such and the protection against the purchase of plots by real estate developers.

Concluding observations

The received view that the actions of the urban poor can be characterized as prompted by material needs has been strongly criticized in the recent literature on social movements. Social movements have been conceptualized as "spaces for the production of meaning" and, especially in the Latin American context of democratic transitions, have been afforded a rôle creating a new political culture and forms of citizenship. In this chapter I have focused on the specific aspect of land rights.

In his discussion of invasions in Recife, Falcão Neto (1985) has suggested that the urban poor have a concept of property rights absolutely distinct from that consecrated in the Brazilian Civil Code by according priority to the right to use over the right to benefit and dispose. The established legality is thus being contested by the normative system of the urban poor, who would be the source and subject of a new legality. The cases reviewed above, however, suggest a much more intricate process. Intermediating agents play an important rôle in shaping and reshaping the discursive framework through which rights and claims are defined. The Church, in particular, tends to assume a prominent rôle in organizing the communities and providing them with discursive, political and legal resources. Rather than a clash between two social forces an image of complex interplay emerges where various imageries are at work, ranging between notions about just treatment of the "poor and humble", expectations engendered by the democratization process and Catholic discourse.

I have presented a series of cases in diachronic fashion, starting with the Movimento Terras de Ninguém and the invasions of the late 1970s, and then moving on to the case of Brasília Teimosa and the PREZEIS project. While this procedure takes into consideration the systemic changes that provided the fuel for conflicts and the conjunctural context that shaped them, it also brings into focus the efforts to move from defensive action and demand-making to prepositive actions, one of the main concerns of the progressive sectors engaged in the transition process. In other words, the approach provides insight into the efforts of hegemonic articulation through the creation of a set of symbolic meanings that signifies an alternative to the existing order.

If meanings emerge from a complex field of competing and overlapping discourses, the issue is to sort out the frameworks of signification present in the cases reviewed. One such framework, as noted, revolves around the notion of justice for the "poor and humble". Although this notion provided discursive conditions for collective action, it relies on a reaffirmation of relations of subordination rather than on a straightforward challenge. In a situation where relations tend to become more exploitative as a result of formalization and monetarization of the land market, as in the case of the Movimento Terras de Ninguém, it is the authorities who are regarded as the subject of justice, rather than the poor and humble themselves. The authorities were called upon to listen "to the voice of the people, which is the voice of God". Although at the same time Arnaldo "the Prophet", one of the leaders of the movement, would remind them that "the earth trembles and the powerful do not want to understand . . . you cannot take what belongs to everybody", and allude to a "true order where all will be equal and humble". As was noted in the case of invasions, frameworks revolving around needs and the obligation to help the poor served to create a common ground for the negotiated solutions by trivializing the event of "invasion". At the same time expectations engendered by the democratization process and a neo-populist policy of trivializing land conflicts and pursuing negotiated solutions contributed to the spread of collective invasions.

It was the proliferation of struggles over urban land generated by this dynamic that created a field for what Laclau & Mouffe (1985) would call hegemonic articulation: the integration of dispersed antagonisms into a discourse that tendentiously constructs the division of a single political space in two opposed fields. The Church, preferentially opting for the poor, and more specifically the Justice and Peace Commission, was a driving force in providing a framework for signifying land conflicts and reconstructing the meaning of urban land in association with the right to a decent dwelling as a citizen's right in the context of the Brazilian democratic transition.

The view on the social use of urban land elaborated by the Brazilian Council of Bishops (CNBB 1982) hinges on an opposition between land for housing and land for speculation. It also involves the closely related opposition between the necessary and the superfluous, invasion and speculation, rights and egoism, the natural community of a city and individualism. This position does not amount to a rejection of private property, which is regarded as a basis for liberty and is strongly associated with family life and the right and duty to work. It does imply, however, a relativization of the absolute property right in the sense that everything beyond necessity, if attained by depriving others, is regarded as a social sin.

Whereas the Council of Bishops referred to a change in the socio-political-economic model, among the more radical groups inspired by Liberation Theology there was a more outspoken anti-capitalist imagery and the desire for "social transformation", a virtual code word for socialism. The framework of signification through which the right of a dwelling is operationalized in this case hinges on an opposition between *terra de moradia* (land for dwelling) and *terra de negócio* (land as a commodity). It is a variation on the opposition between *terra de trabalho* (land to work) and *terra de negócio*, which applies to rural land (Esterci 1990), or between *terra de habitação* (land for housing) and *terra de espoliação* (land for capitalism or plunder; Krischke 1984). Such notions integrate a chain of opposition that divides the political space into two fields by opposing God's Kingdom on Earth with the established order of satanical savage capitalism, an opposition that would ultimately be transcended by the coming of God's Kingdom, liberation or social transformation (see Banck 1990).

Though this discourse played an important rôle in providing a framework for collective action, the selective appropriation of the PREZEIS discussed in this chapter draws attention to the ambiguities of discourse. While people may share a discourse, it should not be taken at face value but with an awareness of the complex variations it may conceal. The tendential division of the political space into two fields can be viewed as a form of boundary construction along symbolic lines. Cohen (1985) has shown how community construction takes place through the acceptance of common symbols embedded in webs of significance not unlike Laclau & Mouffe's signifiers in discursive formations. While interpretation or the meaning attached to symbols is not a random affair, people can find common currency in a symbol while still attaching their own meaning to it and tailoring it to their own needs. This is what seems to take place when lawyers of the Justice and Peace Commission, NGO personnel, neighbourhood leaders and local residents adhere to the PREZEIS scheme as a form of legalizing the land. This shared discourse may serve to cement a coalition that may contribute to guaranteeing the permanence of a squatter settlement, but it conceals the different meanings attached to legalization and the different views on the eventual mode of legalization. Whereas the PREZEIS aimed at institutionalizing the right of possession or use in opposition to property rights, and communitarian management in opposition to individualism, *favelados* appreciate their squat not only as use value but are also aware of its exchange value, which plays a rôle in their household strategies. Ruthless profit seeking and the occupation of plots with the aim of renting or selling are strongly repudiated, but the operationalization of such sensitivities through the CDRU and communitarian land management meets with reluctance. Here, the CDRU is regarded as a step towards full proprietorship rather than an end in itself and, although communities of the urban poor may be mobilized at certain moments, they are not as organic as the Catholic imagery would have it.

This chapter has outlined some of the process of the social reconstruction of the meaning of urban land and the efforts to operationalize the right to dwelling in the context of the Brazilian democratic transition. I have sought to show some of the complexity of this process and how, according to the actors involved and the situation at hand, discursive frameworks are appropriated and modified and meaning is negotiated. Much more could be said about these processes. The approach adopted in my research was tailored to its aim, which was to assess the rôle of social movements in the democratization process and their impact on and intervention in institutional "spaces". This implied a focus on the intermediate "spaces for the production of meaning" between individualized daily life and the political process. Household strategies, therefore, only tangentially came into view and this downward linkage needs further exploration, particularly by paying attention to intra-household divisions along generational and gender lines. This would contribute to a further understanding of the dynamics of the selective appropriation of discourses and how this may contribute to the construction of a social force capable of changing the dominant meaning of urban land. At the same time the Brazilian situation provides a privileged opportunity for a comparative study of the contextual features of such processes. The 1988 Constitution stipulates that municipalities with over 20,000 inhabitants (there are about 1,400 such municipalities) should formulate a Master Plan which, among other things, defines the requirements urban land should meet to fulfil its "social function", including urban zoning regulations and modes of regularization of low income settlements. A comparative study of the assembly of these plans and the intervention by various social actors, the final outcome, and the ways their stipulations are brought into effect under the specific municipal sociopolitical conditions would provide further insight into the ways the meaning of urban land is being socially reconstructed in Brazil.

Notes

1. It is not my purpose to go into the conceptual problems surrounding the term "urban social movements" (see Assies 1990, Salman 1990). Suffice it to say here that, in the Brazilian context, the term is generically used to designate a broad array of urban collective action.
2. The framing of these questions is strongly related to the revaluation of democracy by the Latin American Left which, after the often dismal experiences with guerrilla movements, the abuse of "bourgeois" civil rights by terrorist regimes, and the disintegration of the few examples of socialism, came to view the deepening of democracy and the extension of citizenship as the appropriate strategy for societal transformation.
3. Laclau & Mouffe distinguish relations of domination. These are relations of subordination that are considered as illegitimate from the perspective, or in the judgment, of a social agent external to them, and that as a consequence may or may not coincide with the relations of oppression existing in a determinate social formation.
4. In fact, Laclau & Mouffe refer to tendencies of bureaucratization, commodification and the rôle of the mass media to account for the emergence of new social movements. However, as Geras (1987) remarked, "these concepts belong to another theory". While Laclau & Mouffe may be right in their critique of the Marxist meta-narrative and its deduction of "historical interests", this theoretical position makes it difficult to see what is meant by "progressive". The need for a (socialist) hegemonic project is stressed to define "a set of symbolic meanings which totalize as negativity a certain social order" (Laclau & Mouffe 1985: 190). Large narratives and analyses of societal macro-structures, though less presumptuous than metanarratives, are indispensable for a critical social science (Fraser & Nicholson 1988, also Assies 1990: 44–63).
5. The *terras da marinha* is an often ill defined coastal strip falling under navy jurisdiction. Large tracts are leased out to private agents who used to collect an occupation fee (*foro*) from settlers.
6. Only in 1988, under the government of Miguel Arraes, did titles begin to be distributed under the modality of the *Concessão do Direito Real de Uso*, a form of leasehold which will be discussed later.
7. This might involve a sale and purchase arrangement, renting or the relocation of the squatters in other areas.
8. In São Paulo the CDRU became a stake in the confrontation between the MDF and PMDB Mayor Mário Covas, who sponsored a project that "gave no legal stability to the *favelado*" and envisaged payment for the use of land with no right of inheritance (Boran 1989: 97). The reasons for this stance, according to Boran, were that, in spite of strong power struggles within the PMDB, "the mainstream party members were firm capitalists", and the PMDB did not want to concede to pressure from what it considered a movement led by the radical socialist *Partido dos Trabalhadores* (PT – Workers' Party).
9. Furthermore, in order to provide a platform for discussion of common problems and to consolidate the PREZEIS, a Permanent PREZEIS Forum started to meet in August 1988 and was formalized by municipal decree in December.

117

Micro-level methodologies
Specific techniques in researching land markets and property prices

CHAPTER NINE

Housing the household, holding the house

Ann Varley

Introduction

One of the most difficult issues that researchers face when working at the micro-level is determining the appropriate level of analysis. More often than not the household is adopted, although as we shall observe below, the concept of household is imbued with many meanings. Failure to understand adequately those meanings may result in gender-biased analyses and in the identification of levels of organization that are meaningless to the people themselves. This chapter wrestles with the basic starting point for many studies: what are the best units for meaningful analysis of land- and housing-acquisition processes?

In recent years, established practice in defining and describing the household has come under fire from a number of quarters. Social scientists have favoured the household as an analytical unit because ideal family types derived from theories of kinship do not always match actual social groupings (Wilk & Netting 1984) and because discussion of the household avoids argument about the universal or natural status of the family (Gittins 1985). The household is thought to offer a more objective way of describing the domestic group. However, as Robertson (1991: 9) argues: "Study of the household has tended to circumvent rather than solve the problems which have made study of 'the family' difficult". For example, our seeming inability to do away with the definite article when discussing *the* household suggests that it, too, is vulnerable to criticism about assumptions of universality.

The concept has also been criticized for being too concerned with boundaries when networks of solidarity between kin and neighbours and the intervention of community and government institutions mean that the household is *not* a closed, autonomous unit or separate sphere (Smith et al. 1984, Netting et al. 1984b). This concern with boundaries is one aspect of what, for Wilk & Netting (1984), is too great an emphasis on form rather than function, in spite of households being primarily about what people *do* together: "common residence, economic cooperation, and socialization of children" (Gonzalez 1969, cited in Wilk &

Netting 1984: 3). To introduce these different types of household activity also causes problems because household definitions based on the different activities do not neatly overlap (Gittins 1985). In addition, the emphasis on form has led to an overly static perspective on the household, although in reality it is in a constant process of transformation, associated with both the domestic cycle and the interaction between the household and wider processes of social and economic change (Robertson 1991, Netting et al. 1984b, Smith et al. 1984).

Feminist criticism has presented another strand of argument about the deficiencies of conventional approaches to the household. This concerns the notion of the household as an internally undifferentiated unit whose members share the same interests, and in which there is a single, central decision-maker whose domination of household decision-making is unproblematic (Bruce & Dwyer 1988, Jelin 1991b). On the contrary, it is argued, household members may have conflicting interests, and decisions about distribution of household resources made by a male breadwinner cannot be assumed to serve the best interests of other members. The household "is a unit with shared interests, but in which the division of labour and the distributive processes that accompany it create conditions for divergent interests among its members, including struggles for exercising control" (Jelin 1991b: 33); there are therefore "multiple decision makers with different agendas" (Bruce & Dwyer 1988: 3).

Experts in the field are nevertheless unwilling to abandon the concept of the household as a meaningful analytic category: "our [symposium] participants continued to regard the household domestic group as a part of our social science conceptual vocabulary that can be effectively used. At the very least, the household is more universal and more cross-culturally comparable than many more frequently studied institutions" (Netting et al. 1984b: xxvi).

This chapter does not pretend to offer a new definition of the household for use in land and housing market studies. As Netting et al. suggest (1984b: xxiv), "the boundaries and functions of households cannot be delineated on a priori grounds but must be empirically determined in every case". There are no methodological "quick fixes". What the chapter does try to do is to demonstrate the complex interaction between our definitions of the household and our understanding of settlement characteristics, housing tenure and housing processes. My premise is that by thinking more deeply about the household *in relation to the house*, we can improve our understanding of both housing processes and the nature of the household. My examples are drawn from urban Mexico, and I do not claim validity for any specific arguments I make beyond that context: as Yanagisako (1984: 330) argues, households are first of all "units of cultural meaning", and while cross-cultural comparison is possible, the same household form cannot be assumed to carry the same meaning in different cultural contexts.

Houses and households: mapping complexity

Most definitions of the household include some reference to the dwelling unit, and some take co-residence as the single defining variable. For example, the 1980 US Census of Population and Housing states that "a household includes all the persons who occupy a housing unit". Such definitions are not particularly helpful in self-help settlements, where the absence of professional architects means that there is no externally imposed familist ideology, as identified by Watson (1988: 23), to ensure a neat match between domestic architecture and nuclear family. The concept of a household as a group of people living "under the same roof" is plainly inadequate in such a context. In my work in areas of self-help housing in urban Mexico, I have come across some people who form a single household but occupy more than one building: the different structures serve different functions (for example, kitchen/living/eating area in one, sleeping quarters in another). Conversely, several interrelated but separate households may occupy a single structure, sometimes with minimal physical distinction between the spaces occupied by different households (and certainly nothing as tangible as a "single locked door" – Robertson 1991: 9).

Trying to recognize different households by their occupation of physically distinct dwellings is clearly, therefore, a non-starter where there is a great variety of construction patterns. In some ways, the plot offers a better starting point, because external agencies – subdividers, developers and government departments – as well as the occupier require a more or less precise definition of each unit. Plot areas and boundaries are zealously defended by residents against the encroachment of neighbours or a tax department or regularization agency seeking to charge the residents for more square metres than they actually own. However, when kin occupy adjacent areas of land, it is not always clear what should be recognized as a plot. In Loma de la Palma, a self-help settlement in northern Mexico City now some 20 years old, two brothers purchased a plot of land, divided it into two equal halves, and built separate houses with their own entrances to the street. A wall demarcates the area occupied by each household, so it might be argued that these are now two separate plots; but the wall is only low and there is a gap allowing movement from one side to the other. In San José, another Mexico City settlement of a similar age, a woman has divided her plot between herself and two married sons and their families, whose house occupies half the original plot;[1] again, there is a low wall with a gate between the two halves. If this is still considered one plot, would it make any difference if the two halves were completely separate? In another street in La Palma, there are three adjacent but completely separate houses with their own separate entrances from the street; the land they occupy was originally inhabited by the purchasers as a single property, but they later gave land on which to build a house to two of their sons when they married. Is this one property or three?[2]

Taking the plot as a starting point, we must recognize that it may be occupied by more than one household, and not only where there are tenants. The usual way of recognizing a household employed by recent survey-based studies of urban Mexico makes reference not only to co-residence but also to communal budgeting and/or eating together "from a common pot" (Selby et al. 1990, Chant 1991, Gilbert & Varley 1991, Varley 1992). These two ideas are closely related but do not exactly correspond. For example, old people may be dependent on a married son or daughter living on the same plot but maintain their own house and cook and eat separately. On the other hand, older children in employment may retain a significant part of their earnings, buying their own clothes and consumer goods. They will, however, almost always be expected to contribute towards their keep, i.e. to the cost of the food they consume, and even if they frequently eat at work, they will be acknowledged as having a right to eat at home. Therefore, I give priority to the idea of collective food preparation and consumption as a guide to household definition, even though it is only certain members of a household who actually do the food preparation. Asking people in urban Mexico whether they cook separately (*aparte*) or together (*juntos*) generally elicits a clear and direct response indicating that this approach is a meaningful one to them (Varley 1992).

When multiple occupancy of plots in older self-help settlements is investigated, it becomes clear that it is common for adult children who have married and started a family to form separate households sharing their parents' plot. In two areas of Mexico City about 20 years old, as many as two-fifths of owners

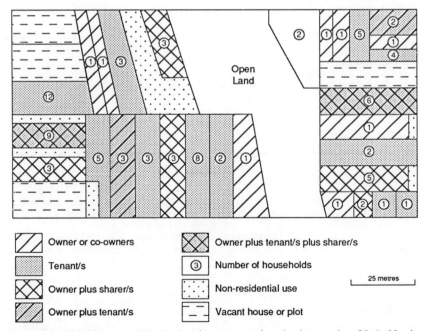

Figure 9.1 Neighbourhood block showing tenure mixes by house plot; 20 de Noviembre settlement in Puebla.

had relatives sharing with them (Varley 1992). When the amount of rented accommodation in consolidated settlements is also taken into account, the combination of multiple plot occupancy and different types of housing tenure can lead to patterns of great complexity. The information displayed in Table 9.1 and Figure 9.1 illustrates this complexity for Veinte de Noviembre, a self-help settlement in the city of Puebla which dates from the 1940s (see Gilbert & Varley 1991).

Table 9.1 Tenure structure, Colonia Veinte de Noviembre, Puebla, Mexico 1986.

Plots occupied by	Plots (%)	Households (%)				
		All	Owners	Tenants	Sharers	Others
Owners	46	22	22	–	–	–
Co-owners	5	6	6	–	–	–
Owners and sharers	10	14	5	–	9	–
Owners and tenants	7	13	4	9	–	–
Owners and tenants and sharers	2	5	1	3	2	–
Tenants (one household)	11	6	–	6	–	–
Tenants (several households)	14	30	–	30	–	–
Tenants, friends/ relatives of owner living rent-free	ng	1	–	1	–	ng
Others	4	3	–	–	–	3
Owners and others	ng	ng	–	–	ng	–
Total (%)	100	100	38	48	11	3
Total N	502	1,041	398	499	114	30

Source: Complete household listing of 502 plots in 29 blocks used for residential purposes (excluding plots for which no information or incomplete tenure not available). See Gilbert & Varley (1991).
Notes: Percentage for households are percentages of table. ng = less than one per cent.
"Co-owners" are where two siblings have bought or inherited a plots and live there with their families as separate households; "Sharers" are (usually) married children or (occasionally) other relatives/friends of owners living on the plot rent-free; "Others" are friends/relatives of the owner living rent-free (where no resident owner), or people living on the plot because of employment by the plot owner (with or without resident owner).

Housing the household

When defining household structure and characteristics in land and housing market studies, some benchmark is often needed to enable comparison between different households to be carried out on a consistent and meaningful basis. At one time, the existence of a head of household was taken for granted. The head of household was defined as the male breadwinner, and only where there was no suitable male present could a woman be assigned this status. This practice has been questioned in recent years, for example by those who point out that the husband will not automatically play the central rôle in a household's survival strategy. Given the impact of economic recession on male employment and the feminization of the workforce, it should not be assumed that the man necessarily earns the largest income. At the same time, women's gender-defined rôle as providers of support for others means that, as Fonseca (1991: 134) writes, "[the woman] is considered by researchers and perhaps the people involved to be the de facto focus of family decisions".

When studying housing processes, moreover, the practice of using the main breadwinner as the benchmark for judging household characteristics may be inappropriate, since they may not be the person who played this rôle when the key decisions shaping the household's current housing situation were taken. Where elderly and now dependent parents bought a plot of land and built the house, the characteristics of the adult son or daughter who is now the main breadwinner in their household may be of limited relevance to the researcher.

The answer to these difficulties is to cut the coat according to the cloth: where housing is the main focus of concern, the household should be viewed *in relation to the house*. Rather than using the main breadwinner or a predefined head of household as the benchmark, I argue that the most appropriate solution is to identify a householder or householders as the benchmark, i.e. the person or couple who acquired or rented a house/plot, and who were responsible for ensuring that their housing strategy was a viable one (whether or not they were personally responsible for earning the necessary income).[3] In many cases, this means that there will be both a male and a female householder. The aptness of this approach can be seen when women's contribution to the self-help housing process is examined. In my work on Mexican self-help housing, it has become increasingly apparent that the woman is often the prime mover in the decision to exchange the relative comfort of rental housing for the discomfort, hard work and lack of security that building a home on an illegally acquired housing plot entails. Her input may be a subtle one: women (and men) have described to me how wives kept "dropping hints" about how nice it would be to own a *lotecito*, not infrequently in the face of male inertia or outright unwillingness. Women may back their campaign of suggestions by saving money without their husbands' knowledge, so that the lack of money for a deposit cannot be presented as an obstacle when an opportunity to purchase emerges. In addition, a woman will often undertake paid employment or other income-generating activities on a temporary basis with the specific intention of funding the purchase of land and materials. Many women who are no longer in employment report that they *had* a job at the time their families were facing the heavy expenses of the early years of construction (see also Coulomb 1992: 115, Massolo 1991: 309). Finally, women's crucial rôle in maintaining households' social networks, which are based on the "daily interchange of favours" (Lomnitz 1975: 148), is important for their families' housing history, given the critical importance of a household's ability to raise the money for a deposit (Gilbert & Varley 1991). Such networks form the basis of the low-income population's ability to mobilize a significant, and even surprising, amount of money without regular, formal savings practices (Coulomb 1992). It is also women who are largely responsible for managing household and community relationships with government agencies with a critical rôle in the construction or upgrading of self-help housing (Moser 1987; for some Mexican case studies, see Massolo 1992).

Using the concept of the householder(s) gives the researcher both flexibility and consistency in describing household characteristics. It enables a sensible distinction to be made, for example, between morphologically identical three-generation households, in one of which a married son or daughter of the owners has found a home for his or her parents as well as his or her own spouse and offspring, whereas in the other the house was acquired long before the person who is now the main breadwinner grew up. This in turn enables the researcher to make meaningful statements about, for example, residents' age or migration characteristics in relation to the housing process.

To anchor the household to the house in this way may also help researchers to respond to criticisms of conventional approaches to the household which, while well founded, could otherwise lead to methodological paralysis. Fonseca (1991: 135), for example, criticizes the overly static nature of the household concept in relation to residential arrangements in the Vila slum in Porto Alegre, Brazil: "residential units appear to metamorphose three or four times, not in a life cycle, but in a single year". She illustrates her point by considering the history of one woman and her 11-year-old daughter, who were originally living on their own, but who then moved through a succession of different residential arrangements with relatives in a short period of time. "Faced with such cases," she comments, "the classification of households into neat categories (female-headed, extended, conjugal) was found to be of little use" (Fonseca 1991: 135). But does this mean that the only way we can describe such a population is in terms of extreme fluidity? While some elements of the population may indeed be extremely unstable, there is presumably a difference, even for the poorest household, with few material possessions, between visiting relatives and moving into, or giving up, even a one-room rented shack: time, organization and money are invested in setting up house somewhere. By identifying householders, and asking how often they, as opposed to other household members, move, and in what circumstances they do so, we may be able to distinguish between what Fonseca describes as different "family systems". For example, it may help us to distinguish between her Brazilian example, in which a high proportion of mother-child units represent "a *transitional* phase between two conjugal unions; they are precarious units liable to be dismantled at any moment upon the mother's remarriage", and a Caribbean example in which a similar proportion of mother-child units exists because "the domestic unit . . . is relatively stable and self-sufficient . . . the sporadic presence of the mother's sexual partners alters but little the fundamental organization of the group" (Fonseca 1991: 136). In other words, an important element of that stability is *residential* stability. In the Brazilian case described by Fonseca, I suggest that the woman in the mother-child unit is less likely to be a householder than in the contrasting Caribbean case.

Another example concerns recent criticisms of the way in which female-headed households are identified.[4] Considering examples from Córdoba, Argentina, and Mérida, Mexico, respectively, Falú and Curutchet (1991) and Peña (1992: 170) have suggested that the proportion of female-headed households in a population doubles if instead of considering only women without a spouse, we also take account of single mothers living in an extended household, usually with their own parents. The latter are termed "hidden" female-headed households.[5] Falú and Curutchet's figures relate to households in a low-income housing project; Peña's findings concern the households of women working in the clothing industry. Table 9.2 presents similar evidence from a number of self-help settlements of varying ages in three of Mexico's largest cities; it concerns only owner-occupiers. It confirms the finding that there are a significant number of single women with children who could be considered as forming "hidden" female-headed households within someone else's (usually their parents') household.

These studies make a valid point, in reminding us of the problem of what Watson and Austerberry call "concealed homelessness" (Watson with Auster-berry 1986: 5). Moreover, concealed homelessness is a gender issue, since, in urban Mexico, single men are far more likely to live independently than their sisters.[6] However, if taken to its logical conclusion, the practice of identifying single women with children as "hidden" female-headed households has some unsatisfactory implications. For example, it is implied that a woman with children should be counted as in some sense an independent unit, whereas her single sister, also living with her parents, is not, even if she is earning a professional salary and is more than capable of supporting herself (perhaps more so than her sister). Conversely, a woman who has children and lives with their father is *not* counted as a separate unit, even though the man's presence in the household is no guarantee that he will be an effective provider for the family.[7] Thus, in one sense, identifying only certain types of women as "hid-den" female-headed households reinforces the notion that women are/should be dependent on their parents (unless they have children) or their husbands. Ulti-mately, this argument would result, conceptually, in an unhelpful atomization of households, with no consistent methodological basis for identification of smaller units within the household. The mother–child unit might appear to offer such a basis, but what happens when the mother is in her 80s, the child in his or her 60s? What happens when the child is married and a parent, even a grandparent? Equally, how should we treat the admittedly rarer father–child unit, or the residual individuals who may be left behind after mother–child units have been separated out for analysis?

Table 9.2 "Visible" and "hidden" female-headed households in six low-income settlements, Mexico 1991–92.

	Mexico City		Puebla		Guadalajara		All
	Loma de la Palma	San José	El Salvador	Veinte de Noviembre	Buenos Aires	Agustin Yañez	
Visible female-headed house-holds[1]	15	11	5	33	8	11	12
Number of house-holds surveyed	78	72	55	33	77	56	371
Visible and hidden female-headed households[2]							
Visible	80	50	75	100	60	67	71
Daughters with children	7	44	25	0	40	11	22
Other female relatives with children	13	6	0	0	0	22	8
N	15	16	4	11	10	9	65

Source: Varley (1992) and further analysis of survey data by author.
Notes: 1. As a percentage of all households surveyed. 2. As a percentage of all such households.
The settlements differ widely in their ages, which partly accounts for the different percentages of female-headed households recorded.

The total number of "visible" and "hidden" female-headed households is not given as a percentage of all households surveyed because in order to do so properly the number of extra households obtained by recognizing mother-child units as hidden female-headed households should be added to the total number of households surveyed. Some "hidden" female-headed households form part of "visible" female-headed households, but they are counted separately in the second part of the table.

To recognize, as most feminist analyses do, that "the household is not an undifferentiated set of individuals", and that "there are structural bases for conflict and struggle within the household" (Jelin 1991b: 33) does not mean that we must reject the notion of the household as lacking any analytic validity. Although there may be secondary groupings (such as a single mother and her child/ren) within a particular household, this does not mean that they would (wish to) see themselves, or be seen by others, as separate units. If single mothers live with their parents, it may be because they are economically dependent on parental support or because they ascribe to, or are obliged to accept, cultural norms according them dependent status. In recent surveys in Mexico City, Puebla and Guadalajara, I found more married children were sharing their parents' plots as separate households than were living with them in extended households; but in only one case was a single daughter with children recognized as an independent sharer household (Varley 1992). The reason why single daughters did not form their own households cannot, therefore, be explained solely in terms of lack of suitable accommodation.

By identifying the householder(s), as a more meaningful alternative to the overly rigid and often sexist concept of head of household, we can begin to make sense of the complexities of household structure in a way that does not automatically ascribe dependent status to some household members on the basis of their sex, marital status or age. For example, a single woman who provides a home for her elderly parents, with income coming from her own income-generating activities, her father's, and her eldest child's, belongs in a different category than the single daughter with a child who has never lived on her own and is dependent on her parents for both accommodation and food. Moreover, in the specific case of householders being home-owners, that status may make a material difference to their status within the household. Meillasoux (1981) and Robertson (1991) have described the practice whereby younger people support their elderly parents as a product of self-interest: by supporting aged relatives, people reinforce a normative system of inter-generational family obligations which they hope will serve them well when they, in turn, are old and have to rely on their children for support. There is, however, no *guarantee* that the younger generation will respect this system. Therefore, the elderly widow who owns the home in which she lives with one of her sons and his family, on whom she is financially dependent, is arguably in a stronger position to ensure that her entitlement to a share of the household resources is respected than is her counterpart who has no material advantages with which to back up her claim on the goodwill of the next generation.

In short, I have argued that to anchor the household to the house by identifying the householders can assist us to design a rigorous methodology for studying housing processes and also to respond appropriately to some recent criticisms of conventional approaches to the household. Any classification scheme will do violence to the subtleties of reality in at least some cases, but we should try to reduce the number of those cases rather than abandon all hope of classification. When housing studies require knowledge about relatively large numbers of households, the concept of the householder/s provides a flexible and sensitive, but none the less systematic, way of identifying a particular person or persons whose characteristics are likely to be important in describing the household and its housing history. By viewing householders as a pivot around which the rest of the household is articulated, the household structure at any given time can be described.

Holding the house

The previous section was concerned with the importance of looking at the house when thinking about the household; this section emphasizes the importance of thinking about the household when looking at the house. Or, to be precise, not so much thinking about the household per se, as thinking, first, about its relation to other households and, second, about the processes of household evolution over time.

Two very similar households that were interviewed on the same street in *colonia* Buenos Aires, Guadalajara, will illustrate the first of these points. It concerns the difficulty of producing accurate descriptions of housing tenure. The first one consisted of a teenage couple and their baby son. They were the only ones living in the house and would be unusually young to own such a relatively well consolidated house. The house was not, in fact, theirs; it had been lent to them by the man's parents, who had a house further down the hill on which the settlement was built, when their son's girlfriend became pregnant. A few doors down the street, a very similar young couple said that they *were* the owners of their house; it was a gift from the man's parents, who also had another property nearby.

The point is that descriptions of housing tenure must often rely on the categories employed by residents,[8] and when, as is by no means uncommon, a household's right to its accommodation derives from its relation to another household, tenure descriptions may not fit neatly into fixed categories.[9] The difference between cases such as those noted above may be more real than apparent: if interviewed, the parents of the young couples might in both cases have said that the property was only lent to their offspring. On the other hand, I have come across enough cases of this type to know that some parents do indeed give property to their children, sometimes as an inheritance (even though the original owners are still alive).[10] It would perhaps be surprising if this were not the case, given the importance Mexicans building their own homes attach to "having something to leave to my children". And significant numbers of houses are lent to relatives or friends, particularly but by no means exclusively when the owners are working temporarily in the USA.[11]

My second argument, about the importance of considering the household when analyzing housing processes, is that some ideas about social change in low-income housing areas depend on implicit models of "normal" household evolution. If these models were to be found unsatisfactory, then our understanding of the processes in question might change.

One Mexican example is not specifically concerned with housing but is nevertheless worth describing as it provides a clear illustration of the point. A number of authors have argued that one response to Mexico's economic crisis of the 1980s was an increase in the proportion of extended households in low-income housing areas (González de la Rocha 1988, 1991; Chant 1991). The extended household, they argue, takes on particular significance during times of economic crisis because of its ability to incorporate extra income earners, "combining resources, increasing household income, goods, and services, and economizing on living costs" (González de la Rocha 1991: 117, see also Hackenberg et al. 1984). In particular, as noted above, married sons or daughters brought their spouses to live in the parental home: "Newly married couples . . . now tend to stay in the home of one set of parents . . . instead of setting up on their own" (González de la Rocha 1988: 211). The model of normal household change implicit in this argument about responses to crisis, therefore, is one in which newly married couples do *not* stay in the parental home, since only if this is the case can an increase in the proportion of extended households be interpreted as the product of economic crisis causing the household to "manipulate the domestic cycle in order to retain able members" (González de la Rocha 1988: 211). But what if low-income urban households in Mexico habitually go through a phase in which married sons or daughters spend at least a few years living with their parents, as they have been widely reported to do in rural areas (Varley 1992)? Then an increase in the proportion of extended households in a particular self-help settlement may simply reflect the fact that the children of people who built their homes there are now beginning to get married and set up home with their parents; it may not have anything to tell us about the impact of changing economic circumstances.[12]

A similar sort of argument can be made concerning the question of whether legalizing and upgrading a self-help settlement leads to a displacement of population from that area, as has been suggested, for example, by Burgess (1982: 78–9; see also Mathéy 1992b: 387).[13] In the first instance, we may investigate whether or not significant numbers of people who built their homes in such an area have moved out as a result of being unable to bear the costs of legalization, servicing and property taxes, or because they are bought out by higher-income groups "raiding" the area after regularization (Durand 1983: 122–3). But even if no such movement is found, displacement may still be occurring. If, in contrast to the model of household evolution implicit in the studies cited above, young people *do* generally live with their parents after marriage, a high rate of households *from the next generation* moving out of an area could also be described as displacement. Hiernaux, for example, describes the Valle de Chalco, a massive area of housing which has grown up in the 1980s on the periphery of Mexico City, as the product of a "generalized expulsion of families" from neighbouring parts of the Federal District (Hiernaux 1991b: 194)[14], and Coulomb (1992: 64) found that two-fifths of the members of various housing co-operatives in Mexico City were currently living either with their parents or other relatives or in a property that had been lent to them. The mechanisms by which the valorization of self-help housing could lead to displacement of the younger generation include parents converting shared into rented accommodation because of the need for extra income (see Gilbert & Varley 1991: 153), or subdividing their property and, instead of giving part to their children, selling it to a third party.[15]

The point of these two examples is not to suggest that an increase in the proportion of extended households did *not* occur in response to economic crises in 1980s in Mexico, or that displacement of second-generation households from self-help settlements *is* occurring. It is, rather, to provide illustrations of the way in which our understanding of processes of interest in land and housing market studies is affected by our understanding of the processes of household evolution over time. Although researchers studying land and housing market processes are accustomed to looking at household variables, we are not, perhaps, accustomed to exploring the implicit models of household change that inform our arguments about housing processes; we might find it helpful to make some of these models explicit.

Conclusions

Although conventional approaches to the household have been subject to considerable criticism in recent years, it is unlikely that researchers studying land and housing market processes will be able or willing to dispense with the concept. Georgina Ashworth, the director of CHANGE, an organization concerned with women's status throughout the world, recently called for the demolition of the household as the unit of economic analysis because it disguises and therefore maintains "the imbalance of power and of time-expenditure and the violation of rights" within the household from which women in particular suffer.[16] But most social scientists, including those concerned with the problems identified by Ashworth, would nevertheless agree with Smith et al. (1984: 8), that the household is "a crucial nexus in the explanation of empirical reality". Arguably, it is because of such problems that we should pay *more,* not less, attention to the household.

The importance of the household to land and housing market studies may be gauged from the fact that the household survey is a central element in the methodology of many such studies. We have, perhaps, tended to make the household a vehicle for our explanations, treating it as unproblematic in itself. As Netting et al. (1984b: xxi–xxii) argue: "We have the decided impression that we can easily discern comparable units in literally any human society", but "this mundane, repetitive, cross-culturally obvious appearance of households may be deceptive, for 'Just the opposite may be true'". It is for this reason that I suggest we need to pay more explicit attention to the household. My twin arguments – that we need to look at the house when thinking about the household, and consider the household when examining the house – simply acknowledge the closeness of the two concepts which is evident in the etymology of the word household itself.[17] Ultimately, what I argue is that cultural norms about who should live together, or how kin should support each other by (amongst other things) the provision of accommodation, should not be dismissed as insignificant by comparison with economic considerations in our understanding of housing. The distinction between what is culturally desirable and what is economically possible is in any case an artificial one: the availability of housing influences the likelihood of certain types of household emerging, but social change in the household also affects the housing market. "Housing the household" and "holding the house" are simply two ways of looking at the same social reality.

Notes

1. One son lives upstairs, the other downstairs. Another, unmarried, son lives with his mother.
2. It might be argued that current property registration (when available) is the acid test of what constitutes a plot. But people may register their property in the name, for example, of a son or daughter living elsewhere, with the clear understanding that the property will not in practice be theirs until the death of their parents. Such understandings are not always respected.
3. This is similar to US Census practice, except that the US Census designates only one person as the "householder": "the person or one of the persons in whose name the house is owned or rented". Where there are two people in whose name the house is owned, etc., it is not clear how it is decided which of them should be the householder.
4. Despite the unsatisfactory implications, this chapter follows the convention in the literature of describing households in which there is no resident male spouse as female-headed households.
5. Falú & Curutchet (1991: 28–29) also count mother-child units as "hidden" female-headed households when they form part of a nuclear household but one or more of their children are from previous relationships.
6. In the settlements considered in Table 9.2, over twice as many sons (aged 15 or over) as daughters of the owners surveyed were reported to be single and living independently (with or without children).
7. Chant (1985, 1991) argues that Mexican women in male-headed nuclear households may actually be worse off than their counterparts in female-headed households because husbands retain a considerable part of their earnings for personal use.
8. The deficiencies of land titles as a guide to property ownership have been noted above. Moreover, titles are not available before a settlement is legalized, and not all residents of a legalized settlement necessarily have land titles (Varley 1985b).
9. In the six settlements considered in Table 9.2, a maximum of 36 per cent of all households enumerated in a household listing enjoyed their accommodation as a result of their relations with those who owned the plots, without paying rent. Questions may be raised about the difficulty of distinguishing sharers from tenants, given the unwillingness of some owners to admit to the presence of tenants on their plots. While some people clearly did conceal the fact that they had tenants, I am confident that those who were identified as sharers really *were* sharers. Thus, even if the omission of some tenants from the listing inflates the proportion of other types of households, the absolute importance of tenants is nevertheless considerable, particularly in Mexico City.
10. I have found some evidence of a custom that has been recorded for rural Mexico (Krantz 1991: 128) of the youngest son remaining on his parents' plot in anticipation of inheriting the property on their death, while other siblings are given assistance in acquiring their own plots. The case of the adjacent plots in Loma de la Palma described above was one example: the father, now a widower, lived alone in a house at the front of his plot; above it, on a terrace, was the house of the youngest son and his family. The two other plots had been given to his older brothers. Four daughters and another son owned homes elsewhere in the city (three of them in nearby streets).
11. Hiernaux (1991b: 194) reports just over 5 per cent of houses in the Valle de Chalco, the south-eastern periphery of Mexico City, as having been "lent" to their residents by the owners, but indicates that in many cases these houses had *never* been occupied by their owners.
12. As Robertson (1991: 169) argues, "we should take care not to mistake a *single stage* in the extended or stem patterns of development for the *compact* pattern", i.e. even where most households in a population are nuclear, many people may nevertheless go through stages of living in an extended household. Like certain agricultural colonization schemes (Robertson 1991: 99), self-help settlements are unusual in that they create a society that consists very largely of a single generation, and we should therefore take particular care in attributing changes in those settlements that may be a product of the domestic cycle to wider economic changes affecting the whole of society or the whole of the low-income population.
13. I am grateful to Gareth Jones for helping me to link the question of household structure and change to that of displacement.
14. Over 80 per cent of the inhabitants of the Valle de Chalco came from the Federal District; only 7 per cent had come to the area directly from other parts of the country (Hiernaux 1991b: 185–7). However, Hiernaux argues that push factors were more important for tenants than for

133

those who had previously lived with relatives, lived in a borrowed house, or owned their home (Hiernaux 1991b: 195).

15. Subdivisions and plot sales affected almost one-third of the plots in an illegal settlement in the south-west of Mexico City in just five years (Varley 1985c: 91).

16. "Raising gender consciousness in development", paper delivered to the Development Studies Association annual conference, 17 September 1992.

17. Although, as we have seen, "households . . . cannot be *equated with* co-residential groups" (Smith et al., 1984: 9, emphasis added).

CHAPTER TEN

Urban land-price research and the utility of land-registration data sources

Amitabh

Introduction

Research on urban land-price changes in developing countries involves hetero-geneous data sources. Overall, there is a lack of uniformity in the data sources that has contributed to a lack of comparability between studies. As it is fre-quently the case that the availability of data sources has informed the methodol-ogy applied in land-price research, one must examine more closely than hitherto the relative utility of major data sources available in each country.[1] Such an exploratory analysis and diagnosis of each data source would give us an oppor-tunity to rule out or accept certain data points in urban land-price research. Without this, one takes a common platform where one can globally compare the findings of one study with another. This leads to assertions and wide-scale gen-eralizations such as that "land prices are increasing rapidly" or "sky-rocketing", or anecdotal assertions based on isolated, highly selective cases that may not be corroborated once analyzed empirically.

A thoughtful analysis of the land-registration data source is urgently required, especially at a time when international agencies such as the UNDP, World Bank and UNCHS show a considerable concern to extend tools for land and housing market management in developing countries (Dowall 1991a). There is already considerable concern that the new conventional wisdom emanating from, above all, the World Bank stresses the desirability of Third World governments considering land values as surrogates for land prices in order that governments can then recoup service provision costs by clawing back a proportion of land value change (Ward et al. 1993). Here, the India data questions the applicability of associating registered land values with some notion of land price.

This chapter aims to examine the potentiality of one particular data source – the land registration office – in urban land-market research in developing countries. The advantage in collecting these data is that they provide information about land-price changes that occur at the city-wide level rather than simply explaining prices for very recent subdivisions at the periphery. As land-registration data are

135

available throughout cities in developing countries, one is dealing with an important potential data source. However, no study completed so far has attempted to explore its potential. In the Indian context the land-registration data are often used as a singular source to examine land-price changes (Wadhwa 1985, TCPO-Government of India 1985). Although these studies often refer to the shortcomings of this data source, they do not attempt to explain whether one can overcome the shortcomings and identify whether it may be used as a primary or secondary source of information. This is all the more surprising if one considers that land-registration data include information on the year of plot sale, plot size, the purchase price and the location of the plot – at face value, a rich data set. This chapter presents an analysis of the land-registration data available in Lucknow city (India) and aims to highlight their utility in contemporary and future studies. Unfortunately, the story is one of optimism that turns sour.

The nature of the land-registration data source

In India land-registration data are available at the Tehsil Office (land registration office) with data broken down to the level of colonies, *mohallas* and villages located within the city limits, as well as settlements located beyond the city.[2] There are usually two main sources at the Tehsil Office that provide land-price information. The first principal source comprises confidential records of what can be termed first-level data. These are unpublished and contain basic details of individual property transactions that have taken place in the city over time. These records have information on each type of property transaction, i.e. house and land (plot), and are used by the state and private individuals for completing property searches in order to ascertain plot or house ownership. One must be careful with this data source because the listings of the house and land transactions are unsorted in the records. Moreover, there are many types of registrations for land and house transactions.[3] With these records, what should concern the researcher is the data for the plot sales which have been registered as a sale deed or agreement. These are the only types of registration under which land is actually sold. In this respect the data reflect land transactions inclusive of (a) plot size, (b) declared price of the plot (also known as the registered price or the consideration money), (c) valuation price (*maliyat*) as assessed by the officials of the Revenue Department (chief-subregistrar), (d) date of the presentation of registry papers (*takmeel ki tareekh*) in the land registration office (i.e. the date the transaction occurs), (e) date of registration in the land registration office, (f) name of the seller and name of the buyer, and (g) location of the plot in the colony (relative rather than absolute location).[4] For research purposes, access to these first-level records can be obtained easily, and the time consumed in collecting information from them is not especially long.

The Tehsil Office in India also collates information, again confidentially, at the so-called second-level. These contain the explanatory details of each property transaction as cited in the confidential records of the first-level. The second-level records are extremely voluminous and are unpublished. Keeping in mind the time limits of research, it may not be wise to opt for data collection from the second-level records over the confidential records of the first level. Also, access to the confidential records of the second level is less assured. When the purpose of collecting land-price data is partly met by the confidential records of the first level, there seems little practical gain in investing huge amounts of time with confidential records of the second level.

The third source consists of the open (public) records. This information is unambiguously in the public domain and is known as the "circle rate" (or area rate) in Lucknow. It is a published data source and contains city-wide *estimated* land prices. The circle rates were designed in 1981 under the Indian Stamp Act (Rule 340-A) and are revised every three years. The main purpose of the circle rate is to minimize the undervaluation of landed property in the registration office and to raise revenues.[5] The fixing of circle rates at the city-wide level is largely contingent upon changes in land and revenue policies over periods of time. Since these policies vary from one state to the other, comparability of the circle rate with the rate and prices prevailing in other states is not straightforward, making comparisons difficult or impossible.

The circle rate is the minimum market price of land expressed in terms of rupees per unit of land.[6] It is determined on the basis of a subset of example land prices as informed by the colonizers, open-market sale deeds and the rates of the urban development and housing authorities in the state sector. Until 1987 the Revenue Department in Lucknow used to fix the rate under the process mentioned above. However, more recently, the revision of the circle rate in Lucknow has been carried out on a different basis. Besides the criteria that were considered in the previous years, the city is divided into three areas consisting of (a) older *mohallas*, (b) *mohallas* at the periphery and (c) country-side areas. Circle rates were fixed in each of these three areas on the basis of the percentage increase in the land prices as collected from a variety of sources over time. Even knowing that the actual market prices are always higher than the "circle" rates, the latter are city-wide kept to the minimum level. The government has taken the conscious decision to maintain a minimum circle rate in order not to discourage plot registration at the Tehsil Office. The Treasury has thus given priority to the extent of registration rather than the technical accuracy of the circle rate assessment. In this way it hopes that revenue will be maximized and not lost through the failure to register land by selling plots on a power-of-attorney basis.[7] Lucknow has learnt from Delhi, where the prices were not fixed to a minimum but allowed to "float" nearer to the market price. In Lucknow, none of the plot registrations could be made below the prevalent circle rate in the concerned colonies/ *mohallas*.[8]

As indicated earlier, there is some variation among states in the nature of their land registration data. For example in Andhra Pradesh the major objective of the Market Value Scheme is to curb undervaluation of properties for collection of the stamp duty, and this is expected to provide realistic land values (Gnaneshwar 1986: 75). The price-assessment process of the market value scheme in Andhra Pradesh appears to be more pronounced and systematic if compared with the assessment of circle rate in Lucknow. Nonetheless, the basic motive behind the design and operation of the circle rate scheme and the market value scheme is largely similar – i.e. to avoid under invoicing (and under valuing) properties in order to reduce stamp duty paid on land transactions.

Limitations of the land-registration data

The information available from the first-level confidential records of the land registration office is rarely intact or complete for every year. It is maintained in handwritten registers that are often found by the researcher to be in a damaged or illegible condition. Damage depends upon the use to which these registers have been put, and that is normally contingent upon the number and frequency of property transactions in a year(s). It is a general practice for lawyers, individuals and property brokers to enquire about the basic information of the property before conveyancing.

It is very unlikely that the valuation price (i.e. registrar's assessment value) of each plot will be shown throughout the confidential records of the first level. Therefore, information on the registrar's assessment values as noted in the registers may not always be available. However, even if sufficient registers were available, the comparability of the registrar's assessment values would be weak in two senses. The first is that the valuation prices determined before the stipulation of the circle rates might be inconsistent since these were decided by the chief-subregistrar under the Indian Stamp Act Rules. Though the rules are quite clear for the plot valuation, actual plot valuation in the land registration office is often quite arbitrary and idiosyncratic. It may be adjusted so as to provide "benefits" to all concerned – the valuer, the appropriator and the buyer. Underassessment of prices in the land registration office records is almost universal (Wadhwa 1985: 116). It is likely to occur whenever taxation on land transaction is stringent and particularly where it is high. Underassessment is not common for the transactions of state institutions or state-based money. However, overassessment may occur for state-based purchases so that part of the additional sum paid to the buyer is returned to the officials through "kick backs" (Wade 1989: 76). Wadhwa (1985: 116) identifies another element of error in price data in Ahmedabad city (Gujrat state, India) which comes through non-correspondence of the dates of registration and actual transaction, thus leaving scope for manipulation of the date of transaction. According to Wadhwa, the time gap between transaction and registration may be as long as 10–15 years, but Wadhwa does not mention the time lapse in more normal circumstances. However, these are exceptions and they do not usually present major distortions of the data source. In the case of Lucknow city these two dates are almost always in the same year.

The second reason for a lack of comparability in the data sources is the addition of one-off statutory reassessments. These reassessments are rarely applied evenly across the city and thus affect a small subset of plots of colonies. They do, however, account for a significant difference in the circle rates among colonies, as some include the additional assessments while others do not. Perhaps the best example of this in Lucknow is the decision in 1984 to assign a 10 per cent valuation premium to plots located alongside a road. Without an intimate knowledge of the city and significant amounts of cross-checking, it is difficult to control for plots that have been subject to this reassessment. Moreover, such additional assessments display a tendency not to be applied equally across the city. The application in 1981, for example, of a minimum and maximum circle rate value in Lucknow was prescribed only for two settlements.[9]

The confidential records of the first level do not show the proper address of the seller or buyer of the plot sold. They tell us about the plot number and the situation on two sides of the plot. Since the address of the plot owner is not recorded in the first-level records, it is hardly possible to cross-check the land prices of one plot (as recorded in the first-level records) to the same plot through a household survey. Of course, an address can be obtained from the second-level confidential records, but one has to overcome two problems; first, to get access through the officials; and, second, the enormous expenditure of time in reviewing these records. Another complication is that in most cases the plot number does not correspond to the present house number, i.e. subdivisions are made on different numbers, and once houses are built, the municipal administration often assigns different numbers to individual houses.[10]

The records are presented in two ways. First, by year, arranged alphabetically by name according to the names of the seller and buyer. Unfortunately these data are not arranged in respect of colonies/*mohallas*. Secondly, data are arranged by year. These records are arranged alphabetically by colony/*mohalla*. This is a problem because records that are held by name cannot be classified on a time-scale basis, while records that are held according to year provide a straightforward method of assessment. Since the concern of most land-market research is to collect information over time, the latter data source is the only effective record of market change available.

Potential applications of the land-registration data

It is clear at this stage that the land prices as recorded in the "confidential records" have various shortcomings. However, this does not imply that the data have little use. The design and implementation of the circle rate provides an opportunity to locate trends in the registered land prices. It is widely accepted that underassessment is an almost universal characteristic in the Indian context and throughout developing countries, but that none of the plot sales (property transactions) would be registered below the circle rates prescribed in the concerned settlements. Thus, the registered prices are likely, at least, to be equal to the prices as determined by the circle rates.[11] The latter being the minimum prices would always reflect a trend in the registered prices that would run either parallel to or below the circle rate.

There are good reasons for this. Since, valuation prices are principally determined by the circle rates, buyers would try to keep the registered prices closer to the valuation prices. This may be practised to avoid disagreement and hassle between the buyer and the land registry officials. Such possible conflict has to be avoided by both parties, as disputes would otherwise be subject to court ruling implying significant delay for the buyer and loss of graft to the land-registration officials. The outcome of this procedure is that, within any jurisdiction, circle rates can be accepted as broadly representative of the registered and valuation prices.

In order to cross-check the Tehsil Office prices and the prices as informed by the households, a comparison of the ratio between different types of land-price information can be developed. If one can ensure and explain the ratio over periods of time, it would be a logical way to support the findings of one data source to the other source. A constant ratio over time between the land-price trends of the two data sources would support the idea that the Tehsil Office prices could be used as a surrogate for real (or actual) land prices. This would then serve as a guide in order to inflate or deflate (depending upon the nature of the ratio) information of the land-registration price data to approximate the land prices from other data sources. Under this situation, despite its severe shortcomings, the land-registration data might have significant meaning and utility. It is necessary, therefore, to cross-check the nature of the relationships among the three sets of land prices, specifically to identify the ratio between the valuation price, registered price and actual price over time. As I argued earlier, the circle rate can be accepted as representative of registered and valuation prices. What I show below is an example of the ratio between the circle rate and the "household-paid prices". Before we proceed further it would be pertinent to provide a brief introduction of the household-paid prices.

The household-paid prices are those that have actually been paid by the plot owner, i.e. the household. A questionnaire-based household survey in 14 colonies of Lucknow was conducted between 1990 and 1991. The colonies have been selected mainly on the basis of the location, age, land-delivery mechanism, level of urban services and "perceived" income level of the households. A total of 521 randomly selected household questionnaires were completed that cover plot (or house) transactions over a 20-year span (1970–90). The questions asked to the households mainly relate to: (a) demographic and general housing information; (b) acquisition of the plot and value of the landed property; (c) legalization of the plot; (d) nature of the land purchased; (e) information on the house construction; (f) provision of urban services; and, (h) threat of displacement or consideration of movement into another colony. In the example below the actual land prices paid by the households are taken to construct a ratio of land price to circle rate.[12]

An example

The thrust of the present example is to show how the ratio can be determined and to what extent the land-price trend of one data source can support the trends of the other data sources. Two types of data sources are under examination. These are: (a) the circle rates; and (b) the household-paid prices. At this point one is not concerned with real price trends, rather with the ratio and conformity between circle rates and the prices as paid by the households. As we are not concerned with the price trend but the relationship, there is no need in this instance to adjust prices for inflation.

Both sets of data have been plotted (Fig. 10.1) for the eight colonies located mainly on the periphery in Lucknow – the capital city of Uttar Pradesh. In these colonies the land has been subdivided by the public, private and co-operative sectors. Although the wider survey was done for 14 colonies, five of these did not have sufficient observations – determined as at least two price readings per year. Hence, they are not represented in the context of the present example. Of the eight colonies, four colonies belong to the public sector, while two are private and two are co-operative colonies. The purpose of dividing the colonies according to the participating sector is to identify any possible variability in the ratio. The distribution of the selected colonies according to the sectors involved in land delivery is presented in Table 10.1.

Table 10.1 Sector-wise distribution of the selected colonies.

Name of colony	Total sample household size	Sector-wise percentage of sampled households (%)		
		Public	Private	Co-operative
Aliganj	51	76	14	10
Indira Nagar	50	88	10	2
Gomti Nagar	32	100	0	0
Rajaji Puram	50	82	18	0
Sanjay G. Puram	43	0	91	9
Triveni Nagar	51	0	73	27
Khurram Nagar	52	0	35	65
Garhi Peer Khan	30	0	37	63
Indralok	34	0	76	24
Hind Nagar	27	30	52	18
Sarojini Nagar	23	0	78	22
Geeta Palli	30	0	80	20
Patel Nagar	21	0	14	86
Ravindra Palli	27	0	33	67

Source: Author's fieldwork 1990–91.

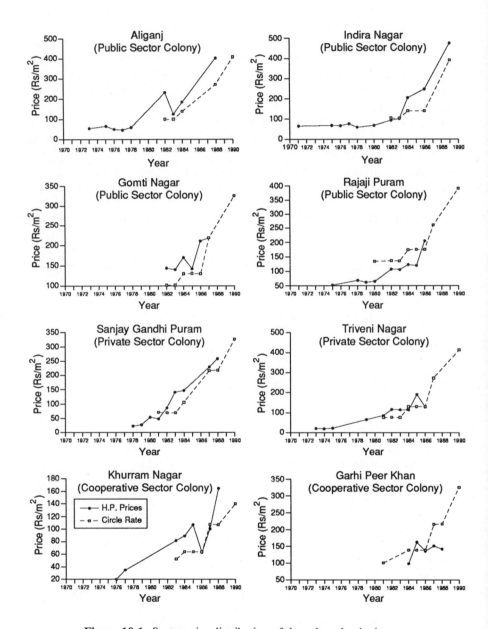

Figure 10.1 Sector-wise distribution of the selected colonies.

142

Broadly, the trend of household-paid prices in the selected colonies is increasing. Nevertheless, the trend fluctuates, particularly in 1986 in respect of Rajaji Puram (public sector), Triveni Nagar (private sector), Khurram Nagar (co-operative sector) and Garhi Peer Khan (co-operative sector). Also, in 1983 and 1985 there is a sharp declining trend in Aliganj and Gomti Nagar (both public sector). This contrasts with evidence for the circle rate, which shows a constant increase over time and throughout all the selected colonies (Fig. 10.1). The circle rate seems to be static only in 1981 and 1983, 1984 and 1987, and 1987 and 1990 owing, as stated earlier, to the revision procedure that takes place every three years.

It is not my intention here to go into the details of land-price changes that have emerged from the two data sources. Rather, I wish to draw attention to the ratio between the household-paid prices and the circle rate, as presented in Figure 10.2. It is clear that the ratio between the household-paid price and the circle rate is not constant over time in any of the colonies, and also that there is no definite pattern with changes in ratio in the public-, private- or co-operative-sector colonies. This suggests that the relationship between the household-paid prices and the circle rate varies significantly over time, such that circle rates may not offer a good approximation of household-paid prices at any one moment in time. Given the problems of assessment, one might suspect as much. However, what Figure 10.2 also indicates is that the discrepancy varies among settlements, such that no particular type of settlement can be said to be consistently under represented.

An effort was made to find out if the ratio between the household-paid prices and the circle rates can be explained. The r^2 values (coefficient of determination) have been calculated on the ratio plotted for the example colonies (Table 10.1). The purpose of the r^2 values is to enable us to explain the variations contained by the ratio between the two data sources. The higher the r^2 values, which would not be considered significant unless greater than 90 per cent, the better the variation in ratio is explained. In the present example none of the colonies has a significant r^2 value. Moreover, the data reveal a wide variation in the r^2 values. There is no obvious reason why this might be so. The data appear not to select values according to whether a colony is public, private or co-operative, according to service provision, location or age. Rather, one suspects that the reason lies within the anomalies and inconsistencies of the fixing of the circle rate that I have already outlined.

The analysis suggests that the land-registration data (circle rates or the registered prices or valuation prices) cannot be used in isolation unless they are thoroughly cross-checked with information from other data sources. The constraints associated with this data source, as discussed earlier, add further doubts about the reliability of the information. Hence, in urban land-price research one must not base sole reliance upon the land-registration data. Given this unreliability with the land-registration data, one ought, perhaps to consider whether other institutionalized data sources should be treated as reliable. This lack of

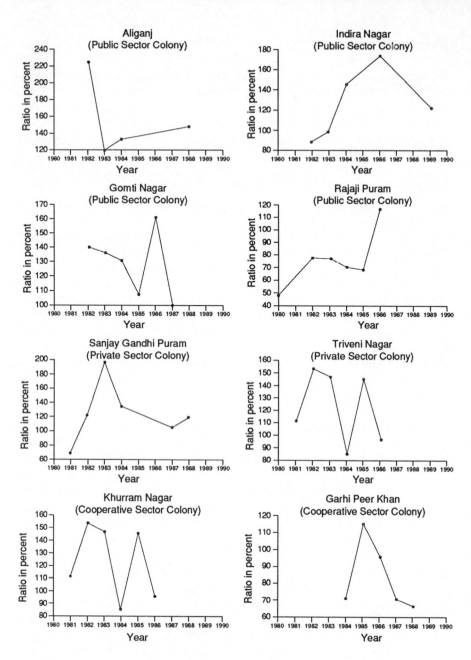

Figure 10.2 Ratio between household paid prices and the circle rate [ratio = (HP prices / circle rate) × 100].

Notes: In 1981 and 1984, the "circle rates" for Gomti Nagar, Rajaji Puram, Sanjay G. Puram, Triveni Nagar and Khurram Nagar have been determined according to the circle rates prevailing in the neighbourhood areas. The names of these colonies do not appear in the circle rate lists of 1981 and 1984. The circle rates of the following neighbourhoods are undertaken for the corresponding colonies: Bari Jugauli for Gomti Nagar; Talkatora for Rajaji Puram; Shiekhpur Kasaila for Sanjay G. Puram; Ahibaranpur for Triveni Nagar; Rahim Hagar for Khurram Nagar.

reliability of the land-registration data in contexts such as Lucknow is disappointing, and it highlights the need for researchers to develop imaginative (but time-consuming) fieldwork techniques that will develop more accurate databases. At a time when local government and international agencies are advocating and, in the more advanced cases, setting out procedures for monitoring the land market through revision and modernization of land-registration and cadastral records, the research from Lucknow points to the need for caution since there appears to be little basis for making comparisons between land-registration data and actual land prices. The former cannot be used as a surrogate for the latter.

Notes

1. The following studies have attempted to co-ordinate methodologies. Dowall (1989a, 1989b) and Dowall & Leaf (1991) have done so for Bangkok, Karachi and Jakarta. Ward et al. (1991, 1993), Jones (1991a), Macoloo (1993) and Amitabh (1993) have co-ordinated methodologies for urban studies of Mexico, Kenya and India.
2. *Mohalla*(s) should be accepted as a synonym of colony. The term *mohalla* is normally used for old settlements that are mainly located in older areas of the city.
3. Types of registrations recorded in the confidential records at the first level are numerous. For example, registrations include gift deed, partition deed, errata, cancellation of sale deed, surrender deed, reconveyance deed, mortgage, return of mortgage, rent deed, receipt, assignment deed, agreement deed, sale deed.
4. For the limitations of these categories see next section.
5. The revenue is realized through the stamp duty payment which is 14 per cent (in 1989–90) of the total amount of the "valuation price" (the price assessed for the plot by the Tehsil Office) (Interviews with ADM [Revenue], Lucknow 1989–90).
6. Before the design of the circle rate system, stamp duty on land was assessed according to the consideration of the chief-subregistrar under the rules of the Indian Stamp Act of 1899.
7. "Power of attorney includes any instrument (not chargeable with a fee under the law relating to court-fees for the time being in force) empowering a specified person to act for and in the name of person executing it" (Malik 1988: 6, Indian Stamp Act 1899).
8. Interview with officials of the Revenue and Land Registration departments.
9. These were Mahanagar and Nirala Nagar colonies. The example that follows considers the average of minimum and maximum circle rates for the determination of 1981 circle rates.
10. A simple policy solution to improve co-ordination would have positive effects on both planning control and revenue collection.
11. Valuation prices are the prices determined according to the prevailing circle rates. Registered prices are the prices reported in the land registration papers by the concerned party. Actual prices are those actually paid.
12. For a detailed information on the methodology of the questionnaire survey as undertaken in Lucknow during 1990–91 and for the explanations concerned with the determination of land prices out of the survey data, see Amitabh (1993).

CHAPTER ELEVEN

Measuring the price and supply of urban land markets
Insights on sources

William J. Siembieda

Introduction

The United Nations Global Strategy for Shelter to the Year 2000 notes that the greatest failure of developing countries in the housing sector has been their inability to stimulate an adequate supply of affordable and serviced land in cities (UNCHS 1989). This and similar arguments form part of a considerable debate that centres on whether the urban poor have less access to land today than in the past (see Doebele, this volume). This debate has already produced some significant questions, some of which are addressed by other authors in this volume and elsewhere (see Ward et al. 1993). For example, does it cost more today to acquire a plot of land than it did 20 years ago? If so, what has contributed to such a rise in cost? It is a theme running through this book that the answers to these questions stem to a large degree from the ideological perspective one adopts as the frame of reference.[1] Moreover, it is argued that the chosen frame of reference will dictate the data collected.

These methodological questions are now, perhaps, all the more important given recent policy changes in many developing countries that put greater emphasis on trying to deal with the land problem (Jones & Ward, this volume, Rakodi 1990b). If policy-makers are to seek better information on land-use policy, then land-market assessments will become a much-used tool (Dowall 1991a). Assessment of the "performance" of urban land markets is seen as useful for local governments since it helps them to manage cities by relating land value to fiscal policy. And it enables social groups to develop strategic approaches to market entry and acquisition of parcels related to their particular needs and circumstances. There is, therefore, a growing consensus on the need to assemble information on land supply and prices. This chapter takes up this challenge by addressing a set of methodologies related to the difficult task of understanding the operation of land markets and determining long-term land prices.

Various methods of assembling information are discussed from a practical point of view. The important idea is that long-term price trends can be established, and that modelling of the supply side can be done in simple ways. This is useful to infrastructure planning, management of urban growth, and the identification of long-term requirements for urban land. In the final section, methodological issues relating to the measurement of land prices and the model of land supply are brought together.

The focus of this chapter is on Mexican land markets outside Mexico City.[2] The context of this research is the behaviour of land-market pricing and supply in three Mexican medium- to large-sized cities: Morelia (500,000 inhabitants); Ciudad Juárez (1,000,000); and Guadalajara (2,500,000). In all three cities access to land is expensive and, therefore, illegal mechanisms to gain access have evolved. Yet, whether land is acquired illegally or not, it is recognized that the land is already substantially commodified and may in certain cases have become a form of investment for all classes of the population. When invasions occur on private land, some form of payment to the owners is usually arranged through negotiation or government intervention. For invasion on government land a per plot cost is commonly paid after some period. In the case of *ejido* lands there is a cost of the land paid to the *ejidatario* or to a promoter or agent. And, in Morelia, the state-level Human Settlements agency that carries out the regularization process charges fees for the services, although these are scaled to the ability to pay. However, it is important to note that, although long-term real price increases have been in the order of 300–400 per cent since the 1950s, it can be argued that buying land in irregular settlements continues to offer a series of "progressive" cost arrangements that facilitate land access (Ward et al. 1993).

The discussion below examines two methodological issues: (a) the establishment of land-price trends over a long period; and (b) estimation of the sources of land supply. For price information, a mixed sourcing technique is described.[3] For sources of land supply, an estimating model is presented.

Methodology issues

From a neoclassical economic viewpoint, it should be possible to explain urban land-market behaviour in straightforward terms (Mills & Hamilton 1989). From an institutional economics viewpoint, urban land-market behaviour should reflect the result of government intervention to ameliorate certain aspects of market failure (Goldberg & Chinloy 1984). From a progressive economics viewpoint, urban land markets should reflect the mechanisms required for the commodification of land to meet the needs of the dominant mode of economic production (Baross & van der Linden 1990, Ward & Macoloo 1992, Topalov 1984). In order to test or examine a particular viewpoint, information on price and the spatial distribution of price is required.

The methodological issues of data collection can be grouped as follows: coverage, time series, conversion to constant prices, reliability, comparability, and the appropriate spatial unit of analysis. In this chapter each of these issues will be addressed, although it is not the intention to resolve all the problems associated with their use, particularly at the micro-level. Instead, a distinction will be drawn between how data are collected and presented at the city scale and at the settlement level.

Coverage

The techniques for price-data and size-estimation assembly described here are attempts to construct data sets for an *entire* city (or central city, plus adjacent city areas). This requires a different approach to that used when working in targeted areas of a city such as low-income neighbourhoods.[4] The establishment of prices for an entire city, or a large area, requires a mixed approach whereby different sources of information need to be knitted together and adjusted to establish an acceptable picture of price transactions.

To establish a realistic understanding of the land market a balanced sample frame is needed. The major subareas of a city can be identified in spatial, socio-economic, functional, and cultural–historic terms. In Guadalajara the city has four main sectors that relate to the compass points.[5] These are convenient for designing the sample frame. However, the areas are quite large and contain many diverse neighbourhoods. A cultural-historical approach was therefore considered to be more useful. This approach allocates neighbourhoods (*colonias* or *barrios*) by the date of development and their significance in the urbanization process. In Morelia, the entire central city area is a UN-designated Historic Human Settlements District. In this case, the city can be viewed as having two distinct functional parts, the old centre and the suburban ring, as well as four spatial sectors that follow the compass. In Juárez, the opening of the Americas free bridge to El Paso, Texas, promoted the development of many new neighbourhoods east of the bridge. Such "dating" of major public investments is one way to structure the data analysis process.

In each of the cities studied the basic spatial area is the neighbourhood (*colonia*, *barrio* or a group of subdivisions) and the basic unit of analysis is the cost per square metre of land. However, the reporting units for various sources differ. Newspaper advertisements generally cite the plot's neighbourhood location. The cadastre has its own spatial unit, as does the Mexican census. Therefore, some matching of these spatial units must be done. For this research the neighbourhood unit, as established by the municipal or state planning agency, was used. The neighbourhood boundary maps from the government agencies were acquired and followed. Adopting one agency's boundaries meant decomposing some cadastral areas into neighbourhoods, determining some neighbourhood boundaries from street addresses in newspaper advertisements, and assigning neighbourhood names to subdivision tracts.

For each city, an electronic map of the major street networks and all the neighbourhoods was constructed using a computer mapping program.[6] The neighbourhood boundaries used were taken from official state planning agency maps. This desktop mapping tool allows for the joining of ordinal data files with geographic files, thus providing for spatial analysis to be conducted and thematic maps to be constructed (Dueker 1987, Levine & Landis 1989).

Mixed sourcing

The approach taken in this study, referred to as "mixed sourcing", uses information from various sources to piece together urban land-market data. The two basic sources of information are documents (files) and field interviews (surveys and focused conversations). In this case the document sources utilized fall into three categories: (a) government data files; (b) newspaper commercial advertisements; and (c) records of private appraisers (*valuadores*). The data obtained from each category are used in two ways: as primary information, and as a gauge from which to check the accuracy of other data sources. Since no single source provides both accuracy and spatial coverage, combining a set of sources can be an acceptable estimation technique (Dowall 1991a). A discussion of each category is presented below with a critique of their its strengths and weaknesses for the analysis of land-market data. Documentary sources are presented first.

Documentary data sources

Government files

The types of government files included here are those that can be accessed at the state level or below. At the state and local level five data sources were utilized: cadastral maps (*catastro público*); subdivision records; tenure and regularization records for irregular settlements; projects of state housing and settlement agencies; and territorial reserve acquisition projects. Certain files of federally operated programmes were obtained at regional offices, including social-housing operations as well as the land-regularization programmes.[7]

Catastro público

The *catastro público* (the mechanism that collects and distributes property taxes to the municipalities) exists in some form in each Mexican state. The published cadastral maps normally provide near complete coverage of an entire city (including areas where there are irregular settlements) as well as assessment values per square metre on the block face. The *catastro* reporting zones (containing a number of neighbourhoods) are usually sequentially numbered according to the date of urbanization. This means that the lower-numbered areas are older sections of the city and the higher-numbered are newer areas. In Guadalajara and Morelia, the *catastro* areas tend to be numbered in a circular fashion, following the pattern of circular expansion from the centre over time. In Juárez, the *catastro* areas are smaller and tend to replicate the census areas.

The major research problem in making use of this data source is that, in many cases, *catastro* data are undervalued and based on various political dynamics within the city. However, the data are not uniformly undervalued. For example, a neighbourhood where unionized workers live may be given special preference in order to secure their voting blocks at election time. Newer subdivisions, developed for social credit housing, will generally reflect less of a distortion with market prices because it is relatively easier to establish the production and selling costs of these subdivisions. The non-uniform nature of the *catastro*, while problematic, can be useful if an acceptable estimate of the variation between neighbourhoods can be established. This can be achieved only on a city-by-city basis, as political manipulation and the degree of rationality will vary. In Guadalajara, the upper-middle-class neighbourhood of Providencia, as a whole, has an assessed tax rate above its actual value, while a nearby neighbourhood of Arco Providencia is levied rates below the market value.[8] In Morelia, patterns of "political taxation" are visible, with lower assessments appearing in well organized areas with strong union representation. In Juárez, nearly all the neighbourhoods represented by a leading opposition social movement, the CDP (Comité de Defensa Popular), had assessments about three times below market value. With this in mind, ranges of variance can be estimated and applied as required.

If the *catastro* is a political as well as a fiscal document, we should observe differences in relation to social class. In this research, the neighbourhood is used as the social class unit.[9] This contention holds true for Guadalajara and Morelia. In Morelia, the poor and lower-working-class neighbourhoods exhibit valuations at about 50 per cent of the advertised newspaper price. For working-class and lower-middle-income neighbourhoods, the differences are 25 per cent. For middle- and upper-class neighbourhoods, the differences are ± 15 per cent. In Juárez the most recent *catastro* valuation (1990–91) of upper-income neighbourhoods has a 10 per cent or less variance from market value.

Subdivision records

Subdivision records provide information on the amount of urban land being developed by the private sector over time. These records are useful in determining the private sector's contribution to the total land supply, spatial preference, size of a typical project in terms of total area, number of lots, and size of lots. These files can serve as a useful reflection of the influence of government regulations on the local land supply and of the demand for housing in the formal market. By comparing the number of subdivisions registered with changes in state and local development codes, the impact of public regulations can be clarified. Simple lot counts on an annual basis produced is a gauge of supply. Mexican subdivision regulations provide for a range of subdivision types. Guadalajara, Juárez and Morelia have luxury middle and popular (working class). Registered subdivision plans (plats) are repositories of data for various aspects of urban analysis. For example, plot sizes are provided as well as the number of lots, the developer's name, and sometimes the initial asking price. Moreover, the plans are spatially specific, allowing one to track urban growth generated by the private sector.

Regularization

Mexico has a long-established policy of land tenure regularization that began near Mexico City in the 1940s. Actual application depends on the original tenure conditions of the irregularly occupied land. Thus, if an irregular settlement is on federal land, the regularization process is carried out by a federal agency. Irregular settlements on private or state land are dealt with by a state agency. In either case, records relating to the amount of land, the prices and costs, and the location are kept by these agencies. These are not regularly reported and are not in the public domain, so that information must be obtained through local offices. For federal procedures, charges are levied for land titles, and valuations are reported. Examination of these records is useful in determining the amounts of land being transformed by the irregular sector as well as the value of the land made available by the irregular sector. In Guadalajara, the city has a special human settlements department that carries out the functions of providing infrastructure to regularized neighbourhoods. Various files contain data on the development of irregular settlements including the year of settlement, lot size and type of infrastructure improvements. In the State of Michoacán there has been a major programme to acquire territorial reserves in the larger cities. These reserves, mostly *ejido* lands, constitute the major areas of future urbanization. The records on the prices paid, the amount of land purchased, coupled with recent history of land-invasion sites provide the basis for establishing rates of transformation on the periphery.

Newspapers

Local newspapers are the major source of information for the research in Juárez, Morelia and Guadalajara. There are two key methodological issues. The first is to decide what pieces of information from the advertisements are to be extracted. Commonly, land sales in local newspapers contain a number of variables (e.g. size, location, services) on the land market other than the land price, but rarely is this information presented in a consistent way. Examples include data on plot characteristics, terms and conditions of sale, and, occasionally, details of the owner (whether a company or individual). The second issue is to decide the base year and the most suitable price index with which to adjust the asking price. This research uses only residential plots (see also Ward et al., this volume). The anticipated sample frame was a minimum of three plots per neighbourhood for years calculated to fall two years before and after the presidential elections. In this case the sample years were 1968, 1972, 1974, 1978, 1980, 1984, 1986 and 1990. In no city was it possible to achieve the anticipated sample frame. In the Mexican context, more land is put on the market by private owners in the late autumn and spring than in other months. This appears to be a culturally determined supply cycle based upon the need for holiday funds. Therefore, reading the newspapers from November–December and April–May yielded a larger data set from which to sample.

People generally settle for less money than they advertise for, and the prices represent market offers, not transactions. Thus, in the true sense, newspaper *prices* are not proper reflections of plot *value*. They reflect the sum of value, profit and various costs related to the sale (commissions and income tax).[10] The key statistic sought is variance (or estimate of variance) from advertised to transaction price. In order to estimate the degree of variance a second data source of transaction price is desirable. In the Morelia case, data from private property appraiser files were used. Newspaper prices were paired with property appraiser prices for as many neighbourhoods as possible and for as many years as possible; then the variances were stratified by economic type of neighbourhood (poor, working class, middle class, and above middle class). This allows some discriminate analysis of variance by economic class. In Morelia, the variance between newspapers and property appraisers for working-class neighbourhoods is 5–8 per cent, and for middle-class neighbourhoods it is 15–20 per cent.

Long-term trends indicate the real prices faced by the consumer. In Guadalajara, newspaper data, adjusted for inflation, show that the real price per square metre more than tripled over a 40-year period (Siembieda 1991). These prices are for the city as a whole and reflect stronger price rises in middle- and upperclass neighbourhoods. Also the data do not reflect the market reality that in Mexico the wage rates have been centrally controlled and thus do not move in concert with inflation.

Private appraisers

Private property appraisers (*valuadores*) have files of actual land transactions and of appraisals generally conducted under contract to individuals or banks. Access to these files is possible only via the strong "recommendation" of personal contacts and colleagues. In the case of Morelia, the president of the state appraisers' association served to "recommend" the project to a small group of appraisers.

Appraiser files usually do not cover the entire city, and the number of appraisals conducted in any one year varies. Therefore, while the information is more precise, there are fewer transactions over a long period of time. A benefit of appraiser files is that they can include transactions that occurred many years ago. This type of data may not be available from any other "neutral" source and represents an important data pool in smaller cities, such as Morelia, where public and newspaper records from before 1970 are scarce and not representative of land-market transactions at the time.

There are many ways to use property appraisers. First, the personal files of appraisers are useful sources of contextual information in themselves. A second, and more important use, is to check and adjust data assembled from other sources (i.e. newspapers, government records). In Morelia and Guadalajara the difference between the newspaper advertisements and the appraiser files was 10–12 per cent for working-class neighbourhoods and 20–25 per cent for middle-class neighbourhoods. Such marked differences between the "asking" and "transaction" prices require explanation that can only be facilitated by the appraiser. This can also provide useful insights into the structure and performance of social groups in the market. Suggested reasons for the difference in prices were that middle-class plot purchasers tend to test the upper limits of the market more than the working class, whose expectations of value may be set differently. Another contributing factor is that the tax structure tends to place a smaller burden on lower-priced houses than on higher-priced houses. This reflects a more general Mexican policy approach of charging more for urban services in upper-class areas than in poor and working-class areas.

A third use for appraisers is to establish a sense of what influences market prices. In this research appraisers were also asked to explain the forces leading the urbanization process in various sectors of the city and to rationalize the local cadastral procedures. In the case of Morelia, a leading factor in rising prices was the movement of professionals and business people out of Mexico City after the 1985 earthquake. Sharp pressure on a limited supply of upper- and middle-class subdivisions appears to have created residential land costs that at times exceed US$115 per square metre. As many appraisers will have been involved in land-market transactions for many years and will possess an intimate knowledge of discrete segments of the market, a fourth use can be to make estimates for neighbourhoods that have few transactions established from other sources. This "fills in" the holes in a long-term data set.

Problems with appraisers as data sources
Data sets of the type described always have problems of comparability between and among units of analysis. While the square metre of land is a good unit to work with, it is not the best theoretical unit. After all, people consume (occupy) a plot and not a single square metre. The best unit would probably be a minimum plot size, say, $150 \, m^2$. A further problem emerges because most data sources, appraiser information included, do not directly reveal the level of urban services provided on a plot. This problem is less acute with data for subdivisions built for middle- and upper-class use, which almost always have complete urban services. However, in the case of plots in irregular settlements, some "progressive" government projects and the occasional private subdivision services are installed piecemeal. Without a precise knowledge of the timing of this service acquisition, it is difficult to assess the value-added effect of urbanization on land prices. As such, it becomes a matter of individual assessment to determine whether the degree to which the installation of urban services has contributed to valorization or whether a favourable location, difficulties in expanding supply, and changes in demand have been more important contributors to change.

Lastly, it has already been noted that land prices recorded from the newspaper surveys and from the appraisers' files may vary considerably (see above).

It would also appear that this difference is not constant over time. Moreover, this would appear to be closely related to the performance of the economy and the stability of local currency. For Morelia, in 1975, when inflation was low, the difference between land prices in the newspapers and private appraisal files was less then 5 per cent. This tells us that there was very little negotiation occurring between offer and transaction price. However, by 1990, the difference between newspaper and appraiser files had increased to about 10 per cent. This range can be explained by a combination of currency values, higher personal income taxes, and the influence of real estate brokerage fees that were not prevalent in the 1970s. While appraiser files offer a useful source of land-price data, the ability to use these data interchangeably with information collected from different sources appears to be limited. In the next section an examination is presented of direct information sources.

Direct methods of data collection

Pricing in irregular and regular settlements

For some researchers collecting land-price and supply information from direct sources, the households themselves, represents an alternative data source. In the case of the present study, however, collecting household data was considered as complementary to the main survey structure. One reason for this was the wish to contribute to the land-policy debate that has focused on the cost of land in irregular versus regular settlements. This debate may be approached from two angles. First, there are those who consider that for the very poor any amount paid for land may be or is too much. Secondly, there are those who look more widely and tend to concentrate upon the social strata above the very poor who, through various mechanisms, find the means to invest in land for the purpose of long-term residence, construction and storage of wealth. It is here that I would argue that the debate on cost is most profound.

The field interviews take the form of sampling owners in each neighbourhood regarding present and past prices. Occasionally it is possible to compare this data with information from interviews with appraisers to provide a "baseline" estimate of the practical realities of pricing in local markets. It is also useful to build up a cost profile of land access or of the effects of subsequent policy on a low-income settlement, say, after regularization of land tenure. In Guadalajara, a single irregular settlement that was originally part of an *ejido* in the northeast sector and which later was regularized was examined. The method was simple: residents of each block were asked the year of plot purchase, the cost of land, and the direct costs associated with the introduction of various services. Using the data from lots sold in 1983, and adding the costs of urban services (electric, drainage, water) and title papers, it was estimated that the plot price was about 20 per cent lower than land offered on the market in lower working-class areas. This confirms a finding elsewhere in this volume that, while "progressive" land purchase can have definite cost advantages, these advantages are not consistently large (Ward et al. this volume). In this case, services and title costs amount to almost 40 per cent of total costs, and these costs are directly borne by the individual lot owner.

Estimating sources of land supply

While it may seem obvious, understanding the sources of land for urban uses is an important task. In the Mexican case the sources are private, government and communal (*ejidal*).[11] How each of these forms of land tenure have been transformed into urban uses through various distinct mechanisms is widely documented (Ward 1986, Ward et al. 1994). Yet relatively little attempt has been made to quantify this transformation. In part this is due to the difficulties with the data and the absence of a suitable model.

In terms of the data needed, the study decided that there were three important components. First, data were required on precisely how much land was owned, or controlled, under each tenure heading (private, public and *ejidal*). Secondly, where this land was located in the context of urban growth, and third, an assessment of whether or not the land was available to be urbanized (to be transformed from non-urban to urban uses). The investigation then attempted to estimate the contribution of each type of tenure to the overall supply of urban land. This was done by establishing, from government agencies, the overall spatial growth in hectares between two points in time (i.e. 1970–80). Then, using archival data on the supply of privately subdivided land to the market (see Subdivision section above), government projects and files on the regularization of irregular settlements, a percentage contribution was made. Any residual was declared to be in the irregular sector. These contributions establish elements for a model of market behaviour. In the cases of Guadalajara and Morelia approximately 60 per cent of all urban growth originated as irregular settlement areas, with the private sector contributing 30 per cent and the remainder being government and the non-reported supply factor. In addition, it has been possible to map the figures to provide an estimate of the distribution of projected land supply. The results bear out the commonly held notion of how contemporary Mexican urban growth occurs; that is, from the informal sector into the formal sector, with final integration being measured in terms of urban services and rights of private property.

The application of these data has an immediate policy use. Once a model of spatial expansion by source is estimated, it can be compared to the structure plans, such as, in Mexico, the ubiquitous Plan Director de Desarrollo Urbano, to cross-check estimates of future land needs. These plans are commonly based on estimates of urban expansion and include ambitious statements on establishing limits to growth and territorial reserves. There is often, however, a feeling that projections of population growth and future land needs are made in isolation from each other. The comparison of a land-supply model to plans is a straightforward way to examine whether land requirements have been underestimated or overestimated and if the spatial components of these plans meet the market reality.

Conclusion

The methodology presented here reports on an ongoing project. Many technical issues of "cleaning the data", establishing high–low estimate ranges, and testing the estimation model have not been discussed. What we now know is that this type of study can be accomplished with existing data, but that more empirical work should be undertaken to complement and to test existing theory. The task of gathering data on price, number of lots produced, years of production by sector (public, private and informal) is essential to accurate evaluation of public-policy impacts and for inductive research. Building the data sets allows for submarket analysis that can more precisely examine relationships between such variables as infrastructure investment and value added (*plusvalia*), social class and price stability, and equity issues of taxing and pricing of urban services.

Long-term data sets also allow for examination of the impact of exogenous events such as the external debt crises on sectors of the land and housing markets (as Jones et al. 1993). Initial analysis in Guadalajara indicates that working-class neighbourhoods are less affected by exogenous variables, at least in price terms, than are middle- and upper-class neighbourhoods. In Juárez, the expansion of the *maquiladora* industry has caused a rise in prices through the submarkets, and a spatial reorganization of land uses in proximity to the new *maquiladora* industrial parks.

By combining price and spatial analysis, other urbanization phenomena may be identified. In all of the study cities, government-financed (social credit mortgage) housing projects tend to produce a "halo" of irregular settlements at their edges (i.e. around the adjacent periphery). This is not unique to Mexico and has been reported in many other countries. However, the impact of this process is to establish zones of transition around government housing projects. These zones create their own submarkets of supply and price and, over time, absorb public infrastructure in locations where such uses were never planned or authorized as part of long-term public works programmes. In Guadalajara, a comparison of the lot sizes of government-sponsored social subdivisions and those of irregular settlement demonstrate that the consumer receives more land for less money in the irregular sector. Clearly, the consumer getting more for less enhances the rationale for irregular settlement.

With the new worldwide interest in improved urban management, there is a greater need for good long-term data about land-market behaviour and spatial development. In many Mexican states there are state agencies that support land and housing projects. These agencies are perfectly capable of utilizing to good effect the data made available to them – as can NGOs working in the urban sector. The methods presented in this chapter can be used by any group, usually at low cost. The key, however, is to develop a systematic approach that allows comparability and replicability, and to embrace as many sources as possible in order to build up a complete data "picture" of land and housing market performance.

Notes

1. If the question of what contributes to rising land cost is approached from a commoditization perspective, the rise in price would be attributed to the penetration of capital into the land-production sector, causing industrial modes of production to articulate the price structure. If this price rise is approached from a demand perspective, the price structure reflects the value occupants place on the location and services attributed to a particular location and on occupants' ability to finance these choices through individual and/or government sources.
2. Studies of Mexico City dominate the Mexican urbanization literature. There are few studies that attempt to determine if Mexico City represents the general case for the country or simply the general case for "mega-cities". By examining smaller cities various exposed theories can be examined and tested.
3. In the Mexico research the initial objective was to establish a 30-year data set (1960–90). Because of the difficulty in gathering data for the 1960s, the data set was shortened to 1970–90, or four six-year presidential terms.
4. Selected areas require a much finer-grain approach to price information because they are sensitive to local externalities such as location of public investment (schools) and commercial centres.
5. The major sectors of Guadalajara are Libertad (the northeast), Reforma (the southeast), Hidalgo (the northwest), and Juarez (the southwest).
6. In this case Atlas*Draw, a program that allows digitizing longitude and latitude, was used to construct the mapping bases: real co-ordinate geographic files. These files were then imported into Atlas*Pro, a program that allows the construction of database files to be matched to geographic files. With these files, thematic maps of the data sets can be made for analysis and presentation. The programs mentioned above are not true geographic information systems but are adequate for this type of work. See Dowall (1991a) for further discussion of this procedure.
7. The primary Mexican social housing programme is INFONAVIT, a national housing trust financed through employer contributions. Project costs in terms of land parcels and costs are available through agency reports. However, these reports are not annual and INFONAVIT does not make land acquisitions or develop sites every year. The primary progressive housing programme is FONHAPO, which provides funds for infrastructure. Various reports are available for this programme. The principal federal land tenure programme is CoRett, which documents costs of regularization and provides an estimation of value at the time the official papers are transferred to the occupant.
8. The analysis is based on interview data from local appraisers and reflects the private appraiser records.
9. It is noted that all neighbourhoods are not entirely homogenous by social class. Therefore, there will be some variance in using the neighbourhood as a unit of analysis.
10. The actual income tax (*impuesto sobre la renta*) varies according to length of tenure, the basis of cost, and the selling price. Since one can assume that every seller faces the same demand curve, the variance is attenuated by actual market forces.
11. The *ejido* system of communal ownership established during the 1930s was changed in January 1992 to allow private ownership rights to be awarded to the *ejiditarios* (members of the local

farming co-operative). Although the federal regulations on the exact nature of these changes in tenure have not been specified, the change means that this class of land-ownership will change from communal to private. For urban areas this is not as drastic as it may first appear. Since 1971, changes in the constitution have allowed the state to declare certain *ejido* areas as "urban zones", allowing for their expropriation.

CHAPTER TWELVE

Measuring residential land-price changes and affordability

Peter M. Ward, Edith Jiménez, Gareth Jones

Introduction

In this chapter our aim is to outline a research strategy that we developed in order to investigate residential land prices in three Mexican cities for the period 1974–90.[1] In the light of price trends observed, we also examine the relative affordability of land acquisition by lower-income groups since the late 1970s. This represents one important dimension of the major research project upon which we have been engaged since 1989 (Ward 1989b, see note 1). Elsewhere in this volume we have included separate discussions relating to other dimensions, namely the rôle of principal land-development actors in creating segmented land markets (Ch. 7), and the valorization impact of public policy on land prices, making use of what we have termed "snapshot" analysis (Ch. 15).

In developing the research strategy described here, we were concerned to address several contentious issues that confront contemporary land-price research as well as the social impact of recession and austerity programmes on the poor. Specifically, we wanted to identify whether the cost of land had risen inexorably over time as some analysts would have us believe. Are changing costs putting access to land beyond the reach of the majority? How did the economic recession that Mexico experienced during the 1980s shape land prices and affordability? Although in themselves relatively straightforward questions, we will demonstrate that they are not easily resolved, but in a relatively short chapter such as this we cannot do justice to a full description of our findings nor can we offer a complete account of the methodology used to gather and analyze our data.[2] Here our concern is twofold: first, to identify specific techniques we used in order to collect and analyze data. This will provide examples of several of the sources discussed by Siembieda in Chapter 11. Secondly, to describe the changes in residential land prices that appear to have taken place in recent years, and to identify whether this has had an adverse outcome in terms of the ability of low-income groups to acquire land and housing. The question of evaluating affordability also invokes major data-handling issues and difficulties that we propose to discuss in detail.

Although the examples upon which we draw are exclusively the Mexican cities in which we worked, we are confident that many of the methods we use are replicable in other contexts. Indeed, other counterpart studies are being conducted by independent research groups working with a similar methodology in India and Kenya, and it is anticipated that ultimately this will allow us to make an assessment of the extent to which one can generalize about land-price trends in different cultural contexts.[3]

Fieldwork was undertaken over two years in three intermediate-sized industrial cities (Puebla, Querétaro and Toluca). Each city has a modern industrial base, has experienced rapid expansion since the 1960s, is located in the central region of the country and has developed in close association with the Metropolitan Area of Mexico City. Moreover, each has a segmented residential land market structure that is dominated by the private sector (see García & Jiménez, this volume). All three cities possess large tracts of community lands established largely during the 1920s and 1930s (*ejidos*) over which peasant communities have agricultural use rights. Individual peasant farmers (*ejidatarios*) are not allowed to sell their land parcels, although they can pass the land on to their heirs. However, although theoretically inalienable, these lands are regularly sold off either by individual *ejidatarios* or by their elected leaders (Ward 1986: 74– 5, Varley 1985c). In many cities throughout Mexico *ejidal* land has provided the principal medium through which the demand for land for self-help housing has been met. On occasions, upper- and middle-income groups have also managed to disestablish these lands for private residential housing estates and for second-home development, but this has usually required presidential or gubernatorial sleight of hand, since formal privatization of part of an *ejido* involves a lengthy bureaucratic process and has to be considered to be in the public interest (Varley 1985b).[4] While its political power has declined somewhat in recent years, the peasant-sector confederation (CNC) continues to be a major force within the Institutionalised Revolutionary Party (PRI), which has governed Mexico (at the federal level) continuously for more than 60 years. Since the 1940s the PRIs influence has been sustained through incorporation of labour, peasant and "popular" worker groups as separate confederations within the party structure.[5] As we shall explain later, this relative political weight and level of organization has an important influence on land prices in individual cities, further underscoring the desirability of taking a holistic or politicaleconomy approach if one is to gain an adequate understanding of land-market behaviour.

One of our principal tasks during fieldwork was to analyze the structure and evolution of the land market for residential purposes among upper-, middle-, and lower-income groups. We identified who the principal agents involved in urban real estate were, as well as their composition, rationale and activities, and the legal and illegal ways in which they sought to develop land (see García & Jiménez, this volume). We examined the organization and impact of local and

160

state governments and the overall impact of public-sector interventions on the operations and dynamics of urban land markets (Ward 1989b, Jones et al. this volume). This included interventions such as the authorizations of residential subdivisions, the effects of state-led housing policies, the provision of urban infrastructure, the legalization of "clouded" (illegal) landholdings, and the whole organization of the property and land taxation records in each city. Through our extensive site visits to all neighbourhoods in the city and detailed interviews with local residents and leaders in some low-income settlements, we were able to develop insights about the nature of the residential land-development process from the "top down" and from the "bottom up" – a research strategy that had rewarded us well in our earlier work (Gilbert & Ward 1985, Jones 1991a).

The land-price information presented in this chapter derives from two principal sources. First, for the period 1974–89 we collected (vacant) plot prices as advertised in the major local newspapers for settlements we had visited and whose socio-economic composition and development history were known to us. These settlements were distributed throughout each city. This source provided us with a large number of separate readings in each city (2,622 in Puebla, 1,504 in Querétaro, and 1,061 in Toluca). The principal local newspaper was consulted for every third month (starting March), and readings were taken for the first and third week in order to avoid multiple recording of same plot. Fewer advertisements in Toluca required us to expand the sample by an additional four months. Advertisements almost always offered the following information: location (an identifiable settlement rather than "near to"); size of plot; the total land price or land price in square metres; and details of telephone number and/or address. If one of these elements was absent, then the reading was ignored. We also set aside readings for plots larger than 1,250 m^2, since these may have represented land parcels for future subdivision rather than actual house plots. Given that we were dealing with vacant plots without any construction, most settlements generated their largest number of readings in the early years after their coming onto the market. Although readings for vacant plots in those settlements also occurred several years later (by which time other externalities would influence the asking price (services, location, cachet, etc.), these readings were few and far between, and their inclusion would not distort the overall analysis we offer.

As Siembieda notes in Chapter 11, there are several potential problems with this type of data source. Newspaper advertisements are the normal medium for land sales through the formal market (i.e. for legally authorized subdivisions), but land availability in irregular settlements is passed on by word of mouth, through personal visits, etc. Therefore the data are partial and cover predominantly middle- and upper-income residential land. Moreover, they are *bid* prices, not *sale* prices; and in using them we have to make the assumption that the ratio of sale to bid price remains approximately the same over time and that the trend we subsequently track reflects changes in average prices and is not heavily distorted by more effective haggling to bring the actual price down in certain locations or at certain times. Siembieda's comparison of advertised land prices and independent assessors' valuations (this volume, p. 158) suggests that an overbid of 10–12 per cent and 25 per cent may occur for lower-income and middle-income residential districts, respectively. Perló reports that the variation between the asking price and the agreed sale price of property was between 5.5 and 15 per cent in Mexico City (this volume, p. 153). Moreover, during periods of low inflation, the price differential between the two sources is much narrower (Siembieda, this volume).[6] In none of the cities in which we worked was it usual for prices to be advertised in US dollars. Only in border cities, such as Tijuana, Ensenada and El Rosario, and occasionally in Mexico City, is it common to find house- and land-prices being advertised in dollars. This might affect land-price trends since rapid inflation requires regular resetting of prices when land is advertised in *pesos*, whereas the stability of the perceived dollar price might generate less frequent adjustments and lower volatility and variability in price-setting. It would be interesting to compare trends in a city in which prices are regularly set in dollars, in order to make an assessment of the independent effect that this may have on overall price trends (see also note 6). However, in our studies we were not successful in gaining access to independent assessors' files, so we were obliged to assume that the ratio of bid-price to sale-price was constant throughout.

Another major data problem related to newspaper advertisements is the fact that plots vary, particularly in their size, aspect, intra-settlement location, and the externalities they enjoy, thereby making direct comparison of unitary land prices difficult or inappropriate. In Mexico, however, this last caveat is not usually a major problem, since individual developments usually offer one "standard"-size plot, and anyone wanting larger plots would usually have to purchase two adjacent plots, or the whole block (both are relatively rare, but see also Varley, this volume, for a discussion of some of the permutations relating to plot or house "holding").[7] Also, in order to minimize the effects of externalities such as those mentioned above, we concentrated our readings around the initial phase of settlement commercialization, when those externalities would be broadly similar for all plots. But if "apples" are not to be compared to "pears", it is imperative that the researcher have a good working knowledge of all the residential areas in the city in terms of their class composition, periods of initial expansion and most rapid commercialization, their mode of land-development process, and so on.

Partly in order to overcome the bias towards middle- and upper-income subdivisions expressed though newspaper advertisements, we gathered data from a second principal source – household questionnaires in low-income settlements that sought general socio-economic information as well as details about the costs of their individual land purchase, and, where applicable, follow-on costs associated with subsequent plot servicing, securing permits and authorizations, the regularization (legalisation of "clouded" title), and so on. Our original intention was also to apply questionnaires to middle-income households, but we quickly discovered that the response rate was very poor. The need to talk into door phones meant that we were much more easily dismissed than where we had established face-to-face contact.[8] Culturally, too, middle-income households appear to find it easier to refuse co-operation with interviewers who, socio-economically, are likely to be their peers, than do poorer people who are less likely to see themselves as social equals. Certainly, the warm response that most researchers receive from most low-income households is an often noted feature among social scientists working in Latin America (Gilbert & Ward 1985). But it does mean, of course, that alternative strategies must be adopted in order to gather information from middle- and upper-income households. Although not widely used in the context of land-price research, telephone and/or postal surveys might represent a rewarding alternative, provided that the number of questions is kept to a minimum (Johnston 1989).

Seventeen settlements were surveyed across the three cities, and we sought to survey at least 50 owner households in each neighbourhood, all of whom had bought a vacant plot without any construction on it. Most (but not all) would have arrived in the period soon after the settlement's development, but the manner of acquisition could vary, and, while most bought from the original land developer or *ejidatario*, occasionally the purchase was made by buying out from a former non-resident "owner" (called a *traspaso* in Mexico). Thus, albeit unwittingly, we were in large part able to "anchor" our analyses to what Varley (this volume) identifies as "house holders", i.e. persons with a common understanding about their relationship to the house and to the land acquisition process. But although before fieldwork we had thought through the need to ensure that our interviews were targeted at genuine "owners" (de facto or de *jure*) at the moment they bought a vacant plot of residential land, at the time, we did not have the benefit of Varley's helpful identification of the diversity of plot-holding, which future analysts are advised to consult carefully. Application of the questionnaire was undertaken by the authors, and the selection of households within each settlement was undertaken randomly according to standard procedures. The settlements included both *ejidal* and non-*ejidal* subdivisions, as well as two subdivisions that had been developed privately and targeted at better-off working class and middle-class groups (Albarrán in Toluca and Satélite in Puebla [hence the higher average plot prices in these two settlements, which are displayed below in Tables 12.2 and 12.3]).

Thus a key element of our survey strategy was to elicit "hard" data about the full array of costs associated with various stages and procedures whereby a plot is acquired – even where this is done illegally. An important objective was to maximize the number of readings both spatially and across time in order for meaningful conclusions to be drawn about overall trends, and in order to identify important differences between various types of land development in what we consider a single, but segmented, land market (see also Fitzwilliam 1991). Another objective was to maximise the different sources used, although in our case we were unsuccessful in our attempt to gain access to independent assessors' archives, and neither the cadastral nor property registers offered us information that we felt we could use satisfactorily (Amitabh, Siembieda, this volume). Therefore, we focused on newspaper advertisements and the household survey.[9]

Of course, these data were not consolidated into a single data set, but were aggregated and analyzed only according to the particular segment of the land market of which they formed a part.[10] A series of controls was established in order to ensure comparability between the various types of settlements. The latter were usually disaggregated by resident income group and by type of land development (private subdivision or *ejidal* land). Land prices were converted to constant *pesos* using the consumer price index, as were other fees and regularization charges. The first half of the following analysis, therefore, is a systematic analysis of changing real land-acquisition costs for different income levels in each city as well as a comparison of aggregated costs for similar types of low-income settlement across the three cities.

Analyzing land-price trends in Mexico

The existing literature on land-price trends in developing countries argues almost exclusively that land prices are rising. For example, Evers (1976), when writing about Asian cities, noted that population increase and other social processes have intensified the pressure on urban land and led, in the 1970s, to a wave of land speculation and spiralling land prices. This skyrocketing of prices is widely perceived to be a normal consequence of market economies, including those of Latin America (Geisse & Sabatini 1982: 162). In São Paulo land prices appear to have increased dramatically between 1968 and 1974 (Haddad 1982). It is certainly true that nominal land prices have risen in Latin American cities, but whether this also represents an increase in real terms, allowing for the effect of inflation, is not always made clear. Indeed, there are major methodological difficulties associated with many of the studies that inform this received wisdom. Often the methods adopted have been confused and imprecise. "Apples" are compared with "pears", most usually by taking areas whose social composition, spatial location at the time of formation, and/or mode of land development are entirely different. The selected time horizons are often too short to pick out genuine trends or are chosen selectively in order to illustrate a priori conclusions. Some researchers have even persisted in analyzing nominal (as against real) prices that take no account of inflation (see Jones 1991a: 131–8 for a detailed review of these shortcomings). In short, much of the body of existing research is sloppy, especially given the complexities associated with accurate land- and property-price investigation, which requires the researcher to pick a cautious path through a statistical minefield that otherwise may explode into spurious conclusions (Fitzwilliam 1991).

Some Mexican researchers have been particularly suspect in this respect. We recalculated Legoretta's (1984) data on nominal (unadjusted) land prices for a range of petroleum cities as well as Castañeda's (1988) data for Mexico City peripheral areas. In contrast to the arguments of each author for a sharp rise in land prices, our recalculations produced a broad "flatness" and even a significant decline in land-price trends over time that totally belie the pattern and conclusions that they drew (Jones 1991a: 140). Legoretta argues that land prices have risen in smaller Mexican cities and that this is due to the intervention of increasingly sophisticated social agents to appropriate land rent. Our studies also contradict this latter point, but that is not an issue for resolution in this chapter. Here our concern is to demonstrate the facts which indicate, in real terms, that land prices have not witnessed a dramatic increase – not even in the rapidly expanding petroleum cities of southern Mexico nor in the Metropolitan Area of Mexico City (see also Hiernaux 1991a, Gilbert & Varley 1991: 93).[11]

Similarly, earlier work by one of us (in Gilbert & Ward 1985), suggested that, although land prices in three Latin American cities appeared to be rising in real terms, the increase was not dramatic. Indeed, the evidence for "tightening" land markets was largely circumstantial, and was best illustrated by other variables, such as declining plot size and by delayed entry into ownership, rather than by a marked rise in the unitary price of land. In that work we expressed some surprise that declining supply was not translated into rising prices, as we had expected and as received wisdom would have had us believe. We suggested that hidden variables, market imperfections in price-setting, and other considerations probably accounted for the lack of a sharp upward trend in prices, given the growing scarcity of land. Whatever the cause, we urged caution not to jump to conclusions about the inevitability of land-price increases. Very recently we have begun to observe the beginnings of a broader acceptance that land prices may be falling in real terms (Gilbert 1991a, Dowall & Leaf 1991). Moreover, it is now recognized that periods of economic recession and austerity can have a sharp negative impact on land prices. Thus, while during certain phases of economic buoyancy and expansion prices may be observed to rise appreciably, it is important to take a sufficiently long-term perspective if the overall trend is to be accurately discerned. If cut-off points are inappropriately drawn or the time span is too short, then one may get a misleading impression about the trend and about the direction in which real prices are actually moving. We believe that a 15-year period is just about long enough for us to begin to gauge the pattern of land-price trends in these three cities, and our data suggest several important findings.

First, it would appear that since 1974 land values have followed a broadly cyclical path. The cost of land rose steadily in the late 1970s, peaked early in the 1980s, and declined sharply thereafter. The data presented in Figures 12.1a–12.1c show the newspaper-advertised average plot prices for middle- and upper-income settlements in each city displayed over time. Although not displayed here, the individual settlement land-price trajectories also move in a similar direction, but inevitably in these cases, the disaggregated data are less complete

(a) Puebla

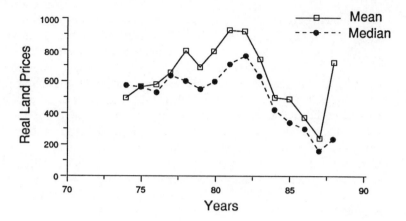

(b) Querétaro

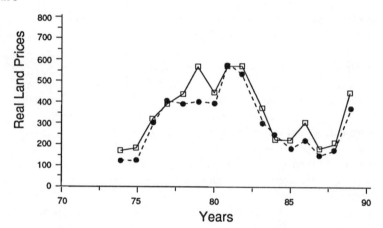

(c) Toluca

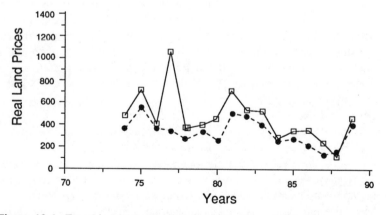

Figure 12.1 Trend in real land prices for study cities, 1974–89.

166

for the full period. There is also evidence of a sharp upturn in the late 1980s that suggests the new administration of President Salinas (1988–94) and the process of economic recovery may be leading to a resurgence of confidence and renewed buoyancy of the residential land market (see Jones et al. 1993). This cyclical pattern emerges consistently across the three cities, although Toluca also demonstrates a sharp rise in 1977, and the decline since 1981 is less pronounced. In short, our newspaper-advertised data suggest that prices in the mid-1980s were broadly similar to those of a decade earlier, with a rise and a fall in between. Similar work to our own by Siembieda (1991) in the city of Guadalajara points to a broad seven-year cyclical pattern of troughs and peaks in real land prices since the 1940s, which he tentatively links with national economic performance and the regular six-year change-around associated with the nature of fixed-term, non-renewable presidential administrations in Mexico.[12]

Secondly, the data suggest that the cyclical pattern is especially marked in middle- and upper-income subdivisions in each city, but it is also apparent when combined data curves are produced for household survey information drawn from low-income neighbourhoods such as private subdivisions and *colonias populares* (figures not reproduced here). With the important exception of Querétaro (where prices are much lower and quite erratic over time), it is also a clear feature for *ejidal* land in each city. Our specific analysis of individual low-income settlements showed considerable atomistic variation which, unsurprisingly, could best be explained in relation to local factors. But the overall trend confirms the cyclical pattern.

A third major observation is that, *prima facie*, prices in middle-income and elite subdivisions appear to be much more macro-market driven and respond more consistently in the expected direction with less likelihood of local perturbation. Illegally generated settlements show a greater inconsistency, but when the data for low-income settlements are combined, land prices also move broadly in a similar direction to the wider market. This suggests that other social factors may also determine price-fixing in irregular settlements, thereby mitigating to a certain extent the overriding effect of the wider market. These may include a lower sensitivity to price-setting by low-income residents and land agents than their more experienced middle-income and formal real estate counterparts. Also, we found evidence that non-monetary considerations enter the negotiation process relating to land transactions among the poor. Sometimes this included another good in part-exchange (a car, a gas cooker and in one a case a suit of clothes!). Also, simply knowing the vendor personally, or having a mutual friend, would result in a lower than market price being struck. Finally, the overall power and level of organization of the principal actors involved in the land-development process shapes the coherence of performance of the illegal land market. Where the *ejidal* sector is relatively strong and well represented through the CNC and in the local branch office of what used to be the Agrarian Reform Ministry, then one can expect a systematic and less atomistic application of market bidding.[13]

Space constraints do not allow us to explore in any depth the possible explanations for these trends. Suffice to mention that macro-level economic considerations set alongside the attractions of alternative investment returns relative to land appear to be paramount. Specifically, factors such as the national and regional economic buoyancy, sustained and/or rising real wages, low real interest rates, combined with the limited alternative investment opportunities during the late 1970s and early 1980s are likely to fuel investment in land and did so until the crisis hit. Thereafter, austerity, a loss of confidence, capital flight, and rising oil prices and interest rates all undermined domestic demand. This led to the decline in land prices and the dramatic slowdown in market activity. In low-income land developments the macroeconomic behaviour is also important, but here the key determinant of land-price fluctuations appears to be principally wage levels. During the austerity programmes 1982–88, wages declined (especially the statutory minimum wage) and land prices dropped accordingly. Also the continued (illegal) supply of land through the *ejidal* sector made land freely available. We will return to the implications of declining wage levels and lower land prices in our discussion of affordability later in this chapter.

Analyzing the absolute price of residential land

It is important to gauge how the absolute price of land varies both between cities and between segments of the land market. Analyzing and explaining absolute land values is likely to shed light on the determinants of prices and the extent to which these are socially derived by the interventions of different groups, or are determined by location and rent that may be derived from different land-use functions. Where absolute land values in different segments of the residential land market are sharply differentiated, then this is likely to shape the degree of socio-economic heterogeneity that exists in any given neighbourhood and the possibilities for mobility between populations in different segments of the market. Other things being equal, and in the absence of concerted state action to redress imbalances, where absolute land prices are sharply differentiated, then *segregation* between low- and middle-income groups is likely to be greater, as is intra-neighbourhood *homogeneity*. Thus far, however, few researchers have analyzed the relationship between land values and issues of urban segregation and residential mobility in less-developed countries.

In terms of elite and upper-income subdivisions, we found that absolute land prices were broadly comparable in each city, although the average cost appears to be slightly lower in Querétaro (Figs 12.1a–12.1c). As one would expect, there are important variations between settlements, which reflect a variety of factors – social cachet, distance from the city centre, and level of social mixing versus exclusivity that has evolved or been created. These variations tended to undermine any consistent pattern from emerging when we sought to map land value changes for the five time horizons mentioned earlier. In particular, the opportunity for low-income populations to acquire *ejidal* land or land in former villages now incorporated into the urban area (*pueblo* cores) has meant that high and low land-value settlements may be in close proximity to each other. Nor does land appear to be valorized over time (through urban development and state intervention), and this also reduces the expected differential between current and past peripheral land. Although land at the periphery is cheaper than that nearer the centre, it is not always markedly so. When we came to map land prices spatially in each city for different time horizons, we found that relatively low-cost land was often available at a variety of locations and not just at the periphery. Nor was the city centre consistently in the highest land-price category. In our view, the price of land is more likely to be determined socially, according to tenure, the type of development, and the social class, rather than spatially according to any distance-decay function of land-use outwards from the city centre.[14]

When the absolute prices of residential land for low-income segments of the market are examined we can observe how, somewhat paradoxically, those contexts in which low-priced land is freely available may actually *accentuate* spatial and social inequality. In Tables 12.1, 12.2 and 12.3, we show how these data may be analyzed in order to provide insights about this apparent paradox. The tables show the average (trimmed mean $\overline{Tx}$)[15] unitary price of land for each of the settlements studied, and the city average ($T\overline{x}$ bottom line) indicates that the land prices in low-income areas are roughly similar in Toluca and Puebla, as Tables 12.2 and 12.3 demonstrate, but are very much lower in Querétaro (Table 12.1). Thus the differential with middle-income land prices is more marked in the latter city. We discovered also that there is likely to be greater social heterogeneity *within* neighbourhoods in Puebla and Toluca. This has led to lower levels of spatial social segregation in these two cities than in Querétaro, where we are dealing with a highly segmented market in which the poor (and the very poor) have had relatively easy access to low-priced land, but where there is little or no possibility for mobility into the middle-income subdivisions. In Puebla and Toluca, on the other hand, that possibility of "filtering" exists, although much more likely is the process of downward "raiding" by lower middle-income households that trade off a larger plot and/or the opportunity of a higher dwelling to land ratio in an irregular and unserviced settlement than they would expect to achieve for their money in a serviced subdivision. But the greater absolute poverty and the greater distribution of poor households in Querétaro irregular settlements make plot purchase by middle-income groups virtually unthinkable (see also Ward 1993). Another factor is that Querétaro experienced an over-expansion of the middle-class residential land market which generated a greater supply of plots. This, in turn, has led to a slightly lower unitary price of land in either Puebla or Toluca, and most middle-income households are able to "shop around" for a plot they can afford; they do not need to consider "raiding" into a lower-class settlement as might their counterparts in the other two cities. This, too, intensifies the differential between the lower and upper segments of the land market.

Table 12.1 The cost of land purchase relative to incomes in Querétaro (October 1989 prices).

Settlement	T̄x plot size (mode)	Corr. size by cost	1978 constant T̄x price of 1 m² (N)	1 min. wage (1978)	1 min. wage	x̄ head household income	x̄ household income
						T̄x total square metres bought with:	
Peñuelas	323 (200)	−0.41	$71.1 (50)	8.9	4.2	7.5	11.6
Bolaños	198 (200)	−0.27	$24.2 (50)	26.0	12.3	21.1	29.0
Echeverría	160 (160)	0.10	$6.1 (47)	103.3	48.9	69.0	120.7
San José Olvera	260 (250)	−0.21	$50.0 (50)	12.6	6.0	13.4	191.1
Menchaca	493 (200 & 400)	−0.27	$23.8 (50)	26.5	12.5	21.5	33.4
Querétaro	293	−0.114	$34.7 (247)	18.2	8.6	16.2	22.8

Notes: Minimum, head and household incomes are per week.

Table 12.2 The cost of land purchase relative to incomes in Toluca (July 1990 prices).

Settlement	T̄x plot size (mode)	Corr. T̄x size by cost	1978 constant price of 1 m² (N)	1 min. wage (1978)	1 min. wage	x̄ head household income	x̄ household income
						T̄x total square metres bought with:	
Oxtotitlán	276 (200)	−0.18	$223.6 (49)	3.2	1.2	2.97	4.2
San Buenaventura	218 (200)	−0.04	$299.3 (50)	2.4	0.9	2.4	3.0
Seminario	188 (200)	−0.02	$255.0 (49)	2.8	1.10	2.1	2.6
Progreso	191 (100 & 200)	−0.02	$148.4 (15)	4.8	1.78	3.9	6.5
Universidad	518	−0.29	$162.0 (9)	4.4	1.63	5.1	7.4
Albarrán	240 (240)	0.014	$691.0 (20)	1.0	0.38	2.3	2.4
Toluca	238	−0.067	$268.0 (192)	2.7	1.0	2.5	3.3

Notes: Minimum, head and household incomes are per week.

Although Querétaro land prices are much lower for low-income settlements, the overall price increases somewhat once one takes into account the additional costs associated with regularization (legalization of clouded titles) and other costs of papers such as full titles, certificates of occupancy (*constancias*) which are given out in some *ejidal* settlements, as well as various other costs associated with state interventions (sundries and taxes). Precise details of these costs are reproduced elsewhere (Ward et al. 1993). However, notwithstanding the slight narrowing between the differentials observed, unitary land prices and plots in Querétaro remain relatively low. We explain the lower absolute cost of land in Querétaro as primarily an outcome of the historical weakness of *ejidatarios* and their allied interest groups (the CNC [see note 5]) in that city, and the relative strength of the "popular" sector (the CNOP/UNE). This balance of forces has meant that the PRI has enjoyed good and conflict-free relations with the irregular settlements, while the state and municipal governments have had far greater success in achieving land regularization and servicing programmes than has been the case in either Puebla or Toluca, where peasant groups have proven better able to resist state interventions that might undermine the land-development interests of their followers (the *ejidatarios*).

Table 12.3 The cost of land purchase relative to income in Puebla (June 1988 prices).

Settlement	T$\bar{x}$ plot size (mode)	Corr. size by cost	1978 constant T$\bar{x}$ price of 1 m² (N)	1 min. wage (1978)	1 min. wage	$\bar{x}$ head household income	$\bar{x}$ household income
				1988 prices (June)			
La Loma	271 (320)	−0.27	$167.0 (57)	4.4	1.8	2.0	2.8
Santiago Momoxpa	715 (1250)	−0.37	$440.8 (42)	16.4	6.6	10.8	14.8
Ampliación Reforma	324 (variable)	−0.17	$118.6 (35)	6.2	2.5	2.8	3.6
Villa Posada	281 (200)	−0.27	$209.0 (48)	3.5	1.4	1.8	2.6
Satélite	160 (160)	−0.18	$776.0 (49)	1.0	0.4	0.7	0.9
Coatepec	120 (120)	−0.04	$236.0 (63)	3.1	1.3	1.5	1.9
Puebla	259 (180)	−0.1	$233 (251)	3.1	1.3	1.7	2.3

Land affordability for the poor

Many of the methodological difficulties associated with the analysis of land prices and land-price trends are compounded further once one seeks to make an accurate judgment about whether land is becoming more or less affordable over time. There are several ways of representing unitary land costs relative to an ability to pay:

(a) against the minimum wage or other standard wage line;
(b) against actual wages (individual and/or household) derived from question-naire analysis;
(c) against a "basket" of basic commodities; or
(d) against price rises in other arenas (building materials, house-building cost indices, and so on).

In our analysis we decided to make an assessment against earnings, using the minimum wage and actual wages as our benchmarks.

The principal assumption built into using these (or other) bases of comparison or "benchmark comparators", is that their relative value is constant over time. Under certain conditions this is not an unreasonable assumption. Where one is dealing with a statutory minimum wage that explicitly aims to ensure a baseline subsistence income, then the value will be maintained, provided, of course, that the state regularly intervenes to adjust the minimum wage in order to protect its purchasing power. The validity of the assumption is also enhanced in less-developed countries by the fact that the profile of individual worker earnings tends to be relatively "flat" over time, since there are relatively limited opportunities for promotion, salary increments, and so on, which would significantly raise an individual's wage and purchasing power as he or she gets older. In circumstances where these assumptions apply, one may successfully measure temporal variations in the independent variable (land cost) against the stable dependent variable (salary) in order to assess changing affordability against wage rates. However, many households have more than one wage earner, and one cannot make the many assumptions about affordability measured against *household* incomes – a point to which we return below. In Mexico, enhanced earnings are more likely to accrue as a result of life-cycle changes or as adjustments are made to the household structure, both of which raise the number of potential workers (and salaries) in any given household (Roberts 1989, Chant 1991, González de la Rocha 1991).

But in Mexico, as elsewhere, recent changes undermine any assumptions that one may, in the past, have been able to make about stable real statutory wage levels. The purchasing power of the minimum wage has been downgraded by government policy (as have all wage levels) since 1982, as part of Mexico's austerity programme. There has been a 45 per cent decline in the real minimum wage since 1982, with especially sharp erosion in 1982 and 1986–87 (Figs 12.2a–12.2c). Although the minimum wage provided a more or less accurate and widely adopted baseline salary for many workers until the late 1970s, and it was adhered to by firms, this is no longer the case. Most firms today pay *more* than the statutory minimum, which is widely recognized as being well below the market rate and below the minimum required for subsistence.[16] Thus one cannot assess affordability in terms of a comparison of the units of land that the mini-mum salary would buy during the 1970s with the units it would buy in the 1980s.

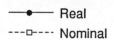

(a) Puebla

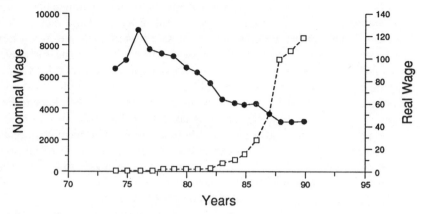

(b) Querétaro

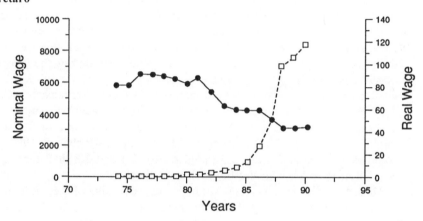

(c) Toluca

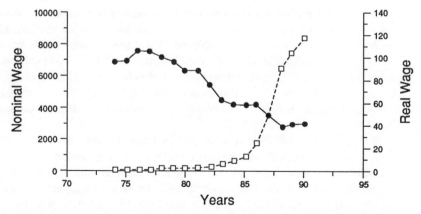

Figure 12.2 Trend in minimum wages for study cities, 1974–89.

173

Nonetheless, in our analysis we first sought to identify how much land a low-income earner could expect to have bought in terms of the real 1978 unitary price of land against the minimum wage as it was in 1978, i.e. when it was set at a realistic baseline level. This provides us with one basis for comparison between cities for the late 1970s. Secondly, we have expressed land-acquisition costs in terms of the proportion of the total head's wage and the total household income at the *moment of our survey* (between 1988 and 1990, depending on the city). "Total household income" was taken to include the earnings of the head and the spouse, second jobs, contributions from other members, rents from subletting, and so on. It does not represent the total earnings of all household members, but rather the disposable income made available to the household for consumption purposes. In this way we hope that the use of "real" (actual) wages, as well as that of the total household income, will provide us with an alternative (albeit different) criterion with which to compare purchasing power during the late 1980s. Thus, although it is now possible to compare affordability for the two broad time horizons, effective interpretation hinges on whether each of the measures accurately reflects reality. We believe that they are sufficiently close as to make comparison meaningful. In order to check this we reviewed the structure of household earnings among the poor during the late 1970s. Specifically we re-analyzed a major database (see Gilbert & Ward 1985) gathered from some 550 households across six irregular settlements in Mexico City in late 1978 and early 1979. At that time the increased ratio of the *head of household's* wage and the *total household* income over that of the statutory minimum was 1.2 and 1.6 respectively. This compares in the late 1980s with a comparable ratio of 1.5 and 2.3 in Querétaro; 2.1 and 2.8 in Toluca; and 1.4 and 1.8 in Puebla – considerably higher in all cases.[17]

Thus, if one accepts the proposition that the real value of the minimum wage in 1978 approximates the value of the head's average wage in 1988 and 1989, then one can begin to make an assessment of how affordability may have changed over time. Of course, this also assumes that expenditure patterns remained broadly similar through the 1980s and that households continue to prioritize expenditures in much the same way as before; and there is some evidence to suggest that, in order to cope with austerity, households are obliged to revise their budgets and consumption towards other basic essentials and away from land and housing costs (González de la Rocha 1991: 121). This, too, must be taken into account, but unfortunately our data do not allow us to make any weighting adjustments to take account of possible changing consumption patterns.

In Tables 12.1–12.3 we display our findings relating to land purchase for each of the settlements. In the first column after each settlement we give the average plot size in terms of the trimmed mean (see note 15) as well as the modal plot size (i.e. the most uniform plot size that a large number hold [usually the majority in Mexico]). As one may observe the modal plot sizes in low-income settlements tends to be around the 200 m^2 mark. Our data suggest that there has been *no significant reduction* in plot size purchased during the 1980s, even though this would have been one way of circumventing declining affordability (cf. Durand-Lasserve, this volume). As expected, there is a negative correlation between unit costs of land and overall plot size (column 2 of the tables), indicating that a unit of land costs less on larger plots (see Table 12.3 for Puebla), but the coefficients are not high. As was noted earlier, however, in all three cities there were marked variations in the unitary cost of land in different low-income settlements as well as in the modal plot size. This suggests that low-income residents generally have some opportunity to select cheaper settlements, or those that offer a variation in plot sizes, and which would cost less in absolute terms.

The remaining columns of Tables 12.1–12.3 contain the average cost per square metre that we discussed earlier, followed by the average (trimmed mean) amount of land that could be purchased assuming the different earning parameters already described (minimum wage, head of household's wage, and total household income). Having identified the principal assumptions and data analysis difficulties relating to affordability, we are now able to return to the original question. Has land acquisition become more costly and more difficult during the 1980s, despite the sharp decline in land prices? Taken at face value the answer would be yes: the amount of land purchased for a statutory minimum wage in 1978 compared with that of 1989–90 has declined by between one-half and two-thirds in most cases (Tables 12.1–12.3). At first glance, the data indicate a very marked deterioration in levels of affordability. But this would be grossly misleading given our earlier point that the real statutory minimum wages in 1978 and 1988–89 are no longer comparable.

We have established that a more appropriate benchmark for comparison with the *minimum* wage in 1978 is the *head's* average wage in 1988 and 1989. When the data are compared in this way, the decline in affordability is marginal, except in Puebla, where it has been cut to almost half its 1978 level. In Querétaro and Toluca, however, the amount of land purchased for one minimum weekly wage in 1978 is very similar to that acquired for one average (trimmed mean) head of household's income in 1989–90 (see Tables 12.1, 12.2). But again we must be cautious, since even in 1978 there was always a small increase in the ratio of average head's earnings over the statutory minimum (around 20 per cent according to our findings reported above). Allowing, too, for minor shifts in consumption patterns away from housing, we conclude that affordability of land purchase as informed by *real* (i.e. actual) wage levels in these two cities probably deteriorated during the 1980s by between a quarter and one-third. In Puebla it has declined by around half.

One of the ways in which households have responded to this relative decline in purchasing power is to raise the disposable income available to them – a finding, as we have noted, underscored by other researchers. Taking into account average total household incomes in 1988–89, and the much greater significance of multiple contributors in the late 1980s than a decade earlier, our data suggest that in Toluca and Querétaro the affordability of land purchase did not deteriorate significantly (see Tables 12.1–12.2). But in Puebla there was a decline of around one-third (Table 12.3). However, a caveat should be inserted here that not all households are in a position to expand their earning power through family extension or by having the spouse, sons or daughters work. Especially vulnerable are young nuclear families (Roberts 1989), many of whom must postpone the move from rental to ownership until they are in their mid-30s (Gilbert & Varley 1991).

Substantive and methodological conclusions

We believe that several important conclusions arise from our analysis. On the issue of affordability we have demonstrated that, although the affordability of land among low-income groups has declined, the decline has *not been dramatic*, with the exception, perhaps, of Puebla, where the land-to-income ratio has almost halved. In each of the three cities it appears that the decline in affordability has been more marked in private subdivisions than in *ejidal* areas, where our interviews revealed that price-fixing was less rigorous. Thus the rising level of production of *ejidal* land in Mexican cities, and the nature of price setting, which may take account of "social" factors as against purely market forces, have also assisted in making available land at affordable rates. We have also found that, for the poor in particular, access to land is primarily a function of real income. Given that land-price profiles tend also to be "flatter" in low-income areas relative to middle-income ones, affordability for the poor is likely to be largely a function of salary fluctuations rather than a mixture of both real earnings *and* real land-price variations. Nor is there much evidence for other adjustments being undertaken in order to alleviate declining affordability. The trend towards smaller plot sizes or plot-sharing in "compound" arrangements between separate but kin-related households is a feature that has been described for owners in Mexico City (Gilbert & Ward 1985). In all three cities the large majority of plots were occupied by a single family, although of course this may change in the future if the market "tightens" and becomes more difficult to enter as a formal owner (de facto or de jure).

Our second broad conclusion is that land prices in Mexico are not steadily increasing, but demonstrate a cyclical pattern closely tied to the state of the macroeconomy. Land prices declined significantly in real terms during the 1980s, but appear to have risen sharply again since 1988–89. Thirdly, the absolute price of land and the segmented nature of informal land markets in Mexican cities may have an important influence on levels of intra-neighbourhood heterogeneity and city-wide processes of social segregation, but not in the expected direction. Cities with lower absolute land prices (i.e. easier access) may be more segregated than those with higher land prices. It appears that the differentials in absolute prices between low- and middle-income segments of the land market are most crucial in determining the propensity for inter-settlement mobility and the degree of mixing of the lower middle classes and better-off working classes.

In addition to these substantive findings, we hope that we have demonstrated the feasibility of data sources such as advertised newspaper prices and household survey in order to begin to track land-price trends in different kinds of residential area. Provided that one exercises sufficient care in order to establish the necessary controls, and that one is sensitive to the difficulties associated with making comparisons among settlements and among plots within a settlement, then we believe that meaningful conclusions can be derived about land-price changes over time and about the relative affordability of land within different segments of the land market. But we also conclude that it is necessary to set this sort of analysis in a broader context provided by a political-economy approach, one that offers a nuanced understanding of the way in which land is socially produced in cities, and about the profitability of its production over time. We are doubtful that neoclassical economic theory and existing econometric models provide sufficient analytical "purchase" on the sort of processes we have described in this chapter, no matter how desirable it might be for us to develop tools that are widely replicable and easily applied to existing data sources. One thing we have learnt along the way is that the data are often "dirty" and require careful disentangling. Moreover, their collection invariably requires the researcher to get his or her feet dirty and engage in detailed and painstaking fieldwork, whether this be archival or through survey of one form or another. Lastly, we concur with Dowall, Siembieda and others in this volume who have argued that land-market analyses must embrace various sources and not focus on a single set of information. Only in so doing is it possible to cross-check data and begin to build up data sets that are sufficiently large and/or cover a sufficiently long period for meaningful trends to be discerned.

Notes

1. An earlier draft of this chapter was prepared for the "International Research Workshop: land value changes and the impact of urban policy on land valorization processes in developing countries", held at Fitzwilliam College, Cambridge 14–19 July 1991. The research and fieldwork for this paper were conducted as part of an ESRC-funded research project directed by Ward and based at the Department of Geography, University of Cambridge.
2. A full account of the research and the methodology is still being prepared and will be published as a book in 1994 (Ward et al. 1994).
3. These investigators are Amitabh (whose chapter on land-registration data is included in this volume), and Chris Macoloo, from the Department of Geography, University of Nairobi, Kenya, who is leading a team funded by the International Development Research Center (Canada) to examine land-price changes in the cities of Mombasa and Kisumu.
4. For further details about the various forms in which illegal land development occurs in Latin American cities, see Gilbert & Ward 1985.
5. These three confederations are the Confederación de Trabajadores Mexicanos (labour sector), the Confederación Nacional de Campesinos (peasant and agrarian sector), and the Confedera-

ción Nacional de Organizaciones Populares, now known as UNE (the acronym has no significance), which covers settlement and local interest groups, small-scale enterprises and workers, schoolteachers, etc. As Mexico has urbanized, so the CNOP has gained influence, often at the expense of the CNC.

6. We are less convinced that it is the rate of inflation that shapes the difference between bid and sale prices than the level of *demand* that exists at a particular time. When demand is very high, then one might expect greater disparities between individually set sale prices and assessors' independent evaluations. When the market is down, people become more realistic about what they can ask and the differential is narrow. Also, casual "test-the-water"-type vendors are less likely to enter the market when it is sluggish, and in part it is this group that beats up bid prices. This is an area that requires further systematic research, as does the possible independent influence of advertising in US dollars.

7. The point is that, even if a purchaser negotiated a special "deal" and lower unitary rate for an extra-large plot, it would not have appeared in the newspaper advertisement as a large plot. If it was advertised as larger than 1,250 m², then it would be excluded from our analysis.

8. This was a particular problem in Querétaro, where the application of questionnaires in Lomas de Querétaro was halted because of a poor response rate.

9. In order to provide contextual support to the empirical work, the authors conducted 85 semi-structured interviews with government officials, leading political decision-makers, community leaders and real estate operators. It became clear that seeking "hard" information from the files of brokers, developers and assessors was too threatening. It should also be noted that few brokers actually maintained any systematic records. Instead, these informants were more useful as expert commentators on the structure and "behind-the-scenes" manoeuvres of land-market agents.

10. The results from an otherwise useful survey of land markets and prices in Malaysia appear to have been distorted by the inclusion of actual land-price data and land-market valuations in the same aggregate data source (Brookfield et al. 1991).

11. Another study in Mexico City that also used advertised sale prices in several middle-income neighbourhoods found that prices increased by between 2.6 per cent and 6.5 per cent per annum over a 30 year period (Makin 1984: 296). In the middle-class neighbourhood of Del Valle, for which the record was most complete, the increase was 4.3 per cent per annum over the whole period, and 2.8 per cent annually between 1970 and 1981. This suggests a steady, rather than a sharp, increase in land values.

12. Our own inclination is not to emphasize the political disjunctures per se, but more the way in which these are translated into the macroeconomic performance of each administration (see Jones et al. 1993).

13. It is too early to say how far President Salinas's reform of Article 27 of the Constitution, which makes possible the privatization of the *ejido*, will shape land-price trends in this particular segment of the market. Certainly one would expect prime *ejidal* land to be open to middle-income and elite residential subdivisions in ways not possible before. Potentially large tracts of land may now come into a part of the market from which they were formerly excluded. This may depress overall land prices, although the unitary price paid for *ejidal* land may rise to take account of the new-found clientele and ability to dispose legally of their land parcels.

14. See Ward 1993 for a comparative account of the inner cities in Latin America and for a discussion of the very sharp differences in demand that have "stunted" their gentrification and reactivation, at least when compared with UK and US experience.

15. The trimmed mean is a method by which the data may be "cleaned", since it removes the top and bottom 5 per cent of values in order to exclude spurious readings prior to calculating the average. Thus, it provides a more representative average reading.

16. It is especially important that anyone undertaking fieldwork in Mexico should understand that many workers will often declare that they are earning the "minimum" but, by that, mean the lowest wage band that the firm *actually pays*. It is necessary, therefore, to obtain details of actual earnings.

17. González de la Rocha's study for Guadalajara also shows that, while male heads of house-hold's incomes deteriorated by 35 per cent in real terms between 1982 and 1985, *total* domestic incomes decreased by only 11 per cent. This recommends our strategy to find alternative (and more realistic) comparators for the 1980s.

CHAPTER THIRTEEN

Bridging conceptual and methodological issues in the study of second-hand property markets in Rio de Janeiro, Brazil

Martim O. Smolka

Introduction: setting the issues

Cities do not change dramatically every day, except perhaps as a result of general catastrophes like earthquakes, flood or war, or because of localized blockbusting as a result of urban renewal projects or other kinds of "creative destruction" interventions. Most cities can therefore be viewed as an ensemble of many highly durable, to a large extent indivisible, and expensive building units owned by a large number of individuals and firms. Moreover, the majority of those residing in these buildings do not change residence often. Even in a lively developing-country city like Rio de Janeiro, buildings tend to last over 50 years and people tend to remain in a dwelling for more than eight years on average.[1] Even in a so-called "boom" year no more than 5 per cent of new housing will be added to the existing stock. As a result about two-thirds of transactions in the Rio housing market refer to second-hand units.[2]

The durability of the existing housing stock is the key to understanding the process of intra-urban restructuring. Given that the value of old housing depreciates very slowly compared with new housing (sometimes it even appreciates, because of the quality of its construction or cultural factors), the existing stock imposes a constraint on the production of new housing. This affects business decisions on the location of developments just as much as it does decisions on what, when, and for whom to build these new units. Product and location differentiation thus become important ingredients for escape from an otherwise highly competitive market and thus the development of different neighbourhoods or subareas in the city, far from being synchronized, tends to follow relatively independent life cycles. For the city of Rio de Janeiro these may have a duration of more than 20 years in amplitude amidst spasmodic new housing develop-

179

ments (Smolka 1989, Abramo Campos 1989). This is to say that the process of land-use conversion is, apparently, not monotonically continuous over space and time, as postulated in traditional neoclassical/ecological diffusion models. Equally, local bandwagon effects have been perceived as characterizing the behaviour of developers who contrive to gain extra-normal profits from the pursuit of "founder's rent" in knife-edge negotiations (Murray 1977, 1978) and from dangerous risks in a highly competitive environment (Smolka 1987).

To further complicate matters, neighbourhoods or urban subareas are not necessarily occupied by a homogeneous socio-economic group and nor is the transition from one social position to another instantaneous. Moreover, tendencies are sometimes reversed or interrupted as a consequence of specific urban legislation or by virtue of spontaneous outbursts of local consciousness leading to resistance or action-oriented social movements. The interplay of these forces responds as much to the emergence of market barriers to change as to the inspirations for developers in setting their marketing strategies. Residential segregation and other forms of urban differentiation can be inferred from these mechanisms.

From this discussion, it is clear that the market for second-hand housing cannot be neglected as a condition of the dynamics of the property market over space. In fact, the very notion of dynamics refers to historical time, as opposed to logical time, in the sense that "today is a break in time between an unknown future and an irrevocable past" (Robinson 1962: 26). In practice, this means that the existing spatial structure of the built environment in general, and of the housing stock in particular, conditions present decisions regarding future changes in land use. Or in Harvey's (1978: 124) words:

> The geographical landscape . . . is the crowning glory of past capitalist development. But at the same time it expresses the power of dead labour over living labour and as such it imprisons and inhibits the accumulation process within a set of specific physical constraints. And these can be removed only slowly unless there is a substantial devaluation of the exchange value locked up in the location of these physical assets.

This chapter forms a part of a larger study on the relationship between the dynamics of the property market and intra-urban structuring of the city of Rio de Janeiro.[3] It deals with the implied empirical data requirements in order to address such issues as the production of the built environment, social segregation and urban renewal and degradation. One of the interesting features of the IPPUR/ITBI/IPTU study is that it attempts to look at the second-hand property market in Rio de Janeiro. The study takes as self-evident that, as transactions involving mortgage-assisted apartments are responsible for about 25 per cent of the total transactions to occur in the housing market from 1968 to 1984, and 52 per cent if confined to newly commercialized apartments, then this cannot be neglected as a conditioning element for the dynamics of the property development and developers over space.

In the context of the difficulties found with all data sources, the relevant issue is not so much of finding the ideal source (it is simply not there) but of selecting the least inadequate one from among what is available. The first section of this chapter analyzes the data sources that were available for the IPPUR study of Rio de Janeiro. In the second section some results of the study are presented that indicate what may be achieved even with "compromised" data sources.

Data source shortcomings and the attractions of fiscal sources

An elementary empirical framework for conducting studies on issues associated with the relationship between the dynamics of the property market and the transformation of intra-urban structures would recommend access to information on prices and quantities of property transactions in different areas over time. This information should in turn be compared with that on the housing stock on given dates. This last data requirement, however, is difficult to satisfy. Not only is the property market said to be atomistic regarding the size and variety of its operating agents, but it is also generally regarded as not very well structured when compared with other capitalist activities. As a result, the sources of information on which researchers have traditionally relied – building permits, records from real estate and/or financial agents, newspaper advertisements, builders' and developers' records – all have serious drawbacks. When such data are available there is a tendency to concentrate on very specific segments of the market, such as upper-income, higher-valued units, on a single type of property such as multi-family buildings, particular city regions such as new developments, definite periods of time (when certain types of mortgage facilities were available) or even only on certain variables. Even when available, most data do not cover a suitable range of criteria. Most commonly, data from building permits do not normally include the value of a building, while newspaper advertisements seldom specify the building's age or the precise location.

These biases or limitations introduce major methodological problems in practice. For example, inconsistencies between sample universes, which might themselves be dictated by the availability of data and therefore defined by different sources, prevent direct comparisons. The most common problem here is the attempt to use data on the land market to compare with trends from the records of new housing sales. Similar difficulties emerge from the regional desegregation of information, since the criteria for defining the supposed regions may not be the same from indistinct data sources. Although one might assume that financial agents, for instance, and builders would define specific regions of the city in a similar fashion, this is not necessarily the case. Thus, drawing data from either source and using them to build a spatial picture of the city can severely compromise the result.

There are also problems when any or all of the data requirements are based upon so-called official statistics. All too often, and especially in underdeveloped countries, relevant information has been distorted, substituted or modified by an "improved" statistic. Thus, after the institutionalization of the Brazilian housing finance system in 1965, the "housing question" became identified as a financial issue and, symptomatically, the publication of other aspects of the housing market (e.g. registrations in public offices) gave way to statistics on the volume of loans per programme or agent. In a further example, the statistics on the value of property transactions for the 1970s appeared to show a convergence and stabilization to a 10-digit figure even though observation indicated that nominal values were accelerating rapidly because of chronic inflation. The reason was the lack of space on the old record cards, which prompted the clerks to omit the last few digits.

Of particular notoriety for use in academic research are data from fiscal records – especially when it comes to property analysis. People tend to under-declare the values involved in property transactions and not all transactions go over what one might term "the fiscal counter". Moreover, the method of valuation used for property taxes is rarely updated on a continuous basis and the relevant fiscal values are subject to all kinds of distortions and inequities. Were it not for these problems, fiscal data could represent an outstanding source, provided that one has permission to access it (see Amitabh, this volume).

Transaction records include information on fiscal value; namely, the value the fiscal authority has for the property being transacted. This is normally the same value used to collect property (ownership) taxes and, as already mentioned, is usually neither systematically updated nor made to correspond to actual market values when this is done. As a rule of thumb, an updating of property tax values occurs only when significant distortions are perceived.[4] These may arise either because of intra-urban transformations (changes in land-use patterns, expansion of the city) or when the political and economic cost of updating is compensated by the additional revenue benefits.[5]

Clearly, there is no secure way of knowing whether, or how closely, the declared values match the actual market values of the properties transacted. But this problem does not mean that declared values are useless. Fiscal records offer large sample sizes that may be sufficient to apply standard statistical techniques.[6] Even though average or median values obtained by type of property, location or time period may deviate from actual market values, one must be willing to assume that any deviation from actual market values is more or less consistent over time (see Ward et al, this volume). Moreover, assuming consistency over space, the data present a surrogate for price indices in order to evaluate the behaviour of certain regions or types of property. In short, for the purpose of analyzing intra-urban transformation, absolute property values are not indispensable. Only by comparison with external statistics such as, for instance, average family income, or by comparison with other real asset port-folio management considerations do absolute values become relevant.

This said, one can see that by comparing fiscal and declared values, an inter-esting indicator is obtained to analyze two current buzz-words in urban research: equity and efficiency. This possibility is enhanced by the ease of calculating this indicator by region, type of property, time period and value range. The higher the ratio of declared to fiscal value, the larger the implied tax evasion and/or injustice. Analysis of the fiscal data bank for Rio de Janeiro revealed that fiscal values tend to be below real market values by approximately 40 per cent on average, implying a proportionately heavier tax burden on low-income families (Dillinger 1989). Moreover, evidence suggests that the higher the property value the greater the lag with respect to fiscal values, suggesting that the property tax is highly regressive (Leal 1990).

Despite these shortcomings, data from property transaction tax forms seem to offer some advantages. First, fiscal data come from a single source that represents a consistent, common statistical universe. Normally, this should be sufficient to provide information on transactions with land (large estates and small parcels), offices or commercial buildings, or single or multi-family housing units (apartments). The information can be further classified according to size (square metres), location, payment conditions (if a private or public loan is involved), the agents involved in the transaction (private individuals or firms), and age (date of transaction). In the case of self-built housing, of course, the registered age of the house does not necessarily correspond to the date of completion, but the date it was first legally transacted. Perhaps the most important classification is declared value.

The second advantage relates to the availability of longitudinal data. Because, for legal reasons, fiscal records cannot be destroyed, they frequently present a more or less continuous time series of data. Thus, in some circumstances, it may be possible to go back several decades to tap the information contained in the forms without major losses in data congruency. This is in sharp contrast to questionnaire or interview techniques which rely on people's memory. In the light of previous comments regarding the slow pace and the subregional variations of transformations of the spatial structure of the built environment, this possibility should be of considerable value. The third advantage is that the monetary and human cost of obtaining the information is substantially lower than, for instance, that of prospecting old newspapers or notary records, not to mention the often unprofessional maintenance of corresponding records in private business institutions. To the author's knowledge there is simply no other source that better satisfies the implied requirements on data coverage and data consistency among different relevant attributes or variables.

A fourth advantage of the property tax database is that it offers the opportunity to analyze important windfall data. Tax forms often provide a very detailed description of the property under review. This may include, for instance, an identification of the parties involved in the transaction, whether private individuals or firms are in the positions of buyer or seller.[7] A switch in the composition of buyers of property in favour of firms may be a telling indicator of what is about to happen in an area in the near future. It may also reveal speculative moves or specific strategies of developers. This information may be compared with eventual increases in new housing production in the area. From their current addresses, an intra-urban mobility matrix can be generated for each period (year) (Smolka 1992). The identification of the origin of buyers of properties in any given area is of relevance to a study of the process of gentrification or degradation. This may be particularly useful in cases where it is possible to control comparisons of prices of properties according to the type of property dealer involved. Comparing the relative value of properties transacted may offer insights into the bargaining power of firms versus private individuals. This latter point needs to be supported by interview data.

The availability of information on the size of the built area of housing units and for the lot where the building is situated can be used to normalize property values.[8] The same information can also be conveniently used to conduct studies on property distribution. Thus, for instance, one may discriminate land parcels from large estates and take the ratio of their relative prices as a proxy for urbanization margins or to calculate profit rates for land assembly (Smolka 1991a). These calculations can then be compared on a time and regional basis.

The timing of transactions can also offer useful insights. An apparent intensification of the rate of transactions is of interest in this respect. Here, the age (fiscal age) of the unit is more reliable when the property refers to apartments or non-self-produced housing, as already mentioned. Nevertheless, data on the age of units do present some useful insights. First, one can gauge the diffusion of apartments by mapping the spatial distribution of units per vintage extracts. Thus one can note, for instance, that most of the 50-year-old apartment units transacted today are located in fewer regions than those of more recent vintage. These figures in turn can be compared with population growth per region to reflect the commodification process in the housing market. Secondly, one may calculate variations in property turnover time. Taking the distribution of the lag between age and the year when the unit was transacted, one can relate variations to market liquidity. This may also be related to specific interventions such as a change in zoning or a rehabilitation project, or to macro-determined factors such as a temporary lack of housing credit facilities or a sudden drop in long-term economic confidence.

Not all fiscal records will conform to the above advantages. Besides the usual problems associated with accessing these records, as a source of information, fiscal records normally exclude all property transactions occurring in the so-called illegal market. In the case of the data bank organized for Rio de Janeiro, property values were accepted on account of three tests.[9] The first test was to ensure that, in more than two-thirds of the property transactions, declared values were found to be higher than fiscal values.[10] A correlation analysis checked that the declared values were not regulated by fiscal values. The second test confirmed whether the overall evolution of property prices obtained from the data follows the same pattern found for other Brazilian cities where traditional survey procedures are employed. An example is shown in Figure 13.1. The remarkable coincidence of the two curves is, one might argue, indicative of a coherence between the two distinct methods.[11] The third test checked the high correlation between the distribution of financed versus non-financed apartment units. This sets out to confirm the quality of the price (per square metre) time-series. For transactions involving financed housing units, it should be assumed that declared values follow more closely the actual market values because financial agents impose a rule, for mortgage security reasons, that registered values are not below the actual ones.[12]

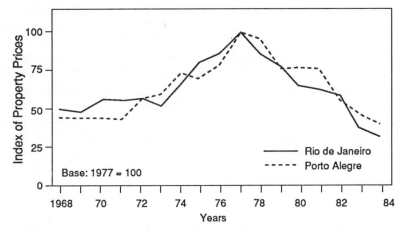

Figure 13.1 The evolution of apartment unit classes 1968–84 (m²).

Utilization of the data bank

As already indicated, each record from the data source provides information on the type of property being transacted (i.e. if land, a single house, an apartment or an office); the unit's size and age, the conditions of the transaction involved, the presence or absence of a financial loan in addition to a declared property value and, of course, the precise location of the property. It is not the purpose here to attempt to suggest all the possible uses for this data bank. The following section, therefore, provides only a brief sketch of some of the analytical possibilities that have already been explored by the author.

Characterization of changes in land use
The identification of which properties have been transacted provides an immediate description of how the city is growing or, in broader terms, a characterization of intra-urban transformations. Where the data set refers to transactions of new properties, there is the possibility of testing urban growth models. The "oil-spill diffusion model" can be tested against other patterns or hypotheses of urban expansion as, for instance, in the modular and spasmodic model whereby new and large areas are incorporated at given dates into the urban fabric, or, in the radial or sectorial path, led by certain infrastructure facilities (e.g. a new transit line).

Similarly, where there are sufficient readings of second-hand property transactions it should be possible to investigate the transformation of local areas or the city as a whole. The succession of land-use conversion can be depicted to characterize or quantify the occupation process of specific areas. Taking one area over time a picture of transformation can be built up following the transition from the initial transaction of land (large estates) at the unoccupied periphery towards a predominance of transactions reflecting land parcel subdivision, and, in turn, substituted by transactions for housing and possibly with apartment units and office units.

The timing and the predominance of each type of property transaction may be associated with land-price change. In this sense, a more rapid transition from land direct to apartment units may be associated with relatively high land prices.[13] This kind of analysis can be further detailed so as to accommodate questions related to the impact of specific interventions on locally defined market segments. By discriminating adjacent from non-adjacent effected areas, one may compare changes in activity (property transaction compositions) and prices provoked by interventions like a subway line or a neighbourhood redevelopment.

The functioning of the property market

The operation of the property market can be examined on a regional basis by comparing data on the level of market activity with the price of property. Over time, one would expect a relative increase in the level of market activity to be followed by a fall in the relative price of property. In order to identify this balance it would be necessary to eliminate distortions from the wider property business cycle and to eliminate undesirable scale effects imposed by existing housing stocks. For comparative purposes, measures may be taken to discriminate according to distance or accessibility to the CBD or to density levels. Then, one may look at standard price elasticity parameters to interpret certain differences among regions. This can be done by the ratio of transactions of new to second-hand housing as the activity-level indicator, and, analogously, to the relative price of new to old housing.

More interesting still, the overall behaviour of property prices over time can be broken down to isolate the effects of macroeconomic factors from the effect of changing regional composition (i.e. intra-urban) on prices. This is virtually the equivalent of comparing the effects of shifts of the price gradient with the effects of changes in the slope of this gradient. The importance of the exercise is that it, again, may provide a test for the permeability of the market or alternatively the resilience of submarkets. Breaking down the property price indices for Rio de Janeiro indicates that, despite major intra-urban transformations in the period 1968–84, the composition effect accounted for only about 9 per cent of overall price variations. In other words, when prices go up, they rise almost everywhere – a synchronicity that is incompatible with the idea of strong market barriers.

Finance as a data source: relationship to the availability of credit
The value of investigating the land market from a credit or finance data source
is that it produces a fairly consistent picture of the flow of funds into the market
against which one can compare market activity. It is implicit in many land and
housing studies that the availability or circulation of finance in the market,
particularly when there is an inelastic supply of land, will fuel price increases.
This data source, therefore, draws together the interrelation of macroeconomic
changes, surplus funds in the financial system, and land or property market
cycles. Of course, one also needs to note that these forces are frequently
distorted or compounded by the presence of highly speculative land agents.

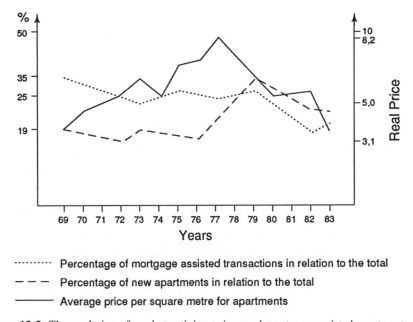

Figure 13.2 The evolution of market activity, prices and mortgage-assisted apartments.

The presence of a strong interrelationship among economy, finance and
property markets is believed to be a common summary of urban development
in developed-world and developing-world cities. From the data collected on Rio
de Janeiro this seems to have little support. Figure 13.2 indicates the evolution
of market activity and prices for mortgage-assisted apartments in Rio de
Janeiro. According to the data, it is difficult to detect any significant correlation
between the percentage of mortgage-assisted apartments and the participation of
new apartments among the total number of apartment transactions. Moreover,
Figure 13.2 appears to indicate that there was a major surplus of available finance at the same time as the market was giving a clear signal of "cooling off".
This is confirmed by the observed trend in Figure 13.3 that the land-price component of property prices appears to be the opposite of the expected trend: the

land-price component is strongly counter-cyclical to activity in the apartment market.[14]

————— Land prices in relation to the price of apartments

– – – Property activity apartments

Figure 13.3 The evolution of the relative prices of land and real estate activity.

The second-hand property market and spatial mobility

In Rio de Janeiro about 45 per cent of the total number of housing units are apartments and about two-thirds of these are registered with the local authorities. Thus, available records contain property transactions of the majority of apartments in the city. A study by the author of the property cycle in Rio de Janeiro for the period 1968 to 1984 found that in 77 per cent of cases the boom in the sale of new apartments preceded that for second-hand apartments (Smolka 1989). That is to say that, arguably, the boom in new apartments appeared to stimulate the boom in second-hand units.

This boom in the supply of new and, later, second-hand apartments appears to work in reverse when one analyses the data on the price of apartments (Table 13.1). Dividing the city into zones, the relative prices of old apartment units increased from 1.11 to 1.18 in Zone B and from 1.38 to 1.54 in Zone C. This contrasted with a fall in relative prices of new apartment units built in the period from 1.30 to 1.16 in Zone B and from 1.59 to 1.38 in Zone C. These data appear to indicate a narrowing of property development opportunities or a saturation of the market. This movement has been backed by a significant gentrification of the area.[15] Thus, in spite of the "revealed preferences" of high-income families for this area, property developers seem to have faced increasing difficulties in profiting from land-use conversion either because of rising land costs as related to a realizable selling price or because of competition with upgraded older apartment units. This interpretation is confirmed by data on the spatial mobility of elite groups in Rio de Janeiro. The main areas for apartment units are the elite zones along the coast of Rio. However, these are precisely the same zones which are the principal exporters of high-income families. Between 1970 and 1980 this submarket has declined from 41.67 per cent to 36.65 per cent of high-income families. This evidence can be understood only as a "closing from within" of a very particular submarket, rather than as the spontaneous movement of high-income families.

Table 13.1 Spatial distribution of the market for apartments.

| Urban zones (RAS) | Average price per m^2 | | | | | |
| | Total | | New | | Used | |
	1970	1980	1970	1980	1970	1980
A (I, II, VII, XXIII)	.69	.64	.45	.55	.88	.75
B (III, IV, V, VIII)	1.13	1.17	1.30	1.16	1.12	1.18
C (VI)	1.54	1.59	1.68	1.59	1.38	1.54
D (X, XI, XII, XV)	.67	.68	.66	.76	.57	.60
E (IX, XIII, XIV, XX)	.89	.92	.91	.92	.71	.81
F (XVII, XVIII, XIX, XXII)	.54	.29	.81	.19	.54	.34
G (XVII, XXIV)	.63	1.04	.53	1.02	.59	.85

Source: IPPUR,ITBI,IPTU Survey.   *Note:* RAS = Administrative regions

From the developers' standpoint, it is apparently more interesting to move to new areas where "founder's-type rent" from innovations in land conversion can be more easily appropriated. Interestingly, the chosen areas are not necessarily those adjacent to the existing urban area or those already substantially urbanized. In fact, as shown in Table 13.2, these lower-income areas (Zone D) do not improve their position regarding the spatial distribution of high-income families, receiving only 13.81 per cent of the additional families from 1970 to 1980 against a 15.09 per cent share of these families in 1970. However, such areas do improve their share of high-income apartment units (7.32 per cent and 1.50, respectively, for added units and pre-existing stock). This evidence, put together, suggests a process of substitution of houses for apartments in lower-income areas with production produced for local and probably existing high-income families.[16] Symptomatically, this greater apparent permeability to capitalist relations has been coupled with a significant reduction in the region's share of low-income families.

Rather than moving to an already equipped area, property developers selected, not surprisingly, one of the less dense and urbanized areas, Zone G.[17] Although short of certain basic facilities, Zone G attracted a formidable number

Table 13.2 Spatial redistribution of families and apartment units for 1970–80 (by class of value).

Urban zones (RAS)	Family income distribution						Slums	Distribution of used and new apartment units					
	Total		> 10 minimum wages		< 2 minimum wages			Total		High value		Low value	
	1970	Variation 1970–80	1970	Variation 1970–80	1970	Variation 1970–80	Pop. 1980	Used 1970	New 1968–84	Used 1970	New 1968–84	Used 1970	New 1968–84
A (I, II, VII, XXIII)	7.12	1.53	7.02	−2.78	5.67	3.35	8.6	8.40	2.26	5.51	1.04	11.55	3.49
B (III, IV, V, VIII)	20.51	10.30	44.75	20.81	8.56	6.56	11.0	54.70	29.87	68.34	43.47	40.35	16.29
C (VI)	4.06	5.62	8.41	13.85	2.42	1.50	6.0	9.02	9.34	15.69	12.95	3.64	5.73
D (X, XI, XII, XV)	27.13	18.41	15.09	13.81	30.03	53.65	38.9	10.95	14.52	1.50	7.32	20.25	21.72
E (IX, XIII, XIV, XX)	16.37	15.52	16.06	28.00	14.38	22.48	14.0	14.69	28.90	8.59	24.40	20.57	33.78
F (XVII, XVIII, XIX, XXII)	19.41	36.95	6.14	9.62	31.96	10.82	17.6	0.87	5.03	0.15	4.09	1.21	15.65
G (XVI, XXIV)	5.04	11.71	2.47	16.66	6.99	4.63	3.9	1.37	9.86	0.15	6.72	2.37	3.34

Source: IPPUR, ITBI, IPTU Survey.

Note: all data are column percentages.

of high-income families. More than two-thirds of the new apartment units built in the area may be classified as of high value. As a consequence, relative prices of used and new apartments increased substantially (see Table 13.1), together with relative family income (Table 13.2). In addition, an immediate consequence of this process was greater selectivity and a more parsimonious scheduling of the programmed developments for the area. This set up a deterrent mechanism reinforcing the gentrification of the area at the same time as it restricted the capacity to fully accommodate all families entering the market. This process, again, can hardly be taken as driven by an autonomous spatial movement of families. The pre-existing stock of apartment buildings is negligible if compared with the significance of the new buildings added in the decade (particularly of the higher-valued apartment units).

Although this description may serve as an illustration of the spatial process of elite family movement and apartment development, it does not typify all movements of property developers in the city of Rio de Janeiro.[18] For present purposes, it suffices to draw from these schematic ideas the fact that the implied selective character of the spatial movement of property developers induced a significant redistribution of high-income families with the corollary, of course, of the expulsion of low-income families from their areas of original residence. One should recall that at the macro-level there is a concomitance of the strong spatial deconcentration process of property developments with their associated high-income markets. At the regional level, there appears to be a relationship between the distribution of new apartment units and the variation of relative family income, with the possible interpretation that the mobility of low-income families is outward.

Although Table 13.2 suggests that, at the aggregated level, zones that improved their relative position in the spatial distribution of new apartment units (especially the high-valued ones) tend also to be the zones showing more significant and relative reductions in the share of low-income families. At the regional level, this association is less clear. In fact, no meaningful correlation was found between these two variables. The explanation for the phenomena may be found in the widely discussed observation that low-income families resort to different and relatively autonomous housing strategies according to location within the city (Valladares 1990).

This has further produced a series of interesting anomalies. One such is the increase in the absolute number of low-income families in the most aristocratic zone, Zone C, even though property prices and family income are growing faster than the average for the city (Table 13.1, 13.2). This is associated with the appropriation by illegal or informal means of land unsuitable for building (e.g. hillside), public land (e.g. ecological reserves), or contested land, by families with no other alternative than to live close to their work to save on transportation costs. It is interesting to note that, as a result of the relative scarcity of similarly accessible irregular settlements, the average income of families residing in the resulting *favelas* is higher than of some families living in legal housings in Zone D (IPLAN-RIO 1985). Thus, displacement from this zone due to land-use conversion (single homes to apartment units) affects mainly low-income families living in regular or legal housing units, but not necessarily the *favelados*. Hence the relative high percentage of these families in 1980.[19]

In fact, indicators such as the flattening of density gradients over time or the increasing family growth rates with distance to the CBD well illustrate the phenomena.[20] Other relevant indicators are displayed in Table 13.3. Comparing growth rates in Table 13.3 it can be further comprehended that the spatial deconcentration of high-income families has been stronger than that of families in general.[21] High-income families, however, have relocated not in a continuous manner over space but to selective areas. A single zone, Zone G, accounted originally for only 2.47 per cent of these high-income families but received 16.66 per cent of the additional families in this income bracket. Copacabana (area V in Zone B), meanwhile, exhibits an inverse phenomenon, with 18.27 per cent original high-income families and 2.69 per cent of new arrivals (Table 13.2).

Granted that the market for apartments is typically high-income oriented, one should expect a strong relationship between the spatial deconcentration of new apartment buildings and the regional variation of family income.[22] Table 13.2 indicates that the spatial deconcentration of the property market (apartments) is stronger than the relative movement of families. Moreover, 31.12 per cent of the new high-valued apartment units were built in areas E and G, corresponding to less than 9.21 per cent of the stock. In the two zones, however, the percentages for the number of families received is 44.66 per cent and 18.53 per cent, respectively. No significant correlation was found relating the spatial distribution of families added in the decade with that of the new apartment buildings.

From the analysis presented in the previous sections, it can be inferred that the dynamics of property developers in the market is responsible for a substantial share of Rio's intra-urban structuring process and residential segregation. The spatial movement of property developers as reflected by the distribution of apartments is shown to be less dependent on family demand than usually argued by neoclassical authors, but also less autonomous than implied in certain analyses pivoted on the so-called "logic of capital". This, I would suggest, is due to a combination of the constraints imposed by the market for second-hand apartment units, the displacement of effective demand exercised by the high-income segment of the market, and developer risk-minimization behaviour. One should note, however, that the relationships referred to above capture no more than manifestations of the residential segregation process, and not the process itself, i.e. the mediating mechanisms.

Table 13.3 Indicators of spatial distribution of families and of apartment transactions in the market.

Urban zones (RAS)	Distance from CBD (km)	Age of apartments (years)	Family growth rate 1970–80		Apartment growth rate		Variation in family average income 1970–80	Variation in average price of apartments 1970–80
			General	High-income families	General	High valued		
A (I, II, VII, XXIII)	3.3	22.1	8.2	0.27	-17.23	0.19	0.83	0.92
B (III, IV, V, VIII)	5.9	21.1	18.5	0.55	20.44	0.63	0.99	0.97
C (VI)	9.4	15.7	50.9	1.05	72.27	0.81	1.14	1.06
D (X, XI, XII, XV)	13.0	17.2	25.2	1.34	40.19	4.78	1.01	1.05
E (IX, XIII, XIV, XX)	12.8	13.5	34.5	2.00	76.23	2.80	1.14	1.12
F (XVII, XVIII, XIX, XXII)	35.5	13.2	69.8	5.82	68.82	26.67	0.95	0.35
G (XVI, XXIV)	25.1	7.5	85.5	7.29	296.10	43.90	1.45	2.65

Note: The relatively low volume of transactions in 1970 implies a certain instability in the market.

Source: IPPUR,ITBI,IPTU Survey.

Conclusion

It is curious that, despite the recurrent centrality of land and property markets within the nexus of questions discussed by those interested in the formation of developing-world cities, there is such an inadequate understanding of two of the markets' basic indicators: price and quantity. This point is all the more important if one considers that studies of land and property imply a broader set of questions, including the distribution of resources, welfare and control. Part of the reason for this ignorance relates, perhaps, to the handicap imposed by the absence of a suitable methodology. The kinds of data sources discussed in this chapter is neither unique nor original. Its main advantage has to do with the variety of information gathered from a single consistent source, its temporal and spatial coverage, and, above all, its relatively low cost and ease of access.

These advantages permit comparative study. In other Brazilian cities of different sizes and characteristics, local research groups are replicating the methodology developed by the IPPUR team for Rio de Janeiro, São Paulo, Governador Valadares, and Salvador.[23] The results obtained for the cities of Presidente Prudente and Uberaba (both with about 250,000 inhabitants) and Vitória (population of about 1.2 million) are encouraging. In the first two cases, a sample size of 100 property transactions per year over the past 20 years has proved sufficient to provide a good understanding of the process of intra-urban structuring along the lines exposed in this chapter. More importantly, the survey and organization of the data bank were both concluded in less than six months with the help of only two part-time research assistants for the data codification and transcription phases of the project, and under the co-ordination of a graduate student (Leal 1990). All this suggests an apparently straightforward assimilation of the methodology under diverse local conditions.

Finally, although the studies mentioned above rely heavily on what I termed earlier a "compromised" data source, it should be possible to devise ways to improve this database. Alternative procedures to improve the information system used for tax purposes is one way forward. The usual method of updating fiscal property values varies significantly from city to city according to legal, political and administrative factors, and even according to tradition or operational convenience. The construction of the fiscal database may rely upon direct evaluations (voluntary or mandatory), samples from newspaper advertisements, field surveys in selected areas, or consultations with building society records.

Nevertheless, few governments or agencies have gone so far as to design updating procedures based on the integration of the information systems used for the different property taxes, i.e. on the value itself of the property, on the transaction and on property appreciation or capital gains.[24] Declared values from transactions taxes can be used, together with information on the property attributes and, through econometric estimations of hedonic price functions, to adjust base fiscal values for property tax purposes. The system could be further improved if the calculation of the appreciation of the property for the income tax were also done at the time when transactions taxes were collected. Sanctions might then be imposed so that declared values would automatically emerge from matching the declared acquisition value to the one obtained at the time when the property was last sold (i.e. based on dated declared values). This should induce buyers not to underdeclare property values. Eventual agreements between buyers and sellers would be checked by the continuous adjustment of fiscal values in a context of highly atomized market transactions. It can be shown not only that the system would rapidly converge fiscal to declared values, but also that declared values would converge toward actual market values.

Notes

1. This is a conservative estimate based on "time of residence" from census data and on rates of property turnover calculated from property transaction data.
2. This figure is an underestimate in as much as the turnover of single-family units is slower than the units of multi-family buildings, even though the stock of the former is at least 20 per cent larger than the latter.
3. The project was initiated in 1986 under the author's co-ordination in the Urban and Regional Planning and Research Institute at the Federal University of Rio de Janeiro.
4. Normally, updating of the fiscal base must be approved by the city council and sometimes stimulates political protest.
5. In a chronically inflationary situation, like the Brazilian one, the updating process is further complicated by the need to index fiscal values on an annual or even monthly basis. Changes in value, therefore, may depend to a large extent on which price index is deemed appropriate by the cadastral agency. In extreme cases, the reliability of using fiscal sources for data collection may depend on this decision; real change may be distorted more by the index than by occasional revaluations or changes in market conditions.
6. Central-limit theorem and purging of extreme values should be used to clean up the distribution, particularly where it is suspected that idiosyncratic values appear due to occasional political manipulation.
7. Although the juridical status can be identified from the names of the buyer and the seller, the collection of data on respective names is of no research use. Thus, confidentiality of records can be maintained.
8. This information is not originally included in the tax forms for the period 1968–84. For Rio de Janeiro it was obtained after a computational exercise designed to complement information contained in the original file with data in the cadastral file. The remodelled tax form now includes these items as well as information on the precise dimensions of a property.
9. Based on a sample of 2,000 records per annum during the period 1968–90. This corresponds to approximately 2 per cent of total transactions.
10. Fiscal procedures regarding property transactions establish the fact that the larger of the two values, fiscal and declared, is taxed at 2 per cent. In the case of a transaction involving a loan from the Housing Finance System, only 0.5 per cent is charged on the financed portion of the value.
11. The coincidence, of course, also suggests the presence of strong macroeconomic determinants in property markets (Smolka 1989, 1990).
12. Legal procedures require that one copy of the paid tax voucher be annexed to the loan documentation. A second copy goes to the public register, and a third one is filed by the fiscal authority. It is this third copy that is used for data collection.
13. Comparing two outer regions of Rio de Janeiro it was observed that, in the region located closer to the expected expansion path of upper-income areas, land prices were higher than in the one where no future expansion was foreseen. Both regions were an equal distance from the

CBD, but the latter was closer to low-income settlements. In the former region there was a rapid transition from land to apartment blocks, whereas in the latter there was a slower transition to single houses.

14. Although not the subject of this chapter, the analysis of the data over time may also reveal whether contracts transacted in cash or credit have become more or less popular or whether this is dependent on the type of property. The latter opens up the possibility of conducting studies on the effects of increasing the liquidity on the second-hand market on new buildings, or studies on socio-economic credit discrimination – comparing the relative values of financed versus non-financed properties transacted, while controlling for the respective locations.

15. In Zone B a relative increase of 100 per cent in the number of families earning over 20 minimum salaries compared with a relative reduction (−15.31 per cent) of families in the 10 to 20 minimum salary income bracket was observed. The figures for Zone C are 222 per cent and −14 per cent respectively.

16. In 1970 there were 1.09 transactions for apartments for every one house transaction. In 1980 the rate was 1.36 apartments to one house.

17. The number of inhabitants per square metre in 1980 was 1,237, whereas for the city as a whole, there were 4,615 and in Copacabana there were 33,948 (Guanzirollo & Bohadana 1983: 14).

18. A closer inspection of the occupation process in Zone G reveals the existence of two sub-markets, one for the top-income families and the other for the middle- and upper middle-income families in Jacarepagua Plains, further from the coast (Smolka 1989).

19. Zone F, in contrast, represents a privileged locus for the provision of low-income public housing (mostly in vertical and horizontal large estates). The share of the city's land plot transactions in this zone increased from 50.32 per cent to 53.14 per cent and in single housing units from 23.27 per cent to 28.38 per cent. This is partly the result of an intense process of land-parcelling by private agents who aim to house, primarily, the displaced low-income families from other regions.

20. The linear coefficient for distance against density decreases from −2.30 to −2.11 in the period, with both coefficients significant at the 5 per cent level. The Spearman rank correlation between the two variables is 82.83 per cent, significant at the 1 per cent level.

21. The dissimilarity indices obtained from a comparison of 1970 and 1980 distributions of high-income families and families in general are 35.03 per cent and 25.57 per cent, confirming the assertion.

22. In the data analysis, apartment units worth more than 400 minimum salaries were taken as corresponding to families earning 10 or more minimum salaries. This became the definition of the upper-income group, which was estimated to comprise about 25 per cent of Rio's families. The corresponding 400 minimum salaries value for apartment units, however, represents the median value for the sample data.

23. The cities are Brazil's planned capital, Brasília; the boom city of Vitória; capital of Espírito Santo; Presidente Prudente in the so-called "California Paulista"; and Uberaba, a traditional city in the cattle region on Minas Gerais.

24. One possible explanation is that these taxes were levied at different administrative levels. Only after the 1988 Brazilian constitution was the collection of transaction taxes transferred to the municipal level. Capital gains on property appreciation are still taxed with income at the federal level.

Assessing the impact of public policy upon land markets and property prices

CHAPTER FOURTEEN

Housing policy impact in central Mexico City

Manuel Perló

Introduction

This chapter presents the methodology and results of a three-year evaluation process examining the impact of housing policies on the real estate market in central Mexico City. These policies were carried out after two devastating earthquakes in September 1985 had killed approximately 4,500 people and had destroyed 412 buildings and damaged a further 5,725. These events left 54,352 people homeless (*damnificados*), whom the government was obliged to rehouse.

The chapter develops three methodological points. The first is the elaboration of a research framework to survey the impact of a major government policy such as the post-earthquake rebuilding programme. The framework developed here is a two-stage study that attempts to evaluate the context "before" the earthquake and the impact "after". The second point is a conceptual link between natural (although man-enhanced) disasters and land- and property-market changes. There is a considerable literature on the human impact of disasters but relatively little on the urban impact even though some of the world's most notorious disaster zones encompass major cities in developing countries (Varley 1994). The third methodological point draws together the first two into an assessment of World Bank policies. In the reconstruction of central Mexico City the World Bank played a key rôle as the principal provider of external funds.[1] An inspection of the property market in this area should serve as a useful indicator of some of the impacts World Bank policies are likely to have on the former and current inhabitants.

The government response and the emerging methodological issues

In the wake of the earthquake a special report produced by the Secretaría de Hacienda y Crédito Público (the Treasury) for Mexico's creditor banks, estimated the financial requirements for reconstruction at 1,000 million pesos (US$300 million). For housing alone the sum needed amounted to 325,000 million pesos. The government responded with four major reconstruction programmes. Two of these were designed as emergency measures to rehouse those most immediately affected by the disaster and a third programme sought to reconstruct a collapsed public housing scheme. In total, the three programmes were to build or renovate 37,821 units.

The fourth reconstruction programme, Renovación Habitacional Popular (hereafter RHP), was the most important and aimed to construct 48,800 units.[2] The action area covered by the RHP programme represented 8.6 per cent of the urban area of the Federal District, 13.5 per cent of its population, and 12.3 per cent of its total housing stock. The importance of the RHP units, together with a second RHP programme called Phase II, within the RHP area must also be appreciated. The population to benefit from the RHP and Phase II programmes represents 20.6 per cent of the RHP zone and the housing units represent 21.4 per cent of the housing stock. In addition, the RHP and other programmes contributed to a major economic rejuvenation of the area involving 3,000 construction sites, 800 construction firms, and, at its height, 114,000 jobs (RHP 1987). Thus, this study seeks to focus on a major portion of a large developing world city and a significant and discrete public-policy intervention in that area.

Although the public sector response was sluggish and erratic initially, a few weeks after the earthquakes, on 11 October, a major step was taken by the government to rehouse those affected by the disaster. An expropriation decree was enacted by the Department of the Federal District (DDF). In the name of the "public interest", 5,476 privately owned buildings covering a total of 2.4 million m² were expropriated (DDF 1985).

Methodological issues emerged from the outset. A few days after the initial decree a second decree reduced the number of expropriated properties to 4,321. Part of the reason was pressure exerted by property-owners on the government (Tomas 1987). However, the absence of adequate property data, even in the most established part of the city which accommodated a great many public buildings, contributed to mistakes in assessing the property damage. "Technical adjustment" to the data took account of a large number of private homes, undamaged buildings, and vacant lots that had been wrongly included in the expropriated list. The assessment also established that there were many damaged buildings excluded from the list and others registered with the wrong address.

Connolly (1987) argues that discrepancies in the housing damage figures do not stem so much from the method used in calculating damage, but rather from the scope of the reconstruction policy the government had in mind. In other words, the extent of the damage depended on the resources available. Certainly, the amendment limited the area subject to expropriation to low-income neighbourhoods, thus excluding the middle-class groups from the type of reconstruction solution the government was offering in the expropriation decree (Azuela 1987b, Duhau 1987).

The study area: central Mexico City

The geographical location of the programme has been analyzed less than its architectural, financial and political aspects. The heaviest earthquake damage centred on an area of $50\,km^2$, of which only $15\,km^2$ was considered a disaster zone. Many studies have vaguely defined the area where the RHP has operated as downtown Mexico City, the historic core, or the central area, and wrongly characterized it as an homogenous zone. Within its wide radius, it actually covers areas that are not part of either the downtown or the historic core. A closer examination of the RHP area reveals that there are three well differentiated zones. The first is located in the truly historic centre of the city and includes the most important historic sites and public buildings. The second zone includes *colonias* (neighbourhoods) urbanized around the turn of the century that display lower densities than the first zone. Land use includes many tenanted buildings, mixed land uses, public housing projects, and a higher number of single-home unit owners. The third zone was formed during the initial steps towards a physical decentralization of the central city that was started in the 1940s. Many of the tenants in this zone live in new, purpose-built, *vecindades* (tenements).

The three zones together accommodated approximately 250,000 people. Most lived in high-density rental accommodation. Ninety-seven per cent of the people were in rented accommodation, compared with 2 per cent in leased homes and 1 per cent who were owners. An RHP study found that the average size of the dwellings was $22.2\,m^2$, and that 32.1 per cent were no bigger than $10\,m^2$. Average family size was 2.99 members, but the average number of occupants per dwelling was 4.37, indicating that many families were sharing their homes with relatives or were subletting. This is partly explained by the area having the highest proportion of low- and controlled-rent units in Mexico City. Although rental accommodation is dominant and family members appear to have been added to the family unit, the majority of the families had been long-time residents in the area, with more than 30 years of residence.

The area is characterized by the heterogeneous nature of the inhabitants. Although an area of decayed rental housing and a traditional reception area of incoming migrants, 17 per cent earn above three times the minimum wage. The average income of the head of the family was twice the minimum wage. Considering that 30–40 per cent of the workers in the Metropolitan Area earn less than the minimum wage, most *damnificados* were relatively well off.

Understanding the structure and heterogeneity of the population most severely affected by the earthquakes is important because one of the strategic goals of the RHP programme was to build units on the same sites as the damaged dwellings and to target the housing to families previously resident in the area. The RHP also sought to integrate nominally the 106 groups representing the *damnificados* into the rebuilding programme in order to quell political opposition and harmonize the architectural goal of preserving the visual and physical surroundings of the *vecindades* and the community *in situ*. As a report on the RHP summarized it:

The strategy of the program is to rehabilitate and reconstruct housing through the permanence of the community . . . through its participation in the decision-making process. By turning the damnificados into owners thousands of families will now have a patrimony of their own. That will ease the process of physical decay of the buildings and facilitate conditions for downtown renewal. (RHP 1986: 3–4)

This aim was confirmed with an extension to the original RHP programme called Phase II. This programme was specifically designed for tenants living in damaged buildings who were willing to organize themselves into civil associations to take the property over in condominium. Phase II could not count on expropriated plots. Instead, the government offered loans up to 1,500 times the minimum wage for the properties to be purchased from the owners. In all, Phase II received 6,478 requests, representing 100,000 families, although limits to the available financial resources and the discovery of many illegitimate claims restricted the final assistance to only 12,000 families.

The impact study of the RHP programme on central Mexico City

The study of the impact of the RHP on central Mexico City considered a number of important questions.[3] The remainder of this chapter will consider just one of these: the impact of the supply of RHP units on the housing market and the consequences for the stabilization of house prices.[4] The study concentrated on the behaviour of property values and market trends in order to assess whether the RHP and Phase II units allocated to the *damnificados* were being sold and, if so, at what price. In other words, is the influence of such a major public construction programme to make the market more active and to shape prices? As stated by a team of international evaluators:

The question becomes especially important because some beneficiaries of the Renovación program will undoubtedly be wishing to sell their newly acquired properties. It will be important to know how they appraise the value of their houses and of their shares in the condominiums and how the market appraises the values. Those findings will help to clarify the level of de facto subsidy the government has awarded the recipients of housing units, for the subsidy may prove to be much higher than the cash outlays from government to beneficiary families. Implicitly they also include the imputed values of the new housing units and the renovated housing units. A land and housing values study would provide an empirical scale to true market values generated by the Renovación program. (RHP 1986: 60)

Methodology for analysis

There are many ways and methods of assessing the impact of RHP on the property market in the area. We have chosen what is fundamentally a quantitative approach in order to address the following questions:

(a) What impact have those units had on the number of real estate transactions in the RHP zone?
(b) What impact did those units have on the price of the offers?

The initial hypothesis was that RHP activity was going to have a direct impact on the transaction volume and on the price of property, increasing both. Two econometric models were designed to measure the impact of the RHP and Phase II programmes on the real estate market of the area. To employ these models the structure of the property market in central Mexico City was simplified. The study broke down the real estate market into different types of submarkets: vacant lots, commercial, industrial and housing. As the main focus of the study was on the residential market, the housing submarket was further broken down into single-family units, condominiums, apartments and flats. Within each category both new and used buildings were included.

Both econometric models use a cross-sectional approach that attempts to gauge the effect of the RHP-Phase II by examining how the different levels of reconstruction activity have influenced the volume of transactions and sale prices. In order to achieve this, data were collected from the classified advertising sections of *El Universal*, *Excelsior* and *Segunda Mano* for the period 22 March–10 May 1987 and 26 January–10 March 1990. Because, clearly, the effect of a programme of the scale of RHP-Phase II on the real estate market will extend beyond the short term, additional data were collected on the number of real estate offers immediately before the earthquake, 7 July–15 September 1985, immediately after the earthquake, 22 September–10 November 1985, and one and one-half years later, 6 April–22 May 1986.

The transaction model

In the transaction model it is assumed that the volume of non-RHP-Phase II residential real estate transactions (offers) in each *colonia* is a function of ten key variables:

(a) the level of real estate construction (number of permits);
(b) RHP reconstruction activity (number of units);
(c) Phase II reconstruction activity (number of units);
(d) the number of earthquake-damaged buildings;
(e) the size of the residential housing stock (number of units);
(f) accessibility of *colonia* to the metro (in kilometres);
(g) accessibility of *colonia* to *zócalo* (main square) (in kilometres);
(h) the economic status of the *colonia* (based on BIMSA data);
(i) cadastral values (pesos per square metre); and,
(j) commercial land prices (pesos per square metre).

In the 1987 research, variable C (Phase II reconstruction activity) was excluded because construction of the RHP units was still under way. It was only in 1990, when all the units had been distributed to the beneficiaries, that this variable was included. However, data for variables D (number of earthquake-damaged buildings) and J (commercial land prices) were excluded for the 1990 model because of the lack of reliable and updated information.

To control for the individual effects of each of these eight (in 1987) and seven (in 1990) variables a multiple regression model was developed. This used the number of recorded residential sale offers per *colonia* as the dependent variable. The models were estimated using data for all 100 *colonias* in the RHP area. To determine whether the level of RHP and Phase II activity significantly affected the volume of transactions, variables B and C were monitored to see if they entered the regression equation with a positive sign and at a level that was statistically significant.

The residential price model

The residential price model is based on the hypothesis that the per unit "offer price" of a residential property is a function of the size and characteristics of the property, accessibility, the extent of earthquake damage, and the level of reconstruction activity. In order to test this, data on a total of 13 variables were collected for each property offered for sale in the study area over two time periods: 22 March to 10 May 1987, and 26 January to 10 March 1990. The variables are:

(a) size of plot (in metres);
(b) area of building (square metres);
(c) number of bedrooms;
(d) number of bathrooms;
(e) age of building (in years);
(f) existence of rent control (1 = rent control, 0 = no control);
(g) use of adjacent property (0 = residential, 1 = other);
(h) number of earthquake-damaged buildings within 0.5 km;
(i) distance to nearest metro station (in km);
(j) distance to *zócalo* (in km);
(k) number of RHP units reconstructed within 0.5 kilometres of property;
(l) number of Phase II units reconstructed within 0.5 kilometres of property;
(m) type of operation (0 = private transaction, 1 = real estate firm or broker).

In the model developed for the 1987 data, variables L and M were not included. For the 1990 version variable H was excluded because of lack of information. To control for the individual effects of each of these variables, a multiple regression model was again developed using the per unit offer price of the property offered in the market. To determine whether the levels of RHP and Phase II activity significantly affect the price of units for offer, it was tested whether variables K (in 1987) and K and L (in 1990), entered the regression equation with positive signs and whether they were statistically significant.

During the 1990 research, additional information was collected on different aspects of each property offered in the market, to be used in the overall analysis of the real estate market. The information includes whether the property offered for sale belongs to the RHP or Phase II programmes, whether the sale price includes a telephone, if the property was sold at the moment of the survey, and details of the real estate firm or broker handling the transaction.[5] In both 1987 and 1990, a follow-up survey was conducted to discover whether the transaction had taken place or not and, if it had, whether the agreed price matched the offer price. In 1987, a total of 75 follow-up surveys took place from the 194 properties for sale (39 per cent) and, in 1990, 308 of the 619 properties were re-surveyed (51.1 per cent).

The dependent variable for the residential price model, that is, the price of residential sales offers, was obtained from the same newspapers and for the same time periods. A list of all the offers of properties located in the study area was made each week, noting the "offer price", number of units in building being offered for sale, size of plot, building area, average number of bedrooms per unit, average number of bathrooms per unit, age of building and making mention of rent control. During the 1990 survey, additional questions included were: does the unit belong to RHP or Phase II; is the transaction handled by the owner or by a real estate firm or broker; has the property been sold; (if yes), at what price; does the asking price include telephone?

The behaviour of the property market before reconstruction, and between 1987 and 1990

Information on the dynamics of the real estate market in the RHP area before and after the reconstruction programmes is very limited. There is no complete and detailed study on the structure and dynamics of the market, and very little is known about prices, the level of transactions, or the type of competition. From the information collected from the few studies that exist (COPEVI 1977), newspaper reports and direct knowledge, it is known that from the 1940s the price of property experienced a permanent recession, especially in the historic core with the exception of a few important commercial streets, that new constructions have not been numerous, and that real estate operations are low in comparison with other areas of the city. This impression was confirmed by the newspaper survey for 28 July–19 September 1985, before the earthquakes (see below).[6]

With information gathered from the newspapers it was possible to quantify the number of real estate offers made for equivalent seven-week periods before the earthquake. In the period 28 July–19 September 1985, the number of offers was 105. This was the lowest recorded figure for any of the years 1985–90. Immediately after the earthquakes (22 September–10 November 1985) the number went up to 143, and one year after (6 April–22 May 1986) the number had decreased to 127.

Closer inspection, however, shows significant variations at a *colonia* level. In a small number of neighbourhoods the quantity of registered offers indicates an active market.[7] On the other hand, the level of real estate operations in 70 of the 100 *colonias* was zero. This second group includes *colonias* across the RHP area from adjacent to the *zócalo*, to up to 7 km away. This distribution is regardless of residential density or the presence of rent control. There appears to be no single factor for the real estate market dynamic. All the explanations based on "single" cause – the existence of rent control, the physical deterioration, distance from *zócalo*, density – miss the complex and, apparently, multi-causal nature of the real estate market.

Table 14.1 presents a comparison of offers for property made in 1987 and 1990. Attention is drawn to the significant jump in the number of offers. From 192 offers in 1987 the number went up to 619 in 1990, an increase of 222.3 per cent. Therefore, the number of offers reached in 1990 has no historical precedent in the previous five years or perhaps longer.[8] The most dramatic growth is for condominiums, with an increase of 426.1 per cent, followed by apartments, with a 289.5 per cent increase, and below average increases for flats (114.2 per cent) and single-home units (106.3 per cent).

Table 14.1 Comparison of number of offers in 1987 and 1990 by type of property.

Type of unit	1987		1990		
	Offers	%	Offers	%	Increase (%)
Single-family house	95	49.5	196	31.7	106.3
Condominiums	42	21.9	221	35.7	426.1
Apartments	48	25.0	187	30.2	289.5
Flats	7	3.6	15	2.4	114.2
Total:	192	100.0	619	100.0	222.3

Source: author survey.

Table 14.2 presents some of the main variables of the offers made in 1990. As one might expect, the price of units varies according to the type of unit on sale. Single-home units are the most expensive, averaging nearly 184 million pesos (US$63,448), followed by flats, at 69 million pesos (US$23,793). Condominiums were the least expensive, averaging approximately 48 million pesos (US$16,552). Although I will return to this issue later, a brief comparison with the 1987 prices proves interesting. Sale price shows up as the single most significant factor. However, if one looks at other variables, one can see that there were significant differences in building and lot size, number of bedrooms and bathrooms, and age of the building. The 1990 single homes on offer were, on average, bigger in built area (from 153 to 227 m²) and lot size (130 to 176 m²) and had more bedrooms (4.02 to 4.41) and bathrooms (2.22 to 2.58) than those offered in 1987. Condominiums, on the contrary were smaller in lot size (69.1 to 61.6 m²), had fewer bedrooms (2.33 to 2.19) and bathrooms (from 1.14 to 1.10), and were newer (from 17.2 to 13.5 years) than in 1987.

Table 14.2 Summary statistics of the main variables of offers by property type.

	Single home	Condominium	Apartment	Flats
Sales price (pesos)	183,979,591	47,990,950	52,020,802	68,600,000
Lot size (m²)	176	61.6	67.5	87.9
Building size (m²)	227.0	60.0	64.5	90.8
Bedrooms	4.41	2.19	1.95	2.0
Bathrooms	2.58	1.10	1.08	1.30
Age of building (yrs)	22.9	13.5	20.6	24.33
Distance to zocalo (m)	3,593	2,674	2,880	3,106
Distance to metro (m)	631	545	527	478

Source: author survey.   *Note:* US$1 = 2,900 pesos (August 1990).

The above analysis supports breaking down the housing market into its various submarkets. It would appear that the trend in condominium offers and sales is different. For an explanation one must turn to an important finding made during the survey. It was discovered that, of all the 221 condominiums offered for sale between 26 January and 16 March 1990, 66 units belonged to RHP and three to Phase II, representing 31.2 per cent of all the condominiums and 11.1 per cent of the 619 offers. One should note that the research project categorized the RHP-Phase II units as condominiums. Virtually all the increase in condominium offers is due to the placement of RHP units on the market.[9]

The evolution of the property market in the centre of Mexico City appears to be becoming more sophisticated. Of all the offers, 512 were handled by the owners (82.7 per cent), 59 by real estate agencies (9.5 per cent) and 48 by real estate brokers (7.7 per cent). In comparison with 1987, when nearly 93 per cent of the sales operations were handled by the owners and only 7 per cent by real estate agencies and brokers, the 1990 survey indicates a considerable increase in the participation of real estate agencies in market operations. The study registered around 40 different types of agencies, ranging from very informal one-person businesses to some of the best-known real estate firms in the city. Such an increase indicates greater real estate involvement in a sector of the market that had been abandoned by the real estate business for a long time.

Analysis of the units sold

The source of information used (newspaper advertisements) indicates the level of real estate offers in the RHP area, but it does not say anything about the number of sales that really took place. How does one know if the quantity of offers reflects market movement or just a one-sided trend, such as a change in supply not matched by demand?

To answer that question, in both 1987 and 1990 a follow-up survey was conducted a month after the main survey was finished to see how many offers had been converted into sales In 1987, 75 property owners were re-surveyed

206

(39 per cent of the total), from which it was found that 22 had sold the offered property. Taking the sample to be representative, one can say with a reasonable level of confidence that over 29 per cent of all offers made in 1987 had been sold a month after being advertised. In 1990, it was found that 28 units had been sold at the moment of carrying out the first survey. A month after the survey was finished 308 property owners (51.5 per cent of the total, less the aforementioned 28) were re-surveyed. A further 87 units had been sold, making a total of 115 units. Considering 51.5 per cent of all the whole as an adequate sample, it can be said that 37.1 per cent of the offered units (230) had been sold a month after the survey. That is a higher rate than in 1987, when only 29.3 per cent of the units had been sold.

The methodology also allowed the study to enquire about the kinds of units sold. Table 14.3 presents the relevant data. Of the units sold, 49.5 per cent are condominiums, 24.3 per cent apartments, 24.3 per cent single homes, and only 1.7 per cent are flats. Again, condominiums emerge as the best-selling units on the market and, in terms of sale, more important than their proportion (35.7 per cent) of all units on offer. Single homes and apartments follow in relative importance, but to a lesser degree than the proportion of offers (31.7 per cent and 30.2 per cent respectively).

Table 14.3 Number and type of units sold.

	Single home	Condominium	Apartments	Flats	Total
Total	28	57	28	2	115
Percentage of total sold	24.3	49.3	24.3	1.7	100

Source: author survey.

The exchange price of the units sold

As in the 1987 survey, the study sought to find out whether there were any differences between the initial asking price and the final price agreed between buyer and seller. Based on information for 98 of the 115 cases, it was found that, on average, the actual exchange price was approximately 5.5 per cent below the initial asking price.[10] Interestingly, in 1987 that percentage was greater (10 to 15 per cent). This might be explained by the fact that the demand for units has been stronger in 1990 and therefore many sellers were in a stronger bargaining position and were able to stick to the original asking price.

Looking at the price of properties sold reveals that apartments and single-home units experienced the greatest price increases, with a 264.7 per cent and 264.1 per cent rise (Table 14.4). Flats, with a 258.2 per cent increase, and condominiums experienced the lowest price increase. Such a difference *could* be explained in simple supply and demand terms: the number of condominiums offered in the market was so great that prices did not increase in comparison to other types of units where fewer offers had been made. However, one must also suspect that the RHP influence has played an important rôle. First, a large number of RHP units sold as condominiums had been brought into the market as potential selling units. Secondly, the prices of the RHP units appear to be higher than the prices at which they were sold to the beneficiaries, but lower in comparison to other non-RHP condominiums – pushing down the prices of all other condominiums in the RHP area. It can be observed in Table 14.5 that the prices of single-home units and apartments are more dispersed than the prices of flats and condominiums.

Table 14.4 Price increases 1987–90 by type of unit (1987 pesos).

Type of unit	1987	1990	Increment
Single home	22,962,105	83,627,086	264.1
Condominiums	7,898,809	21,814,068	176.1
Apartments	6,483,333	23,645,819	264.7
Flats	8,703,704	31,181,818	258.2

Source: author survey.

Table 14.5 Price averages by type of unit (1990 pesos).

Type of unit	Mean	Median	Standard deviation
Single home	183,979,591	160,000,000	93,456,671
Condominiums	47,990,950	45,000,000	17,888,350
Apartments	52,020,802	46,000,000	25,120,462
Flats	68,600,000	68,000,000	30,519,431

Source: author survey.

Results of the transaction and residential price model

The transaction and residential price models serve to isolate the effect of the RHP-Phase II programmes on the real estate market. To isolate the RHP programme's effects on the volume of real estate transactions, the transaction model incorporated nine variables into a multiple regression equation. A stepwise regression model was developed to provide the best-fitting, policy-relevant model. After several interactions, the model presented in Table 14.6 was determined to be the best. It is based on two of the eight variables: the total housing stock in the *colonia* and the number of RHP units constructed.

Overall, the model explains nearly 50 per cent of the variation in the number of real estate transactions taking place during 1987. The regression results indicate that the size of the housing stock positively affects the number of recorded offers. The model estimates that for each 1,000 housing units in a *colonia*, an additional 1.4 transactions will occur. The RHP variable enters with a negative sign, suggesting that the higher level of RHP activity reduces the level of transactions. This was not the expected result (Dowall & Perló 1988). Instead, it was predicted that the RHP action would drive up the residential real estate market and add to transaction volume.

Table 14.6 Regression model results for transaction model, 1987.

	Intercept value	*Colonia* housing stock (000s)	Number of RHP units (000s)	R^2
1987	−1.646	1,374*	−3.571	.49
	(−0.393)	(8.996)	(−5.500)	8
		Colonia housing stock (000s)	Number of phase II units (000s)	R^2
1990		2,333*	−0.04510*	.57

Source: author survey, Dowall & Perló 1988.　　* significant at the 0.001 confidence level.

For the 1990 version of the model, the RHP variable does not enter the equation, meaning that it does not affect the number of real estate offers. Interestingly, the new variable introduced in the model, the number of Phase II units built, enters next and does so with a negative sign, indicating that the higher level of Phase II activity reduces the level of transactions. This result is consistent with the result found in 1987, but, again, not what was predicted.

In both studies, 1987 and 1990, it would appear that the two housing programmes had an initial inhibitory effect on the real estate market. In effect, the presence of the new units has altered some of the normal conditions in which the market usually operates. It is possible that this has worked by withdrawing Phase II programme beneficiaries as potential buyers of private real estate and by bringing in a new supply of units. However, a more subtle explanation would be to argue that the new units have only "potentially" entered the market. That is, they are part of the market, but they are still not "in" the market. Thus, a first reaction is produced even before those units enter the market – an inhibitory effect.

The effect of the RHP programme can be further illustrated by looking at the spatial overlap of RHP construction with market change. There are a number of *colonias* where the relation between the increase in real estate offers and the number of units built by the RHP is strong enough to contradict the result of the model. *Colonias* such as Centro, Doctores, Guerrero, Obrera and Morelos have the highest concentration of RHP units and they also experienced some of the highest growth in real estate offers of the entire RHP area. One could argue that all those *colonias* have a large housing stock, so it would be logical to find the largest number of real estate offers there. However, that does not explain the low performance in 1987. Instead, the answer appears to lie, in part, in the RHP housing market. In 1990, after three years, the RHP units were given to the *damnificados*, and a good number of them became a part of the recorded real estate market transactions. Simply by adding such a massive number of saleable housing units, the number of real estate transactions grew. Therefore, in those *colonias* with significant RHP construction a high increase in offers was expected.

If this is indeed the explanation, a high proportion of the offers should consist of RHP units. Looking at the information on RHP units offered for sale between

25 January and 16 March 1990, it was found that nearly 70 per cent of the RHP units offered were located in four *colonias* – precisely those in which the number of units built was the highest and where the number of offers registered some of the highest increases. The presence of RHP units explains to a large extent why the number of offers grew in the above-mentioned *colonias*.[11] However, it remains the case that the largest number of real estate market offers are in *colonias* with minimal or no RHP-Phase II units. It is clear that in these cases it is the general housing market that has become more active, but not as a direct result of the RHP-Phase II programmes.

To control for those factors that might affect the offer prices, a residential price model was built which again employed regression analysis. Again, a stepwise process was used to determine the best fit of the data. Two models were estimated: one for all *colonias* and one for only those *colonias* where the RHP has been active. The overall fit of the data ranges from 54 per cent to 63 per cent of the variation in offer prices. In both models three factors are highly significant in explaining property prices:

(a) the type of the unit (measured as a dichotomic variable where single-home units are equal to 0, and all other multi-family units are set equal to one);
(b) distance to the *zocalo* or main plaza;
(c) size of the unit.

The type of unit variable is negative, indicating that the price of multi-family units reduces the average asking price. The coefficient indicates that, on average, a unit is 5.8 million pesos cheaper for multi-family units than for a single home. The coefficient of distance to the *zócalo* indicates that, for each metre from the *zócalo*, the price of a unit declines by 1,280 pesos. The size of the unit in square metres adds 67,900 pesos to the offering price for each square metre of space. The fourth factor is the level of earthquake damage.

The 1990 version of the residential price model incorporated two new variables into the list used in 1987: the number of Phase II units built within 0.5 km of the property, and the type of real estate transaction (private = 0, real estate agency = 1, and real estate broker = 2). The number of earthquake-damaged buildings within 0.5 km of the property had to be dropped because the information was not available.

The new version of the model, therefore, determined the individual effects of each of the 12 variables on the asking price of all the housing units offered during the period 26 January–16 March 1990. Three factors are highly significant in explaining the dependent variable:

(a) building area in square metres;
(b) type of unit (measured, as before, where single-home units equal 0 and all the other multi-family units are set to equate to 1);
(c) size of the plot (in metres).[12]

The overall fit of the data is good, explaining 73 per cent of the variation in offer prices. The size of the building unit adds $372,678 pesos to the offer price for each square metre of space. The type-of-unit variable coefficient indicates that the price of multi-family units reduces the average offer price of units by 50,742,704 pesos. The number of units built by Phase II is negative, indicating that the higher level of Phase II construction lowers the asking price of units. The coefficient indicates that each Phase II unit will bring down the offer price by nearly 46,000 pesos. Finally, the type-of-operation coefficient indicates that the offer price of a unit will decline on average by 11,516,953 pesos when the real estate operation is handled privately.

The results of the 1990 version of the models, therefore, seem to confirm the pattern observed for the effect of the RHP programme in 1987. This is particularly so for the transactions model – namely, that the initial effect of the housing programme on the real estate market has been to limit the sales and to reduce the price of other non-RHP transactions. In the following years, one might expect a shift in this tendency as Phase II units become part of the real estate market in the RHP area and perform more closely to other housing offers.

Conclusions

Assessing the effects of a vast project like the RHP programme is a difficult and complex task, primarily because the assessment has to be conducted over a considerable time span before any definitive results can be reached. The study was also conscious of the need to improve and reassess at each evaluation stage the methods used to collect and analyze data. In our first assessment we were able to focus on the immediate effects of the RHP, programme while the second assessment provided us with the opportunity of putting the first exercise into perspective and allowed the whole effect of the reconstruction programme to be seen as a process requiring a long-term outlook. During this process it became clear that a study of this nature would benefit from the combined use of quantitative methods and qualitative analysis.

There is no doubt that the real estate market in the RHP area has undergone a dramatic change in the aftermath of the reconstruction programme. The study's initial observations about this change, however, present a paradox. In 1987, the RHP units appeared not to have entered the real estate market in significant numbers and yet they were shaping the market's behaviour by redirecting buyers to the new units and by inhibiting the owners of the non-RHP housing units in the sale of their properties. Only later, in the 1990 assessment, was it clear that the RHP units had become a very significant part of the market, once again shaping, but this time also being shaped by, market forces, particularly price and demand. The increase in the number of real estate offers at this time, however, is only one symptom of a vast transformation that has taken place in the structure of supply, the type of units offered, the level of prices, and so forth. The level of real estate transactions went up considerably between 1987 and 1990, establishing an historical shift in comparison with the previous trend.

In each of the seven-week periods used to assess the market transactions, an average of 600 to 650 units, or between 4,800 to 5,200 transaction per year, were made. Given the total housing stock in the RHP area (256,771 units) this implies an annual turnover rate of 1.8–2 per cent.

A further effect of the reconstruction programmes on the real estate market has been to help bring down prices. It is evident that in 1987 the presence of RHP units reduced the number of transactions and the prices of those properties offered in the market. In 1990, the impact of the RHP appears not to be performing the same rôle. The most moderate price growth seems to be taking place in condominiums, and there exists a high probability that RHP might be influencing the price. In that sense we can say that RHP has acted as a stabilizing mechanism on market prices.[13]

Finally, the study points to a possible weakness of the methodology of the RHP programme and in the degree of social neutrality of World Bank funding. The study has noted the presence, by 1990, of a significant number of RHP units. Supposing that the number of RHP units already sold or being put on the market represents a substantial proportion of all the RHP units, what does this mean? One should recall that one of the goals of the RHP was to ensure the permanence of the original residents in the area. Moreover, the government placed considerable political emphasis on this objective in the face of severe opposition from the *damnificado* movements. At this stage, we are not in a position to assess conclusively whether these aims have been met or whether the original inhabitants are selling up and moving out. The survey techniques described above are inadequate to make definitive assessments. Other residents of the area might be the buyers. If this is the case, then the RHP and Phase II programmes are retaining families that would otherwise looks for housing options elsewhere. However, if RHP and Phase II units are being purchased for non-residential use, then the programme will have proved ineffective in fulfilling one of its original goals. At present we are poorly placed without further research to determine whether the RHP and Phase II units are being sold or rented, and what the motives of those embarking on this process might be.

Notes

1. The budget of the most important reconstruction programme (RHP) amounted to 274,624.5 million pesos, of which 151,301.7 million (55 per cent) came from fiscal sources and 123,322.80 million (45 per cent) from the World Bank (RHP 1987). The World Bank's involvement was extended to 63.8 per cent of the budget as part of a later extension of the RHP programme called Phase II.
2. The investment of the four programmes together totalled $506,009.5 million pesos.
3. The version of this chapter presented as a paper at the Fitzwilliam Workshop included a discussion of whether the RHP had under- or over-priced the units. Discussion of the detailed impact also related information at the *colonia* level, which is unnecessary for the current chapter.
4. In order to record real price change, the sales price data have been deflated, using 1987 as the

base year.

5. It should be pointed out that the presence of a telephone represents both an indication of the status of the property and a substantial saving in installation costs and hassle to the prospective purchaser.

6. Some authors contend that the explanation for this is the rent control decree enacted in 1942. This appears to have had a particularly negative impact regarding the participation of real estate firms (COPEVI 1977, Moreno 1988).

7. The neighbourhoods are Jardín Balbuena, Moctezuma, Guerrero, Doctores and San Pedro El Chico.

8. At the *colonia* level, a different tendency appears to emerge. In 53 *colonias* the number of offers grew below the average of the RHP area or had no growth at all. Thirteen had fewer offers in relation to 1987, 10 had average and 24 had an above-average growth.

9. The entrance of the RHP units onto the market has also altered the structure of the condominium stock and the offers made in the RHP area, making the average unit, for example, smaller in size. Hence the reason for the condominiums following a different trend from other types of units on offer.

10. Of the units sold, 52 were sold at the asking price, 37 for less and 9 for more than the original price. However, the variations could not be explained according to location, type of unit or type of operation. The survey methodology was inadequate to suggest, with confidence, alternative explanations.

11. In *colonia* Morelos, for example, half of all the offers were RHP units, in Obrera 32 per cent, in Doctores 23.5 per cent and in Centro 18.8 per cent.

12. Additional factors, in order, are the distance to *zócalo*, the number of units built by Phase II, the type of operation (measured as dummy variable), and the existence of rent control (where rent control = 0, no control or other = 1).

13. Of course, factors other than RHP-Phase II are driving up the real estate market in the area. Besides the direct impact of the RHP units enhancing the housing supply, changes in legislation affecting condominium construction and sale, and macroeconomic factors are determining those changes.

CHAPTER FIFTEEN

Snapshot analysis and the impact of public policy on land valorization

Gareth Jones, Edith Jiménez, Peter M. Ward

Introduction: caveats to the measurement of public policy impacts

There is an extensive literature on the supposed impact of public policy on land-price change. The most rigorous evidence for the assertion that government action can affect land prices is provided by neoclassical economics which argues that any government activity in the market must, *ceteris paribus*, influence the distribution and price of commodities (Dowall 1980). Indeed, this proposition was the starting point for the study outlined in Chapter 14 by Perló. In line with the theme of this volume one can, again, clearly observe how theoretical or ideological baggage predisposes the results obtained. In the case of neoclassical-based studies, for example, there would appear to be little control for political conditions. Thus, although individual studies may acknowledge the extent of state intervention, little mention is made of what the state is, other than the neutral provider of public goods. Yet, as Gilbert (1984: 233) notes, for Venezuela, urban transport schemes are rarely a technical solution but rather a fillip to property speculation and the construction industry. An even broader interpretation that might include an appreciation of the state's rôle in impinging on or engendering social conflict is ignored. This has led to a corpus of literature that is largely econometric.

When analyzing the presence or absence of a specific public good most studies have investigated the price differential according to whether a neighbourhood possesses the amenity or not, or to how far away the amenity is located. In this context it has been found that property values in Los Angeles command extra value if they have a "view" (Badcock 1984). Similarly, proximity to local parks or greenbelts affects price depending on the position or distance of the property to the amenity: houses that back onto a park have a lower price than those that face it (Weicher & Zerbst 1973, Correll et al.

1978). Conventionally, it is assumed that structural services and locational advantage are held constant, so that price differences can be attributed to the capitalized value of the externality generated by the amenity (Correll et al. 1978: 208).[1]

In cities in developing countries there is a more up-front concern with the social implications of valorization. The best-documented example is the urban renewal project for Brás, São Paulo, described by Batley (1982). This apparently led to increased property prices and the expulsion of low-income residents. Moreover, both the project and the subsequent valorization of the land altered the physical landscape insomuch as apartments replaced houses, commercial stores took over from corner shops, and even day-to-day financial transactions changed as informal credit gave way to hire purchase. Batley concluded that, "in a situation of great inequality, of rapid urban expansion, of speculative property investment and of insecurity of tenure . . . even the extension of public utilities implies increased property valuation and direct administrative or market-enforced expulsion of residents" (Batley 1982: 234). The displacement of the poor took place even as the result of a policy partly designed to benefit these groups.[2] The problem, however, as Ward (1993) has illustrated, is that even several years after the Brás redevelopment, most land that was cleared for commercialization purposes remained vacant, and construction capital appeared to have focused its attentions elsewhere.

Despite this research we remain poorly placed in terms of identifying an accessible technique to measure public policy impacts on land prices in developing countries. The aim of this chapter is to introduce an original technique that we have developed in our research designed to measure the impact of public policy on land markets at the local scale. The technique is called the snapshot survey. The aim of the snapshot is to identify the ways in which state policies exhibit "definite effects on urban land prices and land uses" (Roweis & Scott 1978: 43). In order to do so, a conscious effort was made to choose spatially and temporally distinct public policies that had been applied to specific areas of the city. In this way, it was hoped that the effect of most exogenous factors would be controlled. The first key feature of the snapshot, therefore, is to disengage valorization effects from other exogenous or market trends.

The second key feature is to build in a sensitivity to how interventions or changes to existing public policy take place. The point of departure is that public policy is a non-technical and, at times, non-rational activity. Although not discussed in detail here, a closer inspection of public intervention and its impact on the land market suggests a complex pattern of state–society and intra-state negotiations that combine strong and decisive actions with occasionally weak interventions and often contradictory outcomes (Ward & Jones 1994). The snapshot, then, is concerned with discovering the extent *and* mechanisms by which the state can influence land prices in controlled settings and under conditions over which the state should have a clear influence.[3]

Building an appropriate methodology

Plainly the measurement of the price effects of state action is exceedingly complex. There are two conventional methods used to gauge the impact that public policies can have on land prices. These are: ex-post measurements, where the effects of government action are assessed by direct fieldwork, taking readings before and after the event; and predictions of land-market impact relating to future government actions (Dowall 1991a: ii). The snapshot falls into the first category.

The reason for selecting this approach relates to the perception that most studies have been overly intent on postulating conclusions in terms of spatial categories, especially rent-distance criteria, such that time has been largely omitted. There are two problems here. First, in policy terms, the concern of governments is more usually to argue that valorization has taken place over time as a result of intervention. This allows calculation of valorization or betterment taxes to recoup some of the costs of specific public-sector intervention. Even for the most technocratic planner, there is little desire to assess the added complication of distance-decay from the city centre, or outwards from the externality designated, as having a positive impact on land prices. While arguably unwarranted, for taxation purposes the valorization impact is often viewed in terms of a given spatial area – usually a settlement or neighbourhood.

Secondly, concentration on the spatial dimension makes it difficult to imagine a clear demonstration of the valorization impact of a given public policy from all other influences. As Bahl notes, perhaps the most difficult problem in assessing the valorization impact of public policy is "that of isolating project effects on land values from all other factors that might influence land values" (Bahl et al. 1973, in Dowall 1980: 23). The most frequent method used to establish the demonstration of valorization is the use of a control. Here, prices are compared between a location where a chosen public policy is present to one (or more) locations where the policy is absent. The tendency, therefore, is to take public policy in isolation, *at one moment in time*, and to ignore the influence of other policies taking place simultaneously elsewhere or in the past. The distance-decay function, for example, might be expected to overlap with many other public policies in other locations.[4]

The use of a control settlement requires the strong assumption that in virtually all other aspects the two settlements could be described as being alike. Yet, as most researchers with first-hand experience of working in developing societies will be aware, this is rarely the case. Indeed, a control selected on the presence or absence of a policy is likely to be different from the survey settlement in every other context. First, in cities of limited resources, the absence (to take an example) of a service from a control settlement, while it would suggest a different type or scale of government attention as in the survey sites, is likely to have received some other form of outside assistance: few governments can afford to exclude settlements from any sort of improvement. Secondly, the fact that a control settlement had not received the chosen form of government assistance might signify something exceptional about that settlement: its unwillingness to be co-opted into the political net, a high degree of self-help, different tenure conditions, topographic problems. For such reasons, therefore, we decided that the most appropriate control would be to compare the survey settlements to a basket of controls that would correspond to the general characteristics of the single settlement (tenure, legality, age), but would not suggest results based on the idiosyncratic land profile of a single settlement. Our snapshot methodology, therefore, proposes a comparison of the land-price trend in the study settlement with the general trend for the city as a whole.

The most comprehensive method to collect these data is the newspaper survey (Ward et al., Siembieda, this volume). If there are sufficient data the analysis can be broken down to provide a comparison with, for example, all private low-income settlements, and illegal or peripheral settlements. In this way it can be quickly established whether the price trend in the study settlement is in accordance with a general, city-wide profile or displays different characteristics. Again, in these cases a more sophisticated analysis can be applied if sufficient data are available.

The need to contextualize the data

Our snapshot survey of 11 projects in 3 Mexican cities confirmed the need to contextualize the data.[5] The methodological point we wish to emphasise in this chapter is that public policy intervention treats each settlement as different. Invariably services are made available in a piecemeal fashion, with the implication that installation or policy adoption usually requires a long process of negotiation, work and payment. This is likely to have considerable influence on the valorization of land in a settlement – not by making it unique and thus providing plots with a price premium, but by obscuring the relationship between service installation and the reaction of land price. Taking this understanding as an assumption with which to investigate the valorization process strongly suggests that any predicted effects are likely only once the service is regarded as "definite". To take one well known example from Mexico City, the renovation of the downtown area of La Merced, rather than increasing real land prices "enormously" as some claim (Reid & Aguilar 1983: 118), has had a far more modest impact. Although a project with strong political backing, the history of the renovation of La Merced has been a long stop-start process. Any pretence to the area being part of a co-ordinated renovation programme has been lost. Rather than improve the area, therefore, many of the undesirable social affects of what was the city's red light district have become more prevalent.

An ex-post investigation such as the snapshot offers the possibility of including a greater level of sensitivity to the *process* of public policy intervention. The traditional lack of concern with discovering how the acquisition of the chosen amenity is introduced to a given area obscures the length of time required to initiate, negotiate and install a project. Thus, the temporal dimension is once more relegated, leading to an unwritten assumption that an amenity arrived overnight – almost as though it was an act of God. In reality, service installation usually occurs after intense political debate. Despite this, analyses have proceeded to examine the economic benefits to accrue from projects on which the political geography of service acquisition is seen to have no effect (Jones 1991a).

Failure to contextualize the data may also present a misleading impression about the correspondence between public policy and land-price change. Some examples can usefully highlight the attraction of such an approach. The consolidation of a middle-income settlement known as Balcones in Querétaro was strongly affected by the inconsistency of the development profile adopted by the developer, Grupo ICA. Although ICA set out to develop Balcones in sections (a conventional method to increase the valorization of plots), the completion of urbanization works and the initiation of plot sales in that neighbourhood coincided with a period during the latter part of the 1970s when there had been an oversupply of plots in Querétaro. ICA therefore decided to "freeze" development of the second and third sections of the neighbourhood, preferring to maintain these areas as a territorial reserve. Given its investment in Balcones, ICA was also reluctant to hand control of the site over to the municipality, since this would also embrace maintenance work, and would, in effect, have meant a deterioration in the "quality" of the neighbourhood's status. At the same time, ICA wished to deny control to the residents themselves. In conjunction with the municipal authorities, therefore, ICA set up a *Mesa Directiva* (Management Board) of ICA representatives to administer Balcones. The *Mesa* was interested in maintenance, but not in consolidation.[6]

The inconsistency of ICA policy has also created a sense of ambiguity over the exact social position of Balcones. In the initial publicity, ICA claimed that electric cables would be placed underground, that there would be colonial-style street lighting, gardens, and *adocreto* (interlocking concrete street paving) and not *adoquín* (cobbles). In fact, Balcones had no water, electricity or telephone service when the first families moved in. Conflict between the residents and ICA occurred in 1986 when ICA requested permission from the municipal authorities to build 14 so-called social interest houses (i.e. rather down-market dwelling units for lower middle-income residents) through a government credit scheme. Although ICA maintained the original designated plot sizes, and did not use the excuse of social interest housing as a means to raise densities, the new houses consisted of two- and three-bedroom, single-storey units – a notably different architectural style to the Swiss-cabin or hacienda-style houses in the first section of the subdivision. Shortly before our questionnaire surveys were undertaken in the settlement, a workshop producing laminated asbestos boards was located toward the entrance of the neighbourhood, and most inhabitants were of the opinion that Balcones had lost its exclusivity and some indicated that the value of plots had fallen as a result.

The selection of public policies for the snapshot survey

Therefore, we sought to build a more appropriate methodology that would allow us a flexible and sensitive basis of data collection. The emphasis was given to building a technique for comparative analysis, and one that would allow both spatial and temporal effects to be taken into account. Thus, it is possible to compare the same amenity in more than one location or different amenities over time in the same city. In our study we chose to divide public projects into three broad types: those that generated intra-settlement improvements, those that improved adjacent areas, and those whose impact was derived from the adoption of more generalized policies. The purpose here was to provide a basis to compare the scale of policy and the location of the policy's application to land-price change over time. It was thought likely that while the valorization effect would probably be influenced by the size of the public investment and the nature of the policy, the spatial relationship of the policy to the affected area would be important. The specific projects looked at under each heading and for each of the three cities are indicated in Table 15.1.

Table 15.1 Sites selected for the snapshot survey.

	Puebla	Querétaro	Toluca
Intra-settlement improvement	Legalization of tenure and water installation	Water installation	Legalization of tenure and water installation
Adjacent improvement/ non-improvement	Bus depot relocation food market public housing	Rubbish dump	
General policy	Renovation historical centre	Renovation historical centre	

Taking a predominantly temporal perspective makes it likely that settlements will have felt the effect of factors other than those for which the valorization impact is being measured.[7] Thus, while in Toluca the authorities have used full legal status of the land as a criterion for service improvement, in Puebla and Querétaro services are extended to sites regardless of the requirement that they be legalized. This complicates any direct correspondence of price change to legal status. In terms of our site selection, this made it virtually impossible in Querétaro, for example, to find a site where the installation of potable water was totally separate from the issue of land legalization. However, we were "fortunate" to be able to select Peñuelas for the snapshot survey, since a section of this settlement had *not* been included in a land legalization programme. The "promise" of land titles was made to this section in 1989, only after water had been installed. Moreover, even when the researcher is content that sufficient controls are in place, the actual background information may be incomplete. In seeking to select a suitable place in which to conduct the snapshot survey of water provision impacts in Querétaro, we were assured by planners that a settlement called Bolaños had no water, whereas the community leader for that settlement had informed us that there was total coverage. In fact, the truth lay somewhere in between: some streets were with water, some were without, and some had water mains – but no water flowed through them.

Therefore, the snapshot survey offers a *synthetic methodology*. We recognize that circumstances are unlikely to permit the rigorous application of a discrete and rigid methodology. Instead, the snapshot substitutes a formula for contingency and pragmatism within a set of guidelines that seek to keep exogenous factors constant or measure them against a series of controls. Where possible, both temporal and spatial analysis is sought – although the Mexican examples concentrated on the former. Land prices were collected by taking actual transaction prices, and once an accurate identification of the date of public policy was set, land prices were collected for at least two years before and two years after the policy programme was implemented. Sufficient readings are required to allow a sensible interpretation to be made, and we required at least three readings for any one year. Once these guidelines are met, additional data can be provided. In Mexico, for example, we also asked for information about land prices by asking respondents to recall an actual recent plot sale (nearby or adjacent) that they knew about (its location, price etc.). These additional "hearsay" data were used to cross-check the information that we had collected, and were not incorporated formally into the data used to identify actual land-price trends.

Positive and negative policies

Most studies of valorization appear to select for study those policies that have a positive impact. Even in cases that investigated the effect of negative externalities such as pollution and crime, it was the *absence* rather than *existence* of these variables that tended to be the focus of study (Diamond 1980). Investigation often also ignores the fact that while public provision of services may be positive for most, it can have negative impacts for some. The construction of high-speed rail links in the USA increased land prices according to the amount saved in transport costs (Boyce et al. 1972). However, there is little appreciation that, for some at least, location "too close" to these amenities may decrease values (Poon 1978).

In applying the snapshot survey to three Mexican cities we took a decision to include at least one negative policy impact. The aforementioned middle-income settlement of Balcones was one such, since although it was an officially authorized settlement and had been developed by one of Mexico's largest engineering and construction firms, it had also been subject to a number of negative externalities. The first was the adjacent growth of a low-income settlement (Bolaños), whose inhabitants were attributed with causing a varied set of problems for the middle-income community: the theft of gas tanks and plants (including trees), the use of vacant plots for burning rubbish or grazing livestock, the illegal encroachment of *combi* (mini-van) bus routes, and begging (especially on Sundays). In response Grupo ICA raised the height of the perimeter wall, but it was obliged by the state governor to create gaps in the wall suitable for public access – including, of course, the residents of Bolaños. A second externality to affect Balcones was the location of a rubbish collection plant (*Planta Transferente de Basura*) opposite the entrance to the settlement. The problems of having a rubbish plant in one's backyard are obvious. The smell and noise from the site, rats, the presence of lorries undergoing repair, increased traffic, and the interruption of the view from Balcones over the city – a view that was the most frequently mentioned reason for first acquiring a plot in Balcones.[8] Families in Balcones have petitioned successive city mayors and made offers to purchase an alternative site for the plant, but these have been rejected. Grupo ICA responded by constructing a "curtain" of social interest houses between Balcones and the plant. Such a move by the authorities to establish the rubbish collection plant at this site is contrary to the received view that there is a close self-serving relationship between Grupo ICA and the state. No reason was offered as to why this policy had been implemented.

Application of the snapshot survey

The impact of intra-settlement improvements on land prices

Land legalization appears to offer a quick and easy solution to a variety of urban problems. Conferring ownership rights on previously illegal occupants is seen to stimulate improvements by offering security against eviction, by resolving boundary disputes, and by providing collateral for loans (Burns 1983, Jiménez 1983, Struyk & Lynn 1983). Beyond the scope of housing improvement, there is also considerable emphasis on tenure legalization as removing the bottleneck posed by illegality for the "good functioning of land markets and urban development" (UNDP 1989: 4). However, critics of land legalization programmes have argued that the issuance of property rights has led to appreciable increases in real property values that the new arrivals have to pay (Burgess 1985b: 281, Nientied 1986, Zetter 1984: 228). Their argument is supported by a double logic. First, the initial illegal status is important in fixing the low level of land prices. Secondly, rent theory suggests that legalization charges represent an absolute rent for land that the occupier has valorized, and that may be appropriated by the occupier when the plot is sold (Legorreta 1983: 93).

The effect of land legalization was studied in two cities: Toluca and Puebla. The Toluca study looked at a comparison of prices between the main part of a settlement called Nueva Oxtotitlán that had mostly been legalized and a later extension called Progreso. In Puebla, a comparison was made between two legalized settlements (La Loma and Santiago Momoxpa) and two settlements not subject to legalization (Ampliación Reforma and Villa Posadas).[9] Data collected from each settlement suggest that land prices have not increased substantially as a result of tenure legalization (Figs 15.1, 15.2). Plot prices in La Loma, for example, appear to have risen over the period but show no marked acceleration either with the onset of legalization or later when most titles were distributed. In Santiago Momoxpa plot prices have actually fallen. There appears to be no marked difference between the land profile of the legalized settlements and the two settlements that have not been legalized. In both Reforma and Villa Posadas land prices are as high as those recorded for La Loma and higher than in Santiago Momoxpa. In fact, from direct observation of the level or trend in land prices alone it is impossible to establish which of the four settlements have been subject to tenure legalization and which have not.

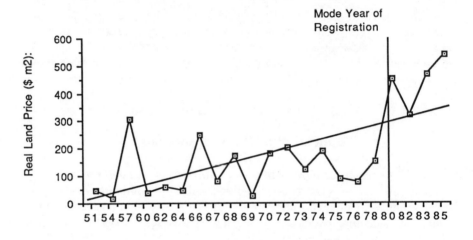

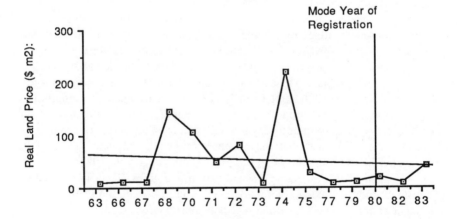

Figure 15.1 Land prices in legalized settlements.

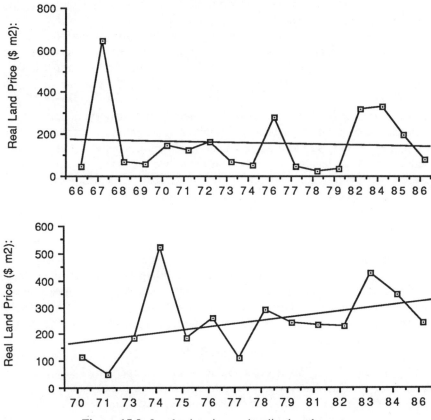

Figure 15.2 Land prices in non-legalized settlements.

The contextual data provide an insight into some of the possible reasons for this. The first reason relates to the cost of legalization. In both La Loma and Santiago Momoxpa the cost of legalization has been low and affordable.[10] A more important tranche of costs has entered with charges for additional legal costs, back taxes and registration fees, as well as a second charge for services, even though these were installed and paid for by the inhabitants. The cost of the legalization, therefore, is not itself significant and is unlikely to enter into the price-fixing equation for families that decide to sell.

Further explanation relates to the ambiguity of legalization as a public policy. In Mexico, land legalization is designed to keep settlements in a subordinate position to the state authorities. The procedure is made complex and drawn out deliberately in order to maximize the political capital from the programmes (Ward 1989c: 143). Instead of instigating a process of land valorization, therefore, legalization represents an ad hoc attempt at urban management. Thus, while most the inhabitants of La Loma and Santiago Momoxpa paid for legal titles in either one payment or by instalments over less than three years, as of 1988 only 68 per cent claimed to hold a full land title even though the legalization programme was officially declared over in 1985.

Given the new cost regime and the length of delays in gaining full title, it is not surprising that legalization is not universally supported by the poor or other interest groups. Neither the *colonos* nor the *ejidatarios* had requested legalization. In both La Loma (Puebla) and Nueva Oxtotitlán (Toluca) the *ejidatarios* had successfully obtained an injunction (*amparo*) to prevent the legalization of tenure. For entrepreneurs, too, there are better business opportunities elsewhere at much less risk, while for better-off families, the legalized settlements continue to offer a poorly serviced environment. Such families could not, in any case, be assured of the legality of the deal. *Ejidatarios*, for example, can remain in possession of significant amounts of land in legalized settlements and continue to sell plots illegally. Yet, there is no evidence in our data to suggest that the *ejidatarios* sold plots at prices higher than would otherwise be the case on the basis of "probable" legalization.

A more highly sought intra-settlement improvement is the supply of drinking water. It was expected that the provision of a regular supply of clean water would be considered an important criterion for settlement consolidation because of the major water supply deficits in virtually all Mexican cities and the increasingly prominent position of water supply on the political agenda. As further support to this claim, research elsewhere suggests that water is the service for which households are most willing to pay (Carroll 1980: 72). However, the inconsistency of government policy made it difficult to apply a snapshot survey for the installation of water. Settlements that apparently had water, such as Bolaños in Querétaro, were, on closer inspection found to have a partial supply only. Others, such as Nueva Oxtotitlán (Toluca), had sections where the water supply was illegally obtained through hoses (*manguera*) buried under light earth or foliage. Illegally dug wells, especially in Puebla, were an added problem. Consequently, households asked "do you have water?" would answer "no", even though large roof-top water storage tanks were clearly visible. An added problem was that, in nearly every settlement, water had been installed in sections. In Nueva Oxtotitlán the installation was "street by street", whereas in Menchaca (Querétaro), water was installed in sections, but plots were frequently left unconnected to the supply. It becomes a delicate procedure, therefore, to deduce what the respondent means by "having a water supply" and to determine the date at which this was "installed".

The snapshot survey looked at three settlements. In the Puebla example, San Rafael (Oriente), the settlement had gone through various stages of the water acquisition process. The settlement was formed in January 1972 from an *ejido*. On 29 March 1977 an agreement was made between the settlement and the municipal department of water (Departamento de Agua Potable) for installation. Many *colonos* opposed the agreement, however, claiming that water had been promised for free after nearby road improvements had been made. Only one street took up the plan. In 1981, a second agreement was reached at a 30 per cent subsidy. The allocated budget, however, was insufficient to supply the entire settlement, so a third phase began in 1982 and a fourth in 1984. Even so, six streets still had no supply in 1989 and relied on a hose-pipe from a local well.

The snapshot data reveal that land prices before and after the introduction of water supplies in San Rafael have been largely in line with the cyclical price trend reported for *ejido* settlements generally (see Ward et al., this volume). In the late 1980s prices were below the average price for *ejido* land (the pecked line) but rose dramatically in 1981, and faster than the general increase in the period, a year after water was first introduced to a part of the settlement (Fig. 15.3). In the following years, however, prices have fallen despite the additional improvements in the water system. Nevertheless, the data suggest that prices in San Rafael are above those of *ejido* settlements generally, presumably because, throughout the period, most households acquired some level of service provision and the settlement as a whole consolidated. The provision of water does seem to have increased prices in the short term and maintained price levels above the general trend. Improvements to the network, however, have not been sufficient to prevent prices in San Rafael from declining after 1981.

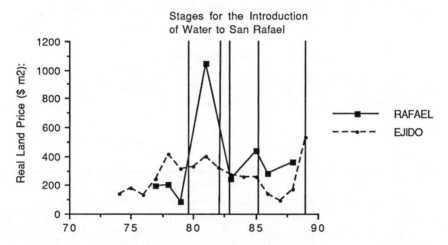

Figure 15.3 The effect of the installation of drinking water to a low-income settlement.

Once again, there appear to be good contextual explanations for this. The first relates to the system of service payment. Inhabitants in San Rafael paid virtually nothing for water – certainly less than the cost of acquiring the supply illegally or from water tankers. In Peñuelas (Querétaro), where the state and local agencies are efficient at payment collection, the inhabitants were paying for the installation of water a year in advance of actual installation. Sometimes, too, these charges appear to vary arbitrarily.[11] A second explanation is that the real cause of the water shortage in Puebla relates to the inefficiency of the supply and the complex political overlaps between competing public-sector institutions. However, while the sporadic and unco-ordinated nature of the delivery system should increase the premium of possessing a water supply, particularly as investment in public services suffered during the crisis, the limited supply that results means that settlements with water often feel as though the service is only temporary. Indeed, San Rafael suffers from frequent water shortages.

The impact of improvements to adjacent areas on land prices
Research indicates that existing properties increase in value after the location of public housing (Bosque Maurel et al. 1985, Rabiega, Ta-Win & Robinson 1984). Because of the ways in which public housing is supplied in Mexico the location of a development near a settlement may be expected to have a significant impact on land prices. Stipulations made by Mexico's leading public-sector housing constructor, INFONAVIT, specify that all sites have complete water, drainage and electricity networks. In areas without these services, INFONAVIT will lay the main from which communities nearby might acquire connections. In addition, areas bought for public housing must also comply with the technical requirements of other government agencies for the provision of schools and healthcare facilities and for zoning requirements. The arrival of an INFONAVIT subdivision, therefore, could herald acceptance for adjacent settlements. In any case, occupants of these settlements will usually be allowed access to services provided for the occupants of INFONAVIT housing.

We examined only a single case of public housing, and that was the development of San José Xilotzingo, Puebla, which aimed to supply 1,464 units for members of the CROM labour union. The adjacent settlement of Las Tres Cruces was formed during the early 1980s from the sale of *ejido* land without services, a condition that remains virtually to the present day. Approximately half the settlement consisted of vacant plots and most housing was less than five years old. The snapshot data show that land prices have fallen consistently over the period, both before and after construction of the housing project (Fig. 15.4). The recovery in 1988 is probably due to the general land-price rises recorded for all areas of the city rather than the project per se. Throughout the study period the price of a plot in Las Tres Cruces was below that of overall prices in ejido settlements (the dotted line). Although it is difficult to identify concrete reasons for the trend, the study points to a number of tentative explanations. First, the development of San José Xilotzingo has not meant the introduction of important new services to Las Tres Cruzes. A regular *combi* bus route was added in 1987, but the inhabitants have to compete with San José for the service. The provision of school places for inhabitants of Las Tres Cruces has not generally been made available in the school on the San José site. The competition for services has also led to conflict between the two communities and gang warfare has occasionally broken out. A second explanation relates to the slow rate of consolidation of the San José site. Although begun in 1980, by 1988, only 808 units had been completed. Figures from INFONAVIT also indicate that the average investment per unit in the site has declined dramatically (Jones 1991a). Certainly, the perceived benefits of the INFONAVIT project have not been appreciated by the inhabitants of Las Tres Cruces and have been more than outweighed by the disadvantages as well as the poor state of services in the settlement.[12]

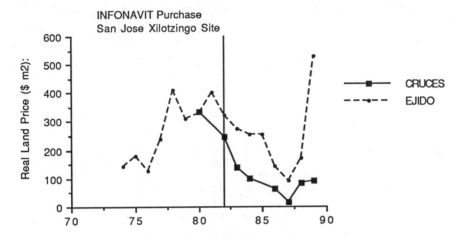

Figure 15.4 The effect of the construction of a public housing project.

When the state does act decisively it appears that valorization can occur in adjacent settlements. For example, the snapshot survey looked at the decision by the Puebla authorities to enforce the relocation of the 30 bus companies from the city centre and to assist the construction of a major bus terminus (CAPU) on the periphery of the city. The project brought to an end a 21-year period of planning and conflict begun 1967 and had witnessed the abandonment of four previous attempts. In 1984, the municipality forcefully supported a single terminal location and linked the construction to a more general policy of commercial decentralization and renovation of the historical centre (see below). Given the political impetus, the 13.75 ha site was rapidly expropriated and re-sold to a holding company run collectively by the bus companies. Opposition from nearby inhabitants, concerned that the depot would become a focus for pollution, was not allowed to interfere with the progress of the project (Patiño 1987: 18). In any case, the government had clearly set out its stall and the preference was for the CAPU location.

Figure 15.5 demonstrates how land prices in the period directly after location of the CAPU changed dramatically. Indeed, one householder interviewed in the settlement behind the CAPU site spontaneously answered that the affect of the terminal would be to raise land prices. What is interesting, however, is that the trend alone says little about the motivation for the valorization effect. What appears to have motivated the land-price change does not appear to be the *start* of construction work. Construction work began promptly in 1985, but up to 1987 there appeared to have been no land speculation in expectation of the impact that the CAPU might have on the area. Rather, we would propose that land prices only changed once the CAPU was *opened*. It appears that it is the actual completion (and visible implementation) of the project that has led to land-price rises being recorded. Uncertainty, in the Mexican situation at least, appears to have a negative impact on land prices and land-valorization processes.

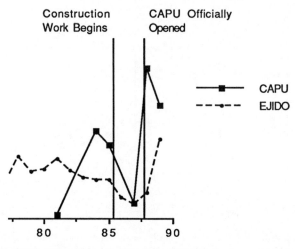

Figure 15.5 The effect of the construction of the bus terminal.

The secondary evidence supports the observed trend for land prices not to continue upward. The image of the CAPU as a "promised land" has been quick to tarnish. In 1988 there was evidence that the CAPU might not be advantageous, especially for residential purposes. Residents in the settlement behind the CAPU regarded the extension of transport facilities in the area as the only significant improvement. Respondents, however, were much clearer as to the disadvantages, with pollution the greatest single complaint. For the inhabitants this is made worse by buses using the access roads to the settlement as an unofficial means to enter the CAPU. Increased trade, in what was formerly a residential area, has also brought additional rubbish and problems of delinquency.

The construction of the CAPU was part of a more general project for the decentralization of informal commercial functions out of the city centre and the renovation of the colonial historic core (Gobierno del Estado 1982). The state had identified the principal problem to be tackled in the city centre as the presence of street traders (*ambulantes*). To avoid political unrest, as past attempts to remove forcibly the *ambulantes* had resulted in violence and the emergence of radical groups to defend and even to extend street traders' rights, the policy solution was to relocate them from the two main downtown markets, which catered for 46 per cent of the city's traders, to 23 markets dispersed through the city (Iragorri 1980: 89; SEDUE 1987: 81). One of the new markets is Emiliano Zapata. The development includes a 216-stall market, a commercial centre and a small shopping plaza. Construction began in 1985 and although the complex was officially opened in 1988, it was still visibly unfinished one year later – the site lacked water, toilets and a paved access road.

The market is bordered by five low-income settlements, one of which, Lomas del Sur, was selected for the snapshot survey. This settlement was formed in 1983 and still has no services, although water and electricity are acquired illegally from supplies nearby. In 1988, there remained plots for sale with only a *minuta* (a receipt of land cession of no legal validity) as proof of ownership. There have been no other improvements in infrastructure in the region other than the market, Emiliano Zapata. It was against initial expectation, therefore, that plot prices in Lomas del Sur appear to have increased, if moderately, to a level equivalent to the price for all *ejido* plots (the dotted line on Fig. 15.6). While it is possible that this has been because of the positive affects of the location of Emiliano Zapata on the local area, it seems more likely that the major part of the increase has been a response to *general land-price* rises for ejido land as a whole in the late 1980s.[13]

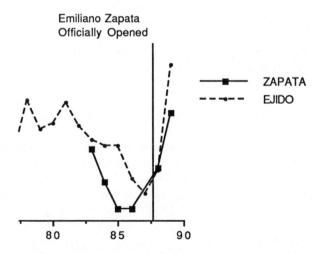

Figure 15.6 The effect of the construction of Emiliano Zapata market.

Our final survey using a snapshot methodology was to investigate the impact of a general public policy. All three cities have begun programmes of urban regeneration in the historic core. The programmes are most advanced in Puebla and Querétaro. In both cases, the programme represents the formalization of a hitherto unofficial public policy that, since the 1950s, had relocated some

229

established central area functions either voluntarily or as part of an unco-ordinated government policy (Estratégia 1987: 46). Traditional activities such as carpentry, leather-working and textiles had left by the early 1970s, while at the same time a series of new markets were built away from the centre (Gormsen 1978). In Puebla, however, the centre remained a principal location of low-income housing with 85,000 people (Gormsen 1978: 8, SAHOPEP 1987: 161), while, in Querétaro, Chant (1984: 98) notes that the centre is "not an area of crumbling rental tenements but a mixture of low- and high-income residents".[14]

The ambition of the renovation policy in Puebla, therefore, has been far greater than in Querétaro where, although pressure has also come from the business lobby and the Church – both blaming the steady loss of status experienced by the centre on the street traders – the renovation has been more straightforward and faster to achieve. The depth of the problems in Puebla required a comprehensive policy to reverse the architectural degeneration of the area, to reduce the concentration of bus terminals, to relieve traffic congestion, to diversify the concentration of markets and to combat pollution and incompatible land uses (Ayuntamiento 1986: 5). An official historic core of 6.99km^2 was identified with a total of 2,487 properties. Most were private residential, but 61 religious and 71 educational buildings were also included (INAH 1986: 31). The government also set about promoting Puebla's cultural identity – giving preference to largely symbolic improvements, public buildings and monuments. In 1986, Puebla was recognized by UNESCO as "Patrimonio de la Humanidad", providing legitimacy to the project and guaranteeing continued support from private foundations and charities to the programme.

Given the enhanced social cachet attached to the historic core the study expected to observe a rise in land prices. Figure 15.7 presents land-price data for two areas of Puebla. The first is the historic core. In this area it was hypothesized that land prices would be the highest for the city and would have experienced a substantial rate of increase. The second area, Zona Juárez, is situated between the city centre and La Paz, a high-income residential and business district. It was expected that land prices would also be high, if lower than the historic core, and would rise over time as the area increasingly competed with the centre.

To some extent the data support the hypotheses. Land prices in both zones are high – the highest for Puebla in general. However, the data also display some tendencies that were not predicted. Most importantly, land prices in Zona Juárez are higher than in the centre despite the renovation of the latter. Rather than compete with the centre it would appear that Juárez has taken over. This has occurred largely without government investment or promotion. Finally, real land prices have fallen in both areas since 1978 – earlier than recorded for residential zones. This is contrary to the expectation that land values in prestigious and accessible locations should "escalate continually" (Roweis & Scott 1978: 41). Despite a minor recovery in 1981, the tendency is one of declining values from 1978. For 1988, estimated land values for the centre were comparable to many other zones of the city at that time.

The study is able to point to some probable explanations of the price trends. The first relates to the position of the historic core in the urban retail hierarchy.

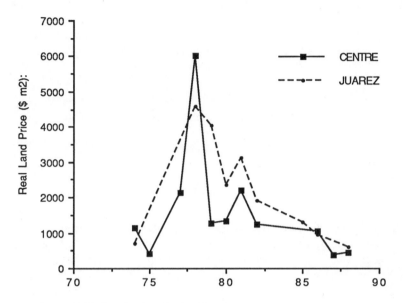

Figure 15.7 Land prices in the historical centre and Zona Juárez.

The construction of commercial shopping malls and the convergence of fewer transport routes on the centre in order to discourage *ambulante* trade have made the centre appear less accessible and less attractive. Secondly, success of renovation appears to hinge on discrete periods of a national construction boom (Benton 1986). In Puebla, the programme to renovate the historic core coincided with a downturn in the national economy and the property market. Thus, until 1986, 21 per cent of the 645 registered colonial buildings eligible for renovation grants had not claimed official financial assistance and 30 per cent of the buildings in the central area were in an advanced state of deterioration (INAH 1986: 33). The more recent quickening supply of *vecindad* property in the centre is probably linked to the desire to spread capital from non-property portfolios that performed badly during the early 1980s, alongside a more determined policy on behalf of the authorities to ensure completion of the renovation programme (Jones 1991a). The evidence therefore suggests that owners may be reluctant to invest heavily in renovation until it is clear that the state is committed to completing the renovation programme (Ward 1993).

Part of the problem is the apparent ambiguity of state policy. Thus, while low-income housing in the centre should be under threat from changes in use, a federal agency has been implementing a policy of *vecindad* refurbishment that would appear to strengthen the hold of low-income families in the area. State policy has also failed to deal with political opposition to the programme. In particular, by 1990 there were probably more street traders than in the past, and these were increasingly politicized in their opposition to removal without completion of the promised markets at the periphery.[15] This ambiguous response is in contrast to that in Toluca, where the main market for the city, 16 de Septiembre, was moved to the (then) periphery in 1976 and was subsequently converted into the city's botanical garden (Jones & Ward 1994).

Conclusion: snapshot methodology, uncertainty, and the unpredictability of valorization

The snapshot survey as a generic methodology

The method of data collection and some of the preliminary results suggest that not enough is known about how the level of land prices is constructed and how change takes place. The received view that land prices and land markets conform to a set of well understood rational rules would appear, at the local level in particular, to be in question. This is not to argue that the "pitching" of land prices and consequent change are not in some way rational – rather it is not very clear what the steps actually are. The snapshot survey has highlighted a number of these caveats. One is that low-income families do not universally respond to service installation in the same way. A number of families in Peñuelas, Querétaro, for example, left the settlement when the urbanization works had begun.[16] Conversely, the majority of respondents stated that the population of the settlement had risen since the installation of major services: the introduction of services had encouraged families holding plots for speculative purposes, and probably renting or living with kin elsewhere, to start building in the settlement.

There is also little understanding of how people make decisions, either individually or collectively, about land occupation. Although almost all respondents to the snapshot questionnaire in Balcones, Querétaro, felt a sense of betrayal by ICA and the municipality, two families interviewed made little mention of either the adjacent low-income settlement of Bolaños or the garbage-processing plant. One of these respondents even went so far as to argue that the lack of consolidation was an advantage or, as he put it, "the fewer people the better". According to him, the fact that Balcones had failed to consolidate meant that it had become a sort of down-market *campestre* (country club) development.

The uncertainty of public policy

The incorporation of land valorization into public policy has, until recently, had limited scope in developing countries (Bahl & Linn 1992). In Bogotá, valorization (or betterment) has been used to fund transport policies, and land readjustment schemes "build-in" a valorization effect to the land development process itself (Doebele et al. 1979, Archer 1987, Masser 1987). Land valorization is increasingly on the agenda and is now a leading issue in the New Urban Management Program of the World Bank and the UNDP (Jones & Ward, this volume). Alarmingly, perhaps, the use of the snapshot as a technique to measure land valorization has produced results to suggest that there is no inevitable land-market response to public policy. This itself has important policy implications. It questions the tendency among governments to use systems of presumed benefits that allow taxation to proceed with only an approximation of land value or price change, rather than actually measure them (Bahl 1979, Doebele & Grimes 1977: 43). Were governments to do so, the data from the Mexican projects suggest that they would find that: (1) the valorization impact is by no means inevitable; (2) even when valorization does occur it is not very substantial; (3) it may be converted into a positive valorization stream only after a considerable lag from project initiation to completion and only once the project is seen to be complete. The fast and flexible use of a snapshot-style technique might help governments ascertain when this point has been reached.

The snapshot examples also tell us something about the types of policies that are likely to produce a valorization effect. First, valorization appears most likely to occur as the result of clear-cut externalities and at a time when the project is open or fully complete. The experience of public policy has more usually been the converse of this general condition. This has left barriers to either the intervention of capital or *in situ* land valorization. The renovation of the historic core of Puebla was held up by the inability of the municipality to remove the street traders. In the other projects, significant deficiencies still exist. The valorization of land in Las Tres Cruces, if it is in any way linked to the development of San José Xilotzingo, would appear to require as a necessary prerequisite the completion of the INFONAVIT development. The problem is not an incorrect interpretation of valorization, but the *uncertainty* surrounding public policy.

It also seems fairly clear that certain so-called improvements are regarded either as unnecessary by those who are affected, or as failing to produce sufficient change to induce a noticeable impact on land price. The valorization effect of the land legalization programme, for example, is weakened by the condition of the security that already exists. Thus, while the legalization agency has sought to maintain the maximum level of insecurity until the moment titles are issued in order to allow the political mileage from the policy to be extended, there is a much broader recognition by most actors that the existence of a legalization policy at all confers a considerable degree of de facto security and, thus, most of the necessary benefits associated with legalization. It would seem to be unlikely that land prices would respond to the formal delivery of the titles.

Overall land-price trends can be predicted with some accuracy where evidence is available on economic performance, public investment and finance, and alternative investment and political conditions (Jones 1991a, Ward et al. 1993). The same does not appear to hold true for land prices locally. The results of the snapshot survey suggest that land prices do not rise as a definite and direct consequence of state intervention. Indeed, the data reveal the limited degree to which "predicted" outcomes are realized from the supposed theoretical implications of state intervention. These preliminary findings highlight the need for an ongoing reappraisal of how data on public policy intervention in land markets are collected and, just as critically, how they are interpreted. The snapshot survey is one route of enquiry. The aim of a snapshot is to get "insights" into the operation of the land market as a consequence of *clearly identifiable* public policy. Its use may indicate whether or not such policies have had any impact on land-price changes and land-market operations and their direction. Although it remains a rather blunt instrument in so far as its ability to measure the precise magnitude of land-price changes is concerned, at the very least it is likely to prove valuable if it encourages critical questioning of many of the basic assumptions relating to land valorization and public policy.

Notes

1. Of course, this is rarely the case. For Karachi, Dowall (1991b) found that there was a strong price differential between plots with good levels of services and those without: provision of infrastructure doubled values after holding distance from centre constant. This leaves a number of factors unspecified. From the published evidence, for example, it is unclear whether the study was able to keep social class constant – was the social status of the new arrivals the same as the resident population?
2. The initial stages of the Brás project witnessed large-scale expulsion as the result of administrative procedure rather than market forces. This is similar to the findings offered by Smart (1986: 40) from his study of Hong Kong. Here, settlement clearance caused property prices to rise as demand increased for plots that would confer the right to government housing for the displaced occupier. Land-price rises, therefore, were not, as in São Paulo, the end of the story, but a mechanism for wider social change and continued conflict.
3. It is important to note at the outset that the snapshot methodology does not seek to discover who has benefited from the specific programmes. As Connolly (1981: 27) points out, sophisticated analyses are not usually required to answer this question, as the clear-cut residential segregation between high-income areas and the rest has been consistently reinforced by government expenditure.
4. The usual analysis employed to measure policy effects is regression analysis. Such a technique is unable to deal well with impacts taking place beyond the measured distance from the particular project (Dowall 1991a: 37).
5. See Ward et al., this volume, for a brief description of the selection of the cities in which this research was undertaken.
6. In 1989 it was clear from the condition of the infrastructure, especially the roads and walkways (*andadores*), that maintenance would soon be a growing issue if Balcones were to retain its middle-income status. In an interesting twist, ICA claimed that it was frustrated by the lack of consolidation in Balcones which prevented the company from capitalizing on the valorization of the sections that it still retained (interview with Ing. Gallegos Diaz, Manager ICA-Querétaro, 28 November 1989).
7. While we are satisfied that the settlement adjacent to the Puebla bus depot (CAPU) was unaffected by any other external influences that might affect its consolidation or the profile of land prices, or that the market Emiliano Zapata was the most dominant influence on Lomas del Sur, other cases will often call for a fine judgement to be made about the effect of exogenous factors.
8. Ironically, the *Planta* refuses to take rubbish direct from Balcones residents, who have to wait for the unreliable collection service.

9. Between 1974 and 1988, 2,678 plots in Puebla were legalized – a total of 270ha.
10. In La Loma the charge was between five and seven pesos per square metre and, in Santiago Momoxpa, 21 to 27 pesos (nominal prices).
11. However, one household claimed not to have paid anything and a further two households to have been charged, in 1989, three times the original figure.
12. It was clear from discussions with the *ejidatarios* that they had not accounted for inflation in pitching land prices leading to real price falls: in 1980, plot prices were 132 pesos per square metre, by 1982, 165 pesos, and, in 1988, 90 pesos (all 1978).
13. According to a *coyote* (illegal intermediary), the price of four plots for sale during 1988 (at 113–180 pesos per square metre) was not notably influenced by the new market facilities.
14. Unlike Puebla, the tenements (*vecindades*) in Querétaro are almost exclusively concentrated in the barrios to the north of the centre. Numbers, however, remain small: of 1,841 buildings surveyed in Tepetate and 645 in Santa Catarina, two of the barrios with the highest concentration of tenements, only 83 *vecindades* were located (INDECO 1979).
15. This is true of all three cities, but especially Puebla, which has an estimated 13,000 *ambulantes*, compared with 3,000 in Toluca.
16. This was possibly the result of a displacement effect. However, although a follow-up survey was not conducted with these families, a study of displacement in five low-income settlements in Querétaro and six in Toluca found that the stated reasons for leaving a settlement were more likely to be personal-, family- or opportunity-led rather than economic (Ward et al. 1994).

235

CHAPTER SIXTEEN

Is under-investment in public infrastructure an anomaly?

Donald C. Shoup

Discovery commences with the awareness of anomaly, i.e.
with the recognition that nature has somehow violated the
paradigm-induced expectations that govern normal science.

Thomas Kuhn

The underinvestment anomaly

Conventional wisdom about urban land and public infrastructure in developing
countries presents an anomaly to an economist trained in the neoclassical
paradigm. The following three propositions contain the anomaly:

(a) Much urban land lacks basic public infrastructure.
(b) Provision of basic public infrastructure greatly increases the value of urban
land, usually by much more than the cost of the infrastructure itself.
(c) The difficulty of financing urban public infrastructure prevents its provision.

The anomaly implied by these three propositions puzzled me when I first
worked for the World Bank on an urban land policy project. *Why is it so difficult to finance public infrastructure that increases the value of the serviced land
by much more than the cost of the infrastructure itself?* If public infrastructure
investment increases the value of the serviced land by more than the cost of the
investment, the investment should, in theory, be self-financing. Yet throughout
the developing world there is said to be such a shortage of serviced land that the
lucky (or politically powerful) land-owners whose sites do receive public services reap great windfall capital gains. For example, many members of the
urban population of Latin America have no piped water in their homes and, as
a result, must rely on higher-cost forms of water supply, such as purchase from
water trucks. Although truck delivery of water is more expensive than piped
delivery, investment funds cannot be mobilized to pay for the cheaper piped-
water supply, even in situations where it would immediately increase the value
of the benefited land by far more than the cost of the investment.

In conventional neoclassical economic analysis, rational investors are assumed
to seek to maximize the present net worth of their assets. If the present

discounted value of public infrastructure benefits is much greater than the cost of the infrastructure itself, why aren't these individually profitable and socially desirable public infrastructure investments being made? Do land-owners in developing countries simply not behave as neoclassical economists assume, I wondered? I did not ask myself this question under any delusion that if the conventional theory's predictions fail to fit the facts, I should consider the theory falsified and should try an alternative (perhaps a Marxist?) theory. After all, how many theories in land economics have been discarded simply because their predictions do not fit the facts?

Quite aside from its rôle as a *positive* theory that can be used to *predict* economic outcomes, neoclassical economics is also a *normative* theory that can be used to suggest what one *should* do to achieve desired economic outcomes. That is, if one *wants* to maximize wealth, or to use increases in land value to finance infrastructure, then neoclassical land economics theory can suggest how to do it.[1] It was in this normative spirit that I approached the problem of trying to discover the reasons for the anomaly of widespread failure to invest in highly profitable public infrastructure. I simply assumed that there was some market imperfection (i.e. the world failed to fit the theory rather than the other way around), and within the conventional neoclassical framework I sought a solution to the problem of underinvestment in public infrastructure.

A conventional neoclassical solution: special assessments

In the neoclassical paradigm, special assessments (also called benefit assessments) are a long-established public-finance mechanism that seems ideally suited to financing any infrastructure investment that increases the total value of benefited property by more than the cost of the public investment. A special assessment is a levy to pay the cost of public improvements in a defined area, with the levy apportioned among the benefited properties according to the benefits they receive. The special assessment is limited to paying the cost of the public improvement, so if the increase in total property value exceeds the cost of the public improvement, and if the cost is apportioned among properties according to the increase in property value, every property's increase in value should exceed its special assessment. Therefore, every property owner should be better off as a result of the *combined* effect of the public improvement and the special assessment that finances it. If so, property owners even in areas of fragmented ownership should be willing to pay for any sort of public improvement that costs less than the resulting increase in the total value of their neighbourhood. In this sense, a special assessment district is a sort of compulsory club of property owners formed to pay for a neighbourhood public improvement that benefits them all.

Ideally, the cost of a special assessment project is apportioned among the benefited properties according to the resulting increase in each property's value, but in practice this ideal is impossible to achieve. Estimating property values is a difficult task, and estimating the increase in property values caused by a public improvement is even more difficult. Therefore, alternative *indicators of benefit conferred* are used to distribute the costs among properties, with the indicator depending on the type of improvement that is being financed. For example, for projects such as sidewalks, curbs, and street lights, where the cost is roughly proportional to the total length of the frontage served, the cost is usually apportioned among the benefited properties according to the number of front feet of each property abutting on the improvement. Secondly, for a project such as flood control, where the cost is a function of the total area served, the cost can be apportioned according to the number of square feet of the benefited property. Thirdly, for projects that benefit each property equally, such as sewer laterals leading to individual properties, the cost can be divided equally among the benefited properties (the "one-each" method). Fourthly, when all or almost all of the benefit from a public improvement accrues to one particular property, the cost can be directly assessed to that one property. often a combination of different methods is used to allocate the different components of the cost of a project, but the aim in each case is to *apportion the cost of the project in proportion to the benefit received by each property*. Financing public investment by special assessment has administrative costs, but these soft costs are typically also assessed against the benefited properties, so no public subsidy is required.

Using special assessments to pay for public infrastructure is different from the more general proposition that the government should "recapture" betterment (increases in land value caused by government action) and redistribute it for the benefit of "the community". Rather, a special assessment is a pragmatic method of using betterment to finance public spending that specially benefits specific properties. A special assessment is simply a way to split the cost of a public project among the benefited parties in some fair way, and it is *limited to recovering the project's cost, even if the betterment created by the project is much greater than this cost*. If the special assessment is not motivated by the ideal that betterment created by society should be recaptured for society's use, however, it certainly contributes to that ideal. Also, a special assessment seems fairer than asking all taxpayers, including renters, to pay for public benefits conferred only on specific private land-owners.

A flaw in the conventional solution

Although, in theory, special assessments seem well suited to paying for public investments that increase property values, in practice they have the severe disadvantage that, because they are levied strictly according to a benefits-received principle of taxation, they ignore the taxpayer's ability to pay. In this century the idea that taxes should be related to the benefits the taxpayer receives has lost ground to the idea that taxes should be related to the taxpayer's ability to pay, and the special assessment seems almost unique among taxes in its total neglect of the taxpayer's ability to pay. It can be argued that if the benefited

238

owner's capital gain exceeds the special assessment, the capital gain itself should provide the ability to pay. The problem with this argument, however, is that the special assessment has to be paid when the project is undertaken, while the capital gain is not realized until the property is sold. Therefore, the *unrealized* capital gain created by the special assessment project at the time it is implemented does not provide the owner a cash flow to pay the special assessment.

Thus, even in cases where each benefited owner's gain in land value greatly exceeds the accompanying special assessment, the *cash-flow problem* can prevent residents who very much want a public improvement from voting for a special assessment to pay for it. The government can ameliorate the cash-flow problem by selling bonds and spreading the assessment payments over time, like a mortgage, but even the regular debt service can present a serious cash-flow problem for some owners, especially in lower-income neighbourhoods where the owners don't have a reliable and predictable cash income. Under such circumstances, property owners can be rightly suspicious of voting for a special assessment to pay for a neighbourhood public improvement if it means that they can later lose their homes to foreclosure if they can't pay the debt. This problem is especially severe in developing countries, where many property owners participate only marginally in the market economy and have no reliable cash income with which to pay taxes. Even if a special assessment is the *only* way to finance a greatly desired public investment, many owners would understandably resist any new tax that threatens the loss of a home by foreclosure. Although special assessments seem to be both a fair and an efficient way to finance neighbourhood public improvements, many voters will not support, and local governments are reluctant to impose, a tax that so completely neglects the taxpayer's ability to pay.

Removing the flaw: deferred special assessments

Special assessment is in theory a sensible, fair way to finance public investment that benefits specific land-owners, but in practice the land-owners' cash-flow problem impedes the use of special assessments. This cash-flow problem seemed to me to be the source of the anomaly of an inability to finance profitable investment in public infrastructure. To solve this cash-flow problem associated with the use of conventional special assessments, I made a proposal in my World Bank research. *The proposal was to allow owners of benefited property to defer paying their special assessment, with accumulated interest, until they sell their property.* The local government would, in effect, offer to lend the benefited owners the money to pay their special assessments for as long as they continue to own their property. Owners could repay all or any part of the debt at any time before they sell their property, but any remaining debt, plus accumulated interest, would be due at sale. If owners pay the market rate of interest on the deferred assessment debt, the present discounted value of all future payments equals the initial special assessment, so the government loses nothing by the delay. Thus the timing of payments entirely at the owner's option distinguishes a deferred special assessment from a conventional special assessment.

The benefits of deferred assessment from the property-owner's point of view are clear. They can obtain desired neighbourhood public improvements without any cash-flow problem or fear of foreclosure. Also, where land values are already high, and where public improvements raise property values even further, the increased property value can be used to pay the deferred assessment due at sale. Of course, there is nothing to stop owners from paying in full the deferred assessment at any time before sale. Indeed, this is likely in cases where real incomes are rising and above the rate of interest. In either event, deferred assessment offers security of repayment to the lender and property borrower. By definition, a deferred assessment can never result in foreclosure for non-payment by the borrower because it will not be due until a property is sold. Because the terms of a deferred assessment specifically exclude the possibility that an owner will ever be evicted for non-payment, a deferred assessment should be more popular than other taxes that are a lien on property.[2]

The benefits of deferred assessment from the government's point of view are also clear. If owners pay a market rate of interest on assessment debt, offering owners the option to defer payment until sale requires no public subsidy. Because deferment eliminates the cash-flow problem caused by conventional special assessment, deferred assessment can encourage neighbourhood self-help improvement without using scarce general public revenues. Local governments run little risk of borrowers' defaulting on deferred assessments because the owner has the cash available from the sale of the property when the assessment is due. If land values are high, and if public investment raises them further, all owners should have more than sufficient equity to repay their initial assessments plus interest at sales, if they have not already voluntarily paid before sale to avoid the interest expense accumulating at a market rate.

The security of deferred assessment tax liens on individually benefited properties has a special importance in the context of international lending for urban investment projects in developing countries. Foreign lenders can now with good cause doubt the ability or willingness of developing countries to repay debt incurred to finance public investment if the only security for the loan is the national government's "guarantee" that the debt will be paid. International lenders would have much greater security of repayment for their loans if the debt were secured by individual tax liens on individually benefited properties. This decentralizing of the responsibility for repayment to the specific land-owners benefited by public infrastructure is both a fair and an efficient way to finance infrastructure. In addition, an important advantage of this "pointillist" method of public finance is that it should remove much of the risk of default on debt incurred to finance public infrastructure investment in developing countries and should thereby increase international willingness to lend for these investments.[3]

Conventional approaches to easing the burden of paying special assessments often misidentify the cash-flow problem as one of low income. Doebele et al. (1979) report that in Bogotá, for example, special assessments are normally due within six months, but low-income owners are granted up to five years to pay in yearly instalments with no interest charges. This offer requires a large subsidy (one-quarter of the capital cost if the market rate of interest is 10 per cent per year), in effect shifting the cash-flow problem to the government. Nor does this wholly solve any owner's cash-flow problem, as it fails to offer the necessary flexibility to overcome the diversity of incomes, ages and family circumstances that are present in any low-income settlement. Not surprisingly, perhaps, the initial apparent success of assessments in Bogotá has now given way to the abandonment of this method of finance collection and cost recovery. Deferred assessments, on the other hand, could completely solve *every* owner's cash-flow problem and yet require no subsidy at all if the government charges a market interest rate on the debt.

If owners wait to pay their special assessments until they sell their properties, they have more money to spend in their community while they own their properties and less to take away from their community when they leave. In this sense, deferred assessment resembles Monty Python's proposal to solve Britain's economic problems by "taxing foreigners living abroad". And if homeowners tend to move to higher-income neighbourhoods as their own incomes increase, financing public improvements by deferred special assessment would tend to increase spendable income in lower-income neighbourhoods and, later, decrease wealth in richer ones. This *voluntary* redistribution of income through time (but not among individuals) requires no subsidy if owners are charged the market interest rate for the right to defer paying their assessments until sale.

Another important advantage of deferred assessment concerns the attitude of the elected local leaders who must impose special assessments. Even if a majority of property owners are willing to pay for improving their neighbourhood by conventional special assessment, the local government is still in the position of imposing on *all* owners, including the unwilling minority, a tax obligation that disregards the owners' ability to pay. The local council can impose a special assessment with a clearer conscience if assessed owners have the option to defer paying until they sell their property and realize their capital gains in cash. In this sense a deferred assessment is a "special assessment with a human face", and elected officials should be less averse to imposing a deferred special assessment than to imposing a conventional special assessment. Thus, by reducing the politicians' "guilt" associated with imposing a property tax lien that disregards the property owner's current income, offering the *option* to defer payment can significantly enhance the political will to finance public investment by special assessment on the benefited property owners.

Deferred special assessment in practice

I initially proposed the use of deferred assessments in developing countries in a book published by the World Bank on urban land policy (Shoup 1983). It then occurred to me that I was guilty of exactly what I disapproved of in some of my academic colleagues. I had seen my colleagues propose for developing countries what I thought were unproved schemes that their own local city councils would probably reject as impractical, unworkable, and utopian. If deferred assessments were a good idea for developing countries, I thought, then why wouldn't they work just as well in poor areas of Los Angeles? Deferred assessment would obviously be much more persuasive for cities in developing countries if they could first be shown to work in California.

The University of California has a programme, the California Policy Seminar, to fund academic research projects that are of practical interest to legislators, and I was able to obtain a grant to draft deferred assessment legislation for California cities. As a result of this research, in 1984 the California legislature passed the necessary enabling legislation for cities to use deferred assessments, and I have since been studying how cities in California have implemented deferred assessment programmes. I have also published a monograph that explains the practice of deferred assessment and includes a case study of its use to finance restoration of the seriously decayed Venice Canals neighbourhood in Los Angeles (Shoup 1990).

The Venice Canals were developed at the beginning of this century by an entrepreneur who bought the land, excavated the canals, installed the infrastructure, and subdivided the land into building sites fronting on the newly created canals. The incentive for the developer to create this unusual residential amenity – housing sites on a romantic system of canals – was the resulting increase in land value, but after the sites were sold to individual owners, there was no mechanism to finance maintenance of the canal infrastructure, and they have been decaying ever since, with the problem of canal-front sidewalks sliding into the water facing many sites. The restoration of the canal infrastructure would greatly increase the attractiveness and value of the sites facing the canals, just as the creation of the canal infrastructure did initially, but the city of Los Angeles has been unwilling to allocate scarce general funds to a project that would primarily enrich a few private land-owners.

With no other funding source available, the owners of more than 75 per cent of the sites facing the canals petitioned for a special assessment project. Almost all of the 386 properties facing the canals are of exactly the same size, and except for corner lots and a few lots facing the Grand Canal almost all have a narrow 30-foot frontage on a canal. The total special assessment for restoring the canals by draining them, relining them, and rebuilding the banks, sidewalks and some bridges was $2.7 million, but the large number of small sites with unusually narrow frontage means that the average special assessment was only about $7,000 per lot.

Almost all the sites on the Venice Canals would benefit equally from the restoration project, but there is a great diversity of household income, household age structure, and housing quality in the neighbourhood. In the 1990 Census, 8 per cent of the families in the census tract had incomes below $15,000 per year and 8 per cent had incomes above $150,000 per year. Also, there is a great diversity in the assessed value of the canal sites for purposes of property taxation. Because of California's famous Proposition 13, properties are assessed for tax purposes at their purchase price, with subsequent increases in assessed value limited to 2 per cent per year, so in an inflationary period properties that have been bought recently have a far higher assessed value than do properties that have been owned by the same owner for a long time. In 1985, the assessed value of vacant lots that were otherwise identical except for the date of purchase ranged from $11,000 to $195,000, a ratio of 18:1. Since the canal restoration would benefit all lots equally, financing the cost by a property tax on assessed value would seem quite unfair, because some owners would be paying 18 times as much as others for the same benefit. At the same time, the high prices paid for the recently purchased lots demonstrates that there is a substantial equity in most properties that could be used to secure any deferred assessment for the restoration of the canals.

In a telephone survey of canal property owners, 85 per cent favoured the special assessment project. After it was explained to the respondents that a new California law authorized local governments to allow property owners to defer paying their special assessments until sale, slightly over half of them said that they personally would be interested in deferring payment, and 70 per cent of those interested in deferring payment said that the cash-flow problem caused by the special assessment would be the most important reason affecting their decision whether or not to defer payment. Finally, of those who were opposed to or were undecided about the special assessment project, 40 per cent said that the option to defer payment until sale would make them more willing to support the special assessment project. This last response suggests that the option to defer paying until sale can reduce the political opposition to a special assessment for public improvements. In addition, many respondents made unexpected but encouraging comments about the deferment option. Although the comments were informal, many owners said that they thought the deferment option was a good idea, not only because they personally might use it, but also because they knew of lower-income neighbours who they felt could benefit from it. And several owners said that their *only* hesitation in petitioning for the project had been their fear that it might impose an undue financial burden on their lower-income neighbours. That is, *it was not merely self-interest, but also concern for their neighbours that generated their support for the deferment option*. If this sentiment is widespread, it is another way that deferment would increase the political acceptability of using special assessments to finance public investments in older neighbourhoods with a diverse population, some of whom lack the ability to pay.

The special assessment was approved in 1991 and the canals are now being restored. When the special assessment bonds (10 years at 6.9 per cent) were issued to finance the project, the average special assessment necessary to retire the debt was only $1,200 per lot per year, so instead of allowing all owners to defer their assessments it was decided to utilize the state's deferment pro- gramme, which allows citizens who are 62 years or older, or blind or disabled, and with a household income of $24,000 or less to defer paying their special assessments until they move, sell their property, or die. All residential property tax bills include an invitation to eligible taxpayers to apply to defer paying their property taxes, and if they meet the income requirements the state controller sends them coupons that they can use to pay any or all of their tax bills. The property owner submits the coupons to the local government in lieu of the property tax payment, and the local government forwards these coupons to the state controller, who reimburses the local government and takes a lien on the property for the deferred taxes and accrued interest. The state charges interest on each year's deferred taxes on a rate based on the rate earned by the state's Pooled Money Investment Fund. In the history of the state programme there has never been a failure to repay the deferred taxes when an owner has died or sold the property, and 40 per cent of the deferred taxes have been repaid *before* the sale of the property or the death of the owner.

My methodological awakening: The Fitzwilliam Workshop[4]

I still believe that deferred assessments will be of great value in developing countries, especially Latin America where conventional special assessments are already familiar, where the infrastructure needs are much more extreme. If my analysis is correct, the cash-flow problem they cause for owners has impeded the use of special assessments, and the option to defer paying the assessment until sale will remove this impediment. And I hope that the case for deferred assessments has been strengthened by first demonstrating that they already work in low-income neighbourhoods in the USA. After all, a successful demonstration project seemed to me to be a pretty good methodology. Thus, I was delighted when I was invited to participate at the Fitzwilliam Workshop that has given rise to the present collection of essays on the methodology of land-market analysis. I looked forward to the Fitzwilliam meeting as an opportunity to come full circle by re-examining the use of deferred assessment to meet the public infrastructure needs of cities in developing countries.

The atmosphere of friendship and trust that prevailed at the workshop made it possible for everyone to exchange ideas, express opinions, and ask questions without any hesitation or fear of seeming ignorant or out of line. Thus I was quickly told, in the gentlest possible way, that what I thought was simply a pragmatic technical proposal was viewed by others as freighted with suspect ideology. What I thought was a method of public finance was viewed by others as tantamount to the privatization of public infrastructure. I learned that I had made a lot of assumptions that I had not spelled out and that might not be met in developing countries. And my neoclassical economic paradigm was a trifle unworldly, even naive. In short, my paradigm faced more anomalies than I had counted on.

I confess that I am as subject as anyone else to the natural tendency to search for evidence that confirms rather than falsifies my paradigm. Methodologists call this tendency the confirmation bias. Fortunately, so much excellent research on the land market was presented at the Fitzwilliam Workshop that it provided me a sterling opportunity to exercise the confirmation bias. Therefore, I would like to conclude by citing evidence presented in the other seminar papers, some of which have been reproduced in this volume, that suggests both the feasibility and the desirability of using deferred special assessment to finance local public investment.[5] I address this by posing some key methodological questions.

The first question to be asked is *are the assumptions in the neoclassical paradigm unrealistic?* One set of criticisms of the special assessment model of public finance centred on the lack of realism of the many unstated assumptions, such as: property lines are neatly drawn, there exists a complete cadastre, property rights are unambiguously established, there is a well functioning real estate market, the system of assessment is professional and fair, an elected local government undertakes public improvements, property owners are taxpayers, and people sell their homes.

Well, obviously not all of these assumptions are satisfied everywhere, but they must be satisfied in many places because conventional special assessments have long been used to finance public investment in much of Latin America. For example, Doebele et al. (1979) describe in great detail how special assessments are undertaken in Bogotá and report that in some years special assessment revenue has yielded almost half as much as total property tax revenue. Macon and Merino Mañon (1975) provide a thorough explanation of how special assessments are levied on benefited properties in several Latin American countries. In particular, Macon and Merino Mañon stress that special assessments are more successful when they are perceived as a price that owners must pay to receive public services, rather than as general taxes on land value increases. Moreover, many papers at Fitzwilliam made implicit or explicit reference to the well established or rapid development of the groundwork for special assessments.

In her exemplary research on the land market in Harare, Zimbabwe, Rakodi writes that: "Deeds to all freehold or leasehold land have to be registered and can only be transferred by means of registered deed of transfer. The register is open to public inspection and is a stand-by-stand record of transfers, giving stand number, size, ownership and amount paid at the time of each transaction."

This sort of land register is exactly the sort of mechanism necessary to enforce the payment of special assessments deferrable until sale. Thus, I would argue that the evidence suggests that there is a strong capacity for deferred special assessment in at least some low-income countries in Africa and Latin America, and that deferred special assessments are at least feasible, even if one does not consider them a desirable way to pay for public infrastructure.

The second question to be asked was, *do public investments increase land values?* Another criticism offered by my colleagues was that it is unrealistic to assume that public infrastructure investments really do increase land values. Fortunately, one of the main topics of the seminar was how public investments affect land values, so there was ample opportunity to answer this criticism. Dowall's paper (Ch. 3) presents careful research on land values in Karachi, with data collected from real estate brokers, and show that the price of land in neighbourhoods where basic public infrastructure has been installed is twice as high as the price of land in similar neighbourhoods where no infrastructure has been installed. That is, providing infrastructure doubles raw land values, after holding constant for distance from the city centre.

Jones et al. (Ch. 15) also studied the effect of public spending on land prices in Mexican cities, using their ingenious "snapshot analysis" methodology. Although they studied six government projects, in only one of the six projects did they find evidence that public investment increased land values. However, what is interesting is that this project, the supply of water to the low-income settlement of San Rafael, appears to have been financed by a special assessment of US$684 per plot. The study of the water supply project had the distinct advantage of providing data on land values before and after the public investment, and land values for a comparable control group of properties that did not receive the public investment.[6]

None of the other five public investments studied by Jones et al. (a bus depot, a public housing project, a facade improvement programme, a commercial decentralization programme) dealt with supplying basic infrastructure for the poor, or with the sort of public improvement that low-income land-owners (or perhaps any land-owners) would ever vote to finance by imposing on themselves a special assessment. And Jones et al. found little or no evidence that these public improvements increased land values. Indeed, they conclude that: "it also seems fairly clear that certain so-called improvements are regarded either as unnecessary by the settlement inhabitants or fail to produce sufficient change to induce a noticeable impact on land price." (p. 233).

From this observation one might reasonably draw the conclusion that financing public investment by special assessments, which must be approved by a majority of the supposed beneficiaries, would help to weed out some unnecessary and burdensome public spending, and would instead direct public spending to higher-priority projects that the inhabitants do regard as clearly necessary.

Jones et al. also observe that "valorization appears most likely to occur as the result of clear-cut externalities and at a time when the project is open or fully complete." (p. 233). If increases in land value do not occur until after a public investment is completed, this finding supports the argument that payment of any special assessments should be deferred at least until after residents are receiving the benefits of the public investment. In another of their papers, Jiménez et al. note for two low-income subdivisions in Toluca: "Although the inhabitants were willing to pay for services, there was no provision of credit or public projects to deal with this situation". The option of a deferred special assessment to finance public services would give the inhabitants of these communities a self-help mechanism they could use to obtain services if they are willing to pay for the services out of the resulting increase in land value. But if infrastructure is financed entirely by higher levels of government, with no payment by the benefited owners, there is no opportunity for self-help, and many important public services do not get provided at all. Also, where infrastructure is financed by higher levels of government, there is ample opportunity for favouritism and corruption in allocating public investment. Jiménez et al. note that state governors "have used their posts to channel public resources into their own private developments" (p. 7). Further, for other private developers "the governors' intervention has been one of the key factors in the valorization of selective plots of land. . ." (p. 8). Similarly, Baross (1991: 60) says that:

It is not accidental that land-owners spend a considerable amount of energy and money to influence planning decisions which will result in "windfall" profits on their holdings. "Political manipulation" is the description most often used in the media and in research studies to account for favorable zoning changes or for the alignment of public infrastructure to serve the financial interest of land-owners.

Greater self-reliance through deferred special assessments would of course shift more decisions concerning public investment away from the governors and directly to the benefited inhabitants. This shift would reduce the opportunity for political corruption of public investment decisions, and would divert energy and money away from the wasteful "rent-seeking" behaviour that Baross describes and into productive payments for the infrastructure itself.

Jones et al. (1993: 21) also observe that under a public works programme known as PRONASOL, urban infrastructure is installed at a cost to inhabitants of only 10 per cent of the total cost. They write that: "The ability of low-income groups to petition for services through PRONASOL will therefore very much depend on the relationship of that settlement to the PRI [Institutional Revolutionary Party]". Thus, when a community has to petition for a subsidy, it has to go either as beggar or as briber. The resulting distribution of services has several undesirable results. For example, García writes that most of the public investment for tourist resorts has benefited private capital and does not produce any revenue for the government. Therefore, public investment is given *free* to private tourist resorts, while, as quoted above, it was made difficult to obtain or denied to low-income communities who were *willing to pay* if offered credit. Charging benefited land-owners for urban infrastructure by deferred special assessment will surely improve the government's cost recovery, at least when compared with a policy of giving public infrastructure away free to tourist resort owners.

The last question is *are special assessments regressive?* Another criticism was that I seemed to assume that taxes and benefits should balance out for individual taxpayers. Some proposed that I had apparently overlooked one of the major purposes of taxation systems, which is to redistribute income. This redistributional function is especially important in Latin America, where the differences in income and wealth are so great. However, although it may appear that low-income families would be harmed by heavier reliance on a tax that ignores ability to pay, it is not clear that special assessments are regressive when compared to local property taxation.[7] Moreover, given the very disappointing record of all previous attempts to tax betterment in order to produce general revenue for redistributing income, it seems to me that the more modest goal of using betterment to finance public investment is far more important than mostly rhetorical and entirely ineffective attempts to redistribute land-value increases for the benefit of society. As Jones et al. (1991: 16) say: "Thus, to come clean, the real motive for policies aimed at capturing land valorization are really intended to strengthen government finance rather than redistribute the valorization gain."

To that, I would say, well, of course, why not? The proposal for deferred special assessments is specifically intended to strengthen the government's ability to finance public investment out of the resulting land-value increases, but in a way that is sensitive to the situation of the taxpayer. Deferred assessment would strengthen the government's ability to finance public investments that increase land values. Deferred assessment would not strengthen the government's ability to pay for the military, for grandiose public boondoggles, or for general social welfare. It might be argued, however, that, by recovering the cost of government spending for public infrastructure that increases private land values, deferred assessment would free up general government revenue to pay for genuine public purposes that have a more legitimate claim on scarce general revenue.

Many of the seminar papers assert that an important goal of urban land policy is to reduce the extreme difference in quality between rich and poor neighbourhoods. From the low-income resident's point of view, the lack of piped water, sewers, electricity, and telephone service would certainly be among the most important differences between poor and rich neighbourhoods, and using deferred assessments to finance infrastructure where it is now lacking is one possible way to reduce the most glaring differences between rich and poor neighbourhoods.

In any case, I would argue that special assessments are ideally suited to redistribute income where that is warranted. Some California cities, such as Santa Monica, exempt individual low-income property owners from paying special assessments (or rather, these cities use their general revenue to pay the assessments for the low-income owners). Thus, cities aid all low-income owners in the special assessment district, but all higher-income owners must pay their own assessments. Contrast this carefully targeted aid to low-income owners with the alternative policy of not imposing a special assessment on *any* benefited owner, and instead paying for the infrastructure out of general revenue. In the first case, benefited land-owners (those with low incomes exempted) pay for public investment when they realize the associated capital gain, and in the second case, all taxpayers, *including renters*, pay right away for public investment that specially benefits only certain identifiable land-owners. Which is fairer? If the goal is really to aid the poor, and only the poor, rather than to aid politically powerful land-owners under the guise of aiding the poor, then deferred assessment with specifically targeted exemptions for low-income owners is far more efficient than paying for infrastructure out of general revenue. As a way to help the poor, using general revenue to pay for public spending that benefits specific land-owners is like spreading a banquet for everyone just in order to provide a few crumbs for the poor.

Conclusion

The research presented at the Fitzwilliam Workshop derived from a number of competing paradigms, but what united all the work seemed to be an agreement on the great value of careful, intelligent description of phenomena in the land market as a primary research method, with a special appreciation for the importance of learning how institutions operate. The findings reported were rich in material both to confirm any existing bias and to challenge any paradigm.

I began with a famous quotation from Thomas Kuhn about discovery commencing with the awareness of anomaly. I would like to conclude with another view of methodology. Aaron Wildavsky argues that you cannot fully understand a problem until you know the solution. Said another way, your approach to a problem, your understanding of it, and your research on it are all influenced by your own preferred solution to the problem. And when it comes to preferred solutions, many of us find it hard to change our minds. On some questions we seem to believe what we believe because we believe it, and we believe it fervently.

The solution I brought to the Fitzwilliam Workshop was deferred special assessments, and I realize that I tend to see the problem of underinvestment in infrastructure in the light of that solution. And I think I came to that solution by struggling with what seemed to me to be an anomaly in my paradigm. Why was it so difficult to finance profitable public investment?[8] As I said earlier, if what I have to say about infrastructure finance has any value, it should have value in California as well as in developing countries, and the most convincing evidence I can present to show that deferred assessment will work in Mexico is that it already works in California. I hope that the evidence from California, together with the confirming evidence that I have selectively quoted from the research presented at the Fitzwilliam Workshop, will arouse interest in using deferred special assessments to finance public investment in poor neighbourhoods everywhere.

Notes

1. Similarly, even if an economic theory that assumes a firm's goal is to maximize profits fails to predict how firms will actually behave, the theory can still be useful to recommend how a firm *should* behave if it wants to maximize profits. And if enough business schools teach enough future managers how to maximize profits, perhaps a theory based on the assumption that firms do maximize profits will eventually come to predict economic outcomes accurately.
2. Lien refers to the right to keep legal possession of a property until a debt held by the occupant of that property is discharged.
3. The property value, not just the betterment created by the public investment, is the security for repayment of the deferred assessment, so the lender can lose only if the owner walks away from the property with nothing.
4. This section quotes from papers presented at the International Research Workshop, Fitzwilliam College, Cambridge. Two of the papers (Baross 1991, Jones et al. 1993) have been published elsewhere. The paper by Jiménez et al., entitled "Incorporation of private urban land into the private residential market: who and how", was presented at the Fitzwilliam Workshop but is not reproduced in this volume. The statement appears on page 4 of the original paper. The remaining papers have been substantially revised for this volume and are quoted here in their revised form.
5. In reading others' papers I have carefully noted anything that reinforces my own point of view. So if anyone feels that I have neglected contrary evidence in his or her own paper, I have to confess that this neglect is probably intentional but should not be taken personally.
6. In any case study that does not use a statistical technique like multiple regression analysis to normalize for other factors, a control group does seem essential. Because Jones et al. did have a control group in their San Rafael study, their finding of land-value appreciation due to investment in water supply is consequently very convincing.
7. Low-income families tend to live in lower-valued property and, therefore, pay a lower property tax per house, but they also tend to live at a higher density, so the burden in average terms may be higher. Because special assessment is paid on equity, the burden on current income is not the only measure of a family's ability to pay.
8. As one of my market-oriented colleagues in the economics department at the University of California, Los Angeles, explained it to me, I had discovered a "hole" in the capital market, not an anomaly in the paradigm.

CHAPTER SEVENTEEN

Urban planning and segmented land markets
Illustrations from Cancún

Priscilla Connolly

Introduction

The tourist resort of Cancún provides almost a caricature of the effects that public policy can have on the urban land market. Its very existence intentionally engendered by the Interamerican Development Bank (BID) and the Mexican government, the speed of its population growth from zero to 170,000 inhabitants in 20 years, its total dependence on particular branches of the economy (first construction and then tourism), and its relative isolation from other urban areas – all these factors, to mention a few, accentuate the processes that may be observed in towns and cities all over Mexico. For the purposes of this chapter, however, the processes we are interested in are a series of government actions that may be usefully described as urban planning.

To start with, Cancún's strictly planned development accentuates land-market segmentation into clearly defined areas. Along with other restrictions, the regulations designed to avoid speculative profits from the subsidized investment in the "planned" areas of the city exclude a large segment of the demand for land. This has been catered for by the well documented process of irregular, then regularized, urbanization of *ejidal* lands,[1] a process that has housed about 70 per cent of Cancún's population. The extreme contrast between the "planned" areas of the city and the irregular settlements highlights the urban segregation produced by this two-tiered land market; it is clear how each kind of urbanization conditions the quality of the environment that is built. These contrasts, however, vary considerably over time. In this case, the rapid development of Cancún as a whole condenses the levelling-out process due to the consolidation of the "unplanned" urban development. Among other things, tenure regularization has gone apace, accompanied by a relatively high level of public investment in settlement improvement programmes – Cancún as a whole has been an extremely privileged recipient of public housing funds. At the same time, Cancún's isolation and the hostile nature of its environs limit the alternatives for

251

territorial expansion. For this reason, the two sectors of the market are mutually conditioned by each other, often with quite bizarre effects on their respective land prices: in certain areas, the price of unserviced, "irregular" land is comparable to that of serviced land in the "planned" area.

Finally, the "artificial" or intentionally planned way that Cancún was created from nothing clarifies the link between property relations and political power; the different kind of property rights prevailing in each fraction of the market are each backed up by one or a combination of different, and often conflicting, political and administrative entities. In this case there is a splendid array of agencies at work: the decentralized federal agency responsible for developing the tourist areas and the "planned" city (Fondo Nacional de Fomento al Turismo, FONATUR), which controls both the planning rules and the finance in these areas; the state government and its own planning rules, dictated basically by SEDUE and substantiated by their consultants; the state housing agency (Instituto de Vivienda del Estado de Quintana Roo, INVIQROO), which owns land that was expropriated for regularization and is also responsible for implementing programmes financed by the federal government agency FONHAPO (Fondo Nacional de Habitación Popular); other regularizing agencies; the expressly created municipality of Cancún, at first a mere puppet of FONATUR, but later to achieve a certain political independence; the *ejido*, belonging to the neighbouring municipality of Isla Mujeres, whose property rights under Agrarian Law provided the base for the initial urban development in the "irregular" sector.

The main thrusts of the arguments posed in this chapter are directed towards this last consideration: the way that "planning" measures are actually implemented by diverse political agencies with particular spheres of influence, defined – among other things – on a territorial basis and how these affect property rights and, therefore, the way that the land market operates. This proposal links straight into a hierarchy of wider methodological issues that need to be made explicit.

The first level concerns the significance of a "case study" such as this one. Clearly, I am not working through the arguments laid out on the following pages merely in order to understand what is happening in Cancún alone. Nor do I propose to generate data to be compared to or compounded with evidence from other cases, thus somehow "improving" the empirical verification of general hypotheses about land markets. Even less would I expect to come up with any kind of universal ahistorical and ageographical theory concerning land markets. What is intended is an "illustration" – and hopefully a constructive revision – of general theoretical principles derived from accumulated collective research experience.

This leads to a second-tier methodological consideration: what kind of "general theoretical principles" am I defending? Do these "general" principles pertain exclusively to land markets in developing countries or are they general to all land markets? In answer to the first question, I would suggest that the way that land markets operate is conditioned, among other things, by the way

252

that buildings are financed and produced, on the one hand, and by the nature of the legal structure concerning property and urban development, including the prevailing attitudes towards the law – compliance and ways of enforcement – and how this is linked to the political power structure, on the other. In the Mexican case this implies recognizing the linkages between the "two-tiered" urban growth structure inherited from colonial times (Lira 1983, Connolly 1990) and reinforced by the post-revolutionary Agrarian Reform which reinstated traditional community properties (*ejidos*), and the Mexican political system. Indeed, certain salient contours of this very idiosyncratic system may help identify similar types of relations and linkages in other societies with colonial pasts. And, to answer the second question, it is at this level, in the development of economic and political institutions, not in detecting some imagined global empirical trend, that we should look for the similarities and differences in the way land markets operate in the developing countries (and the developed, former socialist and so-called Fourth World). This is not to deny the possible existence of similar trends that may be observed simultaneously in different parts of the globe. But these similarities are not the result of cosmic forces. There are, of course, certain economic relations affecting land markets, which for over two hundred years have been subject to theoretical analysis. Thus we might expect, for example, that land prices would drop during a recession or when interest rates increase. There is also a substantial body of knowledge developed over the past century or so that explains, in general terms, the variation of land prices at different locations. Cross-country comparisons of urban land markets clearly cannot bypass conventional economic wisdom.[2]

My analysis of Cancún, however, does not focus on the operation of these general economic principles – which are more or less taken for granted – but rather, on the institutional aspects: the way that economic forces are mediated, and often made unrecognizable, by historically and geographically specific social practices. Hopefully, the ensuing pages can contribute to improving "conventional wisdom" about the way economic and political institutions affect land markets.

A condensed history and geography of an exclusive urban development
Cancún is a contemporary case of planned colonization of what was, from the colonizer's point of view, "virgin territory": low tropical rainforest. The Maya rebellion of 1847–1901 is indicative of the historically low level of territorial integration of this remote coastal strip of the Yucatán Peninsula. In 1970, Quintana Roo was still only a federal territory with a total population of 88,000 inhabitants, of whom 56,000 lived in the border town of Chetumal or the traditional regional centre, Carrillo Puerto (previously Santa Cruz); the rest are distributed in 520 small and very small localities, at very low densities, in mainly Mayan communities. In 1954 the paved road linking Mérida to the Caribbean coast at Isla Mujeres was built, which permitted a limited growth of low-budget tourist development on the island. It also gave rise to two incipient

settlements relevant to our analysis: one at Puerto Juárez proper, the end of the road and jetty for Isla Mujeres with a population of 100 in 1970, and the other, called "Colonia Puerto Juárez", the old roadworkers' camp consisting of about 40 houses distributed between 3 km and 5 km up the road and later to become 70 per cent of Cancún. Some of the residents of these settlements, together with the Island's inhabitants, were *ejidatarios* with rights over the substantial tracts of territory inland which had been established as the Isla Mujeres *ejido*. However, the *ejido* had never been organized on a productive basis; in fact it was not even divided up (*parcelado*) and very few people really lived off the land (INFRATUR 1971a). Fishing, *chicle* (gum) collecting and, for some, tourism on Isla Mujeres sum up the basic economy of the area at that time.

The coral sands, turquoise sea and exotic lagoons made Cancún an obvious primary target for the Mexican government's tourism-promoting policy. This was first pronounced in 1968, and consisted essentially of borrowing money to provide infrastructure and subsidize national and foreign investment in luxury tourist facilities: all aimed at attracting hard currency to be brought by a massive inflow of, mainly North American, tourists.[3] To achieve all this, the Fondo de Promoción de Infraestructura Turística (INFRATUR) was created in 1969. This was empowered to handle all the necessary vital function of tourism promotion, including land acquisition, development investment, and marketing. INFRATUR's seed capital of 30 billion pesos was provided by the Mexican federal government. Later finance was supplied by the Interamerican Development ment Bank (BID). The 6,800 ha made over to the project between 1970 and 1971 was essentially "unoccupied" and in the hands of the then Department of Agrarian Reform (Departamento de Asuntos Agrarios y de Colonización, or DAAC).[4]

In 1972, the Master Plan for Cancún was published (INFRATUR 1972a). This included both the basic layout and land-use distribution, and the rules and regulations that would govern their development. The basic plan clearly defines three zones: the tourist zone, occupying Cancún Island, which encompasses a total of 2,190 ha of dry land, the urban zone, designed to house Cancún's permanent inhabitants, with a total of 3,131 ha, and a "conservation zone" of 6,229 ha of mostly swamps and lagoons (SECTUR/FONATUR 1982). These figures include both urbanized areas and reserves.

It is worth examining the philosophy behind the plan. In its initial version, the main priority was clearly the tourist zone: this was allotted 95.6 ha of net sales area, compared with only 67 ha for the urban zone (INFRATUR 1972a). This priority was closely paralleled in the sequence of investments: first in the airport, then in levelling the tourist zone to provide a golf course and the general infrastructure. However, between the initial plan and 1975, it became clear that the effective demand for land in the urban zone outstripped the initial supply, and both the budget and the actual development of the zone were accelerated. The urban zone was conceived as a model "planned" city to house the population working in the tourist zone (BID 1976, INFRATUR 1971a, SECTUR/

FONATUR 1982). Yet right from the start it was calculatedly clear that at least 39 per cent of this population would not earn enough to qualify for a bank loan for purchasing housing in the urban zone (INFRATUR 1971b, 1972b). In 1975, with 1,322 hotel rooms in service in the tourist zone, the total population of the urban zone was only 1,134 (FONATUR 1975). By this date, of course, Cancún's total population had grown substantially more than that: attracted mostly by employment in construction, Colonia Puerto Juárez had grown to about 5,000 by 1975 and there were a further 4,500 construction workers living in camps in the tourist zone (FONATUR 1975).[5] In 1983, the estimated population figures for the urban zone and the irregular settlements were 19,700 and 63,900, respectively (FONATUR 1983).[6] From quite early on, the precarious living conditions prevailing in the rapidly growing Colonia Puerto Juárez called for many surveys and socio-economic studies. The results of these are fairly contradictory and generally illustrate a lack of understanding of urban demographic processes of this nature. This methodological vacuum contrasts sharply with the know-how and competence demonstrated by INFRATUR and its successor, FONATUR, in predicting the needs of and providing for the tourist population.[7]

The planned urban land market

Any visitor to FONATUR's Cancún will be impressed by the orderly layout, the wide avenues with their well tended roundabouts. With its five-star hotels, luxury condominiums and boutiques, the tourist zone is a veritable monument to the construction industry: not a brick out of place (before the 1988 hurricane, at least). The urban zone also provides a model for successful city planning: the clearly demarcated commercial areas, ample public services, the hierarchical street layout with super blocks and equally hierarchical residential areas: single-family houses for upper- and middle-income areas near to the urban centre and tourist zone and, further away, the neat, brightly painted five-storey flats built under one or other of the federal government's housing finance programmes.[8]

The fact that the Tourist and urban zones of Cancún have actually been built according to plan is due largely to the overall control of the total process by FONATUR. This agency is not only responsible for drawing up and occasionally updating the master plan; it is also in charge of all development investment and subsequent land-marketing, including the definition of conditions of sale. These sales conditions ensure both that the land will be used according to the master plan's land-use and building specifications and that it *will* be used, or at least built on, as quickly as possible. This is unlike other legal specifications in Mexico which make no enforceable requirements of how soon land must be developed. Table 17.1 illustrates the sales conditions for different types of land use. The issue of title deeds is subject to the compliance of these conditions.

The above building requirements are clearly designed to avoid land speculation and, generally, to ensure that the government's effort in providing basic infrastructure is speedily complemented by appropriate investments on behalf of the private sector. There are some anomalies – the odd empty lot in an otherwise built-up area may be observed – but, on the whole, the sales conditions have been fulfilled. The importance of not subsidizing land speculation may be appreciated when considering the magnitude of basic development investment. The scale of earth-shifting involved in the tourist zone is self-evident. Furthermore, the cost of providing even basic services in the area is compounded by natural conditions: ditches for main drainage have to be dynamited through the limestone rock lying only a few inches beneath the sparse topsoil. Alternative domestic solutions, such as septic tanks, are *not* feasible as these contaminate the ubiquitous subterranean streams that are the region's traditional water supply.

Table 17.1 Sales conditions for FONATUR-owned land in Cancún.

Type of land use	Project to be presented by*:	Building to be started by*:	Building to be finished by*:
Hotels and condominiums	6 months	12 months	30 months
Industry	6 months	8 months	24 months
Multifamily housing	6 months	9 months	24 months
Unifamily housing	3 months	6 months	8 months

Source: FONATUR, Gerencia de Mercadotecnia, Lineamientos Para la Adquisición de Terrenos, 1984. (* From date of purchase.)

To counterbalance the strict sales conditions, FONATUR's marketing policy includes measures that ensure that the effective demand is catered for, at least as far as non-residential land uses are concerned. In the first place, both the master plan and the development phasing have been flexible enough to accommodate changes in the market: an increase in demand for hotels and large-scale commercial uses in the urban zone, for example, or for residences and shops in the tourist zone. A more important factor has been the way that sales prices are determined. These bear no relation to their *real* development cost; in fact, the low "subsidized" land prices were designed to attract investors during the initial stages of Cancún's development (INFRATUR 1971b, 1972a). The land prices are prescribed by the Comisión Nacional de Avalúo and calculated as a percentage of total construction costs, given certain assumptions about plot ratios and so forth. As a result, in 1983, land in the tourist zone was available for US$29 to $50 per square metre for hotel development, a price that assumed that 10 per cent of a maximum total cost of US$42,000 per room corresponds to land, with a plot ratio of 120 rooms per hectare (CEDUV 1984). Land for housing was priced at between US$13 and US$37 per square metre, depending on whether it was for luxury residential, middle or "social interest" housing. In the case of these last two categories, the percentage allowed for land costs in relation to total costs was 25 and 20 per cent, respectively, total construction costs were US$208 and $166, and plot ratios were 50 and 60 per cent, respectively. These parameters were entirely compatible with the requirements of the only effective demand for such land: the government housing programmes such as INFONAVIT and FOVI.

This kind of land-price fixing is clearly not the major obstacle barring access to residential land in the urban zone. The requirement that building should proceed quickly and in accordance with certain specifications presents a much more substantial barrier. This effectively limits the potential buyers to two categories: wealthy individuals who build for themselves or for speculation with their own resources, or developers who have access to finance. In Mexico, financial institutions granting mortgages to individual house purchasers or one-off builders practically do not exist;[9] money for housing is channelled through a wide variety of institutions, almost exclusively into new building. This means that, as far as middle- and middle-to-low-cost housing is concerned, the only effective demand for Cancún's urban zone comes from the federal government housing agencies or the developers who are financed by these. The ultimate effective demand is thus limited to those prospective residents who (a) are eligible for credit from one or other of these agencies, (b) manage to obtain such credit and (c) want to live in the houses they produce.

The main factors conditioning eligibility for credits under most of the housing-finance schemes are income and employment. In 1984, it was calculated that between 50 and 70 per cent of Cancún's inhabitants would not have met the minimum family income requirements for the cheapest housing credits provided by INFONAVIT and the National Housing Finance Programme (FOVI) (CEDUV 1984). Normally, having enough proven family income by no means ensures access to a credit; at a national level, the amount of credits available is nowhere near the effective demand (Connolly 1990). However, in Cancún, its highly privileged position regarding public investment means that the reverse is true (or was in 1984): considering only the empty units, buildings in process and approved projects in 1984, the supply of medium- and low-to-medium-cost housing exceeded the effective demand up to 1988 and would fully cover it up to 2000 without a single additional investment in this type of housing (CEDUV 1984). Since then, money has continued to pour into this sector of the housing market in Cancún. There are, however, other obstacles to obtaining housing credit, apart from absolute scarcity: union affiliation, and the requirement of being a conventional "family", for example. Here, a large segment of the housing development has been directly or indirectly controlled by the Confederación Regional de Obreros y Campesinos (CROC) – the strongest union among Cancún's hotel workers.

Even for those who are eligible for housing credits, the kind of home that these provide does not necessarily respond to many peoples' needs and aspirations. In a tropical climate, 40–60 m^2 of concrete and brick with a 2.2 m floor-to-ceiling height, even with running water and drainage, can be fairly uncomfortable.[10] Many people would prefer the 200 m^2 of breezy (albeit unserviced) land on which one can build an affordable house, for example, a traditional stone or wattle and daub thatched hut, which will at least support a hammock. Finally, as a new and rapidly developing city, Cancún attracts migrants from all social classes in search of temporary employment, or just seeing how things will go. These people are not interested in a 10–15-year mortgage.

For these and many other reasons, Cancún's urban zone does not answer the needs, aspirations and possibilities of most of the population. Before turning to the alternative urban land supplied by Colonia Puerto Juárez, it is worth posing the question: who is buying the housing in the urban zone? In 1984, apart from the bona fide middle-class residents, some of the excess middle-range housing supply was being bought up for speculation by outsiders or temporary residents. However, freezing assets in housing is not a good investment: with no mortgages for second-hand purchases, selling property is difficult; neither is renting a going concern, especially during times of high inflation. Nevertheless, in tourist locations, investment in medium-priced flats for rent may be an attractive proposition as "holiday homes" or for short-term lets to tourists. To encourage such investment, there is even a special kind of subsidized credit for purchasing houses for rent. It is notorious that this particular programme has been applied principally in tourist cities; 560 such units were on offer in Cancún in 1984. This kind of speculative investment is, however, strictly for non-professionals; the credits are not available on a large scale and there are still the FONATUR rules and regulations to contend with. In the words of a local real estate agent, investment in property "is a much more interesting prospect on the Colonia Puerto Juárez side of Cancún".

The unplanned land market

There have been no detailed studies of the way land belonging to the Isla Mujeres *ejido* between 1970 and 1975 has been incorporated into the urban area of Cancun. From other studies, it may be assumed that the subdivision and sale of plots were largely in the hands of the *ejidatarios*.[11] It is also known that other political forces were active in the process; not least among these the dominant workers union, the CROC. In fact, the irregular urbanization was not limited to the *ejido*. About this time, the narrow strip of FONATUR land on the other side of the Mérida highway also began to be "invaded". This land, around which a market was located, later known as "super-blocks 60 and 61", was later "disowned" (donated) by FONATUR, from whose iron control it had clearly escaped. In dealing with the counter-face of the unplanned land market I will limit myself here to the development of *ejido* land.

By 1975, the population of Colonia Puerto Juárez was estimated at 4,700, while that of the superblocks 60–61 was near to 200. The housing was almost exclusively built with traditional materials and there were no paved access roads, water supply or drainage. At this point, steps were taken to regularize the situation; in Mexico these inevitably lead to expropriation. In this case, up until 1984, there had been three such expropriations, in favour of different institutions with their respective conditions, procedures and clientele. The first occurred in 1975, when 256 ha were expropriated in favour of the Fideicomiso Puerto Juárez which had been expressly created to handle the regularization. Shortly afterwards, a further 115 ha of the *ejido* were expropriated, but this time the legal justification was the extension of the Puerto Juárez Fondo Legal, so that this land was administered directly by the state of Quintana Roo's cadastre office in Chetumal. Finally, in 1982, another expropriation made over 378 ha of the *ejido* to the State Government Housing Institute, INVIQROO, for the purposes of both regularization and creating land reserves for future urban growth. In fact, the expropriation basically served the latter purpose as the only already occupied land included in this area was one small *colonia* with 190 plots. To this, a further 940 occupied plots, in the superblocks 60–61 donated by FONATUR, were added to INVIQROO's regularization programme.

These legal operations were accompanied by important outlays by the state government in improving the Mérida highway – now a major urban artery – paving a few roads in Colonia Puerto Juárez and the provision of a limited water supply to this area. At the same time, private investment went on apace. Permanent houses substituted the Mayan huts and empty lots were built on; whereas at the beginning of 1982, 53 per cent of the plots were vacant (aerial photo survey by CEDUV 1982), less than two years later, this percentage had been reduced to 30 per cent (CEDUV 1984). In the same short period, commercial buildings sprang up and multiplied along both sides of the Mérida highway and along the paved roads inside Colonia Puerto Juárez.

Of the three regularization agencies active in Cancún, only direct information about INVIQROO's programme was available at the time of writing this chapter. Here, the regularization of already occupied land was given essentially the same treatment as the purchase of plots in the new developments created on the expropriated *ejidos*. This new development, called "New Horizons", and started in 1983–84, involved providing 4,140 so-called "urbanized" lots to be sold with a low-interest five-year loan. The finance for these loans was supplied by the federal agency FONHAPO, which also provided a limited number (479 for 1983–84) of small "self-build" credit packages for the purchase of building materials. The basic development investment was provided by the state government. The "urbanization" provided by such investment was relatively lightweight; it meant bulldozing out the jungle to expose the limestone subsoil, thus creating access roads, providing electricity and water supply, and in the process generating an excruciatingly monotonous urban layout: an exact replica of the street plan of the "unplanned" Colonia Puerto Juárez. The (more expensive) drainage problem remained untackled.

Another potential advantage to planned urban development, also ignored here, is the possibility of procuring so that the city grows in a logically structured way. "New Horizons" effectively pulls the city out towards the south, encouraging ribbon development along the Mérida highway and exacerbating the already serious transport problem between Colonia Puerto Juárez and its population's workplaces.[12] It is, in fact, the antithesis of FONATUR's master

259

plan, which at least prescribes orderly and compact urban growth. But this is not the fault of the state government or INVIQROO; they only act where they can, that is, on the expropriated *ejidos*. Be this as it may, the state government is clearly counterbalancing FONATUR and its master plan as the sole development force in Cancún. For it is not only sites with some services that New Horizons is offering. Over 4,000 new "social interest" housing units were also programmed in 1984 for short-term construction, adding to the already saturated market for this type of housing on the FONATUR side.[13]

The comparison between New Horizons and FONATUR's urban development may be usefully extended to their respective marketing policies. In the first place, the need to avoid speculation was clearly accepted as a basic principle by the state government, and the same kind of measures were applied to this end. Purchasers of lots must build within three to six months of the date of purchase, though provisional construction is allowed. At the time of the CEDUV study, it was unclear how this rule was going to be enforced (whereas in the case of the FONATUR developments, this is very clear). An important line of enquiry is therefore to find out to what extent these conditions have been met in practice. In the second place, unlike FONATUR, the sales prices in New Horizons were not established by the Comisión Nacional de Avalúo on the basis of marginal returns calculated for specific land uses, thus assuring a felicitous encounter between supply and demand. Here, to the contrary, sales prices had to reflect development costs (especially if the World Bank had any say in the matter) and these prices could not fit the pocket of all the demand for land previously accommodated in Colonia Puerto Juárez. In fact, the going prices for land in New Horizons were very similar to those attached to fully serviced plots of superior quality in the FONATUR area. For example, inside New Horizons, in 1984, land was selling at US$8–15 per square metre, compared with US$13–17 for "social interest" housing in FONATUR's urban zone. The price assigned to plots on "New Horizon's" main avenue (the Mérida highway) varied between US$32 and US$48 per square metre, while commercial plots in the FONATUR area were available for US$25–42 per square metre (CEDUV 1984, data supplied by FONATUR and INVIQROO).

Considering both the land prices and the conditions attached to purchase, it is clear that the attempts of the government – in this case, the state government – to substitute the uncontrolled land market for a "planned" and legal land supply can only be seen as partly successful. There still must be a wide spectrum of the market that is excluded from this new development, just as it is from the FONATUR land supply. Among those excluded are individuals or families who cannot or will not pay the established prices (although these are low by all accounts), people who are not eligible for FONHAPO credits, together with a whole host of non-residential land uses, not to mention petty and not-so-petty speculators. How has this demand been accommodated? Among the possible hypotheses is the violation of INVIQROO's marketing norms and/or the continued irregular urbanization of further tracts in what remains of the Isla Mujeres *ejido*.

Who plans, anyway?

At this point, the problem mentioned in the introduction about the multiplicity of government agencies involved in Cancún's urbanization must have become increasingly apparent. But this does not refer only to the contradictory presence of many organisms, all treading on each others' toes and duplicating functions (Ward 1986). A more fundamental issue here is the way that the city is divided up into what amounts to territorial jurisdictions, each "governed" by a different agency or set of agencies. These de facto governing agencies do not necessarily depend on the level of government which sets out the legal faculties for the functions that they perform.

The most outstanding example is the action of the two major development agencies that were responsible for Cancún's initial urbanization: FONATUR and the Isla Mujer *ejidatarios* backed up by the Reforma Agraria. Both of these, in their different ways, prescribed the rules for the first round of the urban land market, thus defining the nature of private property in their respective segments.[14] They also legitimized the property rights acquired by Cancún's first owners. In the case of the Tourist and urban zones, FONATUR still has the power of veto in subsequent real estate operations. It must be remembered that in the early 1970s, alternative institutional mechanisms for controlling urban development hardly existed. Quintana Roo, as a federal state, was only created in 1971; previously it had been a federal territory. The municipality of Cancún – confusingly called Benito Juárez – was created in 1974, carved out of the neighbouring municipalities of Isla Mujeres and Cozumel. Finally, the National Planning System, with its hierarchies of development programmes, land-use maps and property controls, was set in motion only after 1976, reaching a fairly consolidated stage at a national level in the mid-1980s.

During the first decade of its existence, Cancún was politically and territorially divided into two clearly demarcated domains (the dividing line was two blocks east of the Mérida highway): FONATUR and its newly created municipality on one side, and the traditional local forces on the other. The traditional local forces, including the *ejido*, the original inhabitants of Puerto Juárez, the CROC and probably many others were more closely aligned with the state government; at the same time, it was the state government that had to face the demands of Colonia Puerto Juárez's growing population and generally cope with the usual problems associated with irregular development. This division between the territory planned and controlled by FONATUR and the "uncontrolled" development under the wings of the state government is, of course, a schematic description of the original state of affairs. At least three events complicated the situation.

In the first place, as FONATUR progressively handed over urban functions, public services and infrastructure to the municipality, the latter clearly became more empowered economically; in fact, compared with the other municipal governments of the region, Benito Juárez is exceptionally well endowed. Furthermore, a certain degree of political independence was progressively acquired over time through the normal workings of the politico-administrative and party machinery. By 1984, the municipality was by no means a mere puppet of FONATUR.[15] In the second place, the successive expropriations and regularization programmes applied in Colonia Puerto Juárez meant that third parties appeared on the scene with effective control over the most basic of all resources: land for urban development. This effectively tilted the balance of power in favour of the state government but at the same time introduced powerful federal agencies on the scene: CoRett (Comisión para la Regularización de la Tenencia de la Tierra) and FONHAPO. It should be clear that we are not talking about intergovernmental collaboration at an elevated level, but the decisive intervention of agencies who determine the rules of the land market and have face-to-face contact with the inhabitants on matters related to property and land use.

In the third place, on top of this local interplay of government agencies, the consolidation of the Planning System at a *national* level not only provided a new set of rules governing the land market, but also introduced new agencies into the planning scene: the Urban Development Secretariat (SAHOP, then SEDUE) and its regional delegation. The rules essentially consist of an overall development plan that defines basic land uses, territorial reserves and conservation areas, and a secondary zoning plan, which should be accompanied by a legal land-use declaration, prescribing in detail the land use, densities, plot ratios, etc. for each area. After modifications to the Ley General de Asentamientos Urbanos in 1981, property transactions had to conform to the land-use specifications of the Development Plan. The urban development plan also laid out priorities for public investment in services, housing and infrastructure, including indications about regularization and improvements to "irregular" settlements. It should be mentioned that the legal scope of the urban development plans and programmes was (and still is to a certain extent) far from clear, and there were many rival interpretations regarding the significance of such vital components of the planning system as the "land-use declarations" and "partial plans". Not least among these ambiguities was the plans' territorial scope: whether they should apply to the municipality, to the subregion or to the "population centre", as defined by the consultant who was contracted to do the plan. Some of these problems have been ironed out by later legislation. The Constitutional Reform to the Article 115 of December 1983 removed the responsibility of elaborating the urban development plans from the state governments and placed it in the hands of the municipalities. At the same time, the municipalities gained control of the cadastral register and property tax collection. These reforms, instigated at a national level, are not necessarily carried through in state-level legislation, which gives rise to further contradictions and ambiguities regarding planning law and practice. Once again, even under the new planning system, the definition of "regular" (i.e. planned) urban development is by no means cut and dry.

In the case of Cancún, institutionalized planning had various implications. Before the 1984 constitutional changes, the state government achieved more political clout, as it was at this level that the plans were proclaimed and authorized. However, the Quintana Roo government, like many other state entities, was not exactly well versed in drawing up urban development plans; so it was SAHOP (the then federal Urban Development Secretariat) that was responsible for the plans, and these in fact were contracted out to urban planning consultants. For example, the CEDUV (Consultores in Desarrollo Urbano y Vivienda SA) was contracted by SEDUE to draw up an urban development plan for Cancún (Plan Director) in 1982 (or rather, a proposal for same), on behalf of the state government. The scope for this plan was, however, effectively limited to those areas not controlled by FONATUR; otherwise, FONATUR's master plan was adopted and integrally incorporated into the development plan. Nobody really took seriously the idea that FONATUR's land reserves should be used for sites and services programmes to meet the low-income housing demand, although this was in fact suggested by CEDUV. For its part, FONATUR was also active in this new wave of planning effort. In 1983, it also contracted CEDUV's services to do another version of Cancún's urban development plan, or rather, what was called "Diagnosis and Strategy for the Urban Development of Cancún's Tourist Development" (sic), though this was drawn up and presented strictly in accordance with the SEDUE format and SEDUE planning norms were applied. (The fact that the same consultant was contracted was apparently coincidental). This time, there was absolutely no question of suggesting radical changes to the FONATUR master plan. In fact the job – like most planning consultancies of this type in Mexico – consisted mainly of finding out what the various development agencies' plans were and fitting them into the SEDUE planning format.

Clearly, the legal and institutional parameters which divide "regular" from "irregular" settlement processes have evolved rapidly over the past decade in Mexico. Furthermore, the effects of this evolution are by no means uniform across the whole country; marked variations may be observed at a regional, state and even intra-city level. As in the case of the "New Horizons" programme, I have not, to date, been able to obtain information as to how the new planning system has actually been implemented by the municipality, nor how this has affected Cancún's land market.

Concluding remarks

I do not think that it is necessary to spell out all the conclusions that could be derived from this case study. Hopefully, my intentions are clear from the way this is presented. Some comments would, perhaps, be helpful. First, the selection of issues covered here try to reflect the kind of priorities which I, personally, think are important for *evaluating the effect of policy instruments upon the land valorization process*. Here, I suggest that understanding *how* policies are implemented (or not) is more relevant than one-off evaluations of particular kinds of policy instruments. And the way policies are implemented is conditioned by the action of multiple social and political institutions. The complexity of the planning processes relating to land-market controls and housing provision in any one place may be appreciated; which means that under different institutional constraints, the effects of a particular policy will vary.

Secondly, if we are to understand how "irregular" land markets work, it is advisable to understand first why they are not "regular", and what "regular" is? I hope that I have been able to show that this is a variable proposition. Thirdly, a bit of Marxism (or even neoclassical rent theory) can still help. Land, in itself, is worthless; rents, and thus land prices, are generated only by productive processes (FONATUR understands this only too well). It is absurd, therefore, to study the land market without reference to building production and use. In particular, I would suggest (as I have suggested for Cancún) that the "irregular" land-market syndrome is heavily influenced by the types of finance available for housing. This also varies regionally and, of course, nationally (see Connolly 1987 for a more general analysis of the relation between the availability of credit and the extensive or intensive development of the land market in Mexico City).

Fourthly, an important methodological proposition exclusive to Marxist rent theory is its emphasis on the property relation, in that this not only defines who gets the rent and how, but that it actually determines the very existence of rent – thus land prices and land markets – in the first place. Many authors in the 1970s have insisted that there is no universal property relation, just as there is no single category of land-owners (Massey & Catalano 1978). I have tried to exemplify some of the wide variety of property relations at work in Cancún and how these condition the land market; this is why is it possible to talk about a *segmented* land market. Finally, one might add that, following the above arguments, there can be no *model* land market – irregular or otherwise, but especially irregular – still less can we talk about statistical trends or mathematical simulations. There are, however, theoretical principles that elucidate the workings of the land market in different places.

Notes

1. For details of land regularization in Mexico City, see Azuela (1987a, 1989), Connolly (1976, 1982), Varley (1985a, 1985b), and Ward (1986). Cancún's irregular settlements have been regularized by the conventional procedure of expropriation and subsequent re-sale of plots to their inhabitants. As in other cities, the expropriations of *ejidos* for the purpose of regularization extend far beyond the areas actually occupied, leading to the creation of considerable land reserves. These reserves are then administered by a state-level housing agency that, with federal finance, provides a "planned" supply of (unserviced) land to substitute the previous "irregular" urbanization mechanisms: the kind of "housing policy" which national and international experts have been advocating for a long time. Cancún thus provides a good case for evaluating the institutionalization of what was previously called the "uncontrolled" urban settlement process.

2. This observation is related to a basic criticism of certain methodological premises embodied in the way that the Workshop that gave rise to this book was presented. From its original title, it would seem that the Fitzwilliam Workshop aspired to a better understanding of the land market in *less developed countries* or *Third World cities*, on the basis of a handful of case studies, mostly of Mexican cities. From this it might be assumed that underdeveloped countries have some *typical* land market, governed by some indefinable natural force (Third World market forces?), that can somehow be characterized by the accumulating individual empirical research findings. The notable absence of references to general theoretical principles during the course of the Workshop confirmed that this assumption was held by many of the participants in this event.

3. The overt objectives given to the Cancún development project were a bit different: (a) promote employment derived from the "multiplier effect" of the primary investments in tourism, (b) promote regional development (for the same reason), (c) improve and diversify the country's tourist attractions, and (d) increase the short-term inflow of foreign currency (Banco de México 1970).

4. Of this, 115 ha was bought from private owners, and 80 ha was reclaimed lands from lagoons. In addition, the project area includes three lagoons covering 4,829 ha (Diario Oficial 10 August 1971, Banco de México 1970).

5. According to two studies, between 50 and 55 per cent of the economically active population worked in construction in 1975. The rest were occupied in services and agriculture (García Fuentes 1979, FONATUR 1975, CEDUV 1984 II).

6. These figures may be overestimates as they are based on the municipality's calculations, in whose interests it is to exaggerate its population. The 1980 census figure of 33,300 thousand for the whole of Cancún is probably an underestimate. The 1990 census registered 177,300 for the whole of the Benito Juárez municipality.

7. In 1974, INFRATUR absorbed other financial institutions to create the Fondo Nacional para la Promoción del Turismo (FONATUR).

8. Although Cancún undoubtedly is highly privileged as far as public services are concerned, the CEDUV (1984) planning study showed a deficit in certain aspects, such as pre-school facilities and old people's homes, as measured against the planning ministry (SEDUE) norms. But as practically all the public services are concentrated in the urban zone, these deficits affect Colonia Benito Juárez.

9. Important exceptions are the individual credits obtainable under various housing benefit programmes for specific unionized workers, such as those affiliated to the Mexican Electricians union (SME) or the oil-workers union (STPRM). Since 1989, banks have been granting individual mortgages for middle-priced housing.

10. In response to our critical queries as to the (lack of) environmental design considerations in middle- and low-cost housing projects in Cancún, one developer's agent replied: "This is not important; very soon, everybody will have air conditioning".

11. Mostly related to Mexico City's Metropolitan Area: see Connolly 1976, 1982, Alonso 1980, Azuela 1987a, 1989, Varley 1985a, 1985b, 1985c, and Ward 1986, 1989c.

12. The "New Horizons" programme also pulls urban development towards land clearly earmarked for medium- or long-term private speculation: the so-called *fraccionamientos campestres*, consisting of some 2,000 ha bought up (or otherwise acquired) by a developer. In 1984, a project for about 12,200 "small-farm" and "rustic" plots with up-market recreational facilities had been submitted to the state cadastral office. The use of such euphemisms to bypass restrictions on urban development has been carefully documented in studies of Ecatepec, Mexico City (Salazar & Vega n.d.).

13. Cf. the development by AURIS of *ejidos* which had been expropriated for the purpose of regularizing low-income settlements for middle-income housing in the state of Mexico and the Pacific coast tourist resort of Puerto Vallarta (García Peralta 1981, 1990).

14. Even "invasions" or other apparently illegal acquisitions of *ejidal* (or other) land abide by a prescribed set of rules; see Azuela (1987a, 1989).

15. An example of the kind of minor conflict between the two entities concerned the treatment of a group of street vendors, dutifully organized by the local CNOP (the now-extinct Confederación Nacional de Organizaciones Populares, one of the major pillars of the Mexico's ruling party). The municipality supported the street vendors' claim to be allowed to sell in the Tourist and urban zones, while for FONATUR their presence was considered to be an anathema to Cancun's healthy development.

References

Entries in **bold type** are edited volumes of contributions referred to more than once. "(Fitzwilliam paper)" denotes papers presented at the International Workshop on Land Values and the Impact of Public Policy upon Valorization Processes in Less Developed Countries, Fitzwilliam College, Cambridge, 14–19 July 1991.

Abramo Campos, P. 1989. A dinâmica imobiliária: elementos para o entendimento da espacialidade urbana. *Cadernos IPPUR/UFRJ* **4**, 47–70.

Abreu, M. 1987. *Evoluçao urbana do Rio de Janeiro*. Rio de Janeiro: IPLAN.

Agence de Coopération Culturelle et Technique (ACCT). 1988. *La gestion foncière dans les pays en développement: objectifs, instruments et techniques*. Synthèse de la session d'Echange. 30 November– 11 December 1987. Notes et documents. Série syntheses de session no 11. Décembre.

ACT-Consultant (ed.) 1988. *Etude pour une politique de l'habitat en Guinée (Conakry)*. Final Report.

ACT-Consultant 1989. *Etude pour une politique de l'habitat en Guinée*. Phase B: Dossier no 2. Financement du logement; Dossier no 3: Acteurs, institutions et procedures. Unpublished.

Alonso, J. (ed.) 1980. *Lucha urbana y acumulación de capital*. Mexico DF: Ediciones de la Casa Chata.

Alvarez, S. & A. Escobar 1992. Theoretical and political horizons of change in contemporary Latin American social movements. See Escobar & Alvarez (1992), 317–29.

Amitabh 1993. *Urban land value changes in the Indian context: a case study of Lucknow City*. PhD thesis, University of Cambridge.

Angel, S., R. W. Archer, S. Tanphiphat, E. A. Wegelin (eds) 1983. *Land for housing the poor*. Singapore: Select Books.

Archer, R. W. 1987. The possible use of urban land pooling/readjustment for the planned development of Bangkok. *Third World Planning Review* **9**(3), 235–53.

Assies, W. 1990. Of structured moves and moving structures, an overview of theoretical perspectives on social movements. See Assies et al. (1990).

Assies, W. 1992a. *To get out of the mud: neighborhood associativism in Recife, 1964–1988*, Amsterdam: CEDLA.

Assies, W. 1992b. Urban associativism and "democratic transition" in the municipality of Recife (Brazil). In *Urban restructuring and deregulation in Latin America*, M. Carmona (ed.). Delft: Delft University of Technology, Department of Building Sciences.

W. Assies, G. Burgwal, T. Salman (eds) 1990. *Structures of power, movements of resistance*. Amsterdam: CEDLA.

Ayuntamiento de Puebla 1986. *Dirección general de desarrollo urbano y ecología. Estratégia general para la desconcentración de las actividades comerciales y de servicios del centro de la Ciudad de Puebla*. Agency Publication: Puebla.

Ayres, R. L. 1983. *Banking on the poor: the World Bank and world poverty*. Cambridge, Mass.: MIT Press.

Azuela, A. 1987a. Low income settlements and the law in Mexico City. *International Journal of Urban and Regional Research* **11**(4), 522–42.

Azuela, A. 1987b. De inquilinos a propietarios. Derecho y política en el Programa de Renovación Habitacional Popular. *Estudios Demográficos y Urbanos* **2**(1), 53–73.

Azuela, A. 1989. *La ciudad, la propiedad privada y el derecho*. Mexico DF: El Colegio de México.

Badcock, B. A. 1984. *Unfairly structured cities*. Oxford: Basil Blackwell.

Badshah, A. 1992. *Sustainable and equitable urban environments in Asia*. PhD thesis, Massachusetts Institute of Technology.

Bahl, R. & J. Linn 1992. *Urban public finance in developing countries*. Oxford: Oxford University

Press.

Bakani, D. & S. Theunynck 1988. *Etude de faisabilité pour l'aménagement de terrains urbains dans les principales villes de Mauritanie*. Nouakchott, Mauritania: SOCOGIM.

Baken, R-J. & J. van der Linden 1992. *Land delivery for low income groups in Third World cities*. Aldershot, England: Avebury.

Ball, M., V. Bentivegna, M. Edwards, M. Folin 1985. *Land rent, housing and urban planning: a European perspective*. London: Croom Helm.

Banck, G. A. 1986. Poverty, politics and the shaping of urban space: a Brazilian example. *International Journal of Urban and Regional Research* 10(4), 522–39.

Banck, G. A. 1990. Cultural dilemmas behind strategy: Brazilian neighborhood movements and Catholic discourse. *European Journal of Development Research* 2(1), 65–88.

Banco de México 1970. *Proyecto de desarrollo turístico Cancún* [3 vols], Mexico DF: Banco de México/INFRATUR.

Baross, P. 1983. The articulation of land supply for popular settlements in Third World cities. See Angel et al. (1983), 198–210.

Baross, P. 1990. Sequencing land development: the price implication of legal and illegal settlement growth. See Baross & van der Linden (1990), 57–82.

Baross, P. 1991. Sequencing land development: the price implications of legal and illegal settlement growth. (Fitzwilliam paper).

Baross, P. & J. van der Linden (eds) 1990. *The transformation of land supply systems in Third World cities*. Aldershot, England: Avebury.

Barros e Silva, P. E. de 1985. *A questão do solo urbano no Recife: alternativas para uma nova política*. Recife: Camara Municipal do Recife.

Batley, R. 1982. Urban renewal and expulsion in São Paulo. See Gilbert (1982), 231–62.

BCEOM (Bureau Central des Etudes et Equipements d'Outre-Mer) 1990. *Etude pour la création du fichier foncier de la ville de Conakry*. Rapport de première phase. Paris: BCEOM.

Benjamin, S. 1991. *Jobs, land and urban development: the economic success of small manufacturers in East Delhi, India*. Cambridge, Mass.: Lincoln Institute of Land Policy.

Benton, L. 1986. Reshaping the urban core: the politics of housing in authoritarian Uruguay. *Latin American Research Review* 21(2), 33–52.

Bertaud, M-A. 1989. *The use of satellite images for urban planning: a case study from Karachi, Pakistan*. Technical Note Report INU 42. Washington DC: Infrastructure and Urban Development Department, World Bank.

BID (Banco Interamericano de Desarrollo) 1976. *Informe final proyecto Cancún. Préstamo 217/OC-ME*. Washington DC: Interamerican Development Bank.

Bitoun, J. 1991. *Movimentos sociais e a cidade: questões relevantes para a geografia urbana*. Recife: Departamento de Ciências Geográficas UFPE.

Boly, M. & B. Zougrana 1988a. Urbanisme opérationnel et gestion foncière au Burkina Faso. In *La gestion foncière dans les pays en développement: objectifs, instruments et techniques*, 229–55. Bordeaux: Agence de Coopéracion Culturelle et Technique.

Boly, M. & B. Zougrana 1988b. La réforme de la gestion foncière urbaine au Burkina Faso: aspects techniques et juridiques. In *La gestion foncière dans les pays en développement: objectifs, instruments et techniques*, ACCT, 429–39.

Boran, A. 1989. Popular movements in Brazil: a case study of the Movement for the Defense of Favelados in São Paulo. *Bulletin of Latin American Research* 8(1), 83–109.

Bosque Maurel, J., J. Bosque Sendra, A. García Ballesteros, M. Bagazgoitia Barrera, J. Salvador Hernández 1986. The dynamics of land prices and spatial development in Madrid 1940–1980. *Iberian Studies* 15(1–2), 49–59.

Boyce, D. E., B. Allen, G. Desfor, R. Zuber 1972. *Impact of rapid transit on suburban residential property values and land development: analysis of the Philadelphia–Linderwold high-speed line*. [report sponsored by US Department of Transportation]. Philadelphia, Pa: University of Pennsylvania.

Brookfield, H., A. Samad Hadi, Z. Mahmud 1991. *The city in the village*. Oxford: Oxford University Press.

Bruce, J. & D. Dwyer 1988. Introduction. In *A home divided: women and income in the Third World*, D. Dwyer & J. Bruce (eds), 1–19. Palo Alto, Cal.: Stanford University Press.

Burgess, R. 1982. Self-help housing advocacy: a curious form of radicalism. A critique of the work of John F. C. Turner. See Ward (1982), 55–97.

Burgess, R. 1985a. Problems in the classification of low-income neighbourhoods in Latin America. *Third World Planning Review* **7** (4), 287–306.

Burgess, R. 1985b. The limits of state self-help housing programmes. *Development and Change* **16**, 271–312.

Burgess, R. 1992. Helping some to help themselves: Third World housing policies and development strategies. See Mathéy (1992a), 75–91.

Burns, L. S. 1983. Self-help housing: an evaluation of outcomes. *Urban Studies* **20**, 299–309.

Butcher, C. 1986. *Low income housing in Zimbabwe: a case study of the Epworth squatter upgrading programme, Harare*. Department of Rural and Urban Planning Occasional Paper 6, University of Zimbabwe.

Butcher, C. 1989. *Land delivery for low-cost housing in Zimbabwe, phase 1: report of findings* [report for the Ministry of Public Construction and National Housing and USAID]. Harare: Plan Inc. Zimbabwe.

Campbell, J. 1990. World Bank urban shelter projects in East Africa: matching needs with appropriate responses? In *Housing Africa's urban poor*, P. Amis & P. Lloyd (eds), 205–23. Manchester: Manchester University Press.

Carvalho, E. Guimarães de 1991. *O negócio da terra*. Rio de Janeiro: UFRJ Editora.

Castañeda, V. 1988. Mercado inmobiliario en la periferia metropolitana: los precios del suelo. Estudios de caso. In *Estructura territorial de la Ciudad de México*, O. Terrazas & E. Preciat (eds), 219–49. Mexico DF: Plaza y Janes.

Castells, M. 1983. *The city and the grassroots*. London: Edward Arnold.

CEAS 1990. *A lei do PREZEIS, instrumento de luta pela urbanização e legalização da terra – manual para lideranças*, Recife: CEAS.

CEAS 1992. *PREZEIS, um processo de participação na formação da cidade*. Recife: CEAS Urbano PE.

CEDUV 1984. *Proyecto del plan de desarrollo urbano de Cancún, Quintana Roo* [3 vols]. Mexico DF: Consultores en Desarrollo Urbano y Vivienda SA.

Chant, S. 1984. *Las olvidadas: a study of women, housing and family structure in Querétaro, Mexico*. PhD thesis, University College London.

Chant, S. 1985. Single-parent families: choice or constraint? The formation of female-headed households in Mexican shanty towns. *Development and Change* **16**, 635–56.

Chant, S. 1991. *Women and survival in Mexican cities: perspectives on gender, labour markets and low-income households*. Manchester: Manchester University Press.

Cheneau-Loquay, A. 1988. La nouvelle donne économique en Guinée. In *L'année Africaine 1985–1986*, 87–121. Pédone, France: Presses Universitaires de Bordeaux.

Cheneau-Loquay, A. 1992. La Guinée en reconstruction, six ans aprés, redressement ou dérapage? In *Nue Herausforderrungen im Nord-Sud-Verhaltnis: sozio-okonomische und okologishe Krisenfaktorum in Guinea*, 69–107. Loccum, Germany: Evangelische Akademies-Loccum.

Choi, M. J. 1993. *Spatial and temporal variations in land values: a descriptive and behavioral analysis of the Seoul Metropolitan Area (1956–1989)*. PhD thesis, Harvard University.

Christopher, A. J. 1970. Salisbury, 1900: the study of a pioneer town. *Journal for Geography* **3**, 757–66.

Christopher, A. J. 1972. Urban encroachment on a large farm in Rhodesia. *Land Economics* **48**(3), 287–90.

Christopher, A. J. 1973. Land ownership in the rural–urban fringe of Salisbury, Rhodesia. *South African Geographer* **4**(2), 139–56.

Christopher, A. J. 1977. Early settlement and the cadastral framework. See Kay & Smout (eds), 14–25.

CNBB 1982. *Solo urbano e ação pastoral*, São Paulo: Edicoães Paulinas.

Cohen, A. P. 1985. *The symbolic construction of community*. Chichester/London: Ellis Horwood/Tavistock.

Cohen, M. 1990. Macroeconomic adjustment and the city. *Cities* **7**(1), 49–59.

Cole, S. 1989. World Bank forecasts and planning in the Third World. *Environment and Planning A* **21**, 175–96.

Colquhoun, B., O'Donnell & Partners 1985. *Overview of construction and materials production sectors for inclusion in the National Housing Corporation study*. Harare: Ministry of Public Construction and National Housing.

Connolly, P. 1976. *Análisis del comportamiento del mercado de bienes raíces en la Zona*

Metropolitana de la Ciudad de México. México DF: Centro Operacional de la Vivienda y Poblamiento.

Connolly, P. 1981. Towards an analysis of Mexico City's local state (preliminary notes for discussion). Unpublished.

Connolly, P. 1982. Uncontrolled urban settlements and self-build housing: what kind of a solution? See Ward (1982), 141–71.

Connolly, P. 1987. La política habitacional después de los sismos. *Estudios Demográficos y Urbanos* **2**(1), 101–20.

Connolly, P. 1988. Crecimiento urbano, densidad de población y mercado inmobiliario. *Revista de Ciencias Sociales y Humanidades* **9**(25), 61–86.

Connolly, P. 1990. Housing and the state in Mexico. In *Housing policy in developing countries*, G. Shidlo (ed.), 5–32. London: Routledge.

COPEVI (Centro Operacional de Vivienda y Poblamiento AC) 1977. *Investigacion sobre vivienda*, vol. 2. Mexico: COPEVI.

Corbridge, S. 1991 Third World development. *Progress in Human Geography* **15**(3), 311–21.

Cornia, G., R. Jolly, F. Stewart (eds) 1988. *Adjustment with a human face*. Oxford: Oxford University Press.

Correll, M. R., J. H. Lillydahl, L. D. Singell, 1978. The effects of greenbelts on residential property values: some findings on the political economy. *Land Economics* **54**(2), 207–17.

Coulomb, R. 1992. *Pobreza urbana, autogestión y política*. Mexico DF: Centro de la Vivenda y Estudios Urbanos (CENVI).

Cremont, D. 1984. Projet urbain de Bamako, République du Mali: rapport de mission. Washington DC: World Bank (unpublished).

Crocker, D. A. 1991. Toward development ethics. *World Development* **19**(5), 457–83.

Cullen, M. & S. Woolery (eds). *World congress on land policy, 1980.* Lexington, Mass.: Lexington Books.

Cumming, S. 1990. Post-colonial urban residential change in Zimbabwe: a case study. In *Cities and development in the Third World*, R. B. Potter & A. T. Salau (eds), 32–50. London: Mansell.

Departamento del Distrito Federal (DDF) 1985. Decreto por el que se expropian por causa de utílidad pública los inmuebles de propiedad particular que se senalan. *Diario Oficial* 11 October 1985.

De Valk, P. 1986. An analysis of planning policy in Zimbabwe. Paper to Workshop on the Planning System in Zimbabwe, Department of Rural and Urban Planning, University of Zimbabwe.

Diamond, D. R. 1980. The relationship between amenities and urban land prices. *Land Economics* **56**(1), 21–32.

Dillinger, W. 1989. Urban property taxation: lessons from Brazil. *World Bank Report* INU 37.

Doebele, W. 1987a. Intervening in the informal urban land supply: neglected opportunities. Paper prepared for USAID.

Doebele, W. 1987b. The evolution of concept of urban land tenure in developing countries. *Habitat International* **11**, 7–22.

Doebele, W., O. Grimes, J. Linn 1979. Participation of beneficiaries in financing urban services. *Land Economics* **55**(1), 73–92.

Dowall, D. E. 1980. Methods for assessing land price effects of local public policies and actions. In *Urban land markets: price indices, supply measures, and public policy effects*, J. T. Black & J. E. Hoben (eds), 161–83. Washington DC: The Urban Land Institute.

Dowall, D. E. 1981. Reducing the cost-effects of local land use controls. *Journal of the American Planning Association* **47**(2), 145–53.

Dowall, D. E. 1989a. Bangkok: a profile of an efficiently performing housing market. *Urban Studies* **26**(3), 327–39.

Dowall, D. E. 1989b. *Karachi land and housing market study*. Washington DC: PADCO.

Dowall, D. E. 1991a. *The land market assessment: a new tool for urban management*. Washington DC: World Bank/UNDP/UNCHS.

Dowall, D. E. 1991b. The Karachi Development Authority: failing to get the prices right. *Land Economics* **67**(4), 467–71.

Dowall, D. E. 1991c. *A tale of two cities: a comparison of Karachi's informal and formal housing delivery systems*. IURD Working Paper 530. Berkeley: University of California.

REFERENCES

Dowall, D. E. & M. Leaf 1991. The price of land for housing in Jakarta. *Urban Studies* **28**(5), 707–22.

Dowall, D. E. & M. Perló 1988. *Una evaluación del impacto de los programas de reconstrucción sobre el mercado inmobiliario habitacional de la zona central de la ciudad de México.* Instituto de Investigaciones Sociales. Mexico DF: UNAM.

Dueker, K. J. 1987. Geographic information systems for computer-aided mapping. *American Planning Association, Journal* **53**(3), 104–12.

Duhau, E. 1987. La formación de una política social: el caso del Programa de Renovación Habitacional Popular en la ciudad de México. *Estudios Demográficos y Urbanos* **2**(1), 75–100.

Durand, J. 1983. *La ciudad invade al ejido: proletarización, urbanización y lucha política en el Cerro del Judío, DF.* México DF: Ediciones de la Casa Chata.

Durand-Lasserve, A. 1983. The land conversion process in Bangkok and the predominance of the private sector over the public sector. See Angel (1983), 284–309.

Durand-Lasserve, A. 1990. Articulation between formal and informal markets: political issues and trends. See Baross & van der Linden (1990), 37–56.

Durand-Lasserve, A. & R. Pajoni 1992. *The regularization of irregular settlements in cities in the developing countries: techniques, procedures, policies. Synthesis of main findings.* Paris: CNRS.

Durand-Lasserve, A. & J. F. Tribillion 1986. *Pratiques foncières et orientations politiques, Conakry.* Report to Ministère de l'Urbanisme, République de Guinée.

Durham, E. Ribeiro 1984. Movimentos sociais, a construção da cidadania. *Novos Estudos Cebrap* **10**, 24–30.

The Economist 1991. *Sisters in the wood: a survey of the IMF and the World Bank.* Special Supplement, 12 October.

Escobar, A. 1992. Culture, economics and politics in Latin American social movements theory and research. See Escobar & Alvarez (1992).

Escobar, A. & S. Alvarez 1992. *The making of social movements in Latin America.* Boulder, Colo.: Westview Press.

Esterci, N. (ed.) 1990. *Terra de trabalho e terra de negócio: estratégias de reprodução camponesa.* Rio de Janeiro: CEDI.

Estratégia (editorial) 1987. Puebla: patrimonio de la humanidad. *Estratégia: Revista de Análisis Político* **76**, 41–53.

Evans, A. W. 1989. South East England in the eighties: explanations for a house price explosion. In *Growth and change in a core region*, M. Breheny & P. Congdon (eds), 130–49. London: Pion.

Evers, H-D. 1976. Urban expansion and land ownership in underdeveloped societies. In *The city in comparative perspective: cross-national research and new directions in theory*, J. Walton & L. H. Massoti (eds), 67–79. London: Sage.

Falcão Neto, J. de Arruda 1985. O direito de morar – Mocambos do Recife. *Revista Ciência Hoje* **3**(18), 74–80.

Falú, A. & M. Curutchet 1991. Rehousing the urban poor: looking at women first. *Environment and Urbanization* **3**(2), 23–38.

Farvacque, C. & P. McAuslan 1992. *Reforming urban land policies and institutions in developing countries.* UNDP/World Bank/UNCHS Urban Management Program Tool 5. Washington DC: World Bank.

Fitzwilliam Memorandum 1991. International Research Workshop: land value changes and the impact of urban policy upon land valorization processes in developing countries. *International Journal of Urban and Regional Research* **15**(4), 623–8.

FONATUR 1975. *Primer censo de población de Cancún, Quintana Roo.* México DF: Gerencia de Planeación y Estudios Económicos.

FONATUR 1983. *Necesidades de vivienda en Cancún.* México: Agency Publication.

Fonseca, C. 1991. Spouses, siblings and sex-linked bonding: a look at kinship organization in a Brazilian slum, See Jelín (1991a), 133–60.

Fraser, N. & L. Nicholson 1988. Social criticism without philosophy: an encounter between feminism and post-modernism. *Theory, Culture & Society* **5**(2/3), 373–94.

GAJOP 1987. *Projeto de assesoria jurídica popular, relatório de atividades.* Olinda: GAJOP.

García Fuentes, A. 1979. *Cancún: turismo y subdesarrollo regional.* México DF: Universidad

Nacional Autónoma de México.

García Peralta, B. 1981. Estado y capital privado en el fraccionamiento Izcalli-Chamapa. *Revista Mexicana de Sociología* **42**(4), 1439–64.

García Peralta, B. 1988. *La actividad inmobiliaria en la Ciudad de Querétaro: 1960–1982.* Cuadernos de Investigación Social 17. Mexico DF: Universidad Autónoma de México.

García Peralta, B. 1990. El mercado de tierra, el ejido y el turismo: el caso de Puerto Vallarta. Paper presented at the 13th Sociological World Congress, Madrid.

Garza, G. & M. Schteingart 1978. *La acción habitacional del Estado en México.* México DF: El Colegio de México.

Geisse, G. & F. Sabatini 1982. Urban land market studies in Latin America: issues and methodology. See Cullen & Woolery (1982), 149–75.

Geras, N. 1987. Post Marxism? *New Left Review* **163**. 40–82.

Gilbert, A. (ed.) 1982. *Urbanization in contemporary Latin America: critical approaches to the analysis of urban issues.* Chichester, England: John Wiley.

Gilbert, A. 1984. Planning, invasions and land speculation: the rôle of the state in Venezuela. *Third World Planning Review* **6**(3), 225–38.

Gilbert, A. 1987. Research policy and review 15. From Little Englanders into Big Englanders: thoughts on the relevance of relevant research. *Environment and Planning A* **19**, 143–51.

Gilbert, A. 1991a. Some thoughts about land markets and land prices in Third World Cities. (Fitzwilliam paper).

Gilbert, A. 1991b. Comparative analysis: studying housing processes in Latin American cities. See Tipple & Willis (1991), 81–95.

Gilbert, A. & P. Healy 1985. *The political economy of land: the state and urban development in Venezuela.* Aldershot, England: Gower.

Gilbert, A. & A. Varley 1991. *Landlord and tenant: housing the poor in urban Mexico.* Routledge: London.

Gilbert, A. & P. M. Ward, 1982. The state and low income housing. See Gilbert (1982), 79–82.

Gilbert, A. & P. M. Ward 1985. *Housing, the state and the poor: policy and practice in three Latin American cities.* Cambridge: Cambridge University Press.

Gittins, D. 1985. *The family in question: changing households and familiar ideologies.* London: Macmillan.

Gnaneshwar, V. 1986. Land value management: the experience of Andhra Pradesh. *Nagarlok* **18**(2), 71–81.

Gobierno del Estado, 1982. *Plan de desarrollo estatal, Puebla 1983–1988.* Sector de Asentamientos Humanos. Puebla, Mexico: Gobierno del Estado.

Gohn, M. da Glória 1988. Luta pela moradia em São Paulo – movimentos de moradia. *Ciências Sociais Hoje 1988.* São Paulo: Vertice/ANPOCS.

Goldberg, M. & P. Chinloy 1984. *Urban land economics.* New York: John Wiley.

González de la Rocha, M. 1988. Economic crisis, domestic reorganisation and women's work in Guadalajara, Mexico. *Bulletin of Latin American Research* **7**(2), 207–23.

González de la Rocha, M. 1991. Family well-being, food consumption, and survival strategies during Mexico's economic crisis. In *Social responses to Mexico's economic crisis of the 1980s,* M. González de la Rocha & A. Escobar Latapí (eds), 115–27. San Diego, Cal.: Center for US-Mexican Studies, University of California.

Gormsen, E. 1978. La zonificación socio-económica de la ciudad de Puebla: cambios por efecto de la metropolitación. *Comunicaciones Proyecto Puebla-Tlaxcala* **15**, 7–20.

Guanzirolli, C. E. & E. Bohadana 1983. Alguns dados sobre o solo urbano no Brasil. In *A cidade e nossa,* E. Bohadana (ed.), vol. 2, 7–24. Rio de Janeiro: Codecri.

Hackenberg, R., A. D. Murphy, H. A. Selby 1984. The urban household in dependent development. See Netting et al. 187–216.

Haddad, E. 1982. Report on urban land market research in São Paulo, Brazil. See Cullen & Woolery (1982), 201–14.

Hansan, A. 1987. Interviews related to illegal subdivision and development in Yakdoodabad and Orangi Township, Karachi. Paper prepared for UN Economic and Social Commission for Asia and the Pacific.

Hansan, A. 1990. A case study in Karachi, Pakistan. In UN/ESCAP *case studies on metropolitan fringe developments; with focus on illegal subdivisions.* New York: United Nations.

REFERENCES

Hardoy, J. E. & D. Satterthwaite (eds) 1986. *Small and intermediate urban centres: their rôle in national and regional development in the Third World*. London: Hodder & Stoughton.
Harms, H. 1982. Historical perspectives on the practice and purpose of self-help housing. See Ward (1982), 17–53.
Harvey, D. 1973. *Social justice and the city*. Oxford: Basil Blackwell.
Harvey, D. 1978. Urbanization under capitalism: a framework for analysis. *International Journal of Urban and Regional Research* 2(1), 101–31.
Harvey, D. 1985. *The urbanization of capital: studies in the history and theory of capitalist urbanization*. Oxford: Basil Blackwell.
Harvey, S. D. 1987. Black residential mobility in a post-independent Zimbabwean city. In *Geographical perspectives on development in Southern Africa*, G. J. Williams & A. P. Wood (eds), 179–87. Townsville, Queensland: James Cook University.
HCMPTT (Harare Combination Master Plan Technical Team) 1988. Report of study (draft).
Hiernaux, D. 1991a. The process of land occupation, the land market and social agents in Chalco, Mexico City, 1978–1991. (Fitzwilliam paper).
Hiernaux, D. 1991b. Ocupación del suelo y producción del espacio construido en el valle de Chalco, 1978–1991. See Schteingart (1991), 179–202.
Hiernaux, D. & A. Lindon, 1991. Proceso de ocupación del suelo mercado de tierra y agentes sociales en el Valle de Chalco, Ciudad de México: 1978–91. (Fitzwilliam paper).
Hoffman, M. L. 1990. Informal residential land development in Indonesia. Paper prepared for the Workshop on Regularizing the Informal Land Development Process. Washington DC: USAID.
Housing Finance International 1987. Building societies' role in Zimbabwe. November, 20–26.

IBGE 1970. *Censo demográfico, 1970*. Rio de Janeiro: IBGE.
IBGE 1980. *Censo demográfico, 1980*. Rio de Janeiro: IBGE.
INAH 1986. *Convención para la protección del patrimonio mundial, cultural y natural: zona de monumentos de Puebla y Cholula*. Puebla: INAH/UNESCO.
INDECO 1979. *Accrores para la selección de prototipos de vivienda. Programa 1979*. Querétaro, Mexico: INDECO.
INFRATUR 1971a. Estructura de la población de la Colonia Puerto Juárez, Quintana Roo. Encuesta de julio de 1971. Unpublished.
INFRATUR 1971. Bases para el desarrollo de un programa integral de infraestructura turistica en México. Unpublished.
INFRATUR 1972a. *Plan maestro de Cancún*. México DF: Banco de México/INFRATUR.
INFRATUR 1972b. Memorandum sobre las inversiones en vivienda. Unpublished.
Ingram, G. K. 1982. Land in perspective: its rôle in the structure of cities. See Cullen & Woolery (1982), 103–18.
IPLAN-RIO 1986. *Dados básicos do Município do Rio de Janeiro: relatório preliminar*.
Iragorri, R. V. 1980. *Diagnóstico del ambulantismo en la ciudad de Puebla y sus posibles soluciones*. Puebla: Gobierno del Estado de Puebla.

Jelín, E. (ed) 1991a. *Family, household and gender relations in Latin America*. **London: Kegan Paul International – UNESCO.**
Jelín, E. 1991b. Family and household: outside world and private life. See Jelín (1991a), 12–39.
Jimenez, E. 1983. The magnitude and determinants of home improvement in self-help housing: Manila's Tondo project. *Land Economics* 59(1), 70–83.
Johnston, M. 1989. Corruption, inequality and change. See Ward (1989a), 13–37.
Jones, G. 1991a. *The impact of government intervention upon land prices in Latin American cities: the case of Puebla, Mexico*. PhD thesis, University of Cambridge.
Jones, G. 1991b. The commercialisation of the land market? Land ownership patterns in Puebla, Mexico. *Third World Planning Review* 13(2), 129–53.
Jones, G. & P. M. Ward 1994. *The price of uncertainty: the evidence for land valorization in Mexican cities and the implications for public policy*. Working Paper, Mexican Center of ILAS, University of Texas, Austin.
Jones, G., E. Jiménez & P. M. Ward. 1991. The price of uncertainty: the evidence for land valorisation in Mexican cities and the implications for public policy. (Fitzwilliam paper).
Jones, G., E. Jiménez, P. M. Ward 1993. The land market in Mexico under Salinas: a real estate boom revisited? *Environment and Planning A* 25, 627–51.

273

REFERENCES

Jordan, J. D. 1984. *Local government in Zimbabwe*. Occasional papers, socio-economic series, 17. Gweru: Mambo Press.

Joshi, A. 1991. *Plotting transformations: the illegal land subdivision process in Delhi*. Master's thesis, Massachusetts Institute of Technology.

Karst, K. L., M. L. Schwartz, A. J. Schwartz 1973. *The evolution of law in the barrios of Caracas*. Los Angeles: University of California Press.

Kay, G. & M. Cole 1977. The townsfolk. See Kay & Smout (1977), 41–56.

Kay, G. & M. Smout (eds) 1977. *Salisbury: a geographical survey of the capital of Rhodesia*. London: Hodder & Stoughton.

Killick, T. 1989. *A reaction too far: economic theory and the rôle of the state in developing countries*. London: Overseas Development Institute.

Klak, T. 1991. Analysis of government mortgage records: insights for state theory and housing policy with reference to Jamaica. See Tipple & Willis, 96–112.

Koivigui, F. 1986. *Essai d'analyse des budgets familiaux en zone urbaine* [unpublished report], Conakry, Guinée.

Korea Research Institute for Human Settlements 1989. *The final report on the research committee on public concept in land* [in Korean]. Seoul: Government of the Republic of Korea.

Krantz, L. 1991. Peasant differentiation and development: the case of a Mexican ejido. Stockholm: University of Stockholm.

Krischke, P. J. (ed.) 1984. *Terra de habitação e terra de espoliação*. São Paulo: Cortez Editora.

Laclau, E. & C. Mouffe 1985. *Hegemony & socialist strategy: towards a radical democratic politics*. London: Verso.

Landis, J. 1986. Electronic spreadsheets in planning: the case of shiftshare analysis. *Journal of the American Planning Association* **51**(2), 216–25.

Leal, J. A. A. 1990. *Políticas de integração da tributação sobre a renda e sobre a propriedade imobiliária urbana*. MSc thesis, IPPUR, Federal University of Rio de Janeiro.

Lee, D. 1974. Requiem for large-scale models. *Journal of the American Planning Association* **39**(3), 163–78.

Legoretta, J. 1983. *El proceso de urbanización en las ciudades petroleras*. México DF: EcoDesar-rollo.

Legoretta, J. 1984. La autoconstrucción de vivienda en México: el caso de las ciudades petroleras. México DF: Ecodesarrollo.

Lehmann, D. 1990. *Democracy and development in Latin America: economics, politics and religion in the postwar period*. Cambridge: Polity Press.

Levine, J. & J. D. Landis 1989. Geographic information systems for local planning. *Journal of the American Planning Association* **55**(1), 101–8.

van der Linden, J. 1989. The limits of territorial social movements: the case of housing in Karachi. In *Urban social movements in the Third World*, F. Schuurman & T. van Naerssen, (eds) 92–104. London: Routledge.

van der Linden, J. 1992. Back to the roots: keys to successful implementation of sites-and-services. See Mathéy (1992a), 341–52.

Linn, J. 1983. *Cities in the developing world: policies for their equitable and efficient growth*. Oxford: Oxford University Press.

Lira, A. 1983. *Comunidades indígenas frente a la Ciudad de México*. México: El Colegio de México & El Colegio de Michoacán.

Lomnitz, L. 1975. *Como sobreviven los marginados*, México DF: Siglo Veintiuno.

Lostao, S. Soler 1991. *O PREZEIS, um processo de participação popular na formação da cidade*. Thesis MDU/UFPE, Recife.

Lostao, S. Soler 1992a. The intervention of urban social movements in legislation: conquest or concession? *Beyond Law* **2**(4), 63–74.

Lostao, S. Soler 1992b. Participação popular: movimentos sociais urbanos em espaços institucionais (PREZEIS). In *Poder local e particpação popular*, J. A. Soares (ed.). Rio de Janeiro: Rio Fundo Editora.

Macoloo, G. C. 1993. *The determinants and dynamics of land values and their impact upon the equitable development of low and middle income residential areas in Third World cities: a Kenyan case study*. Unpublished report to IDRC.

Macon, J. & J. Merino Mañon 1975. *Betterment levies in Latin America: nature, experience and recommendations for their adoption in the financing of public works projects*. Washington DC: Inter-American Development Bank.

Mainwaring, S. 1987. Urban popular movements, identity and democratization in Brazil. *Comparative Political Studies* **20**(2), 131–59.

Mainwaring, S. & E. Viola 1984. New social movements, political culture and democracy: Brazil and Argentina in the 1980s. *Telos* **61**, 17–54.

Malik, P. L. 1988. *Indian Stamp Act, 1899 (as applicable to the State of Uttar Pradesh) along with Registration Act, 1908*. Lucknow: Eastern Book Company.

Makin, J. 1984. *Self-help housing in Mexico City and the rôle of the state*. PhD thesis, Heriot Watt University.

Malpezzi, S., M. Bamberger, S. K. Mayo 1982. *Planning an urban housing survey: key issues for researchers and program managers in developing countries*. Water Supply and Urban Development Department Discussion Paper 44. Washington DC: World Bank.

Malpezzi, S., S. K. Mayo, D. J. Gross 1985. *Housing demand in developing countries*. World Bank Staff Working Paper 733. Washington DC: World Bank.

Masser, I. 1987. Land readjustment: an overview. *Third World Planning Review* **9**(3), 205–10.

Massey, D. & A. Catalano 1978. *Capital and land: landownership by capital in Great Britain*. London: Edward Arnold.

Massolo, A. 1991. Mujer y vivienda popular. See Schteingart (1991), 305–17.

Massolo, A. (ed.) 1992. *Mujeres y ciudades: participación social, vivienda y vida cotidiana*, México DF: El Colegio de México.

Mathéy, K. (ed.) 1992a. *Beyond self-help housing*. London: Mansell.

Mathéy, K. 1992b. Positions on self-help housing, See Mathéy (1992a), 379–96.

Meillasoux, C. 1981. *Maidens, meal and money: capitalism and the domestic economy*. Cambridge: Cambridge University Press.

Menezes, L. M. 1988. Urban land policy trends in Asia: an overview. *Land Use Policy* **5**(3), 291–300.

Mills, E. S. & B. W. Hamilton 1989. *Urban economics*, 4th edition. Glenview, Ill.: Scott, Foresman.

Moreno, F. 1988. Notas sobre el mercado inmobiliario y la acción expropriatoria de predios urbanos en el centro de la ciudad de México. *A: Revista de Ciencias Sociales y Humanidades* **9**(25), 123–33.

Moser, C. O. N. 1987. Women, human settlements, and housing: a conceptual framework for analysis and policy-making, In *Women, human settlements and housing*, C. O. N. Moser & L. Peake (eds), 12–32. London: Tavistock.

Moura, A. Sobreira de 1987. Brasília teimosa: the organization of a low-income settlement in Recife, Brazil. *Development Dialogue* **1**, 152–69.

Moura, A. Sobreira de 1990. *Terra do mangue: invasões urbanas no Recife*. Recife: FUNDAJ/-Massagana.

Murray, R. 1977. Value and rent theory, *Capital and Class* **3**, 100–22.

Murray, R. 1978. Value and rent theory, *Capital and Class* **4**, 11–33.

Mutizwa-Mangiza, N. D. 1991. The organisation and management of urban local authorities in Zimbabwe: a case study of Bulawayo. *Third World Planning Review* **13**(4), 357–80.

National Council of Savings Institutions 1985. *Housing finance in Zimbabwe*. Washington DC: Report prepared for the United States Agency for International Development.

Netting, R. M., R. R. Wilk, E. J. Arnould (eds) 1984a. *Households: comparative and historical studies of the domestic group*. Berkeley: University of California Press.

Netting, R. M., R. R. Wilk, E. J. Arnould 1984b. Introduction. See Netting et al. (1984a), xiii–xxxviii.

Nientied, P. 1986. The short-term impact of housing upgrading on housing values: methodology and results of a test-control study in Karachi. *Third World Planning Review* **8**(1), 19–30.

Nientied, P. & J. van der Linden 1983. Approaches to low-income housing in the Third World: some comments. *International Journal of Urban and Regional Research* **9**(3), 311–29.

Nunes, E. & P. Jacobi 1982. Movimentos populares urbanos, poder local e conquista da democracia. In *Cidade, povo e poder* J. A. Moisés (ed.). Rio de Janeiro: CEDEC/Paz e Terra.

PADCO 1989. *San Pedro Sula, Honduras land and housing market study*. Washington DC: PADCO.

PADCO & Land Institute Foundation 1990. *Bangkok land and housing market assessment* Washington DC: PADCO.

Panizzi, W. M. 1989. Entre cidade e estado, a propriedade e seus direitos. *Espaço e Debates* **9**(26), 84–90.

Patel, D. 1984. Housing the urban poor in the socialist transformation of Zimbabwe. In *The political economy of Zimbabwe*, M. Schatzberg (ed.), 182–96. New York: Praeger.

Patel, D. & R. J. Adams 1981. *Chirambahuyo: a case study in low-income housing*. Gweru: Mambo Press.

Patiño, E. 1987. *Las elecciones de 1985 en Puebla*. Puebla: DIAU-ICUAP.

Payer, C. 1982. *The World Bank; a critical analysis*. New York: Monthly Review Press.

Payne, G. (ed.) 1984. *Low-income housing in the developing world: the rôle of sites and services and settlement upgrading*. Chichester, England: John Wiley.

Payne, G. 1989. *Informal housing and land subdivisions in Third World cities: a review of the literature*. Oxford: Centre for Development and Environmental Planning, Oxford Polytechnic.

Peattie. L. 1979. Housing policy in developing countries: two puzzles. *World Development* **17**, 1017–22.

Peña, F. 1992. ¿A quienes considerar mujeres jefas de familia en la investigación antropológica? *Nueva Antropología* **12**(41), 159–82.

Perlman, J. 1976. *The myth of marginality*, Los Angeles: University of California Press.

Peterson, G. E., T. Kingsley, J. P. Telgarsky 1991. *Urban economics and national development*. Washington DC: The Urban Institute.

Pineda, J. F. n.d. The valorization system in Bogota: an assessment of recent trends. Washington DC: World Bank (unpublished).

Plan Inc Zimbabwe 1989. *Land delivery for low cost housing in Zimbabwe. Phase 1: report of findings*. Harare: Report for the Ministry of Public Construction and Housing and United States Agency for International Development.

Poon, L. C. L. 1978. Railway externalities and residential property prices. *Land Economics* **54**(2), 218–27.

Pritchard, C. R. 1989. *Rented housing in Zimbabwe: a case study of the development of flats in Harare 1980–8*. BSc thesis, University of Zimbabwe.

Pugh, C. 1989. Housing policy reform in Madras and the World Bank. *Third World Planning Review* **11**(3), 249–73.

Rabiega, W. A., L. T-Win, L. M. Robinson 1984. The property value impacts of public housing projects in low and moderate density residential neighbourhoods. *Land Economics* **60**(2), 174–9.

Rakodi, C. 1990a. Housing production and housing policy in Harare, Zimbabwe. *Journal of Urban Affairs* **12**(2), 135–56.

Rakodi, C. 1990b. Can Third World cities be managed? In *The living city: towards a sustainable future*, D. Cadman & G. Payne (eds), 111–24. London: Routledge.

Rakodi, C. 1992a. Housing markets in Third World cities: research and policy into the 1990s. *World Development* **20**(1), 39–55.

Rakodi, C. 1992b. Urban land policy in Zimbabwe. Teaching Paper, Department of Rural and Urban Planning, University of Zimbabwe.

Rakodi, C. & N. D. Mutizwa-Mangiza 1989. *Housing production and housing policy in Harare, Zimbabwe*. Teaching Paper 3, Department of Rural and Urban Planning, University of Zimbabwe.

Rakodi, C. & N. D. Mutizwa-Mangiza 1990. Housing policy, production and consumption in Harare: a review, part I. *Zambezia* **17**(1), 1–30.

RAL Merchant Bank (various dates). *Executive guide to the economy* (from Sept. 1988 RAL Merchant Bank, *Quarterly guide to the economy*; from June 1990 First Merchant Bank of Zimbabwe Ltd, *Quarterly guide to the economy*).

Razzaz, O. 1991. *Law, urban land tenure, and property disputes in a contested settlement: the case of Jordan*. PhD thesis, Harvard University.

Razzaz, O. 1992. Group non-compliance: a strategy for transforming property relations – the case of Jordan. *International Journal of Urban and Regional Research* **16**(3), 408–19.

Reid, A. & M. A. Aguilar 1983. Las grandes obras del DDF: impactos sociales provocados por la Central de Abasto. *Iztapalapa* **4**(9), 114–29.

République de Guinée. 1980. *Réglementation domaniale et foncière*. Agency Publication, Conakry,

Guinée.

République de Guinée, Ministère du Plan et de la Coopération Internationale DGSI 1986. *Situation économique et conjoncturelle au 31 décembre 1985 et éléments sur la mise en oeuvre de la réforme économique au cours du premier trimestre.* Agency Publication, Conakry, Guinée.

République de Guinée, Ministère de l'Urbanisme, Direction Générale des Domaines 1985. *Avant-projet de législation et de réglementation domaniale et foncière.* Agency Publication, Conakry, Guinée.

République de Guinée, Ministère du Plan 1987 (updated 1988). *Enquêtes sur les dépenses des ménages de la ville de Conakry.* Agency Publication, Conakry, Guinée.

République de Guinée, Ministère de l'Urbanisme et de l'Habitat. Direction Générale de l'aménagement du Territoire et de l'Urbanisme – (Unité de Planification Urbaine de Conakry) 1989. *Plan de développement urbain de Conakry.* Rapport de Synthèse. Groupement BCEOM. Louis Berger. Groupe Huit. Agency Publication, Conakry, Guinée.

RHP (Renovación Habitacional Popular) 1986. *Evaluación del programa de reconstrucción de vivienda popular.* México DF: RHP.

RHP (Renovación Habitacional Popular) 1987. *Síntesis de la memoria del programa octubre 1985– marzo 1987.* México DF: RHP.

Roberts, B. 1989. Employment structure, life cycle and life chances: formal and informal sectors in Guadalajara. In *The informal economy: studies in advanced and less developed economies,* A. Portes, M. Castells, L. Benton (eds), 41–59. Baltimore: Johns Hopkins University Press.

Robertson, A. F. 1991. *Beyond the family: the social organization of human reproduction,* Cambridge: Polity Press.

Robinson, J. 1962. *Essays in the theory of economic growth.* London: Macmillan.

Rodriguez, V. & P. M. Ward 1992. Opposition politics, power and public administration in urban Mexico. *Bulletin of Latin American Research* **10**(1), 23–36.

Roweis, S. T. & A. J. Scott 1978. The urban land question. In *Urbanization and conflict in market societies,* K. R. Cox (ed.), 38–75. London: Methuen.

SAHOPEP 1987. Actualización del plan parcial del centro histórico de Puebla. Puebla: SAHOPEP.

Salazar, E. & E. Vega nd. *Transformaciones del uso del suelo en la periferia de la Ciudad de México: Colonia Emiliano Zapata, Ecatepec, Estado de México.* Thesis, Universidad Autónoma Metropolitana, Azcapotzalco.

Salman, T. 1990. Between orthodoxy and euphoria, research strategies on social movement: a comparative perspective. See Assies et al. (1990).

Santos, B. de Souza 1992. Law, state and urban struggles in Recife, Brazil. *Social & Legal Studies* **1**, 235–55.

Sanyal, B. 1987. Problems of cost-recovery in development projects: experience of the Lusaka squatter upgrading and site/service project. *Urban Studies* **24**, 285–95.

Schteingart, M. 1989. *Los productores del espacio habitable. estado, empresa y sociedad en la Ciudad de Mexico.* México DF: El Colegio de México.

Schteingart, M. (ed.) 1991. *Espacio y vivienda en la Ciudad de México.* México DF: El Colegio de México.

SECTUR/FONATUR 1982. *Cancún: un desarrollo turístico en la Costa Turquesa.* México DF: Secretaría de Turismo/Fondo Nacional para el Fomento del Turismo.

SEDUE 1987. Programa de ordenamiento urbano del area metropolitana de la Ciudad de Puebla, vol.1. Puebla, Mexico: SEDUE.

Selby, H. A., A. D. Murphy, S. A. Lorenzen (with I. Cabrera, A. Castañeda, I. Ruiz Love) 1990. *The Mexican urban household: organizing for self-defense.* Austin: University of Texas Press.

Serageldin, M. 1990. *Regularizing the informal land development process.* Washington DC: USAID.

Shoup, D. 1980. Financing public investment by deferred special assessment. *National Tax Journal* **33**(4), 413–29.

Shoup, D. 1983. Intervention through property taxation and public ownership. In *Urban land policy: issues and opportunities,* H. Dunkerley (ed.), 132–52. New York: Oxford University Press.

Shoup, D. 1990. *New funds for old neighborhoods: California's deferred special assessments,* Berkeley: California Policy Seminar.

Sidaway, J. D. 1992. In other worlds: on the politics of research by "First World" geographers in the "Third World". *Area* **24**(4), 403–8.

REFERENCES

Siembieda, W. 1991. Government policy and local urban land supply. Unpublished paper, School of Architecture and Planning, University of New Mexico.

Silva, O. Pereira da (ed.) 1990. *Pina, povo, cultura, memória*. Olinda: Produção Alternativa.

Singer, P. 1980. Movimentos de bairro. In *São Paulo: o povo em movimento*, P. Singer & V. C. Brant (eds). Petrópolis: Vozes.

Smart, A. 1986. Invisible real estate: investigations into the squatter property markets. *International Journal of Urban and Regional Research* **10**(1), 29–45.

Smith, J. , I. Wallerstein, H-D. Evers 1984. Introduction, In *Households and the world-economy*, J. Smith, I. Wallerstein & H-D. Evers (eds), 7–13. Los Angeles: Sage.

Smolka, M. O. 1983. *Estruturas intra-urbanas e segregaçao social no espaço: elementos para uma discussao da cidade na teoria econômica*. Série Facsimile, 13. Rio de Janeiro: PNPE/IPEA.

Smolka, M. O. 1987. Para uma reflexão sobre o processo de estruturaçao interna das cidades Brasileiras: o caso do Rio de Janeiro. *Espaço e Debates* **7**(21), 39–50.

Smolka, M. O. 1989. *Dinâmica imobiliária e estruturação intra-urbana: o caso do Rio de Janeiro*. Relatório de Pesquisa. Rio de Janeiro: IPPUR/UFRJ.

Smolka, M. O. 1990. Mobilidade dos imóveis e segregação residential na Cidade do Rio de Janeiro: Ou de como o mercado expulsa os pobres e redistribui os ricos. *Anais do VII Encontro Nacional de Estudos Populacionais*, 3. Caxambu: ABEP.

Smolka, M. O. 1991a. *The land market in Rio de Janeiro: some empirical evidence* [unpublished report], IPPUR, Rio de Janeiro.

Smolka, M. O. 1991b. Impostos sobre o patrimônio imobiliário urbano: aprimorando as informações e a sistemática de recolhimento. *Ensaios FEE* **11**(2), 442–54.

Smolka, M. O. 1992. Mobilidade intra urbana no Rio de Janeiro: de estratificão social a segregacão residencial. *Anais VIII Encontro Nacional de Estudos Populacionais* **3**, 311–33.

Sodetegi. 1987. *Etude de cadrage macro-économique* [unpublished report], Conakry, Guinée.

de Soto, H. 1989. *The other path: the invisible revolution in the Third World*. London: Tauris.

South 1990. Up on a property seesaw (cover story). **112**(February), 13–18.

Srinivas, L. 1989. *Proposal for a land market study of Bangalore city*. Professional report submitted to the Department of City and Regional Planning, University of California, Berkeley.

Stren, R. E. & R. R. White (eds) 1989. *African cities in crisis: managing rapid urban growth*. Boulder, Colo.: Westview Press.

Struyk, R. J. 1987. The housing needs assessment model. *American Planning Association, Journal* **53**(2), 227–34.

Struyk R. J. & R. Lynn 1983. Determinants of housing investment in slum areas: Tondo and other locations in Metro Manila. *Land Economics* **59**(4), 444–54.

Taylor, J. L. 1987. Evaluation of the Jakarta kampung improvement programme. In *Shelter upgrading for the urban poor*. R. J. Skinner, J. L. Taylor, E. A. Wegelin (eds), 39–67. Manila: Island.

TCPO (Town & Country Planning), Ministry of Urban Development. 1985. *A study of urban land prices in India*. New Delhi: Government of India.

Teedon, P. & D. Drakakis-Smith 1986. Urbanisation and socialism in Zimbabwe: the case of low-cost urban housing. *Geoforum* **17**(2), 309–24.

Tilly, C. , L. Tilly, R. Tilly 1975. *The rebellious century*. Cambridge, Mass.: Harvard University Press.

Tipple, A. G. & K. G. Willis, (eds). 1991 *Housing the poor in the developing world: methods of analysis, case studies and policy*. London: Routledge.

Tomas, F. 1987. Las estratégias socio-espaciales en los barrios céntricos de México: los decretos de expropriación de octubre de 1985. *TRACE* **11**, 7–25.

Topalov, C. 1975. *Los agentes urbanos y la producción de vivienda*, Documentos de Análisis Urbanos 3, Departamento de Geografía de la Universidad Autónoma de Barcelona, Bellaterra.

Topalov, C. 1979. *La urbanización capitalista: algunos elementos para su análisis*. México DF: Edicol.

Topalov, C. 1984. *Ganancias y rentas urbanas: elementos teóricos*. Madrid: Siglo Veintiuno de España.

Touré, M. 1988. La gestion foncière urbaine au Mali. In *La gestion foncière urbaine dans les pays en développement: objectifs, instruments et techniques*, 289–94. Bordeaux: Agence de Coopéracion Culturelle et Technique.

REFERENCES

Tribillion, J-F. 1985. *Contribution à la réforme du droit foncier et du droit de l'urbanisme engagée par la République de Guinée* [unpublished report], Paris: ACT.

Toye, J. 1989. Can the World Bank resolve the crisis of developing countries? *Journal of International Development* 1(2), 261–72.

Turner, J. F. C. 1976. *Housing by people: towards autonomy in building environments*. London: Marion Boyars.

UNCHS 1986. *Global report on human settlements*. Nairobi: UNCHS.

UNCHS 1989. Twelfth session, Commission on Human Settlements. *Habitat News* 11(1), 3–12.

Underwood, G. C. 1986. Zimbabwe. In *International handbook of land use planning*, N. Patricios (ed.), 185–218. West port, Conn.: Greenwood Press.

UNDP 1989. *Urban management program: overview of program activities*. New York: UNDP.

UMP 1986. *Pesquisa pina*, União dos Moradores do Pina, Recife [unpublished paper].

Urban Edge 1985. New directions in bank urban projects. 9(3), 1–5.

Urban Edge 1986. Housing finance: an urban priority. 10(8), 1–4.

Vainer, C. B. & M. O. Smolka 1991. Em tempos de liberalismo: tendências e desafios do planejamento urbano no Brasil. In *Brasil, território da desigualdade*, R. Piquet, R. & A. C. Torres Ribeiro (eds). Rio de Janeiro: Jorge Zahar Editor.

Valladares, L. P. 1990. *Cem anos pensando a pobreza (urbana) no Brazil. XIV encontro anual da ANPOCS* [unpublished paper], Caxambu.

Varley, A. 1985a. *"Ya somos dueños": ejido land regularization and development in Mexico City*. PhD thesis, University of London.

Varley, A. 1985b. Urbanization and agrarian law: the case of Mexico City. *Bulletin of Latin American Research* 4(1) 1–16.

Varley, A. 1985c. La zona urbana ejidal y la urbanización de la ciudad de México. *A: Revista de Ciencias Sociales y Humanidades* 6(15), 71–95.

Varley, A. 1992. Gender, household structure and accommodation for young adults in urban Mexico. In *Proceedings of the conference on shelter, women and development: First and Third World perspectives, May 7–9 1992*, H. Dandekar (ed.). Ann Arbor: University of Michigan.

Varley, A. (ed.) 1994. *Disasters, development and environment*. Chichester, England: John Wiley (Belhaven).

Wade, R. 1989. Politics and graft: recruitment, appointment and promotion to public office in India. See Ward (1989a), 73–109.

Wadhwa, K. 1985. *Urban fringe land market*. New Delhi: Concept Publishing.

Walters, A. 1983. The value of land. In *Urban land policy: issues and opportunities*, H. Dunkerley (ed.), 40–63. Oxford: Oxford University Press.

Ward, P. M. (ed.) 1982. *Self-help housing: a critique*. London: Mansell.

Ward, P. M. 1986. *Welfare politics in Mexico: papering over the cracks*. London: Allen & Unwin.

Ward, P. M. (ed.) 1989a. *Corruption, development and inequality: soft touch or hard graft?* Routledge: London.

Ward, P. M. 1989b. Land values and valorisation processes in Latin American cities: a research agenda. *Bulletin of Latin American Research* 8(1), 47–66.

Ward, P. M. 1989c. Political mediation and illegal settlement in Mexico City. In *Housing and land in urban Mexico*, A. Gilbert (ed.), 135–55. San Diego: Center for US–Mexican Studies, University of California.

Ward, P. M. 1990. The politics and costs of illegal land development for self-help housing in Mexico City. See Baross & van der Linden (1990), 133–68.

Ward, P. M. 1991. Mexico. In *International handbook of housing policies and practices*, W. van Vliet (ed.), 407–36. Westport, Conn.: Greenwood Press.

Ward, P. M. 1993. The Latin American inner city: differences of degree or of kind? *Environment and Planning* A, 25, 1131–60

Ward, P. M., E. Jiménez, G. Jones 1991. Residential land price changes in Mexican cities and the affordability of land for low-income groups. (Fitzwilliam paper).

Ward, P. M., E. Jiménez, G. Jones 1993. Residential land price changes in Mexican cities and the affordability of land for low-income groups. *Urban Studies* 30(10), 1521–42.

Ward, P. M., E. Jiménez, G. Jones 1994. *The value of land: price setting, valorisation processes*

279

and urban residential development in Third World cities [in preparation].

Ward, P. M. & C. Macoloo 1992. Articulation theory and self-help housing practice in the 1990s. *International Journal of Urban and Regional Research* **6**(1), 60–80.

Watson, S. 1988. *Accommodating inequality: gender and housing*. Sydney: Allen & Unwin.

Watson, S. (with H. Austerberry) 1986. *Housing and homelessness: a feminist perspective*. London: Routledge & Kegan Paul.

Weicher, J. C. & R. H. Zerbst 1973. The externalities of neighbourhood parks: an empirical investigation. *Land Economics* **49**, 99–105.

Wekwete, K. 1989a. *Planning laws for urban and regional planning in Zimbabwe*. Occasional paper 20, Department of Rural and Urban Planning, University of Zimbabwe.

Wekwete, K. 1989b. *Urban local government - the case of Harare city in Zimbabwe*. Unpublished paper, Department of Rural and Urban Planning, University of Zimbabwe.

Whittle, A. G. (ed.) 1979. Management of the physical environment, *Zimbabwe-Rhodesia Science News* **13**(11), 252–69.

Wilk, R. R. & R. M. Netting 1984. Households: changing forms and functions. See Netting et al. (1984a), 1–28.

World Bank 1972. Urbanization World Bank Sector Working Paper. Washington DC: World Bank.

World Bank 1983. *Urban land policy issues and opportunities*. World Bank Staff Working Paper 183, vols. I & II. Washington DC: World Bank.

World Bank (with UNDP & UNCHS) 1990. *Urban management program phase 2: capacity building for urban management in the 1990s*. Washington DC: World Bank.

World Bank 1991. *Urban policy and economic development: an agenda for the 1990s*. Washington DC: World Bank.

World Bank, *DAOC–DOI, and Gouvernement de Guinée* 1990. *Rapport d'evaluation du deuxième projet urbain* [unpublished report], Washington DC and Conakry, Guinée.

Yanagisako, S. J. 1984. Explicating residence: a cultural analysis of changing households among Japanese-Americans. See Netting et al. (1984a), 330–52.

Zetter, R. 1984. Land issues in low-income housing. In *Low-income housing in the developing world: the rôle of sites-and-services and settlement upgrading*, G. Payne (ed.), 221–32. Chichester, England: John Wiley.

Zimbabwe, Government of nd. *Urban housing policy implementation manual*. Harare: Ministry of Public Construction and National Housing.

Zimbabwe, Government of 1985. *Long term plan 1985–2000*. Harare: Ministry of Public Construction and National Housing.

Zimbabwe, Government of 1986. *Report on housing and urban development in Zimbabwe: public and private sector partnership*. Harare: Report by the Ministry of Public Construction and National Housing to the 10th Conference on Housing and Urban Development in Sub-Saharan Africa.

Index